THE PRACTICAL
Dog Owner's
HANDBOOK

Peque
Pequeno

NORTH AMERICAN NATURE HANDBOOKS

THE PRACTICAL
Dog Owner's
HANDBOOK

CONSULTANT EDITOR
PAUL McGREEVY
B.V.Sc., Ph.D., M.R.C.V.S.

WELDON
OWEN

Conceived and produced by Weldon Owen Pty Ltd
59-61 Victoria Street, McMahons Point
Sydney, NSW 2060, Australia

Copyright © 2002 Weldon Owen Pty Ltd
This edition printed 2011

WELDON OWEN PTY LTD
MANAGING DIRECTOR: Kay Scarlett
PUBLISHER: Corinne Roberts
CREATIVE DIRECTOR: Sue Burk
SENIOR VICE PRESIDENT, INTERNATIONAL SALES: Stuart Laurence
SALES MANAGER, UNITED STATES: Ellen Towell
ADMINISTRATION MANAGER, INTERNATIONAL SALES: Kristine Ravn
PRODUCTION DIRECTOR: Todd Rechner
PRODUCTION CONTROLLER: Lisa Conway
PRODUCTION AND PREPRESS CONTROLLER: Mike Crowton
PRODUCTION COORDINATOR: Nathan Grice

SERIES PUBLISHER: Lynn Humphries
MANAGING EDITORS: Janine Flew, Angela Handley
PROJECT EDITOR: Lynn Cole
DESIGN MANAGER: Helen Perks
EDITORIAL COORDINATOR: Jennifer Losco
DESIGNER: Lena Lowe
PICTURE RESEARCHERS: Joanna Collard, Jennifer Losco

ISBN: 978 1 74252 113 8

Printed by 1010 Printing International Limited
Manufactured in China

10 9 8 7 6 5 4 3 2 1

The paper used in the manufacture of this book is
sourced from wood grown in sustainable forests.
It complies with the Environmental Management
System Standard ISO 14001:2004

A WELDON OWEN PRODUCTION

Dogs are not our whole life, but they make our lives whole.

ROGER CARAS (1928–2001),
American broadcaster and writer

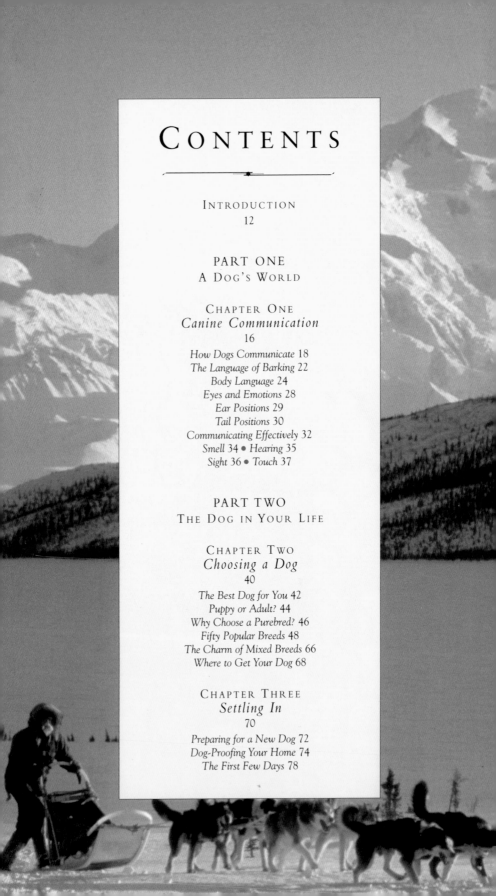

CONTENTS

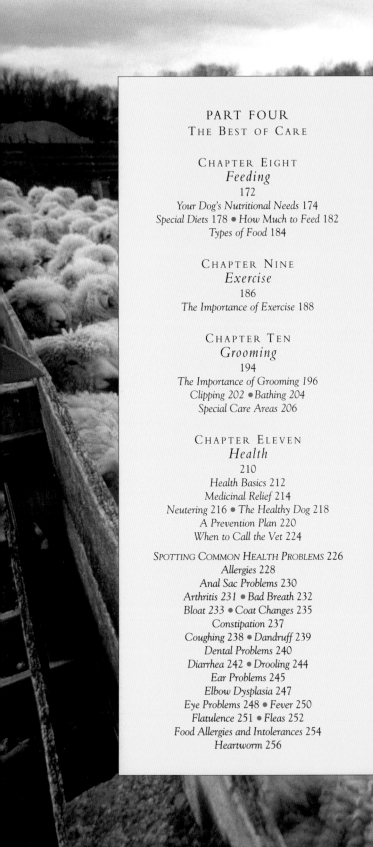

INTRODUCTION

For literally thousands of years, the dog has been humankind's closest ally. It was almost certainly the first animal to be domesticated, and perhaps no other species has been so useful to us, so loyal, nor so well loved. Dogs have guarded our homes and livestock, helped us hunt food and destroy vermin, rescued people who have been caught in avalanches or lost, aided police and customs officers, guided the visually impaired, served polar explorers and even assisted in wartime. Probably their greatest and most enduring role, however, is that of devoted companion.

The *Dog Lover's Companion* provides present and prospective dog owners with all the information they need to care for their pet. From choosing a dog, to understanding your dog's body language and behavior, to health care, feeding, exercise, training and breeding, this book is filled with sound, practical advice. Also included is a guide to the world's most popular dog breeds, which provides helpful information about each breed's history and temperament as well as its feeding, grooming, health and exercise requirements.

For those people who already own a dog, this book will be an invaluable reference at all stages of their pet's life. For those who are deciding what kind of dog fits their needs, it will be an inspiration. A dog's love is a great privilege, and with it comes a genuine responsibility to ensure that every care is taken to make our pets' lives as happy and fulfilling as possible.

THE EDITORS

PART ONE

A DOG'S WORLD

*A dog is not "almost human," and I know
of no greater insult to the canine race than
to describe it as such.*

JOHN HOLMES (1904–62),
American poet and lecturer

The reason why humans and dogs have such an intense relationship is that there is a mutual ability to understand one another's emotional responses. The joie de vivre of a dog may be greater than our own, but it is immediately recognizable as a feeling that we humans enjoy as well.

JEFFREY MASSON (b. 1940),
American academic, psychoanalyst and writer

How Dogs Communicate

Dogs express themselves using their body positions, facial expressions, ear and tail movements, and a variety of sounds.

Dogs and people usually get on very well, but they are still different species with different modes of communication. Humans rely more on words and less on nonverbal communication skills. And they seldom sit back and just look at what is going on. These are the very things you'll need to do if you want to know your dog and how she relates to you and her world. If you observe her and her body language, you'll soon know how things are with her. You'll even get to the point where you can tell what she'll be up to next.

Dog Watch

Some canine signals are pretty universal and mean much the same whether the dog is communicating with a person or another dog. When a dog is play bowing, her rear end up, her front down and her tail wagging, you can be sure she is issuing an invitation, "Let's play," to whomever she's talking to.

Then there are the subtle differences among individual dogs. Watch how your dog's posture changes, how she uses her ears, eyes, brows, lips, nose, mouth, tail and coat. Also take a close look at how her body language changes, depending on the circumstances. You'll soon work out how she expresses herself when she's happy, anxious, proud of herself, sleepy or whatever. But don't assume you can read a strange dog. Picking subtle differences in strange dogs is tricky, even for experts.

FEELING INSECURE This Stumpy-Tailed Cattle Dog signals her uncertainty with an anxious, pleading look and by holding her ears at different angles.

A calm dog and a mildly apprehensive one can be easily confused, as can a dominant dog and an aggressive one. To really grasp the nuances of canine body language, expressions and sounds, you need to be familiar with the characteristics of both the breed and the individual. If a dog's tail is low, for example, it generally means she's feeling insecure, but some sighthound breeds hold their tails this way as a matter of course. A Greyhound or a Whippet with its tail between its legs is probably feeling perfectly fine.

What Her Body and Face Are Saying

Submissive dogs contract, while confident dogs expand. A frightened dog makes herself as small as she can by moving everything inward. She shrinks slightly, tucks her tail, lays back her ears and averts her eyes. She may "surrender" by rolling over and exposing her belly. If she's so scared she wants to bolt for it, she'll pull back her lips and her weight will be back over her haunches.

A confident dog makes herself seem larger by raising her hackles, carrying her tail straight out or up, and standing absolutely erect. She makes and holds eye contact and her mouth is usually closed. If the dog's body appears to be leaning forward (in contrast to an erect stance) and her ears point forward, she may be

PLAY WITH ME! By play bowing, with her front end down, rear end up, and ears pricked, this Australian Kelpie mix tries to entice her owner to romp with her.

FRIENDS AND EQUALS With their extroverted body language—direct eye contact, loosely open mouths and confident body positions—this Rottweiler and Weimaraner indicate that they are entirely comfortable and relaxed with each other.

aggressive and about to attack. An aggressive dog may also have a fixed stare, her mouth closed, top lip pulled up and bottom lip down to show lots of teeth, and a snarl.

A relaxed dog looks quite different. She wags her tail in a neutral position—not stiffly, or raised high or tucked under. Her mouth is often open, her ears are held half-back or relaxed, her weight is evenly distributed on all four legs, and there's no sign of tension or threat in her eyes.

LEARNING HER VOCABULARY

Most dog owners know that their dogs are capable of a variety of sounds: barks, whines, squeals, yelps and howls. But although dogs sometimes sound as if they are trying to talk, these noises aren't attempts to mimic our language. Your dog knows that vocalizing is a great way to get your attention, so of course she will make a noise to make you look at and listen to her.

Dogs also make noises to manipulate other dogs. In a two-dog household, when one dog is snoozing on the sofa, the other dog may cleverly use sound and body language to invite her to come and play. As soon as the first dog is on her feet, the second will jump onto the sofa and steal that prime position. Dogs often seem to bark to distract an opponent, or whimper to put another dog off guard.

A growl, bark or whimper can mean different things at different times. A bark is very effective for attracting attention, and can also signal alarm, happiness, frustration or surprise. In general, the faster and higher the bark, the more excited or agitated the dog. Growls can be deep and threatening, or more like moans of pleasure during a good back rub.

When you listen to your dog, you'll soon know her vocal repertoire. But if you're with an unfamiliar dog, trust your instincts and don't take her owner's word that an alarming sound is actually harmless.

NO TRANSLATION NEEDED It's impossible to misinterpret this Dalmatian's meaning as anything other than a well-mannered request for a walk.

GETTING TO KNOW YOU While the two Cavalier King Charles Spaniels check him out, the terrier mix in the center holds himself stiffly, uncertain of their intentions.

VISUAL CONNECTIONS

Many people think that low-ranking dogs avert their eyes when you look at them, while high-ranking ones meet your eyes and stare straight back. But in different situations a dog may look directly at you, look sideways at you or refuse to look at you at all, whether she is feeling super confident or meek as a mouse.

When your dog stares at you, staring her down won't necessarily convince her that you're in charge. Besides, it's a mistake to assume that a stare indicates your dog is trying to dominate you. Sweet, submissive dogs often stare with melting adoration at their owners. To work out your dog's true intentions, you will also need to look at her facial expressions and at her body posture. It also helps to know something about your dog's background.

What intense eye contact does indicate is that the dog is interested in something that she may like, dislike or be afraid of. If your dog is overexcited or she's easily distracted, pay close attention to her when she makes eye contact elsewhere. She may be getting ready to pull on the leash, lunge, bark, attack or run.

THE SNIFF TEST

Scent is a powerful communication channel for dogs. Each dog has a unique scent, which is contained in a liquid in the anal glands, two sacs located in the anal muscles. The scent is released whenever a dog defecates, urinates or wags its tail. From it, another dog can tell the age, sex and status of the dog whose scent it is. High-ranking dogs will hold their tails high, releasing as much scent as possible. Nervous or submissive dogs often hold their tails between their legs, making their scent less noticeable and so drawing less attention to themselves.

This scent is the reason dogs spend so much time urinating—and sniffing—when they're outside. Urine, or scent, marking is a characteristic of wolves and dogs and is often used to declare ownership of a territory. When dogs are walked, especially males that haven't been neutered, they sniff every tree, post and fence, looking for the scent marking of other dogs. And when they find one, they cover or add to the scent by urinating on it, to stake their claim. That's why a male dog leaves small spurts here and there instead of one big puddle—he keeps a little urine in reserve in case he wants to leave his signature on yet another object. Marking is usually considered a male trait, but some female dogs also do it.

Not every dog that marks outdoors does so to establish territory or declare dominance. Many do it to get and

I KNOW YOU Dogs who know each other, like these young Cavalier King Charles Spaniel siblings, spend less time sniffing than dogs who are unfamiliar with each other.

leave information. From what they sniff, they learn who was there before them, and by leaving their mark, they become news for the next dog passing by.

MIXED MESSAGES

Sometimes you can misread your own dog, or another dog that you don't know well. Not all canine messages have a single meaning. And dogs, like humans, give conflicting signals. Contradictions will always exist among body language, eye contact, vocalizations, actions and intentions, in both humans and dogs. To humans, a smile is a sign of friendship and happiness. The same action in dogs—baring the teeth and drawing back the lips—can signal aggression. However, some dogs, especially Dalmatians, smile when greeting or submitting. This is not to say that you should never smile at your dog; dogs learn to read human signals, even when they differ from their own. But a strange dog may take a different interpretation. In that case, it may be wise to save the smile until the dog knows you better.

Gestures and posture are other areas of possible confusion between dogs and humans. People tend to gesticulate when they talk; to dogs, such quick hand movements can be unnerving, because they don't know what they mean. Humans tend to stand tall when greeting each other, and dogs; dogs don't always appreciate this, because they tend to take a more circumspect approach, sidling up to strangers and acting cautiously until they're sure of their reception.

Watch your dog and note the mannerisms that precede excitable, fearful, silly or aggressive behavior. This will help you to anticipate sudden movements and to keep your dog under control if she gets excited.

LOOK AT THE CONTEXT It's important to take canine body language in context. Exposing the belly is usually a sign of submission, but in this Labrador's case, it's simply a great way to cool down on a hot day.

The Language of Barking

From high-pitched yapping to full-blooded baying,

there's a wealth of meaning in a dog's bark.

Although barking is the most obvious method of canine communication, it made more sense for dogs in the past than it does today. Wild dogs, although they lived in packs, often separated during the day to hunt for food or search for mates. Barking enabled them to keep in contact across long distances. And, unlike scent—which is dogs' preferred form of communication—barking doesn't leave a physical trail for enemies to follow.

Although barking as a biological trait is less useful for pet dogs than wild ones, domestic dogs tend to bark much more than their wild counterparts. This is largely because pet dogs are in a state of arrested adolescence. In general, younger dogs—whether wild or domestic— bark more than adults. Once they have gained some experience of life, and become better at reading the more subtle body language clues that people and other dogs give, they

DECEPTIVELY QUIET Although it is well known for being barkless, the Basenji is far from silent, employing an expressive range of vocal sounds, including a kind of yodel.

tend to bark less. Wild dogs move quickly through adolescence to maturity, when they start taking care of themselves. But pet dogs have humans to look after them, so it is believed that in behavioral terms they never mature entirely—and they keep on barking.

Another reason domestic dogs bark more than wild ones is that they have been deliberately bred to do so. The dog's warning bark was perhaps one of the canine traits that humans first found useful and selected for when breeding dogs for guarding and herding.

WHY DO DOGS BARK?

There are many reasons a dog barks. Barking can mean your dog is having fun, is feeling frightened or lonely, wants attention or hears a noise. It's also his way of warning you of danger or that a stranger is approaching.

The tone of barking changes with the dog's motivation. To tell what a dog's bark means, you need to consider the sound in context.

A series of high-pitched barks often means that a dog is anxious. We recognize this tone and pattern as indicating distress, and this draws us near to help him.

When your dog looks at you and gives a single ear-splitting yap without any other

WHY DO DOGS BARK AT THE MAILMAN?

It's not unreasonable to expect that your dog would recognize the mailman when he comes to your house every day at the same time. Instead, your dog greets him like a stranger with a barrage of furious barks, and you can't figure out why.

To understand this common behavior, put yourself in your dog's position. The first time he sees the mailman coming to the door, he wants to protect his home from this stranger. After a few sharp barks, the mailman leaves and your dog may well feel proud and confident that he was responsible for driving him away. After that, whenever the mailman approaches, your dog woofs out his noisy alarm. It worked the first time, so he thinks it will work again. And it does. The mailman leaves!

IN THE BLOOD Terriers and hounds, such as the Dachshund, were bred to bark to alert their owners to the presence of rats, rabbits, weasels and other vermin.

their voices to call back to their masters during a hunt. Other hound breeds have even more specialized vocalizations. The Black-and-Tan Coonhound, for example, uses one tone of voice when following the scent of an opossum or raccoon, and another to alert its master that it has treed its quarry.

Other breeds are less prone to barking. The Norwegian Elkhound, for example, is totally silent when tracking, so as not to alert its quarry. (When not tracking, however, this breed is very talkative, using a wide range of sounds, each with a distinct meaning.) Irish Wolfhounds, too, tend not to bark to excess.

Some of the scent hounds, in particular Basset Hounds, tend to howl rather than bark, and may have different howls for different situations. Other breeds can hardly bark at all. The Basenji has an unusually shaped larynx, or voicebox, and is unable to bark. However, it makes a variety of other sounds, the most common being a cross between a chortle and a yodel. The New Guinea Singing Dog, one of the world's most elusive wild dogs, is another unusual vocalist, having a strange bark that sounds like a rooster's crow.

stimulus, he probably wants your attention. He might be hungry or want to play. Often, he will bark once and wait to see if anything happens. If it doesn't, he may keep barking until he gets what he wants.

Quick, repetitive, high-pitched barks mean that a dog is in a playful mood, or he has spotted something he wants to chase. Your dog will bark like this from excitement and pleasure or in anticipation of a treat such as a walk or a game.

A low, repetitive bark means your dog is feeling protective or defensive. He will bark in this way when a stranger approaches his territory. This type of bark is the dog's way of alerting his owners to a potential threat and summoning reinforcements in case the intruder needs to be repelled.

While most dogs bark to say something, others do it just for fun, out of habit or because they are frustrated at being left alone. This kind of barking can go on all day and your dog will soon become the neighborhood nuisance. See pages 116–117 for ways to stop excessive barking.

Quiet Breeds, Noisy Breeds

Some breeds were developed to use their voices for a specific purposes. These breeds are often more vocal than others. Terriers, for example, were bred to alert people to the presence of vermin by barking. Some herding dogs, such as Shetland Sheepdogs and Bearded Collies, were bred to use barking to control their flocks. Scent hounds, such as Foxhounds, Beagles and Bloodhounds, were bred to use

SOMETHING TO SAY Dogs need to express themselves, and this Labrador mix finds a barking session even more satisfying when his owner joins in.

Body Language

Dogs use an eloquent range of body language to communicate

with both humans and other dogs.

This guide to some of the most common ways in which dogs express themselves physically explains what they are telling you by each particular behavior.

PLAY BOWING

When your dog is play bowing, his rear end goes up, his front end goes down, his tail wags and his eyes light up. He's saying, "I want to play," whether it's to another dog or to a human. He may perform this friendly, attention-seeking trick when you're serious and he wants to change your tone. Accept his invitation to play if you're in the mood.

ROLLING OVER

When a dog rolls over on his back with his belly exposed and his legs in the air, he's being submissive. If done in front of another dog, he's saying, "You're the boss and I don't want to fight." When your dog rolls over for you, it could have more than one meaning. If done in anticipation of a scolding, it means, "I don't know how to please you and I'm afraid you're angry. Please accept my apology." Or your dog may be trying to avoid something he doesn't want to do. More often, rolling over is a sign that your dog is happy, trusts you and has a pleasant, low-key nature. It just means, "Please pet my belly."

TAIL WAGGING

You're usually right if you assume that tail wagging indicates a friendly dog, but it's not always the case. Dogs also wag their

A WARM WELCOME When his owner bends over and opens her arms, this Samoyed correctly interprets her body language as a welcome, which encourages him to run eagerly toward her when she calls him.

tails when they are frightened, agitated or unsure. A scared dog may wag his tail low and between his legs as he weighs up his next move and wonders whether he should fight, flee or go belly up. An aggressive, angry dog may wag his tail high while he chases or even attacks. Look at what else is going on—is the dog's best friend just getting off the school bus, or is another dog eating out of his dish? Also check how the dog has distributed his weight, before being certain that the tail wagging is welcoming. If he's feeling aggressive, his body will be tense and his weight will be mainly on the front legs. See pp. 30–31 for more information on what a dog is saying with his tail.

IS IT PLAYTIME YET? With her front end down, rear end up, and tail wagging, this Whippet mix is saying that she wants to play.

A QUICK GUIDE TO BODY LANGUAGE

A dog such as this Vizsla (below) can tell a lot about another dog just by looking at him and noting what the different parts of his body are doing.

Eyes
- Direct eye contact means that a dog is feeling bold and confident
- Casual eye contact means he's contented
- An averted gaze means deference
- Dilated pupils indicate fear

Ears
- Relaxed ears mean that a dog is calm
- Erect ears show that a dog is alert and attentive
- Ears that are up and forward mean a dog is challenging or being assertive or aggressive
- Ears that are laid back indicate that a dog is worried or scared

Body movements
- Pawing is an appeasing gesture
- Licking another dog's face is an invitation to play or a sign of deference
- Play bowing (front legs extended, rump up, tail wagging) is an invitation to play and a sign of happiness
- Draping the head over another dog's shoulders is a social challenge
- Freezing in place means a dog is frightened
- Rubbing or leaning against another dog or a human is a companionable gesture

Mouth and lips
- Panting means that a dog is feeling playful, excited or stressed, or he may simply be hot
- A dog with the mouth and lips closed is uncertain or appeasing
- Licking the lips is a sign that a dog is worried or is trying to appease a person or another dog
- A relaxed mouth means a dog is calm
- Lips pulled back are a challenging or warning sign, especially when combined with a snarl

Hackles (the hair on the shoulders and hips)
- Raised hackles indicate arousal, either because a dog is frightened or is challenging another dog
- Smooth hackles show a dog is calm

Tail
- A relaxed tail means that a dog is calm and at ease
- A tail held straight out, wagging rhythmically and slowly, means that a dog is cautious or on guard
- Tail down indicates worry or uncertainty
- Tail held up and wagging fast indicates excitement
- An erect tail is a sign of alertness
- A tail held between the legs is a sign of fear

MOUNTING

When your dog either mounts another dog or stands above another dog by putting his front paws on the other dog's back, he is asserting his dominance over the other dog. Mounting other dogs isn't just a male characteristic. High-ranking females do it, too. Owners wonder why male dogs mount other males or why females mount at all, but mounting is more often related to social status than to sex.

HUMPING

There's often sexual intent in this behavior, even if the dog doing the humping is neutered. You can let dogs interact this way, as long as the dog being humped isn't trying to escape (and, of course, providing the humping dog is not an unneutered male and the other dog a female in season). If a dog does it to a person, break his focus suddenly by making a loud noise to stop him in his tracks.

YAWNING

Yawning in dogs isn't always a sign of tiredness. It may indicate anticipation or stress. Yawning causes instantaneous changes in the body, increasing heart rate and blood flow to the brain, filling the lungs with oxygen and removing carbon dioxide. In short, a yawn helps a dog energize his body, gather his wits

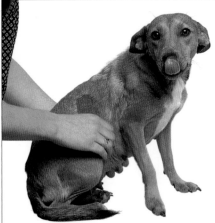

WHAT'S HAPPENING? Dogs will often flick their tongues in and out when they are feeling uneasy or apprehensive, as this mixed breed is doing.

and calm himself down. Your dog may yawn repeatedly when he's waiting in the vet's office, as a way of dealing with nervousness. In training classes, he may yawn to deal with frustration and give himself a mental break. A dog who yawns in anticipation of something enjoyable, such as a walk, is doing so both to boost his energy and to control his eagerness.

TONGUE FLICKING

If your dog repeatedly flicks his tongue up to lick his nose, he's uneasy. He may be assessing a new situation or wondering if he should approach a stranger. Or he may be concentrating hard, trying to master a new obedience command. While a tongue-flicking dog may be friendly, don't approach a strange tongue flicker—the dog is obviously tense. Tongue flicking sometimes precedes biting.

LEANING

Dogs are very tactile and don't always respect personal space. It's common for them to lean against people's legs. Dogs who merely lean, as opposed to a cat-like rubbing back and forth, may be attempting to expand their personal space by taking over yours. Conversely, some dogs lean to express an affectionate kind of possession, or to prevent you from going somewhere else. If your dog rubs against your legs, he is probably just trying to scratch a hard-to-reach spot.

SMILING

Chesapeake Bay Retrievers are known for curling their upper lips whenever they feel happy. Alaskan Malamutes and Samoyeds are also well known for their smiling expressions. Dogs sometimes exhibit what is known as a "submissive grin," which is a type of appeasement gesture. This behavior is particularly common in Dalmatians. Most dogs, however, don't smile in the same way people do. If anything, they tend to assume a grinlike expression when they're feeling threatened or aggressive and want people to see their teeth.

TAIL TUCKED AND EARS BACK

If your dog tucks his tail, lays his ears back, takes a few steps backward or hides behind you, you can be sure he's feeling uncertain. It could be a person or an object that he's not sure of, and you'll need to lessen his fear by introducing him slowly and unthreateningly to whatever he's apprehensive about. See pp. 90–91 and 133 for how to do this.

NOSE NUDGING

Dogs love to push people with their noses. Most of the time it just means they want affection or attention. If you are reading the newspaper, for example, your dog may nudge your hand to try to get your attention away from the paper and back to him. Or perhaps the chair that you're in is his favorite place and he wants you to move out of the way so he can take possession.

PAW LIFTING

If his lifted paw is accompanied by a relaxed, happy expression and a neutral position, your dog just wants attention. Maybe he has been taught how to shake hands and knows he can get positive attention that way. While paw lifting is most likely an invitation to play, your dog might be telling you something else.

SOMETHING ON HIS MIND By panting and putting his ears back, this Norwegian Elkhound shows that he is uncertain or apprehensive about something.

Maybe he has a burr between his toes or ice clumped around his pads that he'd like some help with. Some dogs lift a paw when they are concentrating intently on something, perhaps a ball or a cat. Pointers and setters have been bred to raise a paw to alert their owners to the presence of game. Dogs of these breeds often lift a paw when they see something of interest, even if they have never been used for hunting.

CALMING SIGNALS

Dogs use a number of body language signals, known as calming signals, to soothe themselves, other dogs or people with whom they're interacting. These include yawning, breaking eye contact, tongue flicking, sniffing, turning away, scratching or shaking themselves as though they're wet. To tell when dogs are using calming signals (also known as displacement behaviors), look for an action that's out of context. During a training session, a dog may suddenly scratch himself. If he doesn't have fleas and hasn't been scratching during the rest of the session, he may be trying to relieve stress or to say that he needs a break. These actions are the canine equivalent of the way people will change the subject of a conversation if an argument seems likely to erupt.

I'M THE BOSS This mixed breed puts his head on the other dog's shoulders as a challenge to his rank.

A SIGN OF CONCENTRATION Dogs will often lift one paw and point when they are concentrating hard on something, as this Staffordshire Bull Terrier is doing.

Eyes and Emotions

For those of us who are convinced that dogs think, it is possible

to tell what may be going on in their brains by watching their eyes.

When interpreting what a dog's eyes may be saying, remember to consider this in the context of his body language in general.

Direct Eye Contact

A keen, alert look means a happy and confident dog. The skin around his eyes will be mostly smooth, with perhaps a small crease at the outer corners. This is how dogs look when greeting someone or inviting them to play, or when they've just been given something desirable.

Hard Stare

Dogs stare when they've seen something that warrants closer attention, such as an intruding cat. If they decide that further action is needed, they'll lower their heads a little and squint slightly. This is the same expression wolves use when watching their prey. Shepherds call this "giving or showing the eye"and value it in herding dogs.

Dogs adopt a similar expression when they're being defensive or aggressive. They'll raise their eyebrows, and their foreheads will be slightly furrowed. If they're in behavioral conflict—feeling aggressive yet also a bit fearful—their foreheads will be heavily furrowed. Some dogs show this look when, for example, the vacuum cleaner comes out of the closet and they don't know whether to regard it as friend or foe.

KEEPING AN EYE OUT
This Border Collie's keen gaze shows he has seen something of interest.

LOOKING SIDEWAYS
Dogs look out of the corners of their eyes when they're being coy or asking a person or another dog to play. It's a polite way of expressing interest without being pushy.

Averted Gaze

Avoiding eye contact or looking away is how dogs try to keep the peace. It's how timid or submissive dogs say that they don't want to cause trouble. Dogs look this way when they meet other, higher-ranking dogs or when they sense that their owners are displeased with them.

Dogs may also look away while playing with an object, such as a toy or ball, because this appearance of indifference seems to lure other players into the game.

Eyes Opened Wide

Wide eyes signify astonishment and surprise, and sometimes fear. A sudden noise can cause dogs to jump, turn around, and look wide-eyed at the source of the sound. Dogs who are frightened may open their eyes so wide that the whites show more than usual.

Blank Stare

Blank stares don't need much interpretation; they mean understimulated or tired dogs. If their eyes are open but no one appears to be home, this indicates that nothing of interest is happening around them.

Eyes Narrowed or Half Closed

Dogs who are happy and relaxed will narrow their eyes or half-close them. This is how dogs will look when they're enjoying something such as a tummy rub or a long session of stroking from their owner. These half-closed eyes unmistakably convey total bliss.

Ear Positions

Dogs have wonderfully mobile ears that they can swivel, twitch, raise

and lower to telegraph their moods and intentions.

Some breeds are better at expressing certain emotions because of the shape of their ears. Siberian Huskies, for example, have erect, triangular ears that make them look attentive and alert all the time, even when they're relaxed. A Basset Hound, by contrast, may be just as attentive as the Husky, but his heavy, pendulous ears can't convey the same degree of intensity.

Dogs with cropped ears may be harder to read. Cropping turns hanging or folded ears into erect, pricked ears. This changes a dog's look from placid to intent and aggressive, which can change how people and other dogs perceive him.

All the positions of a dog's ears should be gauged in comparison to the way the dog normally carries his ears when he's relaxed.

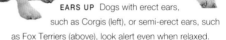

EARS UP Dogs with erect ears, such as Corgis (left), or semi-erect ears, such as Fox Terriers (above), look alert even when relaxed.

JUDGING DOGS BY THEIR EARS

When watching dogs to see what their ears are saying, you need to look closely. Some of the messages can be subtle, and positions that look very similar can mean different things.

Neutral

Every dog, whatever his ear size or type, has a neutral ear position that indicates he's relaxed and content. The skin around the base of the ears will be smooth because he isn't making an effort to move the muscles.

Pricked Up

When stimulated by something, dogs will prick their ears right up and point them in the direction of their interest. Dogs who are feeling aggressive will raise their ears, too. This is easiest to see in dogs with prick ears, such as German Shepherds. In dogs with folded or hanging ears, such as Greyhounds or Labradors, look for creases around the base of the ear, which indicate that the muscles are active. The amount of tension in a dog's ears will tell you how strong his feelings are.

Pulled Down and Back

When a dog's brow and skull muscles are tight and tense, and his ears are pulled down and back, he's probably feeling frightened, anxious or submissive. The more intense his feelings, the more extreme the ear position will be.

Limp

Ears that droop are a dog's way of saying he's tired or understimulated. Dogs with prick ears can't manage the full droop, but will let their ears sag sideways a bit. Those with naturally hanging ears will let them hang even lower.

Multiple Positions

Dogs are sometimes in two minds about things and this will show in the way they hold their ears. They may prick one ear up and pull the other partially back. Or one ear may be folded while the other is flat against the skull. In some cases, the ears keep changing position as a dog's emotions change. You may see this when a stranger comes to the house. Your dog is not sure whether to be excited or nervous, and his ears reflect this conflict.

HARD TO READ Dogs with long or very hairy ears, such as this Chinese Crested, may be harder to read than those with pricked ears.

Tail Positions

The dog wears his heart on his tail, and the movement of his tail will tell you a great deal about what he is thinking.

When dogs are alone, they usually don't wag their tails, no matter how much they're enjoying themselves. This is because tail-wagging is mainly used for social communication. Once a dog is with people or other dogs, the tail really goes into action—how fast and how vigorously depends on the dog's breed and personality. Many spaniels, for example, wag wildly at the slightest provocation. Other breeds may be much less inclined to wag.

Among all breeds, a slight wag, when just the end of the tail moves, is a casual greeting. The happier and more excited dogs get, the more vigorously they wag. Tails that are stiff and not wagging are a signal that dogs are feeling defensive, protective or aggressive.

TAIL COMMUNICATION

Not all dogs communicate equally well with their tails. Some breeds have tails that are less mobile than others. Others have tails that are held close to their rumps. Such dogs can't always say what they mean with their tails.

This can be a real problem for dogs such as French Bulldogs, Basenjis and Pugs, whose tails are small and tightly curled. They tend to rely on other types of body language. When they're happy, they wiggle their bodies back and forth and shake their tails from side to

SIGNS OF FEAR Dogs who carry both their head and their tail low, as this Chihuahua is doing, are afraid or submissive.

side. They also use their heads a lot. They'll wrinkle their foreheads when they're curious, and they have very mobile ears.

Australian Shepherds are born with tails that are very short or non-existent. Boxers, Schnauzers, Rottweilers and Dobermans traditionally have had their tails docked, or cut short. These dogs use their stubby tails as much as they can, but their ability to express themselves is quite restricted.

Some tails, on the other hand, are made for communication because they're easy to see. Dogs with long, bushy tails, such as German Shepherds, Samoyeds and Siberian Huskies, have no trouble expressing their emotions. Their tails move freely, and the luxuriant masses of hair give them an air of authority.

Scottish and West Highland White Terriers are between these two extremes. While their tails are quite short, and short-haired, they're still very expressive because what they lack in size they make up for in mobility and upright positioning.

While a hairy tail can make it easier to communicate by exaggerating dogs' normal tail movements, it can also be a problem for

NO FEAR A tail between the legs usually means fear or submission, but this is the normal tail position for Greyhounds.

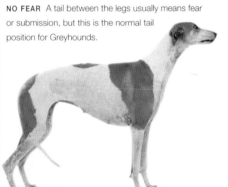

A CURLY PROBLEM Dogs with small, tightly curled tails, such as Basenjis, rely more on other forms of body language.

ON GUARD An Airedale's high-set, stiffly carried tail may look like a signal of challenge to other dogs.

EVERYTHING'S OKAY This Labrador's gently wagging tail shows that he is relaxed and happy.

dogs with very short tails, such as Old English Sheepdogs. Their thick, hairy coats can cover their tails completely. No matter how much they move their tails, the movements may be invisible. To compensate, these dogs will often move their entire rumps back and forth.

Different breeds carry their tails in different positions as well. Fox Terriers and Airedales, for example, naturally carry their tails high and rather stiffly. This can make them look assertive or even aggressive, to both other dogs and people. Golden Retrievers carry their lower-set tails in a relaxed fashion, which makes them look mellow and unthreatening. Greyhounds, Whippets, Borzois and Afghan Hounds usually carry their tails between their legs, but they may not be feeling frightened, timid or unhappy. It's just how their tails are.

TAILS IN ACTION

Tails aren't just for communication. The tail is a vital part of a dog's balance system. Some breeds, such as Afghans, Irish Wolfhounds and Greyhounds, were bred to chase fast-moving

prey. Their tails are thin and very long in proportion to the rest of them. They can run at great speeds, and they use their tails as a counterbalance when turning, giving them agility and the ability to maneuver quickly in response to the movements of their quarry. These dogs' tails are long, tapered and low set, and when combined with their sloping rumps, have something of a rudder effect.

Dogs also use their tails when swimming. Chesapeake Bay Retrievers and Labradors have thick, strong tails that help them move easily through the water. The flexibility of a dog's tail also helps him make quick turns in the water.

Other dogs use their tails as insulation. Nordic breeds, such as Alaskan Malamutes, Siberian Huskies and Samoyeds, have brushy or plumed tails with long, dense fur. When they're lying down, they can pull their tails over their faces to keep out the cold. When they're pulling a sled across ice, these dogs also use their tails as a counterbalance to help them move more quickly.

INCOMMUNICADO Dogs with severely docked tails, such as this Doberman, have a limited ability to signal with their tails.

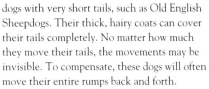

WRONG MESSAGE Malamutes carry their tails over their backs, which may make them look assertive.

Communicating Effectively

Dogs can recognize some human words and body language, but most of the ways we behave and communicate seem a little foreign to them.

People move their hands a lot when they get excited, for example. Dogs know from our expressions that we're happy, yet we may appear angry to them because in the animal world, quick, exuberant movements usually mean aggression or danger.

When dogs don't do what we tell them to, it's not because they're stupid or stubborn; more likely, they've been given confusing signals. Once you understand how dogs perceive you, such confusion should decrease.

VOCAL BARRIERS

Dogs are familiar with the range and volume of their owners' voices, but other voices can be confusing. Dogs don't pay attention to words so much as to tone and laughter, and they're very good at comparing voices with body language—so people can say one thing while their dogs interpret something different.

Tone of Voice

Young or submissive dogs are often the ones with high-pitched barks or yelps, while higher-ranking dogs are more likely to give a low growl. Some dogs get slightly nervous around men with deep voices because they associate that pitch with the imposition of authority, or with the reprimands their mothers gave them when they were young.

People don't have to disguise their voices to communicate with dogs, but raising the pitch a little can help. To a dog's ears, a higher voice sounds happier and less threatening. Trainers often recommend using an energetic, slightly high-pitched tone, because it can help dogs respond with more enthusiasm.

However, high-pitched voices can sometimes cause problems of their own, especially when used for discipline. If you always use a high-pitched voice to encourage your dog and to generally jolly him along, you may find the same tone has little effect when you are trying to stop him doing something. It's worth lowering your voice a notch when giving reprimands. Even if you don't sound angry, the deep, gruff tone will spark your dog's memories of early authority figures, and he'll be more likely to do as you tell him.

Words and Actions

Dogs are experts at reading all kinds of body language, so they can quickly tell when your words or tone of voice aren't telling the whole story. This often happens in vets' offices, where owners try to soothe nervous dogs by telling them that everything's okay. The dogs know perfectly well that's not true, and their owners' attempts to give comfort may have little effect or even confirm the need for alarm.

Similarly, trying to reassure a scared dog who is growling will probably just increase his tension because he'll interpret soothing words as support for what he's doing. He simply won't understand that his behavior isn't appropriate. A better approach is to tell your dog sternly to stop it. He'll respond to the firmness in your voice, and will know that you're in charge and that you'll be able to handle things from then on.

A DOG'S POINT OF VIEW When you understand how your dog perceives you and your actions, it will become easier to communicate with him effectively.

DIFFERENT WAVELENGTHS Dogs try to understand people's words and actions by translating human behavior into canine terms, which may cause confusion.

Laughter

It's important to refrain from laughing when dogs have done something wrong, no matter how amusing, because dogs interpret laughter as a happy sound that means they have your approval. To keep getting your approval in the future, they're sure to do the same thing again.

BODY LANGUAGE BARRIERS

When dogs want to learn more about other dogs, they focus on posture. Dog-to-dog messages are clear-cut because both dogs are speaking the same language. But dogs are in foreign territory when they try to decipher most human body language. When dealing with dogs, be aware of your body language and make sure that it's communicating the same thing as your voice. The two are likely to be at odds when you're trying not to show that you're cross with your dog. Even if your voice is calm, your dog will see that your face, arms, and shoulders are stiff—all signs that you're on edge. He'll be confused because your message isn't clear, and he won't know how to react.

Dogs watch people much more closely than we ever watch them. Should our facial expressions not match the other signals that we're giving, dogs get confused. When you're trying to act stern, for example, but your eyes are twinkling or your mouth is curving into a smile, dogs aren't sure which to believe—your stern voice or your happy facial expression.

Likewise, if you use a serious voice to tell your dog to stay but a few seconds later give him a wink, he may perceive that you're giving him permission to get up and move around.

Putting on a happy face does come in handy when you want to congratulate a dog for following orders. But don't try to fool dogs with "false" expressions, and try not to mix the signals you're giving. Dogs only feel secure when they know what you're feeling; mixed signals make them nervous and uncertain.

MENTAL BARRIERS

It's normal for us to interpret dogs' behavior in human terms, but our judgments usually aren't very accurate. People often swear that their dogs look guilty when they've done something wrong. But as far as we know, dogs don't feel guilt. That means that when you come home and find the trash on the floor and your dog cowering in the corner, you can't assume that he knows he did something wrong. In all likelihood he's simply responding to the cross look on your face. Or maybe he recalls from previous experience that trash on the floor is bad news when you're around.

The important thing is to always make your reaction match the situation. If your dog is to understand what you really mean, he needs to be able to make a logical connection between his action and your response. He may not like being corrected, but at least he'll see that as a predictable response. But starting to scold your dog, then suddenly relenting and indulgently giving his ears a scratch, will seem inconsistent, and that will leave him confused.

Smell

A dog's most important sense is that of smell, which is
many times more sensitive than a human's.

Dogs can identify scents that humans cannot detect and that are incredibly faint. One reason for their superlative sense of smell is their enormous amount of olfactory membrane. Humans have about 65 square inches (420 sq cm) of olfactory membrane. Dogs have about 900 square inches (5,600 sq cm). This membrane is packed with olfactory receptors, cells specially adapted to detect scents. It seems that the bigger the dog, the more acute her sense of smell. A German Shepherd has about 220 million olfactory receptors, a Fox Terrier about 150 million and a Dachshund about 125 million. Humans have a comparatively paltry 5 million.

Dogs must actively sniff to draw in scent molecules, which are then interpreted by various parts of the brain. Much of a dog's brain is devoted to processing and storing scent information. Dogs can remember scent memories for all their lives, and these affect their behavior. Scents tell them where they are, who a person or another animal is, and even that other's mood and state of health.

WHAT SCENT SAYS

A dog's constant sniffing while out on a walk can be tedious for the person on the other end of the leash, but it's a dog's way of gleaning all sorts of interesting information, especially about other dogs. Most of this information is contained in a dog's urine;

TENACIOUS TRACKER
The Bloodhound's phenomenal sense of smell has been used to track criminals, lost children and other animals.

THE NOSE KNOWS Experts believe that larger dogs, such as Great Danes, have a more acute sense of smell than small ones, such as Fox Terriers.

significant amounts are also gained from her feces, anal glands, saliva and paw prints. Each dog's scent is as unique as a person's fingerprints, and a dog only needs a quick sniff of another's scent to work out her status, age, sex, and whether she is neutered or entire, friend, foe, stranger or relation. From these clues, a dog can work out quite quickly what her relationship with another is likely to be.

Your dog also recognizes your scent and those of all the other people she knows. From their scent, she will remember who she likes and who she doesn't, and will react accordingly. Dogs are also believed to be able to detect a person's state of health through changes in his or her body odor.

Although most dogs are attracted by scents that humans find disgusting, such as pungent garbage or rotting fish, there are some scents that they don't like. These include citrus smells (such as lemon, lime and orange), hot pepper and, in particular, citronella. Citronella, a natural plant extract, is commercially available in spray form and can be used to keep dogs away from certain areas.

Hearing

*Dogs can hear sounds from greater distances
and at much higher frequencies than humans can.*

One of the reasons dogs hear so much better than people do is that their ears are bigger. They're also cup-shaped, which enables them to trap all the available sound waves and funnel them into the eardrum. Dogs can also move one ear at a time, allowing them to detect and pinpoint sounds coming from any direction.

Despite their excellent hearing, dogs aren't overwhelmed by the variety or volume of the sounds they hear any more than people are overwhelmed by the range of things they see. A dog's brain filters out anything the dog isn't interested in or doesn't need to know about. That's why they can sleep through a noisy conversation in the next room but will wake up the instant someone says their name or opens the cupboard where their food is kept. Similarly, when someone fills the laundry tub to wash a sweater, some dogs hide because they think it's bathtime—but they'll ignore the sound of the kitchen sink being filled for doing the dishes. They only tune in to the things that might affect them.

A dog's superior hearing can be a real favor to humans, such as when she hears someone slipping over a back fence into the yard. But sometimes it can be too sensitive, such as when a dog erupts in a volley of barking because she hears something that her owners can't see or hear, and wouldn't care about if they could.

Being able to hear high frequencies has surprising benefits for some dogs. The cry of a bat, for example, is way too high for most creatures, including cattle, to hear. That may explain why cattle in South America are often attacked by vampire bats, but dogs seldom are. It seems that dogs are able to hear the bats' cries and so can avoid becoming the source of their next meal.

KEEPING AN EAR OUT
A dog's sharp hearing alerts her to danger, lets her communicate with other dogs and enables her to detect even the smallest and most cautious of prey.

It seems that the distance between the ears may affect a dog's ability to detect ultra-sound. However, ear type doesn't seem to have much effect on hearing. Floppy-eared dogs and prick-eared dogs have fared roughly the same in tests. Surprisingly, dogs with floppy ears can hear almost as well with their ears in the normal, droopy position as when they're taped up to expose the ear canal.

One thing that is breed related is the likelihood of a dog being born deaf. This is caused by a genetic disorder that is associated with white and blue merle coat colors. It can crop up anywhere, but it occurs most often in Dalmatians, Australian Shepherds, Australian Cattle Dogs, Boston Terriers, English Setters, Boxers and Old English Sheepdogs.

However, deaf dogs compensate in other ways. Dogs spend 80 to 90 percent of their time communicating without a sound. They pay close attention to body language, faces and eyes to help them understand each other and people. Dogs who are deaf learn to "read" other dogs and humans very well. They can also be taught to respond to hand signals rather than verbal commands.

I'M HEARING YOU
Dogs' highly mobile ears have 15 muscles that move them up, down and sideways.

Sight

Although sight is not a dog's most important sense, dogs' eyes have various specializations, which even differ among breeds.

Dogs often use their eyesight simply to confirm what their other senses have already told them. For example, a dog may hear her owner's car and dash to the front gate. She is familiar with the sound, so seeing the car simply proves what she already knew. The same thing happens when she smells a squirrel and follows its scent. When she flushes the squirrel, the sight of it stimulates her to chase it, but doesn't give her any new information. It just confirms what her nose already told her.

CANINE EYESIGHT

It has been recognized for some time that dogs, like most domestic species, are dichromats, as distinct from most birds and primates, which are trichromats. This means that dogs see the world in a similar way to a color-blind human.

Studies have shown that the distribution of cells in the retina varies tremendously with skull shape. These findings suggest that dogs of disparate skull shapes see the world in different ways, and helps to explain why all sighthound breeds—such as Salukis, Afghan Hounds, Borzois and Greyhounds—have long noses.

It seems that long-nosed dogs have good peripheral vision, perfect for spotting prey that is on the move. The peripheral vision of short-nosed breeds is less acute, meaning that they are less likely to act like a running predator and to hunt in packs, and instead are more likely to be able to focus on human faces.

Dogs' eyes are more sensitive to light and movement than people's are, but they can't focus on things as well. That's why dogs can see very slight movements in dim light, but they sometimes can't see balls close by in broad daylight. Even brightly colored balls that contrast vividly with the surroundings won't be much easier for them to see due to their poor color vision.

People and dogs have different numbers of receptor cells—called rods and cones—in their eyes. Rods pick up very low levels of light, but only in black and white. Dogs have more rods than we do, which means that in dim light their sight is keener than ours. This is a throwback to their wild days. Most prey animals are most active at dawn and dusk, so wild dogs needed to be able to see in dim light to have any chance of making a kill. Cones, however, are needed to see in daylight and to pick up color. Dogs have fewer of these than people do, because recognizing color isn't very important for dogs' daily lives. What does matter to dogs is detecting movement. When dogs were predators, movement was the trigger that made them pay attention because it meant that prey was nearby. Today's dogs still retain their ancestors' skills and instincts.

Dogs' eyes are set wider apart than those of humans. Their field of vision ranges from 190 degrees for flat-faced dogs, such as Pugs and Pekingese, to 270 degrees for Greyhounds. By contrast, humans can only see 180 degrees.

One thing that doesn't vary much between breeds is the size of their eyes. The eyeball volume of a Chihuahua is comparatively greater than that of a Mastiff, which is why toy dogs' eyes appear to bulge.

ON THE MOVE Dogs have a limited ability to see the color red; it is the movement of the flying disk, rather than its color, to which this Border Collie is reacting.

Touch

More than vision, scent and hearing, touching allows dogs to form emotional bonds and communicate their most basic needs.

Throughout their lives, dogs' interactions with other dogs and with people resemble a contact sport. To us, it all looks like play. But to dogs, a hip nudge, nose bump or paw push speaks as clearly as a shout.

THE MEANING OF TOUCH

Dogs use touch to establish control or rank. When two dogs meet, one dog may push the other with his shoulder or nose. It looks like a playful nudge, which it may be, but it's also a way for the dog to express his high status. Shy, submissive dogs will rarely use these types of touch, while naturally confident dogs use them all the time.

Dogs' social interactions aren't all about status, however. They love to play, and they'll use a variety of touches to communicate their willingness—or their reluctance—to do so.

To know for sure what a dog is trying to say, you have to look at the whole picture. Some of the signals a dog uses to establish status, such as putting his paws on another dog's shoulders or banging him with his hips, are also friendly overtures. A dog who pushes with his nose, for example, and is also wagging his tail or bowing his front end, is saying he'd like to play. Even aggressive-looking touches, such as grabbing the fur around the neck, may be friendly as long as the dogs know each other and they're displaying other play signals at the same time.

LOST IN TRANSLATION

Dogs and humans may interpret the same kind of touch differently. People shake hands when they meet, for example, but

GOOD DOG Touch can be used as a form of praise to reinforce good, compliant behavior, such as this Labrador's, or as a way of calming a stressed dog.

most dogs dislike having their feet touched. We put our hands on each other's shoulders to express affection, but dogs may view this type of touch as a threat. Dogs also dislike hugs, which restrict their ability to move or escape.

When you are aware of how dogs perceive your touch, you can tailor it to avoid these tactile mistranslations. For example, people are much taller than dogs, so we tend to reach down and pet their highest part, the top of the head. Among dogs, this is a clear signal that they're being challenged. A better way to greet a dog is to stoop down, which makes you look less intimidating, and to touch him under the chin or on the chest instead of on the head.

PUPPY TALK From the moment of birth, puppies, such as these Saint Bernards, begin to communicate with their mother and siblings by touch.

We are alone, absolutely alone on this chance planet;
and, amid all the forms of life that surround us, not
one, excepting the dog, has made an alliance with us.

MAURICE MAETERLINCK (1862–1949),
Belgian playwright and poet

*All knowledge, the totality of all questions
and answers, is contained in the dog.*

FRANZ KAFKA (1883–1924),
Czech-born Austrian novelist and short story writer

CHAPTER TWO

CHOOSING A DOG

The Best Dog for You

Choose your pet carefully, taking into consideration your lifestyle,

your home environment and your family situation.

Too often, a dog is chosen with little forethought and does not live up to an owner's expectations—with heartbreaking consequences. The key to a successful relationship between you and your pet is to make the right choice in the first place.

EASY CARE Mixed breeds, such as this Collie mix, are less prone to genetic diseases than purebred dogs. Many of them have plenty of character, too, and make charming pets.

FAMILY MATTERS

Before taking on the responsibility of a dog, make sure that the whole family is willing to care for the new pet. Feeding, play, exercise, training and grooming are all essential canine needs and take time. If you don't have this time, perhaps a cat or smaller animal would be a better choice of pet. Also, make sure that no one in the family is allergic to dogs. Too many dogs are given up each year because of an allergy that was overlooked.

Consider the overall costs of owning a dog. Estimate the price of food, leashes, toys, veterinary care, pet insurance—and the replacement of demolished household items. You may also need to build a fence, hire a dog-walker or sometimes leave your dog at a boarding kennel.

Once it is firmly established that there are enough committed caretakers, it's time to consider exactly what kind of dog you want.

THINGS TO CONSIDER

Learn as much as you can about the characteristics of different breeds so you can narrow your choices to those that best fit your needs. Although dogs vary from individual to individual, dog breeds tend to have distinct appearances and to behave in distinct ways. For example, the sporting breeds were bred for long hours in the field and tend to need plenty of exercise. Therefore, a retriever may not be

NOT JUST A PRETTY FACE Standard Poodles are intelligent, highly trainable, non-shedding and good with children.

the best choice if you live in an apartment. However, if you live in the suburbs and have a large fenced yard and active children, a retriever may be perfect.

For apartment dwellers, a less active breed may be best. However, don't equate the size of a dog with the amount of exercise he needs. A Beagle is a small dog, but an active one that will need plenty of regular exercise. The giant breeds, such as Great Danes and Newfoundlands, on the other hand, require only moderate exercise, and less space than their huge size might indicate. The toy breeds can get much of the exercise they need inside an apartment. But be careful, as some of them are quite noisy.

Coat length should also be considered when deciding upon a breed. Long-coated dogs, such as Chow Chows and Keeshonds, have beautiful thick coats, but they require a good deal of grooming to keep them that way. Short-coated dogs, such as Labradors and Dalmatians, require less grooming but tend to shed hair all year round. The breeds that don't shed, such as Bichon Frises and Poodles, need to be clipped regularly—an additional expense if this is done professionally.

Think about the climate your dog will be living in. The Arctic breeds, such as Huskies and Samoyeds, have thick coats and tend to be uncomfortable in hot, humid climates. On the other hand, Whippets and Greyhounds become very chilled in cold climates. If conditions are extreme where you live, choose a dog whose coat type permits easy adaptation.

You should also consider the dog's sex. In general, males can have more behavioral

BEFORE ADOPTING A DOG, FIND OUT:

- Why was the dog given up?
- Where did he come from?
- How many homes has he already had?
- Is he house-trained?
- Is he used to children?
- Is he used to other pets?
- Is he friendly to people?
- Does he like to be petted?
- Has he had his shots?
- Does he obey commands?
- Does he look healthy?

IN THE SWIM Give your dog a varied exercise regime, tailoring it to his breed if you can. Many of the retrieving breeds, such as Labradors, love to swim.

problems and tend to be more aggressive than females. Although dogs of either sex make wonderful companions, first-time dog owners or families with children might want to look for a female first. Females are usually easier to train and house-train, but they may also be more demanding of your time and attention than a male dog. Males are usually larger than females of the same breed. This difference can be considerable in large breeds—for example, a male Newfoundland may weigh 150 lb (68 kg), while a female may be up to 40 lb (18 kg) less. Males and females make equally good watchdogs.

Don't forget the mixed breeds—they often make excellent, loving pets. The breeding of genetically similar dogs can result in diseases, such as hip dysplasia, and behavioral problems, such as aggression. Adopting a mixed-breed dog is one of the best ways to avoid inherited diseases. Although it is not as easy to predict the adult appearance, size or behavior of a mixed breed, most are very appealing and many are in need of a good home.

SUITABLE DOGS FOR CHILDREN

If you have young children, you may want to consider these playful and friendly breeds:

Bearded Collie	Shetland Sheepdog
West Highland White Terrier	Miniature Schnauzer
Golden Retriever	Labrador Retriever
Cavalier King Charles Spaniel	Beagle

Be aware, however, that children under three may be unintentionally rough with their pets. Dogs, too, can be rough with very young children. Even those breeds listed above require training and positive early experiences with children to be reliable.

Puppy or Adult?

While puppies have obvious appeal, chewed shoes, housetraining and the other rigors of puppyhood are not for every family.

Puppies and adult dogs have different needs and make different demands of their owners. Some people love raising puppies; others will wisely choose to adopt an older dog.

CHOOSING A PUPPY

A puppy is a clean slate, and you can make him what you want him to be. The drawback is that his training has to start from scratch. Because he is a baby, he will need more of your time and patience than an older dog. Do you have enough of both to housebreak and train him, as well as the sense of fun and adventure to play with him? Puppies tend to be destructive when they're bored, so they need plenty of exercise and supervised play.

An ideal match for puppies is a family where one adult is home for much of the day. But if all the household's adults have to go to work, it's still possible to get a puppy. Plan to acquire him when you have some vacation time and spend that time bonding with him and establishing him in a regular routine of exercise and feeding—not a vacation routine, but the kind of schedule you are both going to have to live by once you're back at work. And when your vacation is over, if you can visit him during your lunch hour or hurry home straight after work to spend plenty of quality time with him, he'll grow into a happy and well-adjusted dog.

Early Influences

Try to get your new puppy between six and eight weeks of age. It's important for the development of social behavior that a pup stays with his mother and littermates until this time. However, as a six- to eight-week-old puppy is in the middle of the so-called "period of socialization" (between three and 14 weeks

A HEALTHY PUP

When choosing a puppy, such as this Australian Cattle Dog, examine him all over to make sure he is bright and healthy.

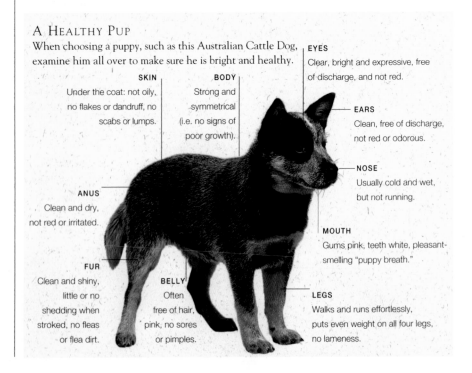

SKIN
Under the coat: not oily, no flakes or dandruff, no scabs or lumps.

BODY
Strong and symmetrical (i.e. no signs of poor growth).

EYES
Clear, bright and expressive, free of discharge, and not red.

EARS
Clean, free of discharge, not red or odorous.

NOSE
Usually cold and wet, but not running.

ANUS
Clean and dry, not red or irritated.

MOUTH
Gums pink, teeth white, pleasant-smelling "puppy breath."

FUR
Clean and shiny, little or no shedding when stroked, no fleas or flea dirt.

BELLY
Often free of hair, pink, no sores or pimples.

LEGS
Walks and runs effortlessly, puts even weight on all four legs, no lameness.

of age), it's equally important that you start to bond with your new pup now. If you can, choose the puppy when he is very young, let him stay with his mother until he is eight weeks old, and in the meantime, visit him frequently so that he becomes familiar with you. This will make it easier for him to adjust once you take him home.

Choose your puppy from a healthy litter. Make sure all the puppies appear bright, alert, active and well fed. If possible, meet your pup's parents and other adult relatives. This will indicate how he is likely to look and behave when he grows up. Are the parents friendly? High-energy? Low-energy? Obedient? This should give some idea of what you're getting.

Watch how the puppies interact with each other. Play with them and pick up each one individually. Although the runt of the litter might be the cutest, he may also have medical and behavioral problems.

If the litter of puppies you are looking at is purebred, consider letting the breeder choose the right match from the litter for you. The breeder has been with the puppies since they were born and will have a good idea of what the different personalities are like.

Many obedience trainers prefer male dogs, but if you're an inexperienced dog owner, or not sure about what sex to choose, pick the middle-of-the-road female puppy in a litter—she'll be a bit more easygoing, not too shy, not too pushy. If you're selecting a puppy from a mixed-breed litter, consider erring on the side of caution by opting for a female, especially if you think the pups are going to grow up big and you don't want an over-large dog.

In many breeds, the size difference between puppies and adults is great. Don't assume that a small puppy will grow into a small adult.

ADOPTING AN ADULT DOG

If the house is empty for much of the day and a new dog will be alone with just his possessions, consider getting an adult dog. It could be the easier option, because more mature dogs are often better at entertaining themselves, and won't miss your company quite so much. Also, a mature dog won't need your absolute and undivided attention when you are home. What's more, he may already be house-trained, and know some basic obedience commands.

One possible disadvantage is that he will be shaped and molded by life experiences that are beyond your control and about which you may know nothing. But if he turns out to have a few bad habits, you can still remold him with the help of obedience classes, a professional trainer, or just a good book on dog training.

Then again, if you "inherit" an adult dog from a family member or friend, there's a good chance you might know a great deal about him. Adopting a dog this way is the perfect solution for all involved, but don't adopt a dog, whether from a shelter or another family, just because you feel sorry for it. Although many adult dogs given up for adoption make wonderful companions, some may have been surrendered because of behavioral problems that might not be obvious. Try to obtain an accurate history of the animal. Observe him at the animal shelter and ask the shelter staff for their opinion of his character. If you choose carefully, an adult dog may be perfect for you. In addition, you will be providing a home for an animal that really needs one.

Why Choose a Purebred?

A dog with a distinguished pedigree isn't necessarily more lovable,

cute, funny or loyal than a mutt. He's simply more predictable.

Purebred dogs have certain specific traits, so you'll know what you're getting. If you decide on a quiet, large, non-shedding dog that's good with children, then you know that a Standard Poodle will fit the bill perfectly.

THE PREDICTABLE DOG

The various dog breeds have been monitored for generations, and their ancestry has been recorded and studied. All that history means that when you decide on a purebred dog, you've got a good idea of what kind of dog you'll be getting, in terms of size and behavior. Once you know your needs and your breeds, you can start matchmaking.

If you want a dog to go jogging with, you'll have to rule out a Bulldog, who is built for strength, not stamina. Opt instead for an athletic dog, perhaps one of the sporting or working breeds, such as a Vizsla, German Shepherd or Siberian Husky.

Although environment and training both play a vital role in molding the adult dog, it remains true that certain breeds, and groups of breeds, are genetically predisposed to certain behaviors. The key is to find out what these are. Purebred dogs are divided into various groups, according to the breed's original purpose. And although the purebreds of today no longer lead the same lives that their ancestors did, they still retain certain qualities and behaviors (see box, opposite).

A SIZE FOR EVERYONE Some breeds come in various sizes. Poodles may be Standard, Miniature or Toy; and Schnauzers Giant, Standard or Toy. The Poodle and Schnauzer pictured are both Toys.

GETTING SOME FRIENDLY ADVICE

Before choosing a dog, get expert advice. Talk to veterinarians about the breeds that interest you. They can give you general impressions of various breeds, and can also probably put you in touch with breeders of that particular dog. Trainers can tell you how easy it is to train certain breeds, which they have had the most trouble with, and which are better suited to first-time owners or to people with more experience, or to people with or without children or other animals.

To see various breeds in action, visit dog shows or events, such as obedience trials or herding tests. Talk to the owners, who will often also be breeders. They will be happy to tell you about their dogs. But be aware that you'll be talking to a real fan of that breed and may not get an

BREED DIFFERENCES
Golden Retrievers need daily, vigorous exercise and frequent brushing. Pembroke Welsh Corgis require daily, moderate exercise and weekly grooming. Both breeds are easy to train, have cheerful temperaments and make good pets for kids.

objective opinion, so ask about what aspects of the breed they don't like—and do your own research if they say the breed is flawless.

PUREBRED HEALTH PROBLEMS

Creating breeds involves concentrating genetic material to obtain certain physical characteristics, appearance, behavior or personality. The downside of this is that a smaller gene pool can increase a purebred dog's inherited predisposition to certain illnesses. Unfortunately, diseases or defects may show up only when the dog is several years old and has perhaps been bred himself.

Every breed is susceptible to some ailment or disorder. Most large breeds are prone to a joint disorder called hip dysplasia. Cocker Spaniels, Akitas and Siberian Huskies, among others, have a higher incidence of progressive retinal atrophy and hereditary cataracts. A blood-clotting disorder, von Willebrand's disease, affects many breeds, including Doberman Pinschers and Scottish Terriers. Newfoundlands are prone to heart defects and Dalmatians to deafness. Dogs with pushed-in faces, such as Pekingese, are prone to respiratory problems, birthing difficulties and painful eye problems.

There are ways to reduce the chance that your purebred pup will suffer from a disease to which his breed is genetically predisposed. Buy him from a reputable breeder, who can demonstrate careful matching of the parents based on their genetic backgrounds to breed out inherited problems. Ensure that the parents have a clean bill of health. The pup should also have been checked carefully by a vet.

It's also wise to find out how old the pup's grandparents lived to be and ask if any of his relatives suffered from diseases or conditions common to the breed. Long-lived relatives are often a good indicator of a healthy line of dogs.

THE SEVEN PUREBRED GROUPS

Sporting dogs The larger spaniels, pointers, setters (such as the Irish Setter, below right) and retrievers; also the Vizsla and Weimaraner. Alert, intelligent dogs that have been, and still are, used by hunters to find and retrieve game. They need plenty of regular, energetic outdoor exercise.

Hounds Once used either their noses to track small game (scenthounds, such as the Basset Hound, above, and Foxhound) or their keen sight and speed to run down prey (sighthounds, such as the Borzoi and Scottish Deerhound). They tend to have great stamina, but differ in their exercise requirements. Most enjoy room to run and sniff.

Working dogs A diverse group that includes guard dogs of both livestock and property (the Mastiff and Kuvasz), sled or cart dogs (Samoyed and Bernese Mountain Dog), rescue dogs (Saint Bernard and Newfoundland), and dogs that serve the military (Doberman Pinscher). Capable and quick to learn, they make dependable companions. Because of their size and strength, it is important that they be properly trained.

Terriers These are dogs that "go to ground"—the name "terrier" is derived from "terra," Latin for earth. Some terriers, such as Fox Terriers and Norfolk Terriers, were bred to dig burrowing animals from their dens. Others, such as the West Highland White Terrier and Miniature Schnauzer, were bred to kill troublesome vermin. Feisty and very active, they need owners who are a match for their strong personalities.

Toy dogs Traditional lap-sitters favored by nobility (Pekingese, left, Japanese Chin and Maltese). Irresistibly cute because of their diminutive size, they can have quite determined personalities. They are ideal for people with limited living space.

Non-Sporting dogs A catch-all group for breeds that were recognized by the American Kennel Club but didn't quite fit any of the other groups. Bulldogs, Dalmatians, Lhasa Apsos, Tibetan Terriers, Tibetan Spaniels and Keeshonds are included.

Herding dogs Intelligent animals bred to herd sheep or cattle. The Old English Sheepdog, Collie and Briard belong to this group, as does the German Shepherd. They make excellent companions, but the instinct to herd is strong; sometimes they can't resist rounding up your children or other pets. They need plenty of exercise.

Fifty Popular Breeds

The chart on the following pages provides a quick-reference guide

to the size, temperament and care needs of some popular breeds.

With so many different breeds to choose from, you want to get the one that's best for you. The following chart lists important features of 50 of the most popular breeds. Firstly, the standard height and weight ranges for each breed are given, along with a personality description.

A dog's height is measured from the ground to his withers, or shoulders. The personality description outlines each breed's basic temperament and includes such information as whether the breed is easy to train or is suitable for a family with young children.

ALERT AUSSIES Herding dogs, such as these Australian Shepherds, tend to be intelligent, easy to train, obedient and loyal. Because they were bred for hard work, they thrive on vigorous, regular exercise.

CANINE COLOR CHART

If someone says, "Look at that harlequin Great Dane," and you're looking for a dog dressed up in a clown suit, then you need some help. Here are the more unusual canine color terms:

Bicolor A coat of two distinct colors.

Brindle An even mixture of dark colors with lighter colors, usually as a striped, tigerlike coat.

Grizzled A roan pattern that is usually a mixture of black, bluish-gray, iron gray or red with white.

Harlequin White with black or blue patches.

Merle A mottled, marbled effect (usually blue, sometimes red).

Particolor An even mix of two or more colors.

Piebald Black and white or two other colors in patches.

Roan An even mixture of white and another color.

Sable Black tips on silver, gray, gold, fawn or brown hairs.

Ticked Small areas of black or other dark colors on white.

Tricolor A coat of three distinct colors, usually black, white and tan.

Wheaten Pale yellow or fawn colored.

The color descriptions indicate coat color. Terms used for color are often common ones, but others may be unfamiliar (see box).

The grooming requirements tell you what kind of coat each breed has and how much brushing it will need. The exercise section indicates how much and what kind of exercise is best for the breed. If you are looking for a low-maintenance dog, these are important sections to help you choose appropriately.

The environment entry indicates whether a breed is suitable for apartment dwelling or needs plenty of space.

The health section summarizes the health problems to which each breed is prone. Also listed is the group to which each breed belongs: sporting, non-sporting, hound, working, terrier, toy and herding. (These are the American Kennel Club's classifications; other countries classify breeds differently. See pp. 320–21.)

Each breed gets a star rating for trainability, city living and whether or not it's good with children. One star is poor, two is fair, three is good, four is very good and five is excellent.

Each of the 50 breeds is photographed, and there is also a to-scale diagram that shows the dog's size compared with that of both a human adult and child, so you can see approximately what size the breed will grow to.

CHIHUAHUA

HEIGHT 6–9 in (15–23 cm)
WEIGHT 2–6 lb (1–3 kg)

COLOR Blonde, white, fawn, patched or black and tan.

PERSONALITY These intelligent and lively dogs prefer their owner's company to that of other dogs. They can bark a lot and be difficult to house-train. Their tiny size makes them unsuitable pets for energetic young children.

GROOMING Smooth coat: brush occasionally. Long coat: brush daily. Bath both types monthly.

EXERCISE A short, daily walk in pleasant weather will make these little dogs very happy.

ENVIRONMENT Chihuahuas are perfect apartment or house dogs and enjoy accompanying their owners on outings.

HEALTH These dogs are prone to dry and bulging eyes, as well as heart disease and tooth and gum problems.

GROUP Toy

TRAINABILITY ★★★
KID'S PET ★
CITY LIVING ★★★★★

MALTESE

HEIGHT 8–10 in (20–25 cm)
WEIGHT 4–6 lb (2–3 kg)

COLOR White.

PERSONALITY For a toy breed, these dogs are particularly hardy. They are intelligent, energetic and good-natured dogs, but can be snappy when handled roughly. They are better pets for homes with older children.

GROOMING The long, silky coat needs daily brushing with special tools to prevent damage.

EXERCISE These dogs like walks but won't mind missing one every once in a while.

ENVIRONMENT Because of their size and low exercise require-ments, these are perfect apartment dogs.

HEALTH These dogs are prone to eye, tooth and gum disorders, as well as hypoglycemia and joint problems.

GROUP Toy

TRAINABILITY ★★★
KID'S PET ★★★
CITY LIVING ★★★★★

POMERANIAN

HEIGHT 7–12 in (18–30 cm)
WEIGHT 3–7 lb (1–3 kg)

COLOR Red, black, white, blue, orange, cream or brown.

PERSONALITY Although they are tiny, these dogs are bold, curious and make good watchdogs. They are also very intelligent and require confident owners for effective training. They are better for homes with older kids.

GROOMING The long, dense coat sheds heavily and, along with the bushy tail, needs daily brushing.

EXERCISE A regular walk or play session is all that these dogs need.

ENVIRONMENT These are the perfect apartment dogs.

HEALTH These dogs are prone to eye, skin, tooth and gum problems, as well as joint and heart disorders.

GROUP Toy

TRAINABILITY ★★★
KID'S PET ★★
CITY LIVING ★★★★★

DACHSHUND

HEIGHT 6–8 in (15–20 cm)
WEIGHT 11–32 lb (5–15 kg)

COLOR One or two colors of red, black, tan or brown. Long coats occasionally come in merles.

PERSONALITY Clever, tenacious and sometimes stubborn, these dogs love to dig. They can be a little snappish around young children. Dachshunds can be difficult to house-train and, if bored, often become destructive.

GROOMING Brush long and wire coats several times a week, and smooth coats weekly.

EXERCISE Frequent exercise will prevent these dogs from becoming overweight.

ENVIRONMENT Their small size makes them highly suitable for apartment dwelling.

HEALTH Susceptible to hereditary eye problems and paralysis of the hind quarters, as well as disk disease, diabetes and skin diseases. These dogs are also prone to dental problems.

GROUP Hound

TRAINABILITY ★★★
KID'S PET ★★
CITY LIVING ★★★★★

YORKSHIRE TERRIER

HEIGHT 7–9 in (18–23 cm)
WEIGHT 3–7 lb (1–3 kg)

COLOR Steel blue with tan markings.

PERSONALITY If pampered, these dogs can become excitable and snappish. If respected for their cleverness and hardiness, their spirited terrier temperament shines through. They are better for homes with older kids.

GROOMING The long, silky coat doesn't shed much, but needs daily brushing.

EXERCISE Yorkshire Terriers don't need much exercise, but will enjoy the chance to run and play occasionally.

ENVIRONMENT These are perfect apartment dogs. Keep them out of cold, damp places.

HEALTH This breed is prone to eye, gum and tooth problems, and to joint disorders.

GROUP Toy

TRAINABILITY ★★★
KID'S PET ★★
CITY LIVING ★★★★★

PEKINGESE

HEIGHT 6–9 in (15–23 cm)
WEIGHT 10–14 lb (5–6 kg)

COLOR Red, fawn, sable, brindle, black and tan, white or parti-color.

PERSONALITY These are the quintessential lap dogs. They are dignified, reserved with strangers and affectionate with their owners. They are hard to train and house-train, and are better for families without children.

GROOMING The long, coarse coat needs daily brushing to avoid matting.

EXERCISE These low-activity dogs would prefer not to take exercise, but will benefit from occasional play sessions.

ENVIRONMENT These are very good apartment dogs. They don't like cold or damp conditions.

HEALTH The flat face makes this breed prone to respiratory ailments, heatstroke and eye problems such as lacerations, infections and prolapse.

GROUP Toy

TRAINABILITY ★★
KID'S PET ★★
CITY LIVING ★★★★★

Shih Tzu

HEIGHT Up to 11 in (28 cm)
WEIGHT 9–16 lb (4–7 kg)

COLOR All colors and blends of colors.

PERSONALITY Unlike some toy breeds, Shih Tzus don't have a problem with snapping and excessive barking. They are feisty but not too difficult to train, and good for new owners.

GROOMING The long, dense coat doesn't shed much, but needs daily attention to avoid matting.

EXERCISE A daily walk is all that is needed.

ENVIRONMENT Their size and low activity levels make these dogs perfect apartment dwellers. Keep them out of cold and damp places.

HEALTH The pushed-in face makes this breed prone to eye injuries, respiratory problems and heatstroke. Also watch for joint, tooth and gum problems.

GROUP Toy

TRAINABILITY ★★★
KID'S PET ★★★
CITY LIVING ★★★★★

Toy Poodle

HEIGHT Up to 11 in (28 cm)
WEIGHT 6–9 lb (3–4 kg)

COLOR Blue, gray, silver, brown, cafe-au-lait, apricot and cream.

PERSONALITY The tiny Toy Poodle is intelligent and easy to train, but can be very demanding of affection and can bark a lot. These dogs are good for first-time owners, but can be snappy around active, younger children.

GROOMING Poodles do not shed, but require regular brushing and clipping every few months.

EXERCISE Toy Poodles require only moderate exercise. They love to go for walks and to run free occasionally.

ENVIRONMENT Toy Poodles make good house pets.

HEALTH Prone to eye and skin disorders, including cataracts, glaucoma, infections and cysts. May be affected by heart disease and epilepsy.

GROUP Toy

TRAINABILITY ★★★★★
KID'S PET ★★
CITY LIVING ★★★★★

Lhasa Apso

HEIGHT 9–11 in (23–28 cm)
WEIGHT 12–18 lb (5–8 kg)

COLOR Gold, red, black, gray, brown, honey, white or cream.

PERSONALITY The cuddly look of these ancient Tibetan dogs belies an independent and bold temperament. They are intelligent, playful and not too hard to train. They are better for families with older children.

GROOMING The dense coat needs almost daily brushing. The eyes water a lot.

EXERCISE These dogs need only moderate exercise.

ENVIRONMENT Lhasa Apsos are good indoor dogs. If you have more than one, provide each with its own toys, as they can be possessive.

HEALTH They are susceptible to skin and eye problems, as well as kidney ailments.

GROUP Non-sporting

TRAINABILITY ★★★
KID'S PET ★★
CITY LIVING ★★★★

BICHON FRISE

HEIGHT 9–12 in (23–30 cm)
WEIGHT 7–12 lb (3–5 kg)

COLOR White, sometimes with buff, cream or apricot shading.

PERSONALITY Good for first-time dog owners, these dogs are generally even tempered and sociable among family and strangers. If they have been socialized early on, they should get on well with young children.

GROOMING The fine, silky coat sheds lightly and requires daily brushing to avoid getting matted.

EXERCISE They are happy to play inside an apartment, but will also enjoy regular outdoor exercise.

ENVIRONMENT They are primarily indoor dogs and so are suited to any climate.

HEALTH These dogs are prone to clogged tear ducts and need to have their eyes cleaned regularly. The condition of the coat needs to be carefully monitored.

GROUP Non-sporting

TRAINABILITY ★★★★
KID'S PET ★★★
CITY LIVING ★★★★★

SCOTTISH TERRIER

HEIGHT 9–11 in (23–28 cm)
WEIGHT 18–23 lb (8–10 kg)

COLOR Steel, iron gray, black, sandy, wheaten or grizzled.

PERSONALITY These very bold, self-possessed and even stubborn dogs dig and bark. They are better for homes with older children as they can be snappy and dominant. They need firm and consistent training.

GROOMING The wiry, dense coat needs periodic brushing and regular shaping by a groomer.

EXERCISE Regular walks and games of fetch are good for these dogs.

ENVIRONMENT These dogs love to travel, and adapt easily to any living situation.

HEALTH These dogs are prone to skin diseases and "Scottie cramp," which makes walking difficult.

GROUP Terrier

TRAINABILITY ★★
KID'S PET ★★★
CITY LIVING ★★★★

PUG

HEIGHT 10–14 in (25–36 cm)
WEIGHT 13–20 lb (6–9 kg).

COLOR Silver, apricot, fawn or black.

PERSONALITY Unlike some toy breeds, Pugs don't have a problem with excessive barking, snapping at children or excitability. They are good natured, easy to train and suitable for first-time owners.

GROOMING The fine, smooth coat doesn't shed much. It needs weekly brushing.

EXERCISE These dogs don't have a great need for exercise but they do like walking and playing.

ENVIRONMENT Pugs are good house pets, but need to be kept out of the extreme heat or cold.

HEALTH This breed is prone to eye injuries, respiratory difficulties and heatstroke.

GROUP Toy

TRAINABILITY ★★★
KID'S PET ★★★★
CITY LIVING ★★★★★

WEST HIGHLAND WHITE TERRIER

HEIGHT 9–12 in (23–30 cm)
WEIGHT 13–18 lb (6–8 kg)

COLOR White.

PERSONALITY These lively and playful dogs are a little easier to train than most terriers. They may bark a lot and will certainly dig, but they are affectionate. This breed is better suited to homes with older children.

GROOMING The hard, straight-haired coat needs brushing several times a week.

EXERCISE A daily walk is good, but these dogs also enjoy romping about in the yard.

ENVIRONMENT These fine apartment dogs are very adaptable and love to travel.

HEALTH They are prone to hernias, skin conditions, copper toxicosis, jawbone calcification and a hip joint disorder called Legg-Perthes disease.

GROUP Terrier

TRAINABILITY ★★★
KID'S PET ★★★
CITY LIVING ★★★★

CAIRN TERRIER

HEIGHT 9–13 in (23–33 cm)
WEIGHT 13–18 lb (6–8 kg)

COLOR Cream, wheaten, red, sand, gray, brindle or black.

PERSONALITY These plucky and curious little dogs are devoted to their owners, sometimes to the point of jealousy. Because of this they are best suited to homes with older children. Some Cairns bark a lot.

GROOMING Brush the coat several times a week. Nails and ears need regular attention.

EXERCISE Regular walks are advised. Because of their curiosity, these dogs are best kept on a leash.

ENVIRONMENT Cairn Terriers adapt readily to apartments, farms and anything in between.

HEALTH Although generally hardy, this breed is prone to skin allergies, blood clotting disorders, dislocating kneecaps and hereditary eye diseases.

GROUP Terrier

TRAINABILITY ★★★
KID'S PET ★★★
CITY LIVING ★★★★

MINIATURE PINSCHER

HEIGHT 10–12 in (25–30 cm)
WEIGHT 8–10 lb (4–5 kg)

COLOR Black, blue or chocolate with rust markings, or solid red.

PERSONALITY These self-possessed, bold and stubborn dogs act like big dogs and may be aggressive with other dogs. They are not always easy to train and require experienced owners. They are unsuited to families with small children.

GROOMING The smooth, hard coat sheds very little and requires only weekly brushing.

EXERCISE These active little dogs need regular walks.

ENVIRONMENT They are well suited to apartment living and prefer not to be outside too much in the cold weather.

HEALTH This is a generally healthy breed, but some dogs may suffer from eye and joint problems.

GROUP Toy

TRAINABILITY ★★★
KID'S PET ★★
CITY LIVING ★★★★★

Pembroke Welsh Corgi

HEIGHT 10–12 in (25–30 cm)
WEIGHT 20–30 lb (11–14 kg)

COLOR Red, sable, fawn, black or tan, with white markings.

PERSONALITY These happy and intelligent dogs fit the bill for those wanting a big-dog personality in a smaller package. They are easy to train and house-train, and make very good watchdogs.

GROOMING The thick, medium-length, weather-resistant coat needs weekly brushing.

EXERCISE These active dogs enjoy playing, walking and running daily with their family.

ENVIRONMENT They need some running room but can adapt to apartment living if adequately exercised.

HEALTH This breed is prone to hereditary eye diseases, bleeding disorders, hip dysplasia and back trouble due to its long spine and short legs.

GROUP Herding

TRAINABILITY ★★★★★
KID'S PET ★★★★
CITY LIVING ★★★

Miniature Poodle

HEIGHT 11–15 in (28–38 cm)
WEIGHT 15–17 lb (7–8 kg)

COLOR Blue, gray, silver, brown, cafe-au-lait, apricot and cream.

PERSONALITY These dogs are intelligent and easy to train and house-train. They can be very demanding of affection and can bark a lot. They are somewhat sensitive and may become jealous of children.

GROOMING Poodles do not shed, but require regular brushing and clipping every few months.

EXERCISE Walks and play sessions a few times a week will keep these dogs fit and happy.

ENVIRONMENT The Miniature Poodle makes a good apartment dog when given adequate exercise.

HEALTH These dogs are prone to eye and skin disorders, including cataracts, glaucoma, infections and cysts. Heart disease can also be a problem.

GROUP Non-sporting

TRAINABILITY ★★★★★
KID'S PET ★★★
CITY LIVING ★★★★★

Beagle

HEIGHT 13–16 in (33–41 cm)
WEIGHT 20–25 lb (9–11 kg)

COLOR Black, white or tan combinations.

PERSONALITY These dogs are known for their stamina and high energy. A good-natured breed, they are happy with kids and other pets, but can be strong willed and sometimes hard to train. If left alone a lot, their barking can become excessive.

GROOMING The coat needs weekly brushing. The ears need regular cleaning.

EXERCISE They need daily walks and some on-leash running in an open area every once in a while.

ENVIRONMENT While their small size may make them seem perfect for indoor living, bored, sedentary beagles can become destructive.

HEALTH Beagles are prone to heart disease, obesity and epilepsy, and to skin, eye and bleeding disorders and some spinal problems.

GROUP Hound

TRAINABILITY ★★★
KID'S PET ★★★★
CITY LIVING ★★

BOSTON TERRIER

HEIGHT 11–15 in (28–38 cm)
WEIGHT 15–25 lb (7–11 kg)

COLOR Brindle or black with white markings.

PERSONALITY These are sensitive, affectionate and sometimes stubborn dogs that are nevertheless good for first-time owners. They adapt well to both an active family or a more retiring owner.

GROOMING Brushing and rubbing daily with a chamois cloth will keep the short coat shiny.

EXERCISE These dogs appreciate daily walks and love to fetch balls.

ENVIRONMENT Well-suited to an indoor life, they are also good watchdogs.

HEALTH Boston Terriers are susceptible to respiratory diseases and eye injuries and ailments.

GROUP Non-sporting

TRAINABILITY ★★★
KID'S PET ★★★
CITY LIVING ★★★★

MINIATURE SCHNAUZER

HEIGHT 11–14 in (28–36 cm)
WEIGHT 10–15 lb (5–8 kg)

COLOR Salt and pepper, black and silver, or solid tan.

PERSONALITY These dogs are playful, smart and stubborn. They combine general terrier behavior (barking, excitability, digging) with general guard dog behavior (territorial and dominant tendencies) and are better for families with older kids.

GROOMING The hard, wiry coat needs combing periodically and shaping about four times a year.

EXERCISE These dogs are happy with regular walks. Provide toys for them to play with indoors.

ENVIRONMENT They adapt very well to indoor living.

HEALTH Miniature Schnauzers are prone to eye and bleeding disorders, kidney stones, heart and liver diseases, diabetes and epilepsy.

GROUP Terrier

TRAINABILITY ★★★
KID'S PET ★★★
CITY LIVING ★★★★★

BASSET HOUND

HEIGHT 11–15 in (28–38 cm)
WEIGHT 45–65 lb (20–29 kg)

COLOR Black, white and tan, or lemon and tan.

PERSONALITY These amusing, mild-mannered dogs are gentle and sociable. However, they are one of the hardest breeds to house-train. They can also be stubborn, so owners will need to be patient.

GROOMING The smooth coat is easy to maintain but the ears need regular cleaning inside.

EXERCISE One or more short walks a day will keep these dogs happy and trim. Discourage them from jumping.

ENVIRONMENT These dogs adapt well to city life, but their howling can be a problem in an apartment.

HEALTH These dogs are prone to glaucoma, spinal disk problems, bloat and skin and ear infections.

GROUP Hound

TRAINABILITY ★★★
KID'S PET ★★★★
CITY LIVING ★★★★

SHETLAND SHEEPDOG

HEIGHT 12–15 in (30–38 cm)
WEIGHT 12–18 lb (5–8 kg)

COLOR Black, blue merle or sable with white or tan markings.

PERSONALITY These dogs are intelligent, affectionate and easy to train. Many bark a lot and some can be a little nervous. They are better with older children.

GROOMING The long and harsh double coat sheds heavily. It needs regular brushing.

EXERCISE They need plenty of exercise and love to run free and frolic outdoors.

ENVIRONMENT If they are given enough exercise, these dogs can adapt to apartment living.

HEALTH Prone to progressive retinal atrophy and other eye problems. Heart disease, epilepsy and deafness (in the blue merle) can also be problems.

GROUP Herding

TRAINABILITY ★★★★★
KID'S PET ★★★★
CITY LIVING ★★★

COCKER SPANIEL

HEIGHT 14–17 in (36–43 cm).
WEIGHT 26–34 lb (12–15 kg).

COLOR Black, any other solid color or parti-colored.

PERSONALITY Energetic and playful, these dogs can also be aggressive. English Cockers are slightly larger and retain more of their sporting instincts than their American counterparts. Both breeds are easy to train.

GROOMING The long, silky coat sheds moderately and needs extensive brushing and clipping.

EXERCISE Both varieties need regular walks, but the English variety needs a little more.

ENVIRONMENT As long as they get out frequently to run off their energy, these dogs are suitable as house pets.

HEALTH Eye problems are the biggest concern. Heart disease, ear infections, hemophilia and epilepsy are also apparent in the American variety.

GROUP Sporting

TRAINABILITY ★★★★★
KID'S PET ★★
CITY LIVING ★★★★

BULLDOG

HEIGHT 12–16 in (30–41 cm).
WEIGHT 35–55 lb (16–25 kg).

COLOR Red and other brindles, white, red, fawn or piebald.

PERSONALITY These are loyal, reliable and gentle dogs with none of the ferocity of their forebears. They don't bark a lot and are known for their sweet temperament. They make fine pets but are not so easy to train.

GROOMING This breed drools a lot. The short coat doesn't shed much and needs little brushing.

EXERCISE Regular, easy walks will keep Bulldogs fit and happy.

ENVIRONMENT These dogs prefer a cooler climate. They are happy indoors and are well suited to small houses and apartments.

HEALTH A short-lived breed, at about ten years, these dogs are prone to breathing difficulties and heatstroke, along with eye, skin and heart problems.

GROUP Non-sporting

TRAINABILITY ★★★
KID'S PET ★★
CITY LIVING ★★★★

BRITTANY

HEIGHT 17–21 in (43–53 cm)
WEIGHT 30–40 lb (14–18 kg)

COLOR Orange and white or liver and white.

PERSONALITY These hardworking and tenacious sporting dogs are favored by hunters. They are good natured and make happy family pets. They are fairly easy to train and are a good choice for first-time dog owners.

GROOMING The medium-length coat needs brushing twice weekly and washing a few times a year.

EXERCISE Happiest working in the field, these energetic dogs need plenty of regular, vigorous exercise.

ENVIRONMENT Like most sporting dogs, Brittanys become bored if confined in small spaces for long periods, and may become noisy and destructive.

HEALTH This breed is prone to ear infections and eye diseases.

GROUP Sporting

TRAINABILITY ★★★★
KID'S PET ★★★★
CITY LIVING ★★

CHOW CHOW

HEIGHT 18–23 in (46–56 cm)
WEIGHT 45–65 lb (20–29 kg)

COLOR Black, blue, red, cream or cinnamon.

PERSONALITY These powerful dogs are aloof and reserved, particularly with strangers. Some are very territorial and prone to aggression. They need firm handling during training and are not suited to first-time owners.

GROOMING They shed heavily and need frequent brushing.

EXERCISE A daily, but not necessarily strenuous, walk is essential for these dogs.

ENVIRONMENT Their thick coats make them uncomfortable in the heat. Chow Chows are clean and quiet indoors.

HEALTH These dogs are prone to eczema and joint and eye problems.

GROUP Non-sporting

TRAINABILITY ★★
KID'S PET ★★
CITY LIVING ★★★

CHINESE SHAR-PEI

HEIGHT 18–20 in (46–51 cm)
WEIGHT 40–55 lb (18–25 kg)

COLOR Fawn, black, cream, apricot, chocolate or red.

PERSONALITY While devoted to their family, these dogs can show aggression toward other dogs. They need firm training and are better suited to experienced owners. They make good watchdogs.

GROOMING The harsh coat needs weekly brushing, but shedding isn't a big problem.

EXERCISE Daily walks are adequate, but a good run every so often will be appreciated.

ENVIRONMENT Because they are such clean dogs they are suited to city living, but will readily adapt to a more rural setting.

HEALTH These dogs are prone to skin and eye problems, as well as hip dysplasia.

GROUP Non-sporting

TRAINABILITY ★★★
KID'S PET ★★★★★
CITY LIVING ★★★★★

ENGLISH SPRINGER SPANIEL

HEIGHT 18–21 in (46–53 cm)
WEIGHT 40–55 lb (18–25 kg)

COLOR Black and white, liver and white, tricolor, blue or liver roan.

PERSONALITY Most of these dogs are cheerful and playful. However, the breed is prone to Rage Syndrome, an inherited behavioral disorder that causes unpredictable aggression. If buying from a breeder, ensure their breed lines are sound.

GROOMING Brush the soft, water-repellent coat weekly and pay close attention to the ears.

EXERCISE These dogs are active and need plenty of exercise.

ENVIRONMENT If they are given brisk walks daily, they are fine to have in the city.

HEALTH These dogs are prone to progressive retinal atrophy, elbow and hip dysplasia, epilepsy and ear and skin conditions.

GROUP Sporting

TRAINABILITY ★★★★★
KID'S PET ★★★★
CITY LIVING ★★★

SAMOYED

HEIGHT 19–24 in (48–61 cm)
WEIGHT 45–60 lb (20–27 kg)

COLOR White, biscuit, cream or white and biscuit.

PERSONALITY These dogs are energetic, playful and friendly. Independent and strong, they are best suited to experienced owners.

GROOMING The thick, double coat sheds heavily and requires daily brushing.

EXERCISE They require robust outdoor exercise every day. In hot weather, exercise them in the cooler parts of the day.

ENVIRONMENT They prefer cooler climates and are best suited to the suburbs or country.

HEALTH Hip dysplasia, skin problems and eye disorders are common in this breed.

GROUP Working

TRAINABILITY ★★★
KID'S PET ★★★★
CITY LIVING ★★

AUSTRALIAN SHEPHERD

HEIGHT 18–23 in (46–58 cm)
WEIGHT 35–70 lb (16–32 kg)

COLOR Blue merle, red merle, red, black or tricolor.

PERSONALITY These highly intelligent dogs can either be friendly or aloof with strangers. They are easy to train but have strong herding instincts.

GROOMING The long coat needs to be brushed thoroughly several times a week.

EXERCISE These dogs will be happiest with real work to do. Otherwise, they require vigorous exercise once or twice a day.

ENVIRONMENT These dogs are not suited to city living. They should be kept in the country, or at least in the suburbs with a large yard to roam in.

HEALTH Eye disorders and hip dysplasia can be problems for this breed. Merles are prone to deafness.

GROUP Herding

TRAINABILITY ★★★★★
KID'S PET ★★★★
CITY LIVING ★★

SIBERIAN HUSKY

HEIGHT 20–23 in (51–58 cm)
WEIGHT 35–60 lb (16–27 kg)

COLOR All colors from black to white, usually with facial markings.

PERSONALITY These energetic and playful dogs love to work. They are friendly but not always easy to train, and they may attempt to dominate. Huskies require confident, experienced owners.

GROOMING The medium-length, double coat sheds heavily and needs brushing twice a week.

EXERCISE They need vigorous outdoor exercise. With insufficient exercise they can be destructive.

ENVIRONMENT Their thick coats make them better suited to cold climates. Because of their size, they shouldn't be kept in a small house or apartment.

HEALTH These dogs can suffer from progressive retinal atrophy and other eye disorders, along with hip dysplasia and skin and thyroid problems.

GROUP Working

TRAINABILITY ★★
KID'S PET ★★★
CITY LIVING ★

DALMATIAN

HEIGHT 19–23 in (48–58 cm)
WEIGHT 45–65 lb (20–29 kg)

COLOR White with black or liver spots.

PERSONALITY These protective dogs have boundless energy and a boisterous nature. When bored, they become destructive, so keep them busy. They are trustworthy with children but rather sensitive. They are not recommended for first-time dog owners.

GROOMING Brush daily to maintain the dog's smooth coat. These dogs are heavy shedders.

EXERCISE Athletic by nature, they need to run as much as possible to keep in shape.

ENVIRONMENT If they get regular outdoor exercise, Dalmatians are happy indoor dogs. They don't like to be outside in the cold.

HEALTH They are prone to deafness, bladder stones and allergic skin conditions.

GROUP Non-sporting

TRAINABILITY ★★★
KID'S PET ★★★
CITY LIVING ★★★

BOXER

HEIGHT 21–24 in (53–61 cm)
WEIGHT 55–70 lb (25–32 kg)

COLOR Fawn or brindle, with white markings.

PERSONALITY Playful and patient with children, Boxers are also courageous and devoted watchdogs. While good for first-time owners, they need firm training and early socialization with other animals and people.

GROOMING The short, smooth coat requires simple brushing. The teeth need regular attention.

EXERCISE Because of their high degree of energy, these dogs need plenty of exercise.

ENVIRONMENT These dogs are clean and relatively quiet and can make good house pets if they are properly trained and given adequate exercise.

HEALTH A short-lived breed, at about ten years, Boxers are prone to skin problems, stroke, heart disease, cancer and bloat.

GROUP Working

TRAINABILITY ★★★
KID'S PET ★★★★★
CITY LIVING ★★★

CHESAPEAKE BAY RETRIEVER	GOLDEN RETRIEVER	LABRADOR RETRIEVER

CHESAPEAKE BAY RETRIEVER

HEIGHT 21–26 in (53–66 cm)
WEIGHT 55–80 lb (25–36 kg)

COLOR Dark brown to light tan.

PERSONALITY These energetic, bold dogs are devoted to their family. They are not excessive barkers, but make good watch-dogs. A stubborn streak makes them tricky to train; they are best suited to experienced dog owners.

GROOMING Brush regularly. Bathe infrequently to maintain the coat's waterproof oils.

EXERCISE This breed needs plenty of strenuous exercise, such as running and swimming, to keep in shape.

ENVIRONMENT These dogs are best suited to an environment where they can spend plenty of time outdoors.

HEALTH These dogs are susceptible to hip dysplasia and hereditary eye diseases.

GROUP Sporting

TRAINABILITY ★★★
KID'S PET ★★★★
CITY LIVING ★★

GOLDEN RETRIEVER

HEIGHT 20–24 in (51–61 cm)
WEIGHT 55–80 lb (25–36 kg)

COLOR Various shades of gold or cream.

PERSONALITY Golden Retrievers are one of the most popular breeds, especially for families. Playful, energetic and not big barkers, they are good with children, fairly easy to train and suitable for first-time owners.

GROOMING The dense, water-repellent coat needs brushing several times a week.

EXERCISE These dogs need regular daily exercise. As their name suggests, fetching is a favorite game.

ENVIRONMENT These dogs will adapt easily to most living situations, but city-dwelling dogs must have daily walks.

HEALTH Golden Retrievers are prone to various eye ailments, as well as hip and elbow dysplasia, obesity and skin conditions.

GROUP Sporting

TRAINABILITY ★★★★★
KID'S PET ★★★★★
CITY LIVING ★★★

LABRADOR RETRIEVER

HEIGHT 21–24 in (53–61 cm)
WEIGHT 55–70 lb (25–34 kg)

COLOR Black, yellow or chocolate.

PERSONALITY These popular dogs are friendly and have a steady temperament. To keep their high energy focused, they need early training. They are suitable for first-time owners.

GROOMING The short, weather-resistant coat needs brushing at least once a week.

EXERCISE These dogs require plenty of exercise and love to play fetch and to swim.

ENVIRONMENT They adapt easily to almost any situation. Apartment dwellers need to be exercised frequently, or they may become destructive due to frustration.

HEALTH Labradors may suffer from bloat, epilepsy, obesity, hip dysplasia, progressive retinal atrophy and other eye problems.

GROUP Sporting

TRAINABILITY ★★★★★
KID'S PET ★★★★★
CITY LIVING ★★★

GERMAN SHORTHAIRED POINTER

HEIGHT 21–26 in (53–66 cm)
WEIGHT 45–70 lb (20–32 kg)

COLOR Solid liver or black, or those colors with white spots or flecks.

PERSONALITY These extremely energetic dogs love people. They can overwhelm young kids, so are better suited to older children. They can be flighty and not always easy to train, and need an experienced owner.

GROOMING Regular brushing is needed. Check ears and feet often for foreign matter.

EXERCISE These dogs need plenty of vigorous exercise, such as running.

ENVIRONMENT Because of their high activity needs, these dogs are not at all suited to apartment living.

HEALTH German Shorthaired Pointers are generally a hardy breed, but are susceptible to hip dysplasia and eye conditions.

GROUP Sporting

TRAINABILITY ★★
KID'S PET ★★★
CITY LIVING ★

AIREDALE TERRIER

HEIGHT 22–24 in (56–61 cm)
WEIGHT 40–50 lb (18–23 kg)

COLOR Black or dark grizzled body, with tan head, ears and legs.

PERSONALITY These playful, faithful and sometimes stubborn dogs are protective of their family members and wary of strangers. With a strong personality, they need firm and consistent training.

GROOMING The wiry coat doesn't shed much, but needs frequent brushing and combing.

EXERCISE A daily brisk walk or other vigorous exercise is essential, even more so if these dogs live in the city.

ENVIRONMENT These dogs are adaptable to any climate and enjoy being outdoors.

HEALTH A generally hardy breed, Airedales have a tendency to develop gastroenteritis and hip dysplasia. Eczema can also be a problem.

GROUP Terrier

TRAINABILITY ★★★
KID'S PET ★★★
CITY LIVING ★★★★

COLLIE (ROUGH)

HEIGHT 22–26 in (56–66 cm)
WEIGHT 50–75 lb (23–34 kg)

COLOR Sable and white, blue merle, white or tricolor.

PERSONALITY Recognized by millions as "Lassie," these dogs are easy to train and affectionate with their family. However, they can be highly strung and aloof with strangers. Some Collies bark a great deal.

GROOMING These heavy shedders require frequent brushing.

EXERCISE Daily jaunts are necessary to keep these dogs fit and happy.

ENVIRONMENT Collies are not well suited to hot and humid climates. They are better suited to an outdoor lifestyle due to their heavy shedding.

HEALTH Collie-specific disorders include Collie nose (an auto-immune disease). They are also prone to hip dysplasia, skin infections and eye problems. Blue merles are sometimes born deaf.

GROUP Herding

TRAINABILITY ★★★★
KID'S PET ★★★
CITY LIVING ★★★

STANDARD POODLE

HEIGHT 15–24 in (38–61 cm)
WEIGHT 45–70 lb (20–32 kg)

COLOR Blue, gray, silver, brown, cafe-au-lait, apricot and cream.

PERSONALITY Standard Poodles are very intelligent and easy to train and house-train. Playful and affectionate, they are good for first-time owners and families with young children.

GROOMING Poodles do not shed, but require regular brushing and clipping every few months.

EXERCISE These active dogs should be taken for a walk daily. They also love to swim and run free.

ENVIRONMENT Standard Poodles will fare well indoors if they are given enough exercise.

HEALTH Standard Poodles are prone to eye and skin disorders, including cataracts, glaucoma, infections and cysts. They can also suffer from heart disease, diabetes, epilepsy and cancer.

GROUP Non-sporting

TRAINABILITY ★★★★★
KID'S PET ★★★★★
CITY LIVING ★★★

GERMAN SHEPHERD

HEIGHT 22–26 in (56–66 cm)
WEIGHT 70–95 lb (32–43 kg)

COLOR Usually black with tan or fawn markings. An all-white coat is unacceptable in show dogs.

PERSONALITY These intelligent and confident dogs are good for families but need an experienced and strong hand for training. They can be aggressive toward other dogs.

GROOMING The dense, double coat sheds heavily and needs to be brushed several times a week.

EXERCISE Without daily walks, these dogs can become restless and destructive.

ENVIRONMENT These dogs are perfect for the suburbs or the country. With adequate exercise, they can cope in the city.

HEALTH Common problems include bloat, hip and elbow dysplasia, skin and eye disorders, epilepsy and heart defects.

GROUP Herding

TRAINABILITY ★★★★★
KID'S PET ★★★
CITY LIVING ★★★

ROTTWEILER

HEIGHT 22–27 in (56–69 cm)
WEIGHT 85–130 lb (38–59 kg)

COLOR Black with mahogany or rust markings.

PERSONALITY These guard dogs are strong, confident and naturally protective. Some Rottweilers can become aggressive. They are suitable for experienced, confident owners.

GROOMING The coarse, short coat needs weekly brushing.

EXERCISE They require vigorous daily exercise or, preferably, work of some kind. Aggressive tug-of-war games should be avoided.

ENVIRONMENT These dogs are best suited to the suburbs or country.

HEALTH Rottweilers are susceptible to bloat, progressive retinal atrophy, hip and elbow dysplasia and eye problems.

GROUP Working

TRAINABILITY ★★★
KID'S PET ★★★
CITY LIVING ★★

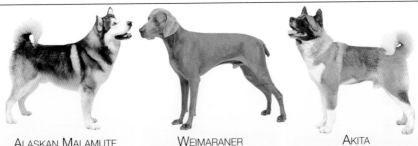

ALASKAN MALAMUTE

HEIGHT 22–26 in (56–66 cm)
WEIGHT 70–95 lb (32–43 kg)

COLOR Light gray to black, or gold to red and liver, with white underbody and face markings.

PERSONALITY A strong personality makes this breed good for the experienced dog owner. Malamutes are very friendly to people but need early, consistent training and should be watched around other pets. They thrive on an active lifestyle.

GROOMING The thick, double coat needs brushing at least once a week.

EXERCISE Known for endurance, these dogs need daily, vigorous exercise.

ENVIRONMENT These dogs are not suited to apartment living—a sedentary, bored Malamute can become very destructive. They prefer a cool climate.

HEALTH Hip dysplasia, bloat, blood clotting disorders and eye problems can affect Alaskan Malamutes.

GROUP Working

TRAINABILITY ★★★
KID'S PET ★★
CITY LIVING ★

WEIMARANER

HEIGHT 22–27 in (56–69 cm)
WEIGHT 50–70 lb (23–32 kg)

COLOR All shades of gray, from silver to mouse.

PERSONALITY These are active and headstrong dogs. They need a firm and experienced hand to bring out their better traits (loyalty and intelligence) while controlling their tendency to dominate and be aggressive.

GROOMING The short, sleek coat doesn't shed much and only needs brushing once a week.

EXERCISE Weimaraners need plenty of exercise, both walking and running.

ENVIRONMENT These dogs are far too active to be living in apartments, and are best suited to the country or suburbs.

HEALTH These dogs are prone to bloat, hip dysplasia and various skin ailments.

GROUP Sporting

TRAINABILITY ★★★
KID'S PET ★★
CITY LIVING ★★★

AKITA

HEIGHT 24–28 in (61–71 cm)
WEIGHT 75–120 lb (34–54 kg)

COLOR Cream, red, blue, gold, white, brindle or pinto.

PERSONALITY This ancient breed of Japanese dog is known for its strength, alertness and courage. Aggression can be a problem, especially around other dogs. Akitas require diligent training and are not suitable for first-time dog owners.

GROOMING The dense coat sheds heavily and needs weekly brushing to keep it in shape.

EXERCISE These athletic dogs need extensive exercise. Avoid aggressive games such as tug-of-war.

ENVIRONMENT These dogs can be quiet, reserved apartment dwellers or equally happy with a large yard to roam around in.

HEALTH This breed can have problems with hip dysplasia and eye disorders.

GROUP Working

TRAINABILITY ★★★
KID'S PET ★★
CITY LIVING ★★★

Doberman Pinscher

HEIGHT 24–28 in (61–71 cm)
WEIGHT 66–88 lb (30–40 kg)

COLOR Black, red, fawn, brown or blue with red markings.

PERSONALITY These are the quintessential guard dogs. They need to be with people and can be good with children if raised with them. They are best suited to experienced owners.

GROOMING The smooth coat doesn't shed much. It needs brushing several times a week.

EXERCISE They need plenty of vigorous exercise, but avoid aggressive games.

ENVIRONMENT These dogs don't like to be in cold weather. They can be fine house dogs if they are given daily exercise.

HEALTH Prone to bloat, hip dysplasia and heart problems. They are also susceptible to a bleeding disorder called von Willebrand's disease.

GROUP Working

TRAINABILITY ★★★★★
KID'S PET ★★★
CITY LIVING ★★★

Saint Bernard

HEIGHT From 25 in (63 cm)
WEIGHT From 110 lb (50 kg)

COLOR White with red or brindle markings.

PERSONALITY These dogs are gentle, calm and generally good with children and other animals. They do not bark a lot, but, like any of the giant breeds, need early and consistent training to quell dominant tendencies.

GROOMING Both the long-haired and short-haired varieties need daily brushing when shedding.

EXERCISE These dogs need daily walks or other forms of regular exercise.

ENVIRONMENT Because of their heavy coats, they prefer cooler climates. They are better suited to the suburbs and country.

HEALTH They are prone to bloat, hip dysplasia, heart disease, eye conditions and epilepsy.

GROUP Working

TRAINABILITY ★★★
KID'S PET ★★★
CITY LIVING ★★

Great Pyrenees

HEIGHT 25–32 in (63–81 cm)
WEIGHT From 85 lb (38 kg)

COLOR Solid white or white with tan or gray markings.

PERSONALITY Traditionally used as guards, these calm and regal dogs have retained their protective nature. While they make good family pets, they need consistent and early obedience training by an experienced owner.

GROOMING The double coat needs frequent brushing. These dogs are big seasonal shedders.

EXERCISE They need plenty of regular exercise to stay fit.

ENVIRONMENT They are not suited to indoor living and prefer a cool climate.

HEALTH These dogs are prone to bloat, hip dysplasia, eye problems and deafness. They have a short life span of about ten years.

GROUP Working

TRAINABILITY ★★★
KID'S PET ★★★
CITY LIVING ★

NEWFOUNDLAND

HEIGHT 25–29 in (63–74 cm)
WEIGHT 100–150 lb (45–68 kg)

COLOR Black, black and white, brown or gray.

PERSONALITY These are gentle, affectionate and protective dogs. Easy to train and house-train, they are great for first-time owners and children.

GROOMING The thick, water-repellent double coat sheds heavily and needs daily attention.

EXERCISE These dogs need regular moderate exercise. They love to swim.

ENVIRONMENT They prefer cool climates to warm ones, and adapt well to an air-conditioned house or apartment.

HEALTH These dogs are susceptible to heart problems, bloat, hip dysplasia and other orthopedic problems.

GROUP Working

TRAINABILITY ★★★★
KID'S PET ★★★★★
CITY LIVING ★★★

MASTIFF

HEIGHT From 27 in (69 cm)
WEIGHT From 150 lb (68 kg)

COLOR Fawn, apricot, silver or brindle.

PERSONALITY These massive, ancient guard dogs combine docility with courage. They like being with people as much as possible, but need a firm and experienced hand in training.

GROOMING The coarse, short coat needs brushing only once a week. These dogs drool a lot.

EXERCISE To maintain good health they need regular exercise.

ENVIRONMENT These dogs are best suited to the suburbs or country, where their size won't be a problem.

HEALTH Mastiffs are prone to hip and elbow dysplasia, bloat and eyelid abnormalities. They have a short life span of about ten years.

GROUP Working

TRAINABILITY ★★★
KID'S PET ★★★
CITY LIVING ★

GREAT DANE

HEIGHT 28–34 in (71–86 cm)
WEIGHT 100–160 lb (45–72 kg)

COLOR Brindle, fawn, blue, black or harlequin.

PERSONALITY These gentle giants love people and, when properly trained and socialized, can make wonderful family pets. They can be territorial and aggressive with other dogs, but they are good with children and other animals.

GROOMING The short, thick coat needs weekly grooming and infrequent bathing.

EXERCISE These dogs need regular daily walks. Don't play tug-of-war or wrestle with them.

ENVIRONMENT Although these dogs can adapt to city living, owners with a yard will find exercising easier.

HEALTH They are prone to bloat, bone cancer, hip dysplasia and heart disease, and have a short life span of about ten years.

GROUP Working

TRAINABILITY ★★★
KID'S PET ★★★
CITY LIVING ★★★

The Charm of Mixed Breeds

The mixed breed, or mutt, is the ordinary, sometimes quirky-looking, everyday kind of dog.

The mutt is a lovable hybrid whose ancestry can be the basis of a long-running guessing game. Because mixed breed puppies are almost by definition unplanned, a disproportionate number of them tend to end up in shelters or for sale from cardboard boxes outside supermarkets. This could be an advantage because they're often inexpensive or free. But despite your lower investment, you're not necessarily sacrificing quality. And all the remaining costs—accessories, feeding and health care—will be exactly the same as those for a purebred dog. Regardless of their pedigree, all dogs need to be loved, valued and cared for in just the same way.

THE ELEMENT OF SURPRISE

Mixed breeds are wonderful, loving and devoted, just like purebreds. And one of the great things about a mixed breed is that he is truly his own dog. He is unique; no other dog will look exactly like him. You really get a sense of individuality with a mixed breed.

"Designer crosses" are increasingly popular, but in many cases, you won't know who such a dog's parent were. This means that factors determined by his genes—including his size, personality, behavior and grooming needs—will be hard to predict, as will any genetic diseases that he may be subject to.

Whatever bubbles up to the top of your four-legged melting pot, the odds are good that the end result will be a great companion. Any dog is trainable if you find out what motivates him. Your new dog's looks will depend on various ingredients in his gene pool. But his personality and manners will mostly depend on the way you train him.

ONE TOUGH COOKIE

A mixed breed dog's birth was most likely unplanned, so he may not have received all the care and knowledge that might be lavished on a purebred, nor been given all the breaks. Some mutts have to survive a pretty tough start to life. Perhaps this is why people tend to think that mixed breeds are hardier and healthier than purebreds. Certainly, the combination of genetic material in a mixed breed will make him less prone to certain hereditary problems, so he may be less likely than a purebred to suffer from some genetic diseases. However, mixed breeds can still get sick from the various non-hereditary illnesses that can affect any dog. Choose a mixed breed for his looks and his personality, not because you think that he'll be free from the hereditary diseases associated with purebred dogs. Remember, any dog's genetic pool will contain an assortment of genes—the good, and the not so good.

A HAPPY MIX This Labradoodle is likely to have inherited the trainability and people-loving nature of her Labrador and Poodle parents. Her shaggy good looks are a bonus.

WHAT A MUTT WANTS This Poodle–terrier mix will require the same kind of love and care as a purebred.

CHOOSING AN ADULT MIXED BREED

Adult dogs, from about nine months of age, are a wise choice for the would-be dog owner. What you see is what you get. You can tell the size they're going to be and how clean they are, and get a good idea of their social skills and temperament.

Knowing a dog's breed or mix of breeds is only part of the equation, however. Any dog's early environment and life experiences will have affected him. So once you're at the dog shelter and have found a mixed breed that looks right for you, pay close attention before allowing yourself to become too smitten. Instead of trying to figure out his lineage, consider the individual dog, his behavior and his reaction to you. Look at the following:

- Does the dog come rushing to the front of the enclosure to greet you in a friendly way, with ears up and tail wagging?
- Does he have the self-confidence to approach strangers, both men and women?

If the answer is yes on both counts and you've got a good feeling about him, then he could be the dog for you. Avoid any dog that acts shy, cowering in the back while growling or showing his teeth. If possible, take a trainer with you to the shelter to help you choose a dog. Good shelters will usually allow you to observe how the dog behaves with other dogs.

Keep in mind that a dog's behavior will differ depending on the environment. It may be friendly in the shelter and snappish at home. This doesn't necessarily mean you've made the wrong choice. It can take a shelter dog a few weeks to adjust and feel secure enough to relax. Give him a little time and a gentle, reassuring approach, but be prepared to take the dog back if he really isn't working out. It's important to give both yourself and the dog the opportunity to find the right fit.

A GOOD COMPANION This short-haired Bull Terrier– Labrador mix should make an affable, easy-care pet.

Where to Get Your Dog

Now that you know the type of dog you want,

where do you find him?

FINDING A PUREBRED

A purebred dog can be very expensive, but if you go to a reputable, knowledgeable breeder, you'll get your money's worth. Responsible breeders know the genetic problems of their breed, keep careful records and try to breed for both good health and good temperament. You may have your dog for ten or more years, so that's a pretty good investment. You're paying for the breeder's years of experience, as well as for ongoing help and advice. Any breeder who cares about her dogs will gladly answer your questions, both before and after you buy the dog.

Not every pup in a litter will live up to the ideal standard determined by a national breed club. Pups that do are "show quality," and can be exhibited in dog shows. Those that do not are often called "pet quality." Don't assume there's anything wrong with a puppy just because the breeder hasn't chosen to show it. The pup may simply have a small kink in his tail, or a coat color that isn't permitted in the show ring—these are serious faults in show dogs, but won't affect the health or temperament of a pet dog. However, if you buy from show litters, you'll know that the health and quality of the pups were the breeder's main considerations. Visit at least three good breeders before buying your pup, so that you have plenty of comparison points.

Breeders to Avoid

Backyard breeders breed their dogs and sell the puppies as a way of making money. They are unlikely to be interested in studying and advancing the breed, so their dogs will not always meet the breed standard. Without a knowledge of the breed and the standard, they may not understand how to prevent unfortunate genetic traits from occurring in their pups. They may still, however, charge prices as high as those of a reputable breeder.

Many classified ads are placed by backyard breeders. Be wary if someone offers to sell you a puppy with no questions asked or if he is

GOOD HOME WANTED Fine dogs can often be obtained from dog shelters and breed rescue groups.

reluctant to answer your questions about the puppy or about the health and temperament of the pup's parents.

Breed Rescue Organizations

In recent years, increasing numbers of purebred dogs have been showing up at shelters. Alarmed at this trend, purebred fanciers have formed breed rescue clubs to give these dogs a second chance. Volunteers who raise a particular breed open their homes and kennels to dogs that have ended up in a shelter or been abandoned. They also take in dogs from people who realize it isn't working out but who want to make sure their dog goes to a good home.

Once in their foster home, these dogs are evaluated for basic obedience, temperament, house-training and health. If a dog has a few flaws, volunteers will often work with him until he meets the requirements to make a good pet. The last thing these groups want is for the dog to go through the cycle of abandonment all over again.

IT TAKES ALL TYPES Your local veterinarian or people from a neighborhood dog-training group may be able to recommend where to get a good dog. Or, if you know someone with a dog whose looks and character appeal to you, such as the engaging collie mix at right, ask where they got him.

Rescue leagues are wonderful places to find a young adult purebred dog. If a purebred puppy is too expensive for you, but you have your heart set on, say, a Norwegian Elkhound or a Papillon, breed rescue may be just the answer for you. Local breeders or your local animal welfare society will be able to refer you to rescue clubs, or look on the Internet.

FINDING A MIXED BREED

The best place to find a mixed-breed dog is at your local animal shelter. To get information about the shelters in your area, talk to your local veterinarian or call your local animal control officer.

Many shelters are well organized and supervised by trained staff, but some are poorly run, so always check out the facility yourself The animals should look healthy, clean and well cared for. The staff should be able to answer your questions about individual dogs and help you to choose the one best suited to you. Make sure you know what kind of dog you are looking for before you visit the shelter. Shelters usually charge a small adoption fee.

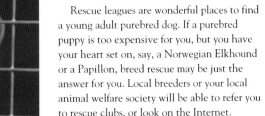

Find out if your chosen dog has been neutered. Shelters are committed to encouraging the neutering of dogs. They may, therefore, arrange through a local veterinary clinic for free or reduced-cost neutering, so check their policy. If possible, get the dog's vaccination record, as this will tell you what shots, if any, your vet will need to administer when you take your dog home.

A local pet shelter is not your only option. If it doesn't have the dog you're looking for, a shelter in a nearby town may have. You can look on the Internet for other shelters, which may have profiles of available dogs.

Many dogs end up in shelters because their previous owners didn't choose an animal that suited their lifestyle. Take the time to make an informed choice, be prepared to put in some work to retrain your dog of any bad habits he may have learned in his former life, and you will be rewarded with a loving companion.

Life without a dog is nothing.

ELIZABETH BOWEN (1899–1973),
Irish novelist and essayist

CHAPTER THREE

SETTLING IN

Preparing for a New Dog

You will need to prepare your home before your new dog arrives.

Think about his basic needs: a bed, food, exercise and health care.

BEDDING

The first thing that your new dog will need is a comfortable bed in a place of his own. For a puppy, a box turned on its side and lined with soft, washable bedding, or a chew-proof pad inside a pen is perfect. A bean-bag type bed or soft mattress will suit most adult dogs, but giant breeds may need a trampoline-style bed for extra support. Make sure the bed is big enough so that the dog can stretch out fully. Put it in a quiet, warm area away from drafts but close to the family. Dogs need an area where they can sleep undisturbed whenever they are tired. Young puppies sleep up to 20 hours a day.

A traveling pen or crate is also a worthwhile investment. If you buy one large enough for your puppy when he is fully grown, you can continue to use it for trips throughout his life. A crate or pen also makes the chore of house-training much easier (see pp. 86–89) and will stop your puppy from getting into trouble when you're not there to supervise him.

FEEDING EQUIPMENT

Your dog will also need his own set of food and water bowls. Try to find the kind that is designed for his breed, so that he can eat and drink without submerging his ears. Some dogs are allergic to plastic bowls; flat-bottomed, heavy-based bowls made of stainless steel or ceramic are the best choice. They're more hygienic and less likely to be knocked over than plastic ones. Put the bowls either inside your dog's pen or close to his bed.

DISHING IT UP Stainless steel or ceramic bowls are more durable and more hygienic than plastic ones.

COLLARS, TAGS AND LEASHES

Other essentials are a collar, leash and identification tag. This tag should be inscribed with your name, address and telephone number and be worn at all times. Even if your dog has an identifying tattoo or microchip (see p. 94), he should still wear a tag. Ensure that is inscribed with the number of the database on which he is enrolled. In some places, dogs may also need to wear a numbered rabies vaccination tag.

The range of collars and leashes available for dogs can be mind boggling. The first type of collar you will need is a plain buckle collar of either nylon or leather, which your dog can wear at all times. Leather or nylon collars and leashes are ideal for mature dogs. As puppies continually outgrow their collars and tend to chew on leashes, the cheaper nylon varieties are preferable. When you fit your dog's collar, it should be loose enough to be comfortable but not so loose that he will be able to slip out of it. You should be able to fit two fingers under a collar that's the right size.

Other types of collars are used for training and for dogs that pull when on a leash. Choke chains and pinch collars should be used only by experienced owners or under the supervision of a dog trainer. If used improperly or with excessive force, they may cause injury.

UNDER CONTROL Various types of collars and leashes are available. Left, clockwise from left: nylon leash; nylon and leather leash; retractable leash. Right, from top: choke chain; nylon clip collar; nylon and leather collar; lightweight nylon collar.

A harness that goes around the body is useful for walking some dogs, such as those with a cough or neck problems, who may find collars irritating.

There is also a wide variety of leashes available. Leashes are generally made of leather, cotton or nylon. Leather leashes are the most expensive, but they last longer and are gentle on the hands. Thick nylon is strong and inexpensive, but is less flexible than leather. Short, lightweight nylon leashes are the best choice for puppies. They're also inexpensive, so if a puppy chews his, it costs less to replace. An extendable leash is another worthwhile investment. Usually made with a comfortable plastic handle, these leashes give dogs freedom to explore while remaining attached to their owners, and enable the dog to be easily reeled in if need be.

Lastly, match the weight of the accessories to the size of the dog. Don't weigh a small dog down with heavy leather items, or expect to restrain a large, powerful dog with a thin, flimsy nylon collar and leash.

ALL IN TOGETHER
These Labrador Retriever puppies may enjoy sharing a bed when young, but each will need his own bed as he grows larger.

HEALTH MATTERS

Most puppies are born with worms or get them soon afterward with their mother's milk. Some cause few problems in their hosts; others cause disease in dogs and humans. Sometimes you will be able to see the adult worms in your dog's feces, but generally your veterinarian will need to do a special microscopic examination of the feces to see if your dog has worms. The vet can then prescribe a medication to get rid of them. See pp. 276–277 for more information.

Adult dogs, especially those that have come from shelters, may have fleas. These tiny pests can cause a lot of discomfort, for both dogs and humans, but there are effective, easy-to-use remedies available. See pp. 252–253 for how to check and treat your dog for fleas.

LITTLE EXTRAS

While you are at the pet supply store, also be sure to buy some safe chew toys and the right grooming tools for your dog's coat type (see pp. 196–201). You may also want to pick up a cleaning solution to deal with the accidents that even mature dogs sometimes have while adjusting to a new home.

73

Dog-Proofing Your Home

*Dog-proofing the home means removing anything that may
be a danger to your dog, or that she may break or damage.*

You may think your house is perfectly safe, but to a dog it's full of fascinating, yet potentially dangerous, attractions. This is particularly true when you get a new dog, since she'll be eager to explore her new home, which means sniffing and probably tasting almost everything she comes across.

It's a good idea to take a tour through your house, garage and yard from a dog's eye view. Get down on all fours and move around and you'll be amazed at the number of chewable everyday items you come across: electrical cords, children's toys, bars of soap, books, dressmaking pins, even jewelry. Use the same precautions for a dog that you would for children, and remember that dogs can be skilled at breaking open bottles and boxes.

The following guide lists some things to watch out for, both indoors and out.

WHAT'S THIS? When you get a new dog or puppy, such as this Norwegian Elkhound, she will be keen to explore everything she can.

THE KITCHEN

Most families spend a lot of time in the kitchen and so will your dog. Dogs have surprisingly agile paws and very determined muzzles with which they can wrest open cupboard doors, so it's important to put cleaning supplies safely away. You may even want to install childproof locks on those cabinets where you store solvents, cleaning materials, rodent poisons and insect sprays.

Keep the garbage safely stored away, or buy a can with a tight-fitting lid. The trash may contain such items as corn cobs, kabob skewers, corks and mango stones, which can obstruct the intestine if eaten. Place especially appetizing—and dangerous—items, such as chicken bones, in the freezer until trash collection day. This eliminates the danger of sharp, splintered bones, and also prevents illnesses caused by eating spoiled foods.

Another common hazard is chocolate, which should be thought of as a poison to dogs. It contains a stimulant called theophylline, which can make dogs seriously ill. The smaller the dog, the less chocolate she needs to eat in order to overdose.

Even such innocent items as towels, throw rugs and dishcloths can be dangerous, as dogs love to chew them. If your dog swallows a big enough piece, it could obstruct the intestine, resulting in serious, even life-threatening problems. To avoid potential harm, find an out-of-the-way spot for all your kitchen linen.

THE BATHROOM

Dogs will often explore the bathroom just to see what's there. All too often, they discover products that have appealing tastes and smells, but which can make them seriously ill.

Bottles and soaps kept along the side of the tub are an invitation to your dog to explore. An elevated shower caddy will keep soaps, shampoos and conditioners out of harm's way. Store all cleaning powders and disinfectants out of dog reach in a cabinet—preferably one that has a tight-fitting latch. Also remember

DANGEROUS FUN Children's toys can be enticing to dogs, but may be hazardous if chewed or eaten.

74

toys when they're finished playing. (Once they've lost a favorite toy or two to sharp canine teeth, this will become easier.)

Dogs often have perverse appetites. They may eat such things as cigarettes from curiosity, and then get seriously ill. If anyone in your family smokes, empty ashtrays regularly and keep loose tobacco in a drawer or tin; paper or plastic packets are easy prey for dogs.

If possible, coil all electrical cords and tuck them out of reach. Or cover cords hanging against a wall with metal covers, available from lighting supply stores. At the very least, you may want to move lamps and other appliances until your dog outgrows that particular interest.

that children's tub toys look very much like your dog's chew toys, but they aren't designed for her strong jaws and teeth.

Sanitary napkins and tampons are highly absorbent, which means they're a problem if your dog chews them and they get inside her intestinal tract. Don't let your dog have access to any cupboard, drawer or trash can that might contain items such as these.

THE LIVING ROOM AND DEN

The number of dog-unfriendly objects in living rooms and dens is as varied as each family. Do you paint? Sew? Knit? Listen to music? Play chess? The materials used for many hobbies can be extremely dangerous to your dog.

The easiest and most practical solution is to store these items in their own special carriers and put them away when you're done. Keep a knitting bag instead of an open basket of needles and yarn. Put your paints in a metal box. Find a high nook for an ongoing game of chess. Also teach your kids to put away their

While chewing cords is mainly a problem with puppies, certain "mouthy" breeds, such as Labradors and Golden Retrievers, may be tempted by them all their lives. In this case, you may want to permanently rearrange your furniture to get all cords out of sight. Taping the cord to the floor doesn't fix the problem. A dog will simply chew through the tape—and it takes only a second for her to be electrocuted.

THE BEDROOMS

Not all dogs sleep through the night. New dogs are particularly prone to wakefulness, and the family bedrooms are a great place to idle away a few hours. Every night before bed, take a few minutes to move any potential hazards off the bedroom floors and out of harm's way.

Children's bedrooms are especially tempting to dogs because of all the toys lying about. Small rubber balls or toys may become lodged in the back of the throat and obstruct the airway. Adult bedrooms harbor two top dangers to dogs: nylon hosiery and medications. Tights and stockings are easily swallowed and can obstruct the intestine. Be sure to keep all medications out of reach; a small dose for a human may be an overdose for a dog, and remember that bottles with childproof caps won't stop her; she may simply chew through them.

Try not to leave loose change and jewelry on the dresser; they may tempt a foraging dog. Instead, place your change in a narrow-necked bottle or sealed jar and put rings, cuff links and earrings in a safely stowed jewelry box.

The Garage

The safest bet, when dog-proofing your garage, is to make the whole area off-limits. Even the best-kept garage can be a hazardous place for a dog, with screws and nails on the floor, as well as paint thinner, insecticide, fertilizer and other poisons lurking about.

Antifreeze is perhaps the biggest danger to dogs. Its sweet smell is attractive to them, but it is deadly. Any dog who ingests it is likely to die unless given the antidote within 24 hours, so store all antifreeze well out of reach. Also periodically check beneath the car; antifreeze leaking from a hose is just as dangerous as that

A CHOICE OF CHEWS
Give your dog plenty of different chew toys and encourage her to chew those rather than household items or your possessions.

in a bottle. You may want to use a new, less toxic type of antifreeze. It's still poisonous, but less so than the traditional kind.

Pay special attention to any poisonous substances lying about, especially slug bait. It doesn't take much to harm even a large dog.

The Garden and Yard

For dogs, gardens and lawns offer a veritable smorgasbord of smells and tastes, not all of them innocuous. Various common outdoor plants can harm your dog (see box), as can some fruits and vegetables. Onions—whether raw or cooked, and even in small quantities—can make dogs quite sick.

Dogs may dig up and eat the poisonous underground parts of spring bulbs, or chew on houseplants. Depending on the height of your dog when standing on her back legs, hanging plants and those on window sills may be safe, but it's best to move any plants off the floor or tables and to put them on higher shelves.

Certain plants traditionally used at holiday times, such as poinsettia and mistletoe, can be extremely poisonous. To be safe, you may want to use the artificial varieties instead.

For a complete list of the poisonous plants found in your area, you could try contacting your county agent or local garden center.

If you keep a compost pile or barrel, make sure your dog isn't able to get to the partially decomposed food inside. Then there are sticks. Dogs love them, but sticks can perforate the roof of a dog's mouth, her throat or intestine. A better alternative is to provide your dog with hard, splinter-free chews, such as Kongs or Nylabones. And while it may be difficult to remove every stick from your yard, it's a good idea to make a careful sweep of the area following a storm, and get rid of any new branches that may have blown down.

PLAY SAFE Sticks often splinter when chewed, and can cause serious injury to a dog. If your dog likes to fetch or chew, rubber bumpers are a safer option.

A COZY HOME Very large breeds, such as Great Danes or these young Newfoundlands, might be more comfortable outside in a kennel than inside the house.

HOME SECURITY

The outside world with all its smells and sounds is enticing to a dog, so if you have a yard, check the fencing to see that it is secure before letting your dog run free. Are there any loose boards in the fence? Gaps that she could squeeze through? A soft place where she can dig? Your dog will spot potential escape routes more quickly than you will, so put her on a leash and stroll around the perimeter of the yard with her. Chances are she might find something you missed, such as a loose board or a small hole that needs fixing.

Is your fence high enough? For a small dog, a fence that is four feet (1.2 m) high should be adequate, while a six-foot (1.8 m) fence will hold most large dogs. Bear in mind that some dogs are natural diggers and will dig under a fence if it is not secure. Make sure the gate shuts firmly and that a small dog is not able to squeeze under it. Swimming pools or ponds should always be covered or fenced.

You may prefer to use an outdoor pen. If so, make it large enough for a good game of fetch. If you plan to keep your dog in the pen for several hours at a time, provide a dog house for shelter from the elements, as well as plenty of fresh water and some toys. There are many different designs, but any kennel should be

POISONOUS PLANTS

The following plants can be toxic to dogs if chewed up or eaten in large enough quantities:

Almonds	Mountain laurel
Apricots	Mushrooms
Azalea	(*Amanita* species)
Black-eyed Susan	Oleander
Boxwood	Peaches
Buttercup	Philodendron
Castor bean (seeds)	Poinsettia (leaves)
Dumb cane	Potatoes (sun-greened
English ivy	tubers, leaves,
Foxglove	shoots)
Jack-in-the-pulpit	Precatory bean
Japanese yew	(seeds)
(needles, bark,	Rhododendron
seeds)	Rhubarb
Kalanchoe	Spring bulbs
Lily of the	Tomatoes
valley	Wandering Jew

sufficiently large for the dog to move around freely inside, as well as easy for you to clean. Stay with your dog while she makes herself familiar with her new yard or dog house, and praise her when she stays and plays where you want her to. If she's understimulated, she's more likely to go looking for excitement on the other side. When you're there with her, however, the temptation to find fun outside the yard will diminish.

The First Few Days

When you first bring your new dog home, he may be somewhat

confused or apprehensive, so let him settle in gently.

As soon as you get your new dog home, but before you bring him inside, take him to the place that will be his permanent toilet area. If he "performs," praise him, but don't be upset if he doesn't get the message just yet. House-training takes time and patience (see pp. 86–89), so don't give up.

Once indoors, restrict your pup to one room. Let him sniff around and familiarize himself with his surroundings. Introduce him to his bed and food and water bowls. Be gentle with him. Praise him for any little thing you can; don't speak harshly or punish him. He needs to trust, not fear you, especially during the first few days. You'll have plenty of time to train him after the adjustment period.

Try not to have visitors until your new pet has settled in. Let him get used to you and your family first, before introducing him to strangers. Teach your children to be gentle and quiet around the new dog, especially if he's a puppy. Children must learn that puppies are not toys and need to be left alone when resting or eating. They should also learn the correct way to pick the puppy up (see p. 85).

MEETING OTHER PETS

Introduction to the household's established pets should be made gradually and under constant supervision. Many older dogs and cats resent the arrival of a puppy, so never leave them alone together at first, unless the puppy is inside a protected pen. Let the established pets sniff the newcomer through the pen. Always give your older animals the most attention, never allowing them to feel that they are being replaced.

BEDTIME

Your new arrival will probably be homesick and lonely. He may whimper and cry, but try not to go to him every time he makes a noise. A puppy may settle down if you imitate his mother's companionship by wrapping a ticking clock and hot water bottle in his bedding. It may help to give the puppy something that he had when he was with his mother—a toy he has played with, or a blanket that carries the smell of his old family, will be comforting to him. Or try Dog Appeasing Pheromone (DAP); this product, a synthetic analog of the

OLD FRIENDS Dogs and cats are not natural enemies and will usually get on very well if encouraged to respect each other.

waxes found in the skin of a bitch's udder, has a calming effect on most dogs. If you're adopting an adult dog, take home one of his toys or his blanket. If he's from a shelter, make him a present of a new toy when you pick him up. Let him sniff it, and when you get home put the toy in or alongside his bed.

Bringing a puppy's bed and crate into your bedroom at night may help the puppy to settle in. But if you get allergies, or the puppy snores, you might need some distance. It's a good idea to start a puppy off in the room you eventually want him to sleep in. An adult dog may have his own ideas about where he'll sleep; as long as that place is okay with you, move his bed to his chosen spot.

PLAYTIME

Most puppies try to play with their owners as they would play with other dogs. They jump up, chase, growl and bite. Play is necessary for the proper social development of puppies, but they need to be taught how to play with people. If your pup starts to bite, say "No!" and turn away from him. If he gets out of control, don't punish him or get angry with him; either leave him alone in a room or confine him in his crate until he calms down.

FEEDING TIME

When you collect your new puppy, ask his former owners what brand of food he's been eating. Feed him the same thing for a few days, even if it isn't the brand you plan to use. A puppy has a sensitive stomach, so make the transition from his old food to his new food gradually. First, give him a few days to settle, then start by mixing the old and new

EIGHT IS ENOUGH Once these Labrador pups go to their new homes, they will depend on their human family for all the care that their mother used to provide.

brands in a ratio of three-fourths of the old with one-fourth of the new. After three days of this mixture, go to half and half for another three days. Finally, feed him one-fourth of the old food with three-fourths of the new for three more days. Then he'll be ready to eat the new food alone.

Feeding other pets at the same time as the newcomer will probably result in "food wars." Feed all the animals separately until they are comfortable with each other.

ADJUSTING TO A COLLAR

A puppy should start to wear a collar right away. Choose a soft, light one to start with. Because many puppies are afraid of collars, the first time you put the collar on, give him his favorite treat. Puppies will take a little time to adjust to collars, so start with short periods and gradually increase the time that your puppy wears his new garb. After a few days, he won't pay any attention to the collar. However, it's a good idea to remove the collar if you put your puppy in a crate. Sometimes, collars can get caught on the crate wires.

GETTING ACQUAINTED Dogs, such as this Border Collie, should be introduced to children gradually and under adult supervision.

CHAPTER FOUR

RAISING YOUR DOG

In order to really enjoy a dog, one doesn't merely try to train him to be semihuman. The point of it is to open oneself to the possibility of becoming partly a dog.

EDWARD HOAGLAND (b. 1932),
American writer

What Is Puppyhood?

The first few months of life are crucial in developing

your puppy's personality, confidence and skills.

Puppyhood is the period when your dog is immature, physically, mentally and emotionally. It lasts until he reaches adulthood at about 24 months, although this can be even later in some large breeds. Here's what to expect in those 24 months, and how to fully develop your puppy's potential.

AT ONE WEEK OLD, a puppy's eyes are still closed and he sleeps much of the time. At three weeks (below left), he can focus his eyes and move around. By six weeks (below right), he is active, curious and starting to eat solid foods.

BIRTH TO 6 WEEKS

A new puppy needs his mother's care and the company of his littermates. At four weeks, he needs about 10 minutes a day outside the puppy pen, being handled gently by a human. This develops his individuality and gets him used to people. At about six weeks, he starts to learn about his place in the pack pecking order. His mother teaches him to respect authority. Roughhousing with his brothers and sisters makes him less sensitive to body contact and noise, and teaches him how to behave socially in the canine world.

7 TO 8 WEEKS

This is the ideal age for a puppy to move into your home. After he has had his temporary immunizations, take your pup to all sorts of places. Put him down, walk away and let him follow you. This will teach him that you're the leader of his pack and he's a faithful follower. Set up situations where he can follow every family member, including the kids. This is the critical time for human socialization. It won't come again, so don't miss it.

Puppies this age can learn what simple commands such as "Sit" and "Come" mean. You can also start gentle leash training.

CHEWING BLUES Puppies, such as this young Labrador Retriever, chew out of curiosity, to investigate new things through their senses of smell and taste, and also to ease the pain of teething.

8 TO 10 WEEKS

More than anything, your puppy needs to feel secure right now. This is the "fear imprint period," when puppies can easily be traumatized and may never forget what frightened them. Some puppies are more affected than others, but this isn't a good time to take your pup to a rock concert in the park.

At this age, puppies love to learn, as long as the teaching is gentle and consistent. Knowing how to please you by coming when called will bolster his confidence, and sticking to a schedule will also make him feel safe. It's also important to continue socializing your puppy: eight weeks is the ideal time to enrol him in puppy-training classes.

A FORMATIVE TIME Interaction with his mother and littermates is crucial for socializing a puppy, building his confidence and maturity and learning essential canine skills.

10 TO 12 WEEKS

Now is the time to add to your pup's social activities and continue gentle training. If he has not been leash trained or learned his puppy "Sit" and "Come," start now. He should accompany you to new places, both indoor and outdoor, and meet friendly people of all ages, other puppies and gentle adult dogs.

12 TO 16 WEEKS

During these weeks, your puppy will continue to need a heap of attention and plenty of social activities. Keep up the training with him, but be gentle. Some pups go through an "avoidance" period at this age, peeping from behind your legs when you go out, or crawling under the couch when guests arrive. If he's been okay around people and other dogs until now, his shyness will probably be short lived. Keep his social life low-key but regular for a while if he keeps hiding.

16 WEEKS TO 6 MONTHS

The juvenile period begins at 16 weeks. While your pup is fully developed mentally, he still has some physical and emotional growing to do, and he won't have an adult attention span. The name of the game is consistency—keep your expectations the same from day to day so he doesn't get confused. Take him out to meet humans and other dogs, and have short, upbeat training sessions. Integrate training into everyday life, for example, by having him sit while you prepare his dinner. He may be clumsy now, but that's just adolescence. He'll be graceful when he's grown.

6 TO 12 MONTHS

Puppies reach puberty, or sexual maturity, during these months, and young male dogs may exhibit some dominant, pushy behavior. You'll notice that your dog's attention span has improved. Training of some kind should be ongoing, whether it's for obedience or just tricks for fun. Some dogs go through a second avoidance period at about ten months of age, but they are usually happy-go-lucky again by one year old.

12 TO 24 MONTHS

This is when your puppy becomes an adult. Smaller breeds reach emotional maturity earlier than larger breeds, some of which won't be fully mature until they're about 30 months old.

Raising a Puppy

Once you've brought your puppy home, he will rely on you entirely for his physical and emotional needs.

You should always be gentle with a puppy, but you don't need to treat him as though he's fragile. Healthy, vaccinated puppies are vigorous, and the bigger they grow, the hardier they get. Before they're vaccinated, they are susceptible to certain diseases, so it's important to keep your puppy away from unvaccinated dogs until he's had his first shots. Otherwise, give your puppy plenty of opportunities to love, learn, and play; he will respond willingly.

BUNDLES OF FUN In return for your love and care, puppies such as these Australian Shepherds will give you a lifetime of loyalty and pleasure.

HOW TO ACT AROUND YOUR NEW PUP

Take pleasure in your puppy's antics. If he dashes across the room in a madcap race, pounces on his toy and plays "kill" with violent shakes of his head, laugh and enjoy it. And incorporate his schedule into your regular household routine. If he is napping and you want to watch television or play the piano, do so. He will learn to sleep through normal household noises. If he's contentedly gnawing his chew toy and you have an irresistible urge to hug him, do so. Puppies understand spontaneity and can give us lessons in having impromptu fun.

COMMON SENSE

In dealing with your puppy, let common sense be your guide. When the neighbor's kids want to share their nachos with him, encourage them to give him a dog biscuit instead. If he wriggles to get off your lap, place him on the floor. A puppy can be hurt jumping or falling off your lap or the furniture, because it's a long way down. Be as cautious with him as you would be with a human toddler.

KEEPING AN EYE ON THE KIDS

When a friend wants to bring her toddler and three-year-old over to see your puppy, supervise closely. Hold your puppy, sit on the floor with the kids, and show them how to pet him before giving them a turn. Never let young children, no matter how gentle, walk around with a puppy in their arms. Squirming puppies can easily slip out of uncoordinated little hands. And if you have children, you'll need to supervise closely whenever their friends come over. Not all people teach their children how to handle animals or that they have feelings. Peer pressure is a potent force; your child may be unable to stop friends from treating the puppy roughly, so you may need to step in. You don't want your puppy being hurt, either physically or emotionally, by any kind of rough treatment.

TEETHING TROUBLES

Puppies tend to be pretty stoic about teething pain, but loose teeth, inflamed gums and sometimes even a lack of appetite will give the game away. Teething puppies are especially prone to chewing, so be aware of this. Put away your chewable belongings and buy him a few chew toys as teething aids. Or you can try making your own. Wet and twist old washcloths and freeze them solid. Give one to your puppy to chew whenever he seems to be suffering from the new-tooth blues—the cold will help relieve the pain. As soon as the washcloth thaws or your puppy has finished chewing, wash the cloth well, give it a twist, and put it back in the freezer for next time.

HANDS-ON CARE

Your pup has to get used to being handled on all parts of his body. He'll need this for a lifetime of grooming and paw checks, ear exams and all the other hygiene routines. To get him used to this, pet him all over. Touch him from the top of the nose to the tip of the tail and every place in between.

Many puppies are sensitive about having their feet touched, but he'll get over it if you deal with it the right way. Sit down with your puppy on your lap or beside you. Then stroke him in places he enjoys being petted until he relaxes so much he's nearly asleep. Continue stroking his body, but include his feet as well. If he tenses, go back to petting only his body until he's sleepy enough that you can try his feet again. After he falls asleep, gently massage the toes of all four feet. Soon he will relax and let you touch his toes when he's awake too.

When doing daily or weekly grooming, such as brushing or trimming nails, be gentle but matter of fact—not apologetic or cajoling. Use just the amount of firmness it takes to stay in control and get the job done. If you stop brushing because he struggles, you're letting him control the situation. Next time, he will simply struggle sooner and harder.

WHO'S IN CHARGE? Don't buy a dog for a child on the condition that the child alone must care for it. You must be willing to accept responsibility when necessary.

PICKING UP A PUPPY

Picking up a puppy needs two hands, so that you can support him at both ends (left). Scoop under him with your right hand pointing forward so it is under his chest, and use your left hand or arm to cradle his rear end. Reverse this if you are left-handed.

Carry your puppy close to your body in both arms. Don't hold him away from you so that his rear dangles. A pup should never be picked up by the scruff (nape of the neck) or the front legs or under the armpits, as this can cause permanent damage to his joints.

AROUND THE HOUSE

Many puppies are initially afraid of vacuum cleaners, so introduce them gradually. First, turn the machine on in another room for a short while and let your puppy get used to its noise. Repeat this for slightly longer periods each day until he seems unconcerned, then gradually bring the machine closer to, and finally into, the same room as him.

Puppies must also learn what they can and cannot play with. When your puppy picks up a non-toy item, such as one of your shoes, avoid giving chase; this will excite him and make him think you're playing a game. Instead, offer him a toy or a food treat, and praise him when he drops the shoe to accept it.

House-Training

Unless your dog is going to be kept entirely outdoors,

early and thorough house-training is essential.

Whether your dog is a puppy or an adult, good house-training should be established from the first day you bring her home. Dogs are naturally clean animals, so once your dog gets the message, she'll be happy to oblige.

HOUSE-TRAINING A PUPPY

Begin with a good feeding and watering routine. Establish set times for eating from the outset. A young dog needs to eat several times a day, so this means that she will also need to eliminate several times a day. Whenever possible, feeding should be scheduled when people will be home to allow your puppy access to the proper elimination location.

Your puppy is most likely to eliminate within 10 to 20 minutes after eating or immediately after waking or playing. Your house-training will be most successful if you can take her outside at these times. The focus of house-training should then be teaching her, by persistence and praise, where to go—outside—and what kind of surface to go on—grass, gravel or concrete (whichever surface is most available).

Inside the Home

Supervision and confinement are the most important tools in successful house-training. When you are home, watch your pup at all times. Keep her in the room with you; if necessary, leash her

JUST IN CASE These Australian Shepherds are confined to a crate when they can't be supervised indoors.

to you or to a piece of furniture to prevent her wandering off. When you notice restlessness or whining, or if she is sniffing, especially in circles, take her outside; she may be telling you that she has a full bladder or bowel.

If you cannot supervise your puppy, she may need to be confined. Try child gates or a dog crate if the puppy is used to it and is not left in it too long. A small, puppy-proof room, full of toys and chews but devoid of dangerous items that the puppy could eat and with an easily washable floor, will work well. Do not confine the puppy so frequently that she feels isolated. A puppy is a sociable animal and needs to be with people or other pets.

Going Outside

Allow plenty of time for house-training. Take your pup outside whenever you see warning signals or simply when she is due to eliminate. When she begins to eliminate, praise her profusely. Use a key phrase so that she will begin to associate it with elimination. Once she has eliminated, it is time to play.

A GOOD ROUTINE These Golden Retriever pups are taken outside soon after meals to encourage elimination.

Training Troubles

What can you do about a puppy that goes outside and does not eliminate? Or worse yet, comes inside and eliminates in the house? There could be several contributing factors. First, the puppy was not outside when she needed to eliminate. Second, she was not given enough time to eliminate. Third, someone was not supervising her inside. Fourth, she was allowed to play and wander and did not eliminate while outside. You want to send the message "eliminate first, play second."

If your puppy does not eliminate when you take her outside, wait a little longer. If still nothing happens, bring her in and either confine her or watch her closely for any signs that she may need to go. When she begins to exhibit any of these signs, whisk her outside to the correct location. Don't forget to praise her when she eliminates.

What should you do if your new puppy has an accident inside? If you did not see it happen, do not punish her for it. Remember, unless you reward or punish a puppy within

HANDY HINTS FOR REMOVING STAINS

It's one thing for your dog to make a mess, but another when you can't get the stain out of the new carpet. Luckily, there are a number of cleaning products that have been created for this specific purpose. Some are colorless and odor neutralizing, and all will safely remove these types of stain.

Commercial products made from concentrated orange peel work well. Or try adding a quarter of a cup of white vinegar and a few teaspoons of liquid laundry detergent to 1 quart (1 liter) of warm water. Spray the soiled area with this solution, let it sit for a few seconds, then rub it in. Dry with a towel.

Neutralizing the odor is important, and not just because it's unpleasant. Dogs are attracted to the smell of urine and will urinate where they, or other dogs, have gone before. Removing the smell entirely will remove this motivation.

15 seconds or less, the puppy does not know what she is being rewarded or punished for. Just clean up the mess and vow to supervise her better in the future. However, if you are right there and your puppy begins to squat, this is the time to use a loud, firm voice and

WHAT A RELIEF Dogs who are given plenty of chances to urinate outdoors, in an approved place, are less likely to do so in the house.

New Home, Old Smells

If you bring a new adult dog to your home and you owned a dog before her, you might not be aware that your previous dog leaked some urine on the carpet here and there, which soaked through to the padding underneath. Despite your best house-training efforts, your new dog will be attracted to the odor only she can detect, and will think it's okay to eliminate indoors. Although they are not 100 percent effective, UV lights available at hardware stores can reveal urine spots you can't see but your dog can smell; under the lights they will glow bright green. To show her that the carpet is off limits, keep her out of that room. You could also consider having the carpets steam cleaned.

On the other hand, you can use your dog's attraction to urine to mark out areas outside that are appropriate, by laying out pieces of soiled newspaper in a corner of the yard.

shout "Outside!" Then swiftly take your puppy outside to the appropriate location. If elimination then occurs, immediately switch gears and praise her lavishly.

HOUSE-TRAINING AN ADULT DOG

If you adopt an adult dog who isn't properly house-trained, train her as you would a pup: by routine and prevention. The only difference between an untrained adult dog and a puppy is that an adult can hold her bladder or bowel for much longer.

Take your adult dog to the same outdoor spot morning, night and after meals, and wait with her while she eliminates. When she's indoors, keep your eye on her as much as possible. If you see her sniffing about or just about to go, make a loud, distracting noise and take her outside. When you can't watch her, confine her to a small space, such as her crate or the laundry or bathroom.

GETTING OLDER

Older dogs, no matter how fastidious, may become a little incontinent and can't always wait to get outside to eliminate. The best thing you can do is to quietly mop up the mess and visit the vet for a checkup. If she could help it, she wouldn't be doing it, so this is not the time to reprimand her.

There are several medical problems that might cause incontinence. These include diabetes, urinary tract infection and, more commonly, memory loss. It's wise to have the dog evaluated by a veterinarian so that you are in a position to make choices regarding treatments or changes in diet or exercise that can help re-establish your dog's routine.

AN INDOOR OPTION This Maltese mix lives in an apartment and can't be let out frequently, so she has been trained to urinate on newspapers.

Moving Confusion

A move to another house can sometimes confuse an adult dog. She hasn't established her scent there yet and may want to mark her territory by urinating in all the wrong places. If this behavior continues, put her food dish next to her favorite new spots. Dogs don't like to soil where they eat and sleep.

Be aware, too, that persistent house-soiling may have other underlying causes; see pages 134–135 for how to deal with this problem.

TIPS FOR FULL-TIME WORKERS

Trying to house-train your new dog when you work full time can be difficult. It will take a little longer than if you were supervising all day, and you may have to juggle your schedule a bit, but it can be done.

Get up a little earlier in the mornings so you have some extra time before you leave for work to take your pup out in the yard once or twice.

Choose a safe area where you can leave your pup while you are gone during the day. The easiest solution, if you have a secure yard, is to leave your pup outdoors (make sure she has shelter, food, plenty of water and a few toys). If she must stay indoors, the kitchen, bathroom or laundry are the easiest rooms to puppy-proof and they can usually be blocked off from the rest of the house with a baby gate. Put her open crate, some toys and a water bowl close to the baby gate, and spread some newspapers down on the floor at the back of the room.

Until she is six months old, someone will need to come and feed your puppy at lunchtime and take her outside afterward. If you don't have family or friends who can help, hire a puppy sitter to come by.

Occasional Mistakes

If visitors bring an adult dog to your house, this might trigger a urinating contest in the house and your dog may return to those spots long after the other dog has left. If possible, don't let the visiting dog inside unless you can watch both dogs constantly, or they are crated.

Sometimes a dog you've owned for years may suddenly eliminate in the house. Perhaps she was too distracted or excited when she was outside to concentrate on eliminating. Maybe she wanted to get back in for a meal or to greet a special visitor. Unless the act is repeated, consider it an isolated incident. If it continues, retrain her as you did when she was a puppy.

DON'T GO CHANGING Dogs, such as this Golden Retriever, are creatures of habit. Changes to their routine, such as moving house, stress in the home, or staying with friends, may upset them and cause a lapse in house-training.

Socializing Your Puppy

*To grow up happy and confident, a puppy needs exposure
to as many different people, places and objects as possible.*

Socializing your puppy means getting him used to people, places and things. Every time your puppy does something he's never done, goes somewhere he's never been, encounters a new object, or meets a new person or a friendly dog, he's being socialized.

Between three and 14 weeks of age is a critical time in a dog's life. A dog will never forget what he learned in those few weeks. His experiences, both good and bad, will leave a permanent mark on his personality, making him outgoing or shy, happy-go-lucky or cautious, curious or fearful, eager to learn or resentful of authority.

Your puppy needs to be exposed to the world outside so he can learn how to live happily with all that goes on around him. He will decide for himself what's safe and what isn't, but he needs your steady guidance. With you there to help him, he will be introduced to a non-threatening world and will grow up confident and outgoing.

OUT AND ABOUT

Taking your puppy with you when you visit a friend socializes him. So does meeting a friendly stranger at home or while on a walk, playing with another animal or examining a soccer ball. Your puppy needs to meet senior citizens, toddlers, bearded men, women in sun hats, teenagers with skateboards and people pushing strollers. He needs to walk on carpet, grass, linoleum and pavement. He needs to learn to climb steps (start by placing him on the third or fourth step and letting him walk down) and to ride contentedly in the car.

COPING WITH HIS FEARS

There are two cardinal rules for socializing a puppy. Never pet him when he's afraid and always praise him for being brave.

When your puppy seems fearful, do not reassure him with petting and soothing words because he will interpret your actions as praise. He will repeat what he is praised for over and over, so a hesitant stance could become his learned reaction to anything new. On the other hand, never jerk him toward the object he fears. Treatment like that could turn a little trepidation into total terror.

Encourage your puppy by setting an example. If he is afraid to go near something, leave him where he is and go yourself. Handle the object as if it were a winning lottery ticket, talk about it excitedly and invite your

TWO FOR ONE This German Shepherd pup gets two socialization lessons on this walk, by meeting both a child and another dog.

YOUNG ADMIRERS Dogs need positive early experiences with children. These young Golden Retrievers are enjoying the gentle attention.

puppy to join you. Sitting down beside the feared object works well. Your puppy will probably start creeping over, but hold your praise until he at least touches the thing with his nose. If the object isn't breakable or too large, roll it away from, never toward, your puppy. This might awaken his chasing instinct and entice him to play with the object himself.

If your puppy is afraid of people, have a friend toss a dog treat his way. She should then ignore the pup and chat with you. When your pup comes nearer, as he surely will, your friend should kneel down and make herself seem friendly and nonthreatening. When your puppy comes in for an exploratory sniff, your friend should hold her hand low, reach under the puppy's chin and tickle him on the chest. Reaching over the puppy's head could make him back up in fright. If your puppy doesn't approach, don't force him, but give

him a lot more socialization. Get other friends in on the act and set up situations where your puppy will be enticed into approaching.

If loud noises send your puppy scurrying, try announcing his favorite things with sound. If he loves to eat, mix his meal in a metal pan with a metal spoon before giving it to him. There's no need to make a racket; keep the volume realistic. Eventually, he'll learn that loud noises can mean pleasant things and will be less likely to jump out of his skin.

I THINK I LIKE YOU ...
This Labrador mix still looks a little timid, but is well on his way to accepting this stranger's friendly approach.

The First Checkup

*Your puppy should visit the vet within two days of your bringing
him home, whether his vaccinations are due or not.*

Put the puppy in his crate for the journey,
and pack a roll of paper towels just in case
he gets carsick or eliminates in the car on the
way. If you have your puppy's health record,
take it along. Also take a sample of his stool.
(A quick tip: Turn a resealable plastic bag
inside out, pick up a small section of your
pup's stool with the bag, turn the bag right
side out and close it.)

When you arrive at the clinic, give the
puppy's health record and stool sample to the
receptionist. The sample will be checked
under a microscope to see if the pup should be
treated for worms. Keep your puppy in your
arms or in his crate while you wait for the vet
to see him. It's easy for young pups to pick up
germs, so don't let him sniff around on the
floor or play with strange dogs.

Keeping Him Happy

When it's your puppy's turn in the examining
room, be matter-of-fact about putting him on
the table. Hold him in place gently, but as
firmly as necessary, for the checkup. Don't
console or coddle him or he'll be sure something terrible is about to happen. Instead, talk
to him in a happy, upbeat voice.

Even if needles make you nervous, don't let
it show, because your puppy will take his cue
from you. If you're tense, he will be fearful, but
if you act naturally and seem to like the vet,
he will feel more comfortable and will be
disposed to like the vet, too.

The Checkup

On your puppy's first trip to the vet, he will be
checked over thoroughly to make sure everything is okay. Your vet will take your puppy's
temperature and listen to his heart, as well as
examine his eyes, nose, ears, throat, stomach
and skin, and check for swollen glands.

FIRST TIME ROUND Try to make your puppy's first
meeting with his new vet a positive one, so that future
visits will go more smoothly for all concerned.

A male puppy will be examined to see if his
testicles have descended into the scrotum,
which they usually do at birth or within ten
days of birth. If they are going to descend, they
will always do so before six months of age.
About 10 percent of dogs have a problem with
either one or both testicles being undescended.
The condition is hereditary, and affected dogs
should not be bred.

Your pup will also be given any vaccinations
that may be due. The whole examination is
painless and will be over in five to ten minutes.

Any Questions?

If you've noticed anything about your puppy
that you especially want to have checked, or if
you have any questions, be sure to bring them
up with your vet. You've already spent a day or
two with the puppy and may sense something
unusual that your vet maybe won't see during
a routine exam unless you mention it.

This is also a good time to discuss heartworm prevention, a vaccination schedule and
neutering, and to find out how the clinic
handles after-hours and weekend emergencies.

92

VISITING THE VET

Once you have found a veterinarian that you trust, don't change vets unless you really can't avoid it. The better the vet knows your dog, the easier it is to recognize a change in the dog's health, diagnose the problem and commence appropriate treatment. The dog will also be more at ease being treated by a familiar person.

Vets will not usually make house calls to domestic pets. They prefer to treat dogs in their clinics. This is because of the convenient access to the appropriate equipment and drugs, and also because dogs tend to be better behaved there than in their own territory. If you cannot drive the dog yourself or get a friend to drive you, some large cities have pet taxis or animal transportation services that you can phone for help. Veterinary ambulances can be of assistance in case of emergency or accident.

Your dog should see the vet at least once a year for his annual checkup. Many dogs will see their vet much more frequently than this, so every dog should be trained to allow the vet to do the following things without resisting:

- To lift him up onto a table;
- To lift and examine his paws;
- To examine his mouth and ears.

A dog who has been trained to be cooperative in these matters will be less likely to become stressed himself when visiting the vet, and also will allow the vet to do his job more easily and efficiently.

There are a few other courtesies you should observe during visits to the vet:

- Your dog should be clean.
- He should be restrained—either on the leash or in a crate—in the waiting room.
- Tell your vet exactly what is worrying you about your pet's health, but avoid long-winded descriptions of symptoms.

Responsible Dog Ownership

Along with the pleasures of owning a dog come various legal and social obligations of which you should be aware.

LOCAL LAWS

Laws regarding dog ownership vary from place to place. In some countries, certain breeds are banned, or allowed only under severe restrictions. It is common for owners to be required to keep their dogs on a leash in public places and certain breeds may also be required to wear muzzles. Familiarize yourself with any local laws and obey them. While dogs may be allowed to exercise off the leash in certain locations, never let your dog loose without supervision.

Most towns and cities in the US require that dogs be licensed or registered, and many also require that dogs be vaccinated for rabies. In addition, your dog should always wear an identification tag on his collar. In Britain, registration and rabies vaccinations are not required, but dogs must wear a collar and tag in public at all times. For permanent identification,

UNDER CONTROL In some places, certain breeds are required by law to be muzzled in public.

a veterinarian can inject a computer microchip under your dog's skin or tattoo him. Both procedures are relatively painless.

When walking your dog in public, make sure that you always clean up after him. In many cities in the U.S., and throughout Britain and Australia, it is now an offense not to do so. If possible, train your dog to defecate on your own property before the walk.

If you are not planning to breed professionally, then it is both sensible and responsible to neuter your dog. Neutering both addresses the growing problem of pet overpopulation and can have many beneficial effects on your dog's health and behavior (see pp. 214–215).

A GOOD CANINE CITIZEN

You must train your dog from an early age to behave well around people and other dogs. All dogs should be taught to obey the basic commands, such as "Come," "Sit" and "Stay," and to walk on a leash without pulling. Allow your dog off the leash only where regulations permit. Even in designated off-leash areas, make sure your dog will not be in danger, or endanger others, before you let him run free.

CROPPING AND DOCKING

The cropping (partial removal) of ears and the docking (partial or total amputation) of tails are becoming increasingly controversial practices and you should be aware of any regulations regarding them in your country. The cropping of ears to make them erect is actually forbidden by some national kennel clubs, including The Kennel Club of Britain and The Australian National Kennel Council.

The docking of tails is still allowed by most kennel clubs. This practice is traditional for many breeds (such as Schnauzers, left, some sporting breeds and many terriers) and

involves removing part of the tail shortly after birth.

If you wish to show your dog and his breed standard in your country specifies cropping or docking, you will have no choice in the matter. However, some owners of pet dogs prefer not to have their dogs' ears cropped or their tails docked. If this is important to you and you intend buying a puppy from a breeder, ask them if they will save you an undocked or uncropped pup from their next litter.

If in doubt about whether cropping and docking are permitted in your country, contact your national kennel club.

CLEANING UP HIS ACT Cleaning up after your dog prevents the transmission of diseases and makes public places more pleasant for other users.

Avoid tying your dog up in the yard away from people for long periods. Such isolation can lead to barking and aggression problems. If your dog is noisy and likely to disturb the neighbors, don't let him outside between 10 pm and 7 am. If your dog does bark a lot when alone, see pp. 116–117 for ways to prevent this behavior. If it persists, consult a veterinarian or animal behaviorist.

Health and Grooming
Your dog depends on you to ensure that he is adequately fed, housed, exercised and kept in general good health.

It is your responsibility to provide regular veterinary care for your dog. Annual vaccinations and check-ups are essential for good health and also to prevent the transmission of diseases to people and other dogs. In addition, always keep your dog clean and groomed. This

keeps him looking good and helps to detect skin parasites. Grooming is also linked to stress reduction in dogs, and helps to consolidate the dog–human bond.

Feed your dog a balanced premium diet and provide plenty of fresh water at all times. Try to exercise or play with your dog for at least 20 minutes a day. Regular exercise and play will keep him healthy and also stop him from being lonely or bored. This, in turn, will help avoid many behavioral problems.

WELL GROOMED Regular grooming controls skin parasites and helps prevents skin diseases. Long-haired breeds, such as this Great Pyrenees pup, generally require a considerable amount of grooming.

Caring for Latchkey Pets

A little care and preparation will ensure that your home-alone dog will be kept safe, stimulated and happy.

Dog are very social creatures and they crave companionship and stimulation. While you're at work, your dog will be stuck at home, trying to find ways to pass the hours until your return. Each dog handles this separation differently. Some dogs cope quite easily, while others have trouble dealing with loneliness. The good news is that there is much you can do to help your dog deal with the temporary separation.

KEEP HER ENTERTAINED

Pay plenty of attention to her when you are home. A few hours a week of occasional interaction just isn't enough for a dog that stays home by herself. When dogs spend a lot of time alone, they also need to spend plenty of time with their owners, getting both exercise and attention.

Schedule regular exercise for dogs left alone during the day. Try giving your dog two good aerobic workouts each and every day, one in the morning and one in the evening. Exercise reduces stress and tires her out, so she'll spend more time resting during the day and less time feeling lonely and perhaps being destructive.

Another way to help your dog cope is to give her something to do, such as providing her with toys that can be filled with kibble, cheese or other foods. She will be occupied for hours working on one of these toys as she tries to get the food out. This food can replace part of her regular meals.

CONSIDER THE BREED

Some breeds of dog are generally better able to deal with being alone all day because of the temperament they have inherited as part of their breed characteristics. Dogs that were bred to work alone, such as terriers, cope better with isolation because they are more independent and less reliant on their owners' attention. Breeds such as German Shepherds and Golden Retrievers were meant to work closely with humans, and are not good candidates for keeping themselves company. You'll need to consider your dog's personality before you decide how well she can handle being left alone.

THE OUTDOOR LIFE

Your first instinct may be to leave your dog outside, where she can eliminate at will and

THE BEST PET DOORS

If keeping your dog exclusively indoors or outdoors doesn't appeal, you need a pet door. This is a panel that allows your pet to exit when she needs to relieve herself or get a breath of fresh air, then re-enter when the weather threatens or things get scary outside.

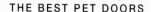

Pet doors come in a number of different styles. If you are concerned about the risk of theft to your home, consider purchasing one with a magnetic or electronic locking device that responds to something on your dog's collar. Only your dog can gain entry.

Don't expect her to know automatically how to use a pet door. Some dogs are initially afraid of them. You may have to teach her how to use the door with treats, a leash and lots of encouragement and praise.

QUALITY TIME This Golden Retriever enjoys regular visits from his petsitter, who feeds him and also spends some time playing with him.

Preparations and Provisions

A dog who is to stay outdoors must have a securely fenced yard, shelter from the elements and plenty of fresh water that can't be spilled. You can do this is by attaching a bucket to a fence or placing an eye bolt on the side of her doghouse to hold it. Or use a heavy ceramic water dish. The indoor dog will need water too, and toys to keep her occupied.

No unsupervised dog should ever wear a choke collar; it may catch on something and entrap her. Use a flat-buckle collar instead.

PET-CARE SERVICES

Dog day care and pet-walking services are excellent ways of helping lonely dogs through the day. The company of people and other dogs in these environments can make all the difference to a dog that is blue without you.

Pet sitters are professionals who will come to your house while you are away. They will walk your pet, feed her, give her fresh water and spend time petting her and talking to her.

Dog day-care centers are places where you can drop your dog off each morning and pick her up again at night. Here, she will be walked and played with and will have both human and canine company while you are absent.

When choosing any service, always check the reputation of the individual or company— ask for references and follow up on them. Make sure walks are included at dog day-care centers, and be aware that some dogs may forget their house-training if they have to eliminate indoors at a day-care center.

Choose a center that requires proof of immunization, screens dogs for good temperament and puts only compatible dogs together. Also check that the facility, play area and enclosures are secure so that dogs can't escape or be stolen.

LOOKING FOR TROUBLE Should this Bullmastiff become bored, he may become destructive or try to escape.

where there are fresh air, passersby to look at and intruding birds and squirrels to chase. This may sound ideal, but there are some risks to leaving a dog outside all day alone. To relieve her boredom, your dog may find a way to escape from the yard; or she could be stolen, teased or harassed by passersby.

Behavioral problems may also develop. Occasionally dogs become aggressive when left outside all day; they can get very frustrated with people passing by. Another emotional hazard is fear, which can be brought on by larger dogs or loud noises. Thunderstorms and fireworks can be particularly scary to your dog; if she is trapped outside while they are going on, she may become so panicked that she will literally claw her way out of the yard.

THE INDOOR LIFE

Your dog is safer indoors, where she can escape from loud noises and other scary things. The downside of being indoors is that she won't be able to relieve herself when her bladder is full. Adult dogs can physically cope with this, but may still be uncomfortable. Also, if your dog is lonely and lacking mental stimulation, it's the furniture that is likely to bear the brunt of her boredom and frustration.

Dogs feel very strongly that they should always go with you in the car, in case the need should arise for them to bark violently at nothing right in your ear.

DAVE BARRY (b. 1947),
American humorist

CHAPTER FIVE

OUT AND ABOUT

Life on a Leash

Being able to walk correctly on a leash should be

part of every dog's repertoire.

One of the responsibilities of dog ownership is making sure your dog does not
make a nuisance of himself in public. The
easiest way to control his behavior is with
a leash. In many places, dogs are required by
law to be leashed in public. This is for the
safety of other people as well as that of the
dog himself—a dog who is not restrained can
easily run off and get lost or be hit by a car.

Putting your dog on the leash won't destroy
his enjoyment of the outdoors, but you will
need to train him to accept the leash; many
dogs resent leashes at first. A dog who is not
properly leash trained is frustrating to walk;
you'll spend your time battling him as he tries
to go one way when you want to go another.

NO SNIFF! When out walking, don't let your dog sniff
everything he passes. His attention should be on you.

LEASH TRAINING

The first step in leash training your dog is to
make sure he has a comfortable collar and that
he is used to wearing it (see pp. 72–3 and 79).
Your dog will need a 6- to 8-foot (2–3 m)
leash that fits comfortably in your hand. For
a small dog, a quarter inch (8 mm) may be
wide enough; for a larger dog, choose a leash
that is one-half to three-quarters of an inch
(12–20 mm) wide. Avoid a chain or a flimsy
nylon leash—they will cut into your hand.

Just as he did when he first wore a collar as
a puppy, your dog will need to become familiar
with the leash. Don't rush outdoors right
away; let him drag the leash around the house
for a while so he can get used to the sound and
feel of it. Keep your eye on him all the time
so he doesn't get it caught up in anything.

Every few moments, bend down and pick
up the end of the leash and gently call your
dog to come to you. When he does, praise
him. Once he comes to your side while he's
on the leash, you're ready to start taking steps
with him. Holding the leash, walk away from
your dog for a bit, then stop and call him to
come. When he comes to you, reward him
with a treat, either some food or praise.

Your dog might resist this exercise by trying
to bite the leash or by digging his paws in and

LEASH MANNERS
A dog who knows
how to heel nicely,
such as this Shiba
Inu, is much more
pleasant to walk
than one who pulls
his owner all over
the place.

CHOKE CHAINS

A choke chain (also known as a choke collar or check chain) is a length of metal chain that tightens around a dog's neck whenever pressure is applied to it, usually via a leash. When put on the right way, choke chains loosen automatically when the pressure is released. However, when put on or used incorrectly, or left on an unattended dog, they can damage a dog's neck or even choke him to death.

Choke chains come in many different shapes and sizes. The finer ones are more likely to cut in and damage the delicate structures (including the carotid artery) under the skin of the neck.

In the past, choke chains were more popular with professional trainers and handlers, especially when teaching a dog to heel, but in recent times they have lost favor. Many obedience trainers and judges are now appreciating that dogs work better when they have never felt neck pain in association with heelwork. It is easy to be heavy handed with a choke chain; it takes skill to use one with sufficient subtlety to be consistently humane. For most training purposes, a dog will need no more than an ordinary collar and leash and appropriate rewards and encouragement.

RIGHT WAY
When put on the right way, the chain will automatically loosen when you stop pulling.

WRONG WAY
When put on backward, the chain will not loosen when you stop pulling.

refusing to budge. These are all normal reactions. To discourage him from chewing the leash, you can spray it with a commercial pet repellent. If he refuses to move, don't scold or pick him up; this just reinforces his reluctance. Be gentle and persistent, and try to entice him to move with a toy or food.

After performing this exercise successfully a few times, move to the outdoors. Gradually coax your dog into moving at a regular speed with you. As he begins to accept this and moves in the same direction and at the same pace as you, stop and praise him. Keep repeating the exercise, making sure you have his full attention. Give a short correction on the lead if his concentration wanders. He will soon understand that whenever you put his leash on him you want him to pay attention to you and to walk at your pace beside you.

If he rushes ahead, stop dead and pull your arms in close to your body for support. You don't need to say anything. Dogs don't like the sensation of straining without making progress and will soon back off. When your dog relaxes and there's slack in the leash, praise him, then keep walking. Repeat until your dog is comfortable with the leash and is no longer trying to pull your shoulder out of its socket. Most dogs will get the message in two or three days.

UNDER CONTROL Good leash training is especially important when walking several dogs at once, such as these Italian Greyhounds.

When You Go Away

While taking your dog on vacation can be a great experience,

the difficulties may outweigh the benefits for both of you.

Before deciding whether to take your dog on vacation with you, consider his health, the mode of transportation and the nature of the destination. Dogs who get nervous or carsick when they travel, those who are sick or aggressive and females in heat are all best left at home or in a boarding kennel.

In many countries, trains and buses will not take dogs as passengers or cargo unless they are specially trained to assist handicapped people. Most U.S. airlines accept dogs, but those over 10 inches (25 cm) tall must usually travel in the baggage compartment.

Find out if the hotel or campground you're going to allows dogs. Also, are you willing to involve your pet fully on your vacation? While dogs love to go camping, most don't enjoy being cooped up all day in a strange hotel room while their owners are out sightseeing.

Think especially hard before taking your dog to another country. Many countries require dogs to be quarantined for as long as six months.

Most dogs do not need tranquilizers when traveling.

UNDER CANVAS Active dogs such as Malamutes generally enjoy camping.

In fact, a tranquilized dog traveling in the baggage area of a plane may have difficulty breathing. If you feel that your dog really should be sedated, consult your veterinarian. Always test tranquilizers at home before your trip.

BOARDING AND KENNELING

If you decide to leave your dog behind, and you can get someone to feed, walk and keep him company, then he can stay in his own home. Another option is to try to get a person to live in your home while you're away, or hire a petsitter to visit him regularly.

Otherwise, find a reputable kennel; get references from friends or your veterinarian. Inspect the housing, feeding and exercise areas thoroughly. Make sure there is someone on the premises at all times and a veterinarian available if needed. When you leave your dog at the kennel, make the transition easier by bringing along a favorite bed or blanket, his usual food and a couple of his toys.

TRAVEL NECESSITIES

To satisfy local laws and to make your pet as comfortable as possible, always organize the following before going on vacation with your dog:

- A current health certificate, proof of vaccination and medical history
- Have your dog checked by a veterinarian before you go and ask about any diseases you could encounter that your dog might not be protected against

- Your dog's medications (write down the names and dosages so they can be replaced if lost)
- Your dog's leash and collar with an identification tag (with both your permanent and temporary addresses), and his license
- Food and water bowls
- A supply of regular food and treats to last the whole trip
- Plenty of water, preferably from home

- A can opener for dog food
- Grooming tools, including a flea comb
- Flea and tick repellent, plus tweezers for removing ticks
- Toys and a favorite bed or blanket
- Photos of your dog in case he gets lost
- Plastic bags or newspaper to clean up after him
- A pet crate, if your dog is trained to use one

Driving with Dogs

*Good preparation will ensure that a road trip with your dog
will be a pleasure for all concerned.*

When you're traveling by car with your dog, half the fun is getting there. He will enjoy roadside scenery almost as much as you do, and he may even spot a few other traveling dogs cruising down the same roads. To ensure that your dog, and the rest of the family, has a comfortable trip, get him ready well in advance for his time in the car and for the new sights and sounds he'll encounter.

PREPARING YOUR DOG

Several weeks before you're due to set off, start acquainting your dog with the sorts of things he may encounter on vacation. To reduce the stress of his first trip, your dog should be introduced to a wide array of situations.

New Sights, Surfaces and Sounds

Focus first on people. Have your dog meet a variety of people: young and old, thin and heavy, bearded and clean-shaven, folk with eyeglasses, with canes or in wheelchairs. It's also important for your dog to be comfortable around animals; if you can, introduce him not only to other dogs, but also to horses, cats and various farmyard animals.

Be sure your dog is comfortable stepping on all types of surfaces. Moving walkways, floor grates and elevators may scare him.

A traveling dog needs a tolerance for traffic noises. Desensitize your dog by taking car rides on a busy thoroughfare. Open the windows to let the noise in, and gradually work up to a walk along that busy street.

Exotic Food and Drink

Your dog will likely jump at the chance to try the local cuisine, but a sudden change of diet could give him diarrhea. So when on the road, play it safe and give him his usual food.

STRAP ME IN A special dog harness that attaches to the seat belt keeps this mixed breed safe on the road.

If it's just a short trip, take along his regular food. On longer trips, take enough of the dog's usual food to mix gradually with whatever he will be eating. This also goes for water. Take a supply of your dog's usual drinking water. After 24 to 36 hours, start mixing it gradually with the new water he'll be drinking.

FEELING QUEASY

People are not the only ones who get carsick. Dogs can suffer from motion sickness, too, with disastrous consequences. You can help your dog avoid getting sick, or at least help him to feel better if he does succumb.

"SETTLE" Dogs who roam in the car are a nuisance and a danger. Teach your dog "Settle," which means "Find a good spot and lie down—then stay there."

can be given. Don't let him get thirsty or dehydrated, but do remember that a belly full of water can quickly become a backseat full of water.

If these tactics don't work, your vet can prescribe drugs to counter carsickness, or he can recommend over-the-counter products designed for humans that can be given in dog-sized doses.

If your dog is sick when you're on the road despite all your efforts, pull over and take him for a walk. Or try opening the windows if it's cool out, making sure not to let your dog hang his head out the window. If it's hot in the car, turn on the air conditioner and point it at the dog. Some dogs like an ice cube to chew on. Or get his mind off his sick feeling by giving your dog some of his favorite toys to play with.

Time for a Break

If your dog is quiet in the car, you can take him out as often as you wish for breaks. If he's hyper, hold off on frequent breaks, since this may only aggravate his problem. However, you'll still need to stop stop every four to six hours to give him a toilet break. Some roadside rest stops have a special area for dogs to relieve themselves, and places where your dog can run about. Keep your dog on a long leash while he romps, and maybe even play a game of ball. Unless he has been trained to come without fail every time he is called, don't take him off the leash or you could risk losing him.

Dog-Proofing the Car

If you know your dog is prone to carsickness, or if it's his first long-distance trip and you don't know how he'll react, dog-proof the car before you set out, with a plastic tablecloth placed on the backseat to protect the interior.

Better still, keep your dog in a pet crate when traveling. If he doesn't already have his own crate, you'll need to get him used to it for a month before you travel. Do this by feeding him in it. A crate is the safest way to ride in a car, for both the dog and you. If you have to stop suddenly or there's an accident, your dog will be safe in his carrier. A wire barrier between the back and front seats of the car is also a good security measure.

Anxiety Overcome

Many dogs vomit in the car simply because they are anxious—they don't like things whizzing past them in an alarming way. To get your dog used to riding in the car, first spend some time in it when it's stationary. Let him check out the car while you read a book. Give him a dog treat and a pat, then take him out of the car. Once he accepts this routine, take him on a quick trip around the neighborhood. Gradually increase the length of the journeys, and he will eventually be a calm traveler.

Easing the Queasies

Withholding food helps deal with carsickness. Don't feed your dog for at least eight hours before the trip. Empty stomachs might get sick anyway, but at least there's not much to expel.

Don't give your dog anything to drink for the two hours before you set off. Once on the road, ice cubes or small, frequent sips of water

Flying with Dogs

Plane travel is not recommended for dogs, but if it can't be avoided, you must make proper preparations for the journey.

Air travel is stressful for dogs and should not be undertaken lightly. The first requirement is an airline-approved pet crate. If your dog is not accustomed to using a crate, acquire one and begin getting him used to it at least one month before your trip.

HEALTH CHECK

Take your dog to the vet for a checkup and a health certificate. Health certificates are required for all pets that are transported by air, and are usually valid for 30 days for domestic travel and 10 days for international flights. If you are flying to another country, contact that country's consulate and ask what inoculations he'll need and whether he must be quarantined before or after entering the country.

You can also discuss with your vet the possibility of giving your dog tranquilizers, although these are not recommended in most situations because they can interfere with your dog's breathing and ability to cope with changes of temperature.

TICKET TO RIDE

Make your reservations well ahead of time. A possible bonus of booking early is that your dog may be able to fly in the cabin with you, provided his carrier is small enough to fit under the seat in front of you. Only one or two animals per flight are usually allowed in the cabin, so the earlier you book, the better your chance of securing one of these spots.

In most cases, your dog will be placed in the cargo hold, where you won't have access to him. At least make sure he has a familiar blanket for both comfort and warmth.

Book a nonstop flight, if possible, and fly at a time of year and time of day when there is less likelihood of outdoor ground temperatures being hot. For dogs in the cargo hold of a plane stuck on a runway, heat can be a killer. On a direct flight, there is less likelihood that your dog will be in this situation. Night and pre-dawn flights are the safest for pets traveling in

UP AND AWAY This Belgian Tervuren may never actually enjoy flying, but adequate preparation will lessen the llikelihood of a traumatic experience.

summer. Finally, make sure you book yourself on the same flight as your dog. Don't send him ahead of you, or on a later flight.

FLYING TIME

Give your dog nothing to eat for eight hours before the flight, and nothing to drink for two hours before. Get to the airport early. Dogs are usually shipped as freight, which means you should check in two hours before you fly. Your name, address and phone number should be written clearly on the crate, including your destination address in case there's a mix-up.

Once you're on the plane, advise the crew that there is a dog in the cargo hold and insist that they tell the pilot. Then, if something happens that could endanger your pet's well-being, such as the plane being held for some time on a hot runway, the pilot can arrange for your dog to be cared for.

If such a situation arises and you are at all worried about your dog, don't be afraid to speak up. Let the crew know that your dog's safety is of the utmost importance to you.

Staying Away from Home

When staying in strange places with your dog, research and plan

your trip to ensure a positive experience for everyone.

Taking dogs to hotels or friends' houses can be a challenge, for the dog himself and for the people who have to deal with him. He needs to know how to behave in various situations and he will also need some extra care from you, both before and during your stay.

STAYING AT HOTELS

An increasing number of hotels are willing to welcome dogs, but don't just drive somewhere and trust to luck. Check hotels in the area you're visiting before you leave home, book in advance and get confirmations in writing.

There are many guidebooks available on where to stay with your pet. The World Wide Web has databases for dog-friendly holidays. Your local automobile association may have listings, and you can also call the local humane society in the area where you will be staying and ask for the name of a good hotel that allows dogs. Many bed-and-breakfast hotels are also happy to have dogs. Start by picking a place that sounds good to you, then do a little research. Call and talk to the owners to get a sense of how they cater to canine guests. If dog treats or other canine services are provided, chances are your dog will be very welcome.

TWO'S COMPANY Even hotels that welcome dogs prefer them not to turn up unannounced. When you make your reservation, let the staff know that your dog will be accompanying you.

for a short time, confine him to his crate and inform the hotel manager so cleaning staff don't get a surprise when they enter the room.

If your dog tends to bark at strange noises, ask for a room where there's little foot traffic. And, if your dog usually sleeps in or on the bed with you, bring a sheet from home to put on the bed so he doesn't leave his hair on the bedclothes.

Most importantly, your dog must be infallibly house-trained. If he isn't, then he's not hotel-trained, either.

The Well-Behaved Guest

Dogs can make excellent guests—if their owners know how to handle them. This means taking some precautions to ensure that your dog does not disturb other guests, ruin the room or make too much mess.

Whatever you do, don't leave your dog alone in a hotel room. An anxious dog can tear a hotel room apart in no time. If you must leave your dog alone

LEAVING LESS MESS Brush your dog thoroughly, outside or on a balcony, to reduce the amount of hair that he will shed on your hosts' carpets and furniture.

STAYING WITH FRIENDS

Even a dog who is impeccably behaved at home may not be when staying in a strange place, simply because the rules are different there. She may be used to early-morning walks at home, but she won't understand that her hosts aren't. People who love you may not love your dog, or the social limitations that dogs impose. Find out if your dog is truly welcome in your hosts' home, then make an effort to ensure her stay goes smoothly.

Perhaps the most contentious issue for a dog's hosts is neatness. They won't want pet hair everywhere, so bath your dog before you leave home. Once you're at your destination, be sure to brush her thoroughly, outside or on a balcony, as often as is necessary.

If your dog sleeps on the bed at home, take your own sheet for her to lie on. Better yet, if she usually uses her own pet bed or crate, take it along. You can put it on the floor next to your bed. She'll feel secure, and you won't have to worry about her making a mess.

If your dog is a drooler, control the slobber with a pet bib, available from pet supply stores, or a bandanna tied around her neck.

A PORTLY POODLE Familiar touches, such as her own basket and blanket, should make this Tenterfield Terrier feel quite at home in a hotel room.

Making the Introductions

Visiting a pet-free household is easy, but you will need to work harder to ensure harmony if you stay where there are other animals. Cats will often simply disappear until you and your dog have left, but dogs will have to deal with the new arrival.

Dogs are social animals, and most of them really enjoy meeting other dogs, but don't just throw them together and hope for the best. Instead, try easing them into the acquaintance. Make sure they meet on neutral ground. A park or the street is best, or, at a pinch, outside in the yard. Dogs are territorial, so the resident dog may feel that she has to defend her property from strangers.

Many dogs dislike being leashed when meeting other dogs; it seems to make them more likely to react aggressively, so remove their leashes. Then stand back and let them sniff each other for as long as they need to. This is an essential part of their getting to know each other. A little bit of blustering is normal, and generally gives way to friendship or at least tolerance.

Once they have got their sniffing over with, the dogs will probably relax and accept each other, and they can then be taken inside. But if they really can't stand each other, you'll have to make other plans.

The Great Outdoors

*Even city-bred dogs love a chance to get out in the wilderness
and go hiking with their owners.*

Dogs enjoy open spaces, fresh air and new and intriguing scents. But some get so overexcited that they bark madly and race up and down wilderness trails, frightening away wildlife, disturbing people and exhausting themselves before the hike has barely begun. Park rangers get many complaints every year about noisy, aggressive or overexuberant dogs. For your dog to enjoy his day in the outdoors, and not annoy others, he will need a bit of special preparation.

BEFORE YOU LEAVE HOME

Some dogs are much better suited to hiking than others. Most athletic breeds, such as sporting dogs, will relish a long hike. Those with short noses, such as Pugs, Bulldogs and Pekingese, often have difficulty breathing and can be stressed by too much exercise. They are unlikely to enjoy or benefit from hiking, especially in hot weather.

PACKED AND READY Dogs can be trained to carry their own supplies in a special canine backpack.

TEMPORARY ID Pet supply stores sell small containers that attach to dogs' collars and contain papers on which you can write your vacation address and contact details. Your dog's usual tags will be useless if she gets lost, as you won't be home to get the call.

Ask your vet to make sure that your dog is fit for the trip. Also get a copy of your dog's health certificate and proof of vaccinations. Some campgrounds and border crossings won't let dogs pass unless they have these documents.

Unless your dog is used to regular, vigorous exercise, you'll need to increase her exercise in the weeks leading up to the trip.

You'll also need to pack enough food and fresh water and perhaps some anti-motion sickness drugs for the drive there.

ON THE TRAIL
Under Control
The simplest way to prevent most behavior problems on the trail is to put your dog on the leash. On most public lands, dogs are required

If bicyclists or runners also use your trail, they may trigger a dog's chase instinct. If your dog is a chaser, tell her to "Sit" when runners or bicyclists approach from either direction and reward her for looking away.

The Right Gear

Pet supply and camping stores stock a range of hiking accessories for dogs. You may want to equip your dog with some special items.

Try using a flat nylon collar (with a quick-release catch in case it gets snagged on something) and a nylon or cloth leash. Leather leashes are heavy enough to weigh down your arm on a long day's hike.

Your dog will also need protection from ticks and fleas. Try using a flea spray before you leave home. Sprays containing pyrethrins are safer than some chemical sprays. Rather than spraying it directly onto your dog, spritz some onto a cloth and wipe it over her; this enables you to control the application so that it doesn't get in your dog's eyes, nose or mouth.

Consider fitting your dog with a canine backpack. Even a small dog will be able to carry her own food and collapsible food and water dishes. Get your dog used to wearing a backpack at home first. It's not only the weight that she needs to get used to; the pack will also make her wider than normal, meaning that she won't be able to fit through the same spaces that she usually can. The first time, put the pack on her when it's empty and let her wear it for a short time. Gradually increase the time she wears it, while also packing it with an increasing weight, until eventually she is carrying the same weight that she will be required to take on the trail.

by law to be on the leash, for the convenience of other hikers and for their own safety. Some public hiking areas are also grazing areas, and dogs may be shot for chasing livestock or wildlife. Putting your dog on a leash won't destroy her enjoyment of the outdoors, but make sure she is properly leash trained before you go (see pp. 100–101).

Outdoor Etiquette

Most people go to wilderness areas expecting peace and silence. Dogs who bark too much can spoil that, so keep your dog's barking to a minimum. Before leaving home, teach your dog the "Quiet" command (see p. 117). Or put your hand on her muzzle when she barks; this should stop her, but it is only a short-term solution, as she will soon learn to dodge your hand.

Another issue on wilderness trails is that of not crowding other users. Many such trails are too narrow to allow two users to pass comfortably. You may need to teach your dog to get out of the path of an oncoming hiker by swapping sides. If, for example, your dog is walking on your left and you want her to swap sides, use the leash to direct your dog to the right, then tell her, "Side," while patting your right thigh. Most dogs quickly learn to associate the word with the gesture and will move to the required side.

STAND ASIDE Teach your dog to swap sides on command, so that she can get out of the way of oncoming hikers or cyclists.

No animal should ever jump up on the dining-room furniture unless absolutely certain that he can hold his own in the conversation.

FRAN LEBOWITZ (b. 1950),
American writer and humorist

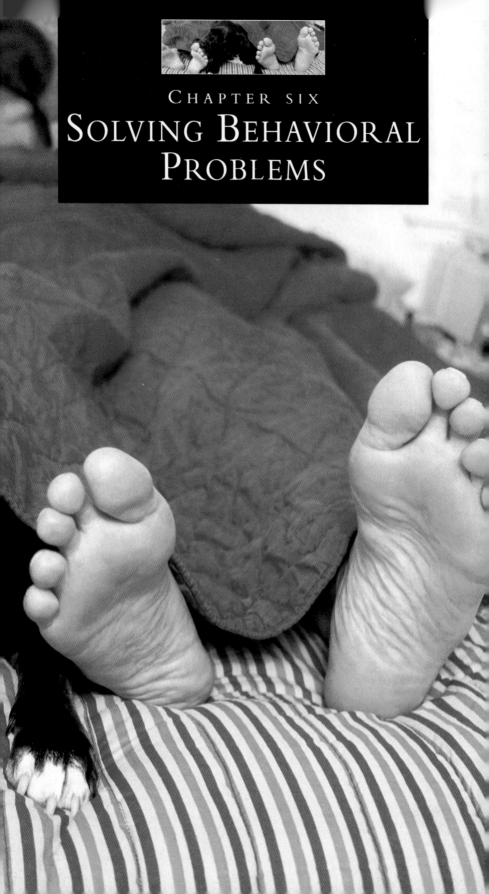

CHAPTER SIX

SOLVING BEHAVIORAL PROBLEMS

Aggression

Aggression in dogs covers many behaviors, including growling,
barking, snarling, lunging, snapping and biting.

Sometimes a dog will indicate its aggressive intentions by staring and standing tall with its ears and hair erect. Unneutered male dogs often behave aggressively to other males, resulting in dog fights.

Fear, pain and nervousness may also make a dog behave aggressively. If your dog is displaying aggression and threatening family members, visitors or strangers, or has bitten people, the intervention of a qualified behaviorist is essential. Don't think that the problem will disappear on its own. Until you feel your dog is reliable, don't leave him around toddlers unsupervised.

JUST PLAYING Not all apparent aggression is due to fear or anger. These two mixed breeds are snarling and biting as part of a play-fight.

With a new puppy, establish yourself as his leader from the start, by setting rules that are humanely but consistently enforced. Get him used to your handling of his food, toys and body. Do this when he is calm, not excited.

If you need to take something from a puppy, do so in a firm but gentle manner and offer him an alternative, more appropriate toy. If you yell and reach quickly for him, you may scare him and prompt aggression in return. Remember, harsh punishment can cause aggression based on either fear or pain. If you must reprimand, a firm verbal rebuke is enough. Always reward your dog with treats and praise for calm, subordinate behavior.

Between the ages of three and six months, puppies begin teething. At this time, they also become more playful with people, and a soft, fleshy hand feels soothing on a puppy's gums. A little playful gnawing isn't aggressive, but it can increase to hard bites and this can lead to aggression. So can other games, such as wrestling and tug-of-war. To prevent your puppy from developing aggressive tendencies, avoid playing games that encourage winning.

EARLY INTERVENTION

The best way to deal with aggressive behavior is to prevent it in the first place. The first time he growls, don't be afraid to tell your dog "No!" When you do this, your dog will know that you're serious with the correction. Act as soon as you hear a rumble in your dog's throat. He'll get the message more quickly if he knows that the outburst he's about to make will not be tolerated. When you tell him "No," it is important to offer him an alternative, preferred response so that he can be rewarded for performing it.

PREVENTING AGGRESSION

Some animals will be wary of new people and exhibit aggression toward them. Frequent and early socialization with many different people in many locations is a good start in avoiding this behavior; a sheltered existence does not prepare a dog for street noise, other dogs or strangers. Use a calm but happy voice to encourage your dog to be friendly with people.

YOU'RE IN CHARGE Regular obedience training teaches dogs to respect their owner's leadership, which makes them less likely to behave aggressively.

When people visit, teach your dog to sit or lie down for attention. Make meeting new people fun by using treats and praise. Keep a treat jar by the front door and have visitors give a treat to the dog on arrival. Your dog will soon learn to associate good things with people coming in the door. Your dog will pick up signals from your attitude, so relax and praise him when he accepts the treat and

PLAY NICELY Although many dogs love rough play, it can stimulate them to act aggressively. If your dog tends to be aggressive, avoid rough play and games with a win-or-lose outcome, such as tug-of-war.

doesn't shy away. If you're nervous about your dog's response, he'll be nervous, too.

If your dog becomes frightened, don't pick him up or coddle him in a baby-talk voice. The worst thing to tell a fearful dog is, "It's okay, don't worry." This will only reinforce his timid behavior. Just stay relaxed and your dog will follow your cue.

If you have adopted an older dog who is aggressive around people or other animals, you may need to use a leash for control, even in the home. This will at least prevent injuries to people visiting your home.

In public, keep your dog on a leash if you are not sure how he will react. If you suspect your male dog dislikes other male dogs, don't let him go nose to nose with one while out for a walk. If your dog is nervous of children, build up his confidence by making him sit and stay near to a public playground where there are children running about. If he is obviously anxious and fearful in a situation and cannot be calmed, remove him at once. If this kind of behavior occurs repeatedly, you may need to seek qualified help. Don't assume that your dog will grow out of the behavior.

WATCHDOGS AND GUARD DOGS

Many owners want a dog that will bark and alert them to intruders. So, how can you create a dog that barks, but does not engage in excessive and annoying displays? The important conditions here are control and early training. Do not let your puppy bark excessively either indoors or outside. Excessive barking can get a dog agitated and increase aggressive behaviors. When excessive displays begin, you must go outside and stop them. You may even need to keep the dog on a leash so you can get him to stop more easily.

Some breeds were developed as guard dogs, so certain traits, such as obedience, loyalty and aggression, were actively selected by breeders. While many of these breeds make natural watchdogs, they must be handled carefully. Training must be firm but never harsh. A good watchdog should learn from the outset to control its aggressive instincts.

LOOKING FOR TROUBLE Certain breeds, including Jack Russells and some other terriers, often tend to be aggressive around other dogs.

A MATTER OF TERRITORY

Dogs are very territorial creatures, particularly if they are tied up in the yard a lot. Some dogs will become very protective of that small space and can become aggressive. Also, dogs that are tied up cannot escape from teasing or other annoyances. As a result, they may resort to aggressive behavior to stop such intrusion. Dogs that were bred to guard are particularly prone to excessive territorial behavior.

Dogs aren't only territorial about their house and yard. They will regard any place they visit regularly, such as a park or even a street they often walk along, as part of their territory. To prevent this, vary your walking routes and the parks and other outdoor areas that you visit as much as possible.

MEETING OTHER DOGS

When two dogs first meet, they'll immediately want to establish the pecking order. If one dog asserts his authority and the other dog reacts submissively, order will reign. The trouble starts when both dogs want to be the leader.

When you take your dog for a walk, keep him on a loose leash. If he becomes aggressive when a strange dog approaches, try to distract him by changing your pace or turning to the right or left frequently. If you see him spot another dog up ahead, don't tense up or tighten your hold on his leash. Your dog will sense that something is wrong from your behavior, and he'll prepare himself for potential danger. If you remain calm, your dog will also feel more relaxed. Sometimes, however, it may be better to avoid the situation.

In many cases, it is better to introduce dogs to one another off the leash (see p. 107).

FIGHTING

It's fun to watch two dogs play together. Their romping, rolling and noisy games of tag can keep them busy for hours. Two dogs who live together will usually work out their own rules and take turns at being in charge. However, the play growling and chasing can get out of hand very rapidly if a new dog comes on the scene or one dog becomes too excited and escalates the level of play. If one dog continually grabs the other one by the neck and rolls him to the ground, or nips him hard enough that he lets out a yelp, that isn't acceptable. If one dog is smaller or younger, he may become frightened by such rough play.

To avoid fights starting, be on the lookout if both dogs are sparring—that is, standing on their back legs and biting one another around the ears or head. Dogs that are very dominant, fearful or that have been attacked before are more likely to get into fights.

How to Break Up a Dog Fight

If you see your dog fighting with another dog, don't reach in to grab his collar, even though it may seem the logical thing to do. Your dog may think your hand is just another part of the other dog, and so aim for it and bite you. Instead, try clanging two metal items together and shouting loudly at the dogs to stop.

You can also douse the combatants with water from a garden hose, bucket or even a pitcher. The cold sensation will startle the dogs and distract them for long enough for you to call your dog to you, put a leash on him and remove him.

If you have a male dog, the best way to prevent him from getting into fights is to have him neutered. This decreases his natural tendency toward aggression, and also means that other dogs won't see him as competition in the perpetual quest for higher status.

THE FIGHT'S OVER Dousing fighting dogs with a jet of water will startle them and make them break apart for long enough for you to separate them.

Attention Seeking

Any dog that has a strong bond with its owner is a ca.
for attention-seeking behavior.

All canids are opportunists: they experiment with a wide range of new behaviors to see if they bring any benefits. This accounts for the enormous variety of responses—notably stealing objects, tail-chasing, nudging owners and whining—that can be diagnosed as attention-seeking behaviors.

Dogs also attach fundamental importance to social interaction. This is why attention from key members of the social group, especially the leaders, is so valuable. If the leader engages with the lower-ranking members of the group, they sense a considerable reward. In human–dog interactions, praise is an obvious example of a reinforcing form of attention, but sometimes even just looking at a dog can reward it for whatever it has just done. The dog learns how to gain and maintain its owner's attention by repeating the behavior, whether it be barking, jumping up or just fooling around.

These two factors—opportunism and the value of social interactions—explain why attention seeking is so common. Many owners find attention-seeking behaviors amusing, especially the first few times they appear. They may laugh and point out the dog's latest trick to someone else, or may simply just smile. This provides enough feedback for many dogs to know that they are on to something. They will offer the response again to see what happens; if they get the reward they are seeking, the behavior begins to become established in their repertoire. Even when they have been rewarded irregularly, they will persist. Indeed, infrequent rewards make behaviors more likely to last in the absence of continued attention.

How to Prevent It

The challenge for owners of attention-seeking dogs is to learn how to take away the reward—that is, the attention—that reinforces the unwanted behaviors. This is not as easy as it

LOOK AT ME A smile from his owner may be reward enough to keep this Miniature Schnauzer dropping a toy at her feet every time he wants attention.

may sound. Even pushing a dog away after it has jumped up to greet you can be perceived by the dog as a reward, because it is an outcome that involves physical contact.

The maxim for owners who want to prevent attention-seeking behavior is that "nothing is free." During their everyday contact with their humans, dogs should work for rewards, be they physical interaction, verbal praise or visual contact. Once owners realize how powerful these seemingly minor rewards can be, they simply have to dispense them on their own terms. Dogs that demand attention should be ignored. This means that all attention-seeking stunts (new and old) should be met with the same disinterest. This doesn't mean that the bond between the dogs and their owners has to suffer; rather, it means that the owners are in control. They can tell their dogs when it is appropriate for them to seek attention and this has the added benefit of enhancing their role as gentle but impressive leaders.

Barking and Howling

Dogs bark or howl to communicate, to indicate excitement, to relieve boredom, stress or anxiety, and to alert people to intruders.

While most dogs bark to say something, others do it just for fun or out of habit. This kind of barking can go on all day and make your dog the neighborhood nuisance.

When you have a dog that barks to excess, it is important to determine the motivation. Some dogs bark incessantly when left outside all day by their owners. This barking is very difficult to stop and you should instead look at why the dog needs to be left outside in the first place. Is it because you can't trust your dog in the house? If so, then there are other problems that need to be treated first.

If your dog is barking while you are home, and you can't make him stop, then you need to teach him the "Quiet" command. If you have tried yelling at him to be quiet without success, you can assume that he hasn't associated silence with the word you are using. You need to establish a clear link between your command and the desired response (see box).

If you are having difficulty teaching your dog the "Quiet" command, you might want to try using a headcollar. When the dog is wearing a headcollar, you can attach a leash to it and use it to close the dog's mouth while you give the command.

SPEAK NOW Dogs such as this Vizsla can be taught to bark on command, which will help you to control their barking when you are with them.

HOW TO STOP YOUR DOG'S BARKING

To help your dog expend the energy he might otherwise use for barking, give him plenty of physical outlets for expression. Long daily walks will both satisfy him mentally and tire him out, as will taking him to a large fenced-in dog park where he can run, play and bark in a controlled environment.

If your dog is left alone for long periods, barking may be his way of expressing himself. Dogs are social animals, so they should never be left alone for long periods of time. But if you can't avoid leaving your dog at home by himself, try turning on the radio or television before you leave. Some dogs associate the o sound with the presence of their owners and will be comforted and quiet.

You can also give your dog "puzzle" games, such as a hollow plastic toy filled with peanut butter or dog biscuits, to play with while you are gone. These will keep him busy for hours as he tries to extract the food. This mental stimulation will also tire him out, so he'll probably spend the rest of the time snoozing.

Barking is often elicited by sound or sight. If you have no control over the source of the sound that your dog barks at, you may need to keep him inside. If he barks every time he sees a stranger in the street or a cat in the yard, keep your window shades drawn or make sure your backyard fence is solid to prevent him from seeing what's going on outside.

When he barks, don't pet him or reassure him that everything is okay. If you do, he'll think that you are praising him for his bravery and

116

ON THE LOOKOUT Many dogs will bark at things they see outside. A simple solution in the case of this Bull Terrier mix might be to move the sofa away from the window, taking away his lookout point—and with it, his motivation for barking.

that barking is a good thing to do. Yelling at him to stop barking will just convince him that you're joining in with his alarm call.

If your dog barks because he's frightened of something, such as the vacuum cleaner, the lawn mower or a large trash can, try desensitizing him to those objects. If you feed him next to these common items or while the motors are running, he'll eventually associate those scary things with the positive act of being fed. Densensitizing him to objects he is frightened of will not only reduce his barking but will also give him confidence. See pp. 85 and 133 for more hints on desensitizing.

Another way to stop a dog barking is to make a sharp sound that's at least twice as loud as his barking. Clang two cooking pots together or use an air horn, the kind that is commonly used on boats. Work out your dog's motivation before you use this method; it may work if he is barking to get your attention or because he is bored, but if he is distressed, the sharp sound will increase his stress and also increase his barking.

A last-resort method to control barking is to use products that administer a correction when the dog barks. Bark collars that use a noise deterrent or those that use a citronella spray can be effective. Shock collars are not recommended. If all else fails, seek the advice of a professional behaviorist.

TEACHING "QUIET"

To train a dog to stop barking, you must first get him to start. So, find something that will reliably make him bark, such as the doorbell. Then, standing in the doorway, ring the doorbell and allow your dog to bark a few times.

Hold a treat over the dog's nose while saying "Quiet," "Hush" or the like. (It doesn't matter what the word is, so long as you use the same one every time.)

When your dog stops barking to sniff, praise him and give him the treat. Repeat, each time requiring the dog to be silent for longer periods before he receives the treat.

Begging

Dogs learn quickly that pleading eyes and a paw raised

in supplication are their best hope of getting extra food.

Dogs beg because they lust after what we're eating—they see us enjoying it so much, and they want to join in the fun.

It's hard to resist a dog's pleading eyes, but if you give in just once and feed your dog even a tiny morsel from the dinner table, you'll scarcely ever be left alone during mealtimes again. Your dog will soon act as if he's starving all the time and the begging will progress to drooling, whining, jumping up on your lap and frantically scrambling all over the room every time someone accidentally drops a bit of food.

WHY BEGGING IS BAD

Sharing your calorie count will ensure that you never have another moment's peace. It will also make your dog gain weight, because on top of his regular portion of dog food, he'll be eating the odd buttered roll, piece of meat, serving of pasta, slice of cake and anything else he can manage to mooch from you.

A canine's digestive system isn't the same as a human's, so your dog can get sick from eating too much human food. You may think you are being loving to your dog by feeding him fried foods or sweets, but love is keeping your dog healthy and feeding him properly.

Not all leftovers are bad for dogs; you just need to monitor the type and quantity. If you do feed your dog mealtime leftovers, choose raw or cooked vegetables, rice, low-fat cottage cheese or small pieces of fruit. A small piece of skinless, broiled chicken can be given as a treat. Put the leftovers in his dish in place of some of his regular ration the next day or after you've finished cleaning up in the kitchen.

TIPS TO STOP BEGGING

- Never feed your dog from the table and make sure that even small children keep this rule.
- Ask visitors not to feed your dog, or put your dog outside or in his crate when guests come to dine.
- Ignore your dog's begging. Whenever he is quiet and doesn't beg, praise him and offer him a dog treat after you have finished eating.
- If your dog jumps up on you, barks or drools on your lap during mealtime, command him to "Down" and "Stay" in a special spot for the duration of the meal.
- Take your dog to his special spot and give him a bone to chew on or a rubber toy filled with food to play with while you are dining.
- Feed your dog before you sit down to eat. If he's full, he's more likely to leave you alone.
- Give your dog some vigorous exercise before you sit down to meals. If he's tired, he'll sleep.
- If you must feed him leftovers, place them in his dish with his regular food the next day. Don't forget to reduce the amount of his regular food to counteract the extra calories (kilojoules) that the leftovers provide.

WHAT ABOUT ME?
All dogs will try begging, as this Fox Terrier is doing. If they are rewarded with food, they will continue until their begging becomes a nuisance behavior.

Biting

Biting is a normal form of canine communication, but around humans it needs to be controlled or it can get out of hand.

When a dog wraps her muzzle around your hand without using her teeth, she is greeting you in a friendly way. This behavior is common in Labradors and other retrieving dogs who have been bred to gently carry game back to their owners. When dogs are playing, one will often use her mouth to gently shut another's muzzle.

However, dogs should never be allowed to use their teeth on people, even in a controlled way, as this type of behavior is often followed by other forms of aggression. You will need to be able to recognize the various types and causes of biting so that you can avoid situations in which your dog may bite. And, if your dog does bite you or anyone else, don't ignore it—act immediately to stop the behavior escalating.

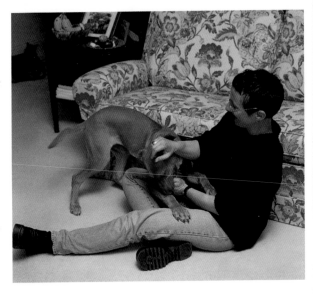

NOT ALL IN GOOD FUN Young dogs, such as this Rhodesian Ridgeback, easily become overexcited and are likely to bite people who are playing with them.

PUPPY BITES

Puppies love to chase and nip, but this should be discouraged around people. One of the things that puppies learn when they bite other puppies is how much pressure causes pain. When one puppy bites too hard, the other will yelp. This usually results in the first puppy being more gentle. People, too, need to let pups know that those bites hurt. When your puppy uses her teeth on you, yelp sharply, like a puppy would, and say "Ouch" or "No."

The line between canine and human can become especially blurred for puppies when they're around children. To a puppy, kids may seem to act more like other puppies than humans. When they are running around and squealing, this can make the puppy excited. If one of her littermates were playing in that way, she would probably nip at him.

Explain to your children that when they play roughly, the puppy can lose control in her eagerness to join in. If this happens with your kids, teach them to squeal like a puppy, even if the nip didn't hurt much. This will teach the puppy bite inhibition, and the children will be less likely to be accidentally hurt. It's best to encourage children to play quieter games around the puppy, and to confine her when they are playing boisterously.

When a puppy bites, hitting her, holding her mouth closed and pushing her away may be ineffective. You may only get the puppy more excited and result in increased biting as she misinterprets your harsh methods to mean you wish to play harder. If all else fails, leave. Social isolation is a powerful tool for puppies. They do not like to be alone, and if you leave, they lose their playmate. Each and every family member must follow these rules. Never encourage your puppy to jump and bite at any family members, even in play.

FEAR BITING

In a frightening situation, any dog may bite, no matter how calm, friendly and obedient she normally is. In such cases, biting usually results from mishandling a terrified dog. The dog is nervous and is trying to stop you from making her do something she is too scared to do. For example, if your dog cowers under the bed after a particularly loud thunderclap and you try to drag her out, she might snap. Instead, wait for her to calm down and emerge by herself. Don't punish a fear biter. All you'll do is add to her terror. If such behavior occurs on numerous occasions, check with your vet in case there's a serious reason for it.

Dogs also bite when they are in pain. This is another type of reaction to fear—the fear of being hurt more. Because your dog is in pain and doesn't understand what's going on, she will be scared. No matter how gentle she normally is, the fear that accompanies an injury can turn her into an out-of-control biter. Your dog won't be able to understand that you are trying to help her. A dog is afraid that your approaching touch will only worsen the agony. If you look at it from her point of view, she's only trying to stop you and the pain she thinks you are causing her. The surest way for her to do this is to give you a good bite—so the surest way to avoid being on the receiving end of her distressed teeth is to put a muzzle on her. You can use a store-bought muzzle, or improvise with a tie, a pair of tights or a piece of cloth (see p. 279).

MAINTAINING CONTROL

If an adult dog who is not frightened or in pain bites you or someone else, don't treat it as an isolated incident and hope it will never happen again. A dog who bites and is not reprimanded for it will assume that what she has done is acceptable. Even if you can see a reason for the behavior—for instance, if you try to remove your dog's food bowl before she has finished and she bites you—do not tolerate it. Biting is an attempt to control you; it is what a high-ranking dog will do to a lower-ranking one, and may indicate that your dog is trying to get the upper hand in your relationship. Don't assume that this will go away on its own. A dog who successfully pushes the boundaries with her owner once will keep doing so, because that is what a dog's pack mentality has programmed her to do.

You should never be afraid of your dog. If you are, take immediate steps to remedy the situation. Talk to your vet, or call in a trainer to help reinforce your dog's obedience training and teach you how to take control.

THE SAFE OPTION
Before you help a dog in pain, you may need to muzzle him to stop him biting you. If he is large, like this mixed breed, or particularly agitated, you may need another person to help you.

Chasing

If it moves, most dogs will chase it. Balls, bubbles, sticks or falling

leaves are just a few of the stimulating things dogs love to pursue.

Chasing is instinctive in dogs; in their wild past, it was how they caught their prey. Even now, although their food is provided for them, they still like to chase. Young dogs, in particular, love the challenge of moving objects. They make perfect toys and it's fun to watch a pup entertaining himself by trying to catch a fly on the window or investigating a tuft of cotton blowing around the yard.

As they mature, some dogs become territorial. They try to protect their home from intruders, and the chase game that was once so cute soon develops into barking and running back and forth as they try to scare away anything that moves. To a territorial dog, cats and squirrels are just as menacing as kids on bicycles and noisy skateboards.

The first time your dog succeeds in chasing something away, he swells up with confidence and this makes him want to demonstrate his chasing ability again. Dogs who chase cats are a nuisance, especially if their quarry lives in

VICIOUS CIRCLE In some dogs, chasing shadows, insects or their own tails can become a compulsion.

the same household. But when a dog gets enough confidence to start chasing cars, he has become dangerously aggressive and is risking his own life and those of other road users.

To prevent a dog from becoming a chaser, don't encourage inappropriate chasing. If your dog steals something of yours, don't run after him. Instead, call him to "Come," and reward him enthusiastically—or with a game of chase-the-ball, which will satisfy his motivation—when he does. Obedience training will help firmly instill the "Come" response.

THE THRILL OF THE CHASE A way to avoid nuisance chasing is to channel your dog's chasing instinct into an acceptable form, such as fetching balls and sticks.

TO CHASE OR NOT TO CHASE Dogs who have been raised with cats are much less likely than others to chase them.

DETERRING CAT CHASERS

Not all dogs are cat chasers. Older dogs or those with relaxed temperaments are likely to let a passing cat alone, as are dogs that have been raised with cats. Even those dogs who do chase cats may not hurt them if they corner them; most modern dogs love to chase, but have lost the follow-up urge to kill. However, there are good reasons to discourage cat chasing. No cat likes being chased by a dog, and if the chase is indoors, it can cause damage to furniture, possessions and human nerves.

Give your cat a better chance by installing a barrier (such as a baby gate) at the entrance to a cat-only room. Hang it a few inches off the ground so that your cat can slip underneath, leaving the dog on the other side. Of course, this method only works if the dog is considerably larger than the cat. If they're a similar size, install the barrier flush with the floor, not raised, and firmly nail or screw a perch to the top. The perch can be as simple as a piece of board. Cats are better jumpers than dogs, and the perch will provide your cat with a springboard to safety.

Another way to discourage a cat chaser is to interrupt his fun. Keep a leash on him at all times, and if you see him about to lunge, step on the leash. He won't enjoy the jolting sensation when his movement is arrested. A few such leash jolts may make him think again the next time he's tempted to give chase.

PREVENTING CAR CHASING

If your dog has already taken to chasing cars, make sure you keep him in a fenced yard or on his leash when he is outdoors. Giving your dog plenty of exercise is another way to curb the chasing instinct. Teach him to retrieve, then spend plenty of time throwing balls and sticks for him to chase after and return to you. Never encourage him to run after anything without bringing it back to you.

If a moving car still fascinates your dog, ask a friend to slowly drive a car by the front of your house. When your dog begins to run after it, have your friend throw water balloons or something noisy (but harmless) from the car. It should startle your dog enough to make him change his mind.

You can also try attaching a 15-foot (5-m) leash or rope to his choke collar. Again, ask a friend to drive slowly by your house. When your dog begins to give chase, let him run a little way, then briefly tighten your grip on the leash, say "No!" then quickly release your grip so as not to hurt or choke him. Reward him with a ball game as soon as he turns round. Repeat this exercise until your dog catches on.

WALKING A CHASER

To stop your dog chasing things while you are out walking, keep him on a leash and develop his attention span by making him follow your commands and getting him to watch you (see p. 161). If he begins to run after a moving object while walking on his leash, turn sharply in the opposite direction. When he follows you instead of going after the object, reward him with praise and a food treat—or better still, a ball game that meets his need to chase.

Chewing Objects

Whether it's food, chew toys, chair legs, tennis balls or their owners' shoes, dogs love to give their teeth a workout.

Chewing is an entirely natural behavior in dogs. It stems from their days as hunters, when they had to chomp whole carcasses into manageable chunks. The urge to chew remains in today's dogs. If it weren't for the fact that dogs occasionally destroy things they shouldn't, chewing is a good habit because it keeps their teeth clean. It's also a great way for dogs to release energy and relieve stress.

Dogs bred for hunting and retrieving, such as spaniels and Labrador Retrievers, have an instinctive urge to put things in their mouths. However, they have been bred to have "soft" mouths, which means they tend simply to hold or carry items in their mouths, rather than ripping and destroying them.

CAUSES AND SOLUTIONS

Chewing wouldn't be a problem if dogs stopped doing it once they were out of their puppy phase, or if all they chewed were their own possessions. But some dogs keep chewing all their lives, and it seems as though some of them chew everything except their own toys.

Puppy Problems

Puppies start chewing at about three months, when their puppy teeth are loosening and their adult teeth are erupting. Their mouths are sore and gnawing relieves the pressure. Puppies have all their adult teeth at about six months, but they usually keep chewing for a while as the teeth settle into the gums.

HOURS OF FUN
Some dogs can chew the same object for hours. If it's an acceptable item, such as this mixed breed's favorite ball, let them go for it.

Apart from keeping your possessions out of your puppy's reach, about all you can do is provide her with a rich variety of suitable chew toys. Also try putting one of her chew toys in the freezer for an hour or two, then giving it to her to work over. Most puppies like chewing cold things, and the cold acts as a temporary anesthetic and numbs the gums.

Once dogs have finished teething, they go through a phase of more strenuous chewing as they use their teeth to explore their world. Their paws aren't much use for handling and investigating things, so they use their teeth. Most dogs outgrow their chewing phase by the time they reach adulthood, but some never

AN ACCEPTABLE ALTERNATIVE To dissuade this German Shepherd from chewing a shoe, her owner offers her a tennis ball instead.

give it up, usually because their owners put up with it and it becomes a habit. If you let a puppy chew your possessions, she'll keep on chewing when she's an adult. But rather than scolding dogs for chewing the wrong things, it's more effective to give them objects that they can chew, then reward them when they show an interest. Every dog has different preferences, however, so expect some trial and error while searching for acceptable chew toys that your dog prefers to your sneakers.

Anxiety and Boredom

Many dogs become lonely or anxious when they're alone and chewing provides a useful distraction. Chewing their own toys helps, but chewing their owners' belongings is more appealing because they carry a familiar human scent, which helps dogs feel less lonesome.

Dogs also chew things out of frustration and boredom. Dogs were not designed to sleep on the rug all day, and need plenty of physical and mental activity. When they don't get them, they quickly become bored and start looking out for ways to amuse themselves. Chewing fits the bill perfectly. Anything that's conveniently lying around is fair game for their questing jaws. Dogs enjoy chewing and find it very satisfying to work their jaws and sink their teeth into a variety of objects— if not their toys, then shoes, garden hoses, electrical cords or furniture.

Dogs who are anxious or frustrated—a group that includes nearly every dog who isn't physically or mentally active—are desperate for stimulation. Apart from taking them for more walks, an excellent solution is to give them more exciting toys. Brands such as Kongs and Buster cubes are good choices because they're made of hard materials that give a satisfying level of resistance to canine jaws. They can also be loaded with food, such as dog biscuits, low-fat cheese or peanut butter. These toys give dogs a mental challenge as they try to get to the goodies

THWARTING DESTRUCTION If you don't want your dog to chew your new shoes, don't let her chew your old ones. She can't tell the difference between the two.

inside. As a bonus, the hidden food rewards them for chewing their own toys, making them less likely to return to your possessions. The mental effort also satisfies them and tires them out, taking away their need to chew to relieve stress.

Like children, however, it doesn't take dogs long to get bored with their toys. Rather than buying them just one or two chew toys, buy several. But don't put them out all at once. Each day, put one toy away and bring another one out. That way, your dog will always regard each item as being reasonably novel.

The Sabotage Solution

While some dogs chew anything and everything, others develop a powerful urge for one particular thing. They may start chewing it because its size and texture are appealing, and then keep returning to it because they're attracted by the personal smell they've left behind. By coating the object with a commercial pet repellent or even some chili sauce, you can break the dog's fixation for the object. Start by coating an inconspicuous place to make sure the object won't be stained.

Dogs dislike surprises, which is why some experts recommend booby-trapping their chews of choice by putting a few coins in an empty soda can and running a string from the can to the object you're trying to protect. The can will come clattering down as soon as your dog touches the object, and the noise may startle her into better behavior.

PLENTY OF CHOICE Provide your dog with a variety of chew toys—such as rope, plush and squeaky toys—to keep her amused and exercise her jaws.

Climbing on Furnitur

Most dogs can share the furniture without causing problems,

but others will need to be discouraged.

At some point, nearly every dog will attempt to stake a claim to the furniture. If you call your dog even once to jump up beside you on the bed or sofa, he'll believe that's where you want him to be all the time.

If you ignore him the first time he tries the sofa or the bed, or laugh and tell him how cute he looks, he'll think you approve of the new arrangement. This isn't a problem if you don't mind your dog being there next to you. But if you decide later you don't want him there, or if he starts overpossessively hogging the furniture and trying to repel you from it, you'll have to convince him that the furniture is uncomfortable. To do that takes some effort and consistency, so it's better to make a firm decision in the first place and stick to it.

NOT SO COMFY

To discourage your dog from jumping up and sitting on the furniture, lay plastic bubble wrap on top of your sofa or bed. The next time he jumps up he will be startled by the new sound and feel, and jump right back off. For some dogs, that's enough to make them think twice about ever trying to get up again, but others will recognize the bubble wrap and just jump on the sofa when it's not there. In that case, tuck a bedsheet on top of the wrap and leave it on all the time, or at least until your dog decides to stay off for good.

You can also place plastic (not metal) mouse traps under the sheet. These will make a loud snap the minute your dog jumps on the couch and will scare him into jumping back down. Lightweight plastic mouse traps are not dangerous to your dog because there are no metal pieces.

There are also special mats designed to be placed on top of furniture to deter your dog from jumping up. As soon as your dog jumps up, the mats give a very mild electric shock.

THE COMFORT ZONE Dogs love to climb on furniture because it's soft and comfortable and allows them to be close to their people. The people may not always appreciate this closeness, however, especially if the dog is large, like this mixed breed.

DOGS ON BEDS

Many dogs like human beds. Because dogs are pack animals, they like the warmth, security and companionship of sleeping with other creatures, be they other dogs or people. Beds are also high off the ground, making them a good vantage point and giving dogs a feeling of power. Most dogs can sleep on the bed without it going to their heads, but others will take advantage of what they see as their increased status. They may start growling defensively when the cat, another dog or even the bed's human owner tries to get onto the bed. This dominant behavior may escalate to aggression, and should be discouraged.

Off the Bed, on the Floor

If you want to get your dog off your bed, there are several steps you can take. A compromise is to put his bed on the floor of your room. He will be able to smell you and hear your breathing, and will enjoy sharing your general space even if he can't share the bed itself. For extra emotional comfort, put one of your old blankets or an old garment that you've worn in with his bedding. Your scent will make him feel secure as he sleeps.

An additional tactic is to make his bed a special

A PRIME POSITION Beds provide a good vantage point, especially for small dogs such as this Toy Poodle, as well as a chance to be with their humans.

place to be. If what he wants is your company in bed, then give it to him—but in his bed, not yours. Sit on the floor next to your dog's bed, or on the edge of it, if it's big enough. Pet him, talk to him and feed him the odd treat. Occasionally stash a food treat or a favorite toy in his bed, too, as a surprise.

Also, make sure that your dog's bed is both comfortable and big enough for him. He may covet yours simply because his own is too small, too hard or is not in a sufficiently sheltered location. Old dogs or those with joint problems will appreciate a softer bed.

Although dogs mostly sleep curled up, they need space to sprawl out when they feel like it. Your dog's bed should be at least as long as he is when he's at full stretch. Giant breeds, such as Great Danes and Irish Wolfhounds, may require extra padding in their beds, to help support their weight and cushion their joints. A trampoline bed may be a comfortable choice for very large dogs.

TIME'S UP This Australian Kelpie mix knows that "Off" means he must give up his place on the sofa.

WHY YOUR FAVORITE CHAIR IS HIS FAVORITE CHAIR

Your dog will like to sit in your favorite armchair for some of the same reasons you do. It's probably the most comfortable piece of furniture in the house. It's softened up in all the right places and there may even be cushions or a blanket for extra padding. It will also have your smell, which may mean nothing to you but will be comforting to your dog, especially when he is home alone.

You will have positioned it in a spot where there isn't a draft, and if it's a window seat, there'll be an outdoor view. Or it may be located in a quiet corner of the room where your dog can just relax.

Destructiveness

Chewing and digging are fun and natural activities for dogs, but some dogs take them to extremes, causing chaos.

Destructiveness isn't limited to naughty puppies. Even a dog who is always on her best behavior when you're at home can change drastically when you go to bed or to work.

It's no coincidence that dogs are usually at their most destructive when they're left by themselves. Dogs are sociable animals, and they don't like spending time alone. When you leave the house, your dog has no way of knowing if you are ever coming back, and may feel abandoned. Her anxiety may mount until she feels the need to relieve her stress. Some dogs do this by barking incessantly; others do it by destroying anything they can get their paws and teeth on.

Unless you spend your days at home, there's no easy way to monitor your dog's goings-on. It takes time and patience, but there are ways to help her cope with being on her own.

KEEPING HER MIND OFF MISCHIEF

Boredom and anxiety are the greatest causes of destructive behavior. Keeping your dog's mind active will help her feel better and keep her away from your garden and possessions. Dogs who are confident and secure are much less likely to become destructive when they're alone. You can boost your dog's confidence by giving her plenty to do while you're with her—anything from walks, to canine sports such as flyball, to visiting hospitals or nursing homes. Also, active dogs are tired dogs, so they're more likely to sleep than look for trouble when you're gone.

Dogs chew when they're upset because that's their way of relieving tension, and also of passing the time. A good way to stop a destructive dog who enjoys chewing is to give her acceptable alternatives, such as chew

BEDSIDE MANNERS Some dogs will concentrate their destructive behavior on one item. The wicker of this mixed breed's bed has been protected with wire mesh, but the foam still needs to be replaced regularly.

toys or tennis balls. A good choice is the Kong toy or Buster cube. Made of stout plastic with a cavity inside, these are designed to hold small amounts of food, such as cheese, dog biscuits or a spoonful of peanut butter. Dogs can happily spend hours just trying to get the food out of the hole.

When selecting chew toys, don't give your dog discarded socks or shoes. She can't tell the difference between old, rejected items and brand-new ones. If you let her think that one shoe or sock is acceptable, she'll conclude that all footwear is fair game.

If your dog keeps chewing a particular piece of furniture, put a box full of her toys right next to the furniture that she's been working over. Every time she heads for the furniture, tell her, "No chew," then tell her, "Look in the toy box," while putting your hand in it and waving one of her toys to get her attention. Most dogs will quickly learn what the words mean, especially if you get them started by sometimes salting the box with a couple of dog biscuits.

MIND GAMES A Buster cube will keep this Vizsla's mind off destructive behavior while she tries to extract the food inside.

USING A DETERRENT

Some dogs have a favorite object and will keep returning to chew it. Spraying the object with something that tastes or smells bad, such as citronella or commercial pet repellents, will help keep them away.

Or you can booby-trap the objects your dog chews by putting coins in an empty soda can and tying it to the object of her desire. When she grabs it, the noise will startle her and she may think twice about chewing it next time.

It's harder to discourage a dog that likes digging, but you can make it less fun for her by burying small rocks or her own (or another pet's) feces in the area; she won't like the way the rocks feel when she hits them, and the feces will act as a repellent, too. Or sprinkle the area with ground red pepper; she won't like the way it smells when she digs it up.

COMPANY AND EXERCISE

If you live close to work, perhaps you can occasionally drop by at lunchtime. This will

THREE'S COMPANY Dogs who have company—be it that of humans or other dogs—are much less likely to become bored or frustrated, and thus destructive.

interrupt your dog's isolation, and she'll be less likely to be anxious when you're gone. Just be sure not to arrive during an episode of unwanted behavior, or your dog may perceive your return as a reward for what she was doing.

Another option is to arrange with a friend or a professional dog sitter to come by your home during the day. Giving your dog someone to play with, even if it's only for a few minutes, will help keep her entertained while taking her mind off your belongings. If a friend or neighbor has a dog that your dog gets on with, you might even be able to arrange with her for your dog to have regular or occasional "play dates" at the other's house.

While dogs often use destructive behavior to relieve stress, they also do it simply because they have more energy than they know what to do with. A good solution is to give your dog plenty of vigorous exercise just before you leave in the morning and again when you get home at night. A dog who has used up all her energy is much less likely to be destructive.

PAPER CHASE Some dogs enjoy playing with toilet paper. It's easy to chew and unrolls into long, soft, fluttery ribbons that are fun to chase and paw at.

Digging

Most dogs love to dig. Some breeds dig only when
they're young, while others will continue all their lives.

Digging is instinctive in dogs. In their wild past, it was a survival tactic. They dug to make dens in which to sleep and raise their pups. They also dug to catch burrowing prey and to bury leftovers. Humans later enhanced the digging instinct by selectively breeding the most enthusiastic diggers, so creating terrier breeds to catch rats and other vermin, and Dachshunds to hunt badgers. Although pet dogs have little practical need for any of these skills, many of them still continue to dig.

A DESIRE TO DIG For a dog who loves to dig, such as this Australian Shepherd, toys, boots and anything else he can find may end up in the ground.

WHY DIG?

Dogs enjoy digging and they do it for many reasons. Some dogs dig just because they enjoy it, and others because they're bored and they want to feel busy. And if there's an odor in the earth, a dog will want to find out more about it. A rodent could have tunneled far underneath and your dog will want to go after it, especially if he likes to guard his territory or he's a terrier whose ancestors have been digging out small creatures for generations.

If he sees you gardening, he may copy your behavior. To a dog, new plants may smell good enough for a close inspection. And bitches who are about to give birth or who are going through a false pregnancy like to dig a cozy hiding place for their puppies.

The type and location of the hole will sometimes indicate your dog's motivation. Holes by the fence show that he's trying to escape; he may be bored and frustrated, or perhaps there's something out there that he wants to investigate. Shallow holes around the yard show that he is trying to get comfortable. If it's a hot day, digging, especially under bushes, can provide your dog with a cool place in which to lie. Earth provides warmth on a cold day, too.

HOW TO CONTROL DIGGING

The first step is to meet your dog's motivation to dig by giving him his own digging area full of buried treasures, such as his toys and some food treats. If you see him working away in non-approved spots, tell him "No!" Then give him a toy to distract him. You'll probably have to repeat the correction a few times before he understands where he may and may not dig. To deter him from digging in certain places, put heavy bricks over that area. Salt the earth with small rocks, which will feel unpleasant to his paws, or ground red pepper, the smell of which will deter him. Place chicken wire mesh around plants or shrubs you want to protect.

A busy dog is less likely to dig, so take him running with you or throw a ball for him until you've worn him out. This will burn off energy he might otherwise use churning up the earth.

If it's hot outside, leave a small wading pool for him to cool off in. And when the weather turns cold, make sure he has adequate shelter or bring him inside to warm up.

Dislike of Being Handled

Some dogs will take all the attention you can give them;

others maintain a strict hands-off policy.

Your dog may like to be petted, but may try to wriggle away when you touch his feet to clip his toenails. He may also be reluctant to have his rear end examined or his teeth inspected. It will be difficult to properly groom a dog who hates being handled, or have him examined by a vet.

When puppies are not handled much from birth, tactile sensations are new and strange to them. They're unsure what will happen, so they flip their heads from side to side to see what you're doing with your hand. Sometimes female dogs are uncomfortable about their rears being touched, especially if they're in season or soon will be. Other dogs might have had a lot of early stroking but are very strong-willed and dominant and want to control their own bodies.

FEEL IT, DON'T FIGHT IT

Trying to get a grip on a dog who is struggling to free himself is not easy. Besides scratching you, he might also try to bite your hands. If this happens, tell him sternly, "No bite!" Keep holding him and praise him when he stops.

Accustom your puppy to your touch by giving him gentle massages from the moment you bring him home. Talk softly to him as you soothingly stroke all over his body. Apply very little pressure at first. When your dog begins to enjoy it, he'll respond by leaning his body into your fingertips.

LOOKING GOOD This Bearded Collie mix is so accustomed to being handled that he doesn't even mind when a hand-held vacuum is used to remove his excess hair.

With an older dog, put his collar and leash on. While holding the leash, talk softly to him as you pet him where he feels comfortable. Confidently move your hand to other areas of his body, while telling him what a good dog he is. If, like many dogs, he doesn't like his paws to be handled, offer him a treat while softly touching one of them. When he allows you to do this, say, "Good dog." If he still resists, tell him in a low, strong voice, "Stop it," and give him a little leash correction. Touch the remaining paws one at a time. Repeat this process until you can lift each foot slightly and are able to rub his toes very gently without him protesting. Practice this several times a day.

Try making a game out of giving your dog rough pats and tickles after running your hands over his back and tail. Be sure to laugh so he knows it's supposed to be fun. The goal is to make him feel secure enough to accept your authority.

130

Eating and Rolling in Dung

Once a dog develops a taste for the unspeakable,

it becomes a habit that's difficult to break.

There are a few reasons why your dog may eat dung. It may fill a nutritional need that isn't being met by his conventional everyday dog food. Or he may have seen another dog do it and copied the behavior. If your dog is a retriever breed, then he has been genetically programmed to pick up objects in his mouth.

As for rolling in dung, this behavior is a leftover from the time when dogs roamed wild. Some experts believe that to put predators off the trail, wild dogs covered themselves with foul-smelling messes to mask their own scent. Rolling and twisting in dung may even feel like a good back massage to your dog.

FOLLOW THE LEADER Puppies learn from older dogs by imitating what they do. If this adult Kelpie mix finds some dung in the bushes and eats it, the Pomeranian-mix puppy is likely to copy his behavior.

HOW TO STOP IT

If your dog homes in on dung while you are out walking, command him to "Leave it" (see box). If he picks it up in his mouth, try the "Drop it" command (see page 142). Back in your own yard, supervise your dog's toilet time and clean up immediately afterward. If it's not there, he won't eat it.

If your dog still persists in eating dung, try spraying it with a commercial pet repellent. Or there are products that you can sprinkle on your dog's food before he eats it and which will give his dung a taste even he won't be able to stand. Ask your local veterinarian or pet supply store about these.

To stop your dog rolling in muck, keep your yard free from all messy substances. If your dog is prone to rolling in filth while you're out on walks, keep him on a leash.

If you're exercising your dog outdoors and you see a problem area up ahead, call your dog to "Come" immediately and distract him with a game or a few obedience drills.

TEACHING YOUR DOG TO "LEAVE IT"

When you tell your dog to "Leave it," you're really saying "Ignore it immediately." Teaching him not to go near dung or anything else that takes his fancy is a big challenge, so begin teaching this command indoors where it's quiet. Ideally, you want your dog to ignore the item that draws his attention the minute you tell him to.

1. With his training collar and leash on, command your dog to sit in front of you. Show him a piece of food and tell him to "Leave it."

2. Shorten the leash, then throw the food a short distance away, again saying "Leave it."

3. When your dog rushes to get the food, tug the leash. When he stays by your side, praise him and reward him with a treat. Repeat the process until he understands the command. Test him with all his favorite foods before taking the act on the road.

Fearful Behavior

When a dog doesn't understand something or finds herself

in an unusual situation, she may become fearful.

A well-adjusted dog who has been handled by plenty of different people and exposed to a wide variety of things will take unusual situations in her stride. However, a dog who was not so fortunate and was left alone too much when she was young will be confused, and may have a difficult time making sense of the world around her.

THE FEARFUL DOG

A fearful dog is one who gets nervous about many things—people approaching her, going for a ride in the car or loud noises such as thunder or the drone of the vacuum cleaner. The sight of a dog who is so afraid that nothing can calm her down is disturbing. She may growl, shake or try to run and hide. And if you don't solve the problem, her fearfulness can turn into aggression and fear biting.

HOW TO CURB FEAR

Changing a fearful dog into a stable one is not easy and may take a long time, but it's worth the effort. Don't reassure your frightened dog by hugging her or telling her everything is okay. It's not, and she knows it. She may be so panicky that she tries to bite you.

Instead, act calmly and your dog will most likely follow your example. If you can laugh while your dog is struggling to escape a vet's examination, your upbeat mood will probably rub off on her. It's okay to give her a gentle touch when she's nervous, but don't make too big a deal out of what's bothering her.

To help a fearful dog, socialize her more by taking her everywhere you go. Bring along some dog treats and when people approach, ask them if they wouldn't mind giving one to your dog. While she may not take it at first, she will eventually. If you do this often she will soon come to enjoy meeting strangers.

It also helps to handle your dog a lot. Rub your hands all over her as an examining vet might. This will relax her and accustom her to being touched. You can also enrol your dog in obedience classes, where she will learn the basic commands of sit, stay, down, heel and come. This builds her confidence, and also gives you a technique to use with her the next time she gets spooked. She'll regard you as the one in charge and the next time she gets worried, she'll look to you for reassurance.

Fear of Loud Noises

A dog's sense of hearing is far more acute than a human's, so everything sounds much louder to them than it does to us. Common loud noises, such as a plate being dropped or the alarm going off, can send a dog rushing off to cower in the corner or under a bed.

CHASE THOSE FEARS AWAY If your dog exhibits fear, try distracting her with a favorite game or toy. Act in a happy, upbeat way, as this Miniature Fox Terrier's owner is doing, to reassure your dog and take her mind off what was bothering her.

BETTER GET USED TO IT If a dog, like this Collie mix, reacts with trepidation to an everyday object, it will be necessary to desensitize her to it.

To overcome such behavior, desensitize your dog to loud noises by playing noise games. While she's eating, for example, laugh and clatter some pots and pans. Or pump up the volume on the radio and dance around the room while giving her food treats. She'll soon realize that noise is no cause for alarm.

Fear of Objects

All sorts of objects may frighten a young pup: a large vase placed on the floor, a garbage can or a tire in the yard. Until she becomes familiar with them, your pup will regard most objects with suspicion. She may stare at a strange object for a while before barking and running backward. If she's feeling brave, she might even creep forward slowly and quietly so as not to disturb it. To familiarize your dog with new things, go over to the object and sit beside it. Talk to her in a very upbeat tone of voice and run your hand over the object. When your dog sees that it doesn't attack you, she will gradually become less afraid.

TAKING COVER When frightened by loud noises, such as thunderstorms and fireworks, dogs like this Australian Shepherd may be prompted to hide.

Fear of Strangers

Some people look scary without meaning to. The way they walk might seem menacing, or they may be wearing a big hat that can intimidate a young puppy that hasn't seen much of the world yet. Some dogs are nervous just seeing people other than their family.

If your dog is frightened of people, take her with you when you visit a friend. Ask your friend to offer your dog a treat. Stand nearby and be calm. Don't yank your dog's collar or leash to prevent her from backing away. If she doesn't want to take the treat, your friend can toss it to her. It can take some time for dogs to be comfortable around other people, so be patient. Don't try to rush her progress.

Once your dog improves, start asking other people to hold her leash while you stand by. This teaches your dog that others can be leaders too. With practice, your dog will soon be confident enough to sniff strangers' hands for treats the minute new people approach.

House-Soiling

Well-trained dogs who are constantly having accidents in the house

nearly always have a problem—one that won't disappear on its own.

Most dogs are house-trained by the time they're five months old. And once they understand the rules, they rarely break them—unless they feel they have no other choice.

PHYSICAL CAUSES

The most common cause of mistakes—one that has more to do with owners than with dogs—is staying inside too long. Even dogs with excellent bowel and bladder control can't restrain themselves indefinitely. Most adult dogs can go for as long as 10 to 12 hours—but that's really pushing their limits.

For many dogs, going outside more often is all that's necessary to stop messes in the house. It's most important to let them out first thing in the morning and after meals, when the urges are strongest. You should also let them out before you go to bed, because some dogs can't wait until morning. Puppies need to eliminate more often—at least every two hours during the day and every four hours at night. If you can, install a dog door so that your dog can let herself out as needed.

Older dogs may experience lapses in house-training due to muscle weakness. Most muscles—including those controlling the bladder and bowel—weaken as dogs get older. This tends to be more of a problem in older females who have been spayed because they have very little estrogen, a hormone that helps keep the muscles strong. But any older dog will probably have less control than she did when she was younger. In addition, older dogs may have arthritis or other conditions that make it

TERRITORIAL INSTINCTS After another dog has visited, the resident dog may feel the need to scent-mark inside the house to re-assert it as her territory.

difficult for them to get outside as quickly as they should. You can prevent many accidents just by putting your dog's bed a bit closer to the door or the dog door, or simply put her bed where you can see it. This will improve your chances of getting her outside in time.

Dogs who are urinating in the house—not just once, but several times a day—often have a urinary tract infection. These infections irritate the delicate tissues lining the bladder or urethra, giving dogs a sense of urgency that they can't control. A similar thing happens in dogs who have the flu. As with some other viral infections, flu can cause diarrhea to come on with almost no warning. When accidents are happening daily, or when your dog is having frequent diarrhea or is dribbling small amounts of urine, call your veterinarian. Diarrhea that persists for more than 24 hours should be taken seriously because of the risk of dehydration. Urine dribbles may indicate a bladder disease, diabetes or one of several other conditions. Play it safe and take your dog for a checkup.

UNWELCOME VISITORS Most dogs limit their scent-marking to outdoors, unless they feel threatened when another dog has been inside the house.

TERRITORIAL MARKING

Dogs instinctively mark their territory so that other dogs know who it belongs to. Most dogs understand that urine-marking is only supposed to occur outside, but sometimes they feel the need to protect the inside of the house as well.

If your dog is a domineering type and a friend brings another dog over, this might trigger housesoiling. Territorial marking can be confusing because it doesn't necessarily happen at the same time as the original "threat." Some dogs will continue to feel threatened for days, weeks or even months, and so will keep marking to make their point. Once dogs start doing territorial marking in the house, it can be very difficult to make them stop. Neutering will often stop territorial marking in both males and females, especially if it's done when dogs are young. Even then, however, some dogs will always get defensive or aggressive when other dogs are around, and they may express their feelings by marking inside the house. About all you can do in these instances is leave the dogs outside or keep one or both of them in a crate.

SUBMISSIVE URINATION

Among dogs, this behavior—in which they roll on their backs and urinate on the spot—is a way of expressing respect. It is usually done by puppies and adult dogs who are particularly shy or submissive. Dogs who behave this way in the human family are generally insecure or frightened. Stress in the home can also cause a dog who lacks confidence to lose control.

Submissive urination is natural among dogs, but inappropriate in human families. Making submissive dogs a little more confident is one way to deal with the problem. Each day, spend a few minutes practicing basic obedience drills, such as "Sit" commands, and praising your dog when she does the right thing. Dogs who are insecure often crave human approval. Teaching them simple things and rewarding their successes is the best way to bolster their confidence. Also try taking them out in public where they'll see new places and meet new people. Dogs who urinate submissively are often afraid of all sorts of things. The more they experience, the bolder and happier they'll be.

REMEDIAL TRAINING

Dogs who are suddenly making messes often need a refresher course in basic house-training (see pp. 86–89). Treat your dog as though she is a puppy again. Keep an eye on her whenever she is in the house. Your goal is to catch her before she lifts her leg or squats on the carpet, since it's more effective to praise her when she goes in the right place than to punish her for making a mistake. You don't have to wait until she's almost in the act before heading for the door. Letting her out more often will give her more opportunities to eliminate, and the praise you give will help her understand what she is supposed to do in the future.

Humping

Dogs who try to hump arms, legs, teddy bears, cushions

or sometimes even cats don't always have mating on their minds.

Even a dog who is frenzied by hormones knows the difference between a receptive partner and someone's leg. Humping is not about pleasure, although that may play a role. Dogs often hump because they're trying to assert themselves. The longer they are allowed to get away with it, the higher status they may assume.

COMING OF AGE

Humping usually starts during adolescence—between six months and two years of age, depending on the breed (larger breeds mature later than smaller ones). Humping is not strictly a male behavior, although males are the worst offenders. Unlike females, whose hormones ebb and flow with their reproductive cycles, males maintain fairly steady hormone levels all the time. The hormones themselves don't cause humping, but they make dogs more likely to do it. That's why neutering (see pp. 216–17) is the best way to reduce or eliminate this unpleasant behavior.

YOUNG REBELLION

Males are also more competitive than females. They're always trying to prove—to people as well as to other dogs—how tough and independent they are. Humping is just one way in which they push the boundaries and assert their dominance within a family.

When puppies are at play, they spend quite a bit of time climbing on top of each other. The more assertive dogs may take advantage of their position and throw in some humping. It's their way of saying that they are, quite literally, top dogs. The same instinct remains once dogs are living among humans. Human legs don't have any special appeal, but they're accessible and easy to wrap paws around. In the wild, dogs never mount dogs who are higher in rank than they are. The only time that a dog tries this with people is when there's some confusion about who's in charge and who isn't.

It's not that dogs make conscious decisions to assert their authority. Humping is just something they do. Even those who understand that they're not supposed to do it may forget themselves—when visitors come to the house, for example, or when people are on the floor playing with them.

If your dog wants to lord it over his stuffed toys or other dogs, you may not care. But it's never okay for him to do it to a person.

PREVENTING HUMPING

Humping is generally the last link in a chain of physical liberties. Maybe your dog is always pushing against or leaning on your legs. Or he may insist on licking your face or climbing onto your lap. Physical pushiness is a sign that dogs are feeling free to do pretty much whatever they want. Once they get away with some aggressive physical contact, it's natural for them to push the boundaries further. You may want to encourage your dog to keep his distance, by pushing him away with your knee when he leans, for example, or by walking away when he's getting in your face. Once he understands that you only get physical when it's your idea, he'll be less likely to take liberties in other ways.

Dogs need to understand that no matter how exalted they feel around other dogs, they're always second banana in their dealings with people. Rather than dealing with the humping directly, it may be more effective to deal with the underlying attitude. One way to do this is to make dogs work for everything they like. Have your dog sit before you give him food or take him for a walk. Have him lie down before you give him a toy. Have him do something—anything—before you do anything for him. When you reinforce your position of authority, your dog will be less inclined to be disrespectful.

If your dog does start humping, discipline him by turning away. Reward him as soon as he sits or walks away.

Hyperactivity

Hyperactivity is not a common problem in dogs, but a dog who has energy to burn needs more exercise and mental stimulation.

Young dogs are naturally excitable, and there'd be something wrong with them if they weren't. But adult dogs who have so much energy that they can't sit still are often considered hyperactive. Some people believe that with so many dog treats being high in calories (kilojoules) and sugar, diet might play a part in raising a dog's energy levels. But there is no evidence to suggest that hyperactivity in dogs is related to diet. If you think your dog is hyperactive, blame his ancestors. Years ago he was probably bred to run all day herding sheep or hunting game. If you take this same dog and leave him at home alone for eight hours in a small backyard with nothing to do, it's not surprising that he will have oodles of energy to burn off when you get home. Running from room to room without being able to settle down is a sign that your dog needs a job to do.

KEEP HIM BUSY

To deal with a hyperactive dog, you'll need to channel his energies into behavior you can live with. Getting upset and yelling won't help. Your dog will sense your mood right

KEEP HIM ACTIVE Hyperactive dogs, in particular, need plenty of physical and mental occupation.

away, and this will agitate him even more. Instead, give him lots of physical exercise. Take him for long walks or go running or cycling with him. If you have to leave him alone while you work, hire someone to come during the day and take him out jogging or play a vigorous game of fetch with him until he starts to flag. With some physical activity during the day, your dog won't be all over you the moment you walk in the door. Try to get up a little earlier in the morning to allow yourself more time with him, too.

Mental exercise is as important as physical exercise for a hyperactive dog. Giving him an activity to focus and concentrate on will slow him down, so take him to agility or obedience classes regularly. You can even make a small obstacle course in your backyard. Puzzle feeders will also exercise his mind. Hyperactive dogs need constant work to keep their energy levels on an even keel, so make these activities a permanent part of your dog's life.

Ignoring Commands

Inconsistency is often to blame when dogs begin to ignore commands that they have previously obeyed.

One of the chief sources of inconsistency is repetition. Your dog regards a repeated command as being a completely different stimulus to the original command. Issuing a command repeatedly trains him to expect the command to be repeated. In a sense, it means that each repeated command is nothing more than a warning that things will become serious before too long.

Being consistent when issuing commands is critical because it is the very best way of avoiding confusion in your dog. So, once you have decided on a command for a certain behavior, stick with it. Changing a command is usually advisable only if the dog has been retrained to offer a different or better response. A common mistake is to issue a series of commands that change, sometimes slightly, sometimes radically, from one to the next simply because the first didn't work. This is what humans do when making themselves clear to one another. However, what may, to a human, seem an obvious connection between one command and another is never as straightforward to your dog.

Think about how you use your dog's name before a command. Adding the name can upset your attempts to be consistent and can confuse a dog that has just learned a new response to a particular command. The problem is that the name and the command together may sound very different from the command alone.

Giving a command and then failing to ensure that it is obeyed is particularly bad practice because it effectively trains the dog to ignore commands. Confused dogs learn to avoid responding altogether. They learn to filter out the noise (including commands) coming from their humans because it is

EFFECTIVE COMMANDS

To avoid your dog learning to ignore commands, remember the following:

- Use a single command for a single response
- Issue commands only once
- Ensure your dog responds to each command
- Never call in vain

largely irrelevant to them. Commands become irrelevant when they lose their association with predictable events. Moreover, they actively encourage ignorance when they lose their association with pleasant consequences or become associated with undesirable outcomes. It is a rare dog that willingly subjects itself to unpleasant outcomes without at least trying to dodge them, even if only experimentally. The experiments a dog conducts to avoid unwanted events are sometimes labeled defiance, but really they represent a natural response to discomfort and are far from calculated.

Many owners set themselves up for failure when they disregard their dog's current motivation and issue a command that runs counter to what the dog is enjoying at that moment. The best example is calling a dog when it is clearly focused on running away to play with another dog. The called dog may experiment with ignoring the command and be rewarded by getting closer to its playmate. So, the outcome of such ignorance is immediate pleasure. Effectively the owner has trained the dog to run away when it is called. In this context, there are important lessons to be learned from falcon trainers, who have the maxim: never call in vain. This reminds them to avoid calling a bird back to them when it is clearly focused on departure.

The key to success involves the use of exquisite timing. In the case of a recall command ("Come"), the challenge is to time the command so that the animal is about to leave the object of its desire; you thus pitch the odds in favour of the instruction being obeyed. Timing and consistency are the hallmarks of good trainers, regardless of the species being trained.

Jumping Up

A puppy's exuberant, physical way of greeting people can seem cute—until he grows into an adult who can knock them over.

Many people complain about their dog jumping up on them or their visitors. However, owners often inadvertently reinforce this behavior in their pets. A common error is to let your dog jump up in certain situations and not in others. It's very difficult for a dog to understand when jumping is acceptable and when it is not. If you allow him to jump up on you when you're playing ball with him on the weekend, then yell "Down!" at him at other times, he won't understand why it's okay one day and not the next.

You may think it cute and harmless when a puppy jumps up on you, but this behavior may be much less appealing when the puppy grows into a large, strong, mature dog capable of knocking people over. If you allow your dog to jump up on you when he is a puppy, he will expect to continue doing so when he is an adult—no matter what size he grows to. His intentions may be friendly, but a dog who rushes at and jumps on people, especially children or the elderly, can be frightening, intimidating and potentially dangerous.

When greeting one other, dogs always sniff each other's faces first then move to each other's rear ends. When they greet people, they also like to try to sniff their faces. However, because dogs are generally smaller than humans, for most of them, jumping up is usually the only way to reach that high.

HELLO THERE You may not mind if your dog jumps up on you when she's invited to and when you're ready for her, but it could be dangerous if she launches herself at someone unexpectedly.

Furthermore, jumping usually gets attention—even if that attention is just pushing the dog away—and this may be enough to maintain the behavior. For young animals, pushing may be interpreted as a signal for play. Crouching down to greet your pup is a good way to start training him not to jump. If you do want your dog up on you for petting, you can even teach him to jump up on command. That way the behavior is under your verbal control.

Some breeds, such as Chow Chows, are much more reserved in their greetings than others, and therefore less likely to jump up. Terriers, Golden Retrievers and Labradors, on the other hand, will jump on just about

A LONG WAY UP Dogs like to greet others by sniffing their faces. Because people are generally much taller than they are, dogs jump up to try to reach them, as this terrier mix is doing.

WORTH TRYING AGAIN If dogs get a good reaction to a behavior, they are prompted to keep doing it. Her owner's laughing response to this terrier's action will encourage the dog to do it again, whether or not her owner really wants to be jumped all over.

anyone. To eliminate unwanted jumping behavior successfully, you need to identify any and all reinforcement for the behavior. If the jumping occurs when you come home, a good strategy is to ignore your dog until he obeys a command, such as "Sit". Don't give him any attention until he is sitting calmly.

Another similar technique is to anticipate the jumping behavior and to physically turn away. This often gets the dog to move sideways so you can then command him to sit before giving him attention. For some dogs,

it may be even more effective to rush at them just as they approach you. Many dogs will back away to avoid being stepped on, at which point you can command them to sit.

What about the dog that jumps up on visitors? There are several ways to discourage this behavior. Keep your dog on a leash when greeting people or have your dog practice "Sit" and "Stay" in the doorway of your home. Get people he knows to approach him with a food treat and pet him if he does not jump. Then practice with people he is less familiar with. What is important is practice and patience. It is not enough to make your dog sit to be greeted only once in a while. For your dog to learn, he should always sit to be greeted, even if only by members of the family.

For persistent jumpers, headcollars can be a very helpful additional control. These devices encircle both the muzzle and the neck and control the movement of the dog's head. If you control where the head goes, you can make the dog sit, stay and not jump up. These collars do not require strength to use, nor do they choke the dog as training collars, or choke chains, do.

TEACHING "OFF"

Every dog should understand the word "off." This simple command can be used to keep dogs off doors, couches and counters as well as off guests. Here are two ways to teach it.

1 When you're expecting guests, put a leash on your dog and let it dangle behind her. When people arrive and she jumps up to greet them, step on the leash. She won't achieve the height she's looking for, and her forward momentum will pull on her collar. In essence, she'll be correcting herself. When she quits jumping, praise her.

2 Put a leash on your dog and hold the free end. When she jumps up to greet someone, firmly tell her, "Off!" and pull the leash firmly to one side. When a dog is jumping up, she is standing on two legs, which means her balance is off. Pulling the leash sideways will force your dog to put her feet back on the ground. Once she's down and relaxed, if only briefly, praise her.

Licking

When a dog licks your face, it's a greeting. It's also the way young dogs show submissiveness to older dogs.

When dogs lick them, some people just laugh and say it tickles, while others find the feeling of their dog's wet and rough tongue on their skin unpleasant or even revolting. Whatever the human reaction, when your dog gives you a lick on your hand or your face, it's usually a sign of affection, although it can sometimes get out of hand and require correction.

A LIKING FOR LICKING Although these dogs are not related, the Labrador-mix puppy reacts to the friendly adult Vizsla as she would to her mother, by licking her face in a gesture of affection and appeasement.

AN EARLY EXPERIENCE

The first lick a dog experiences is right after he is born. A mother licks her newborn pups to clean them and to stimulate them to urinate and defecate. Licking is also her way of letting them know that she is their mother. They will always be able to recognize her by the smell of her saliva. The mother's saliva may also help to make all the littermates smell similar and thus help the litter stay together.

Licking can be a way of begging for food, too. When wolf cubs greet their mother when she returns from a hunt, they lick her muzzle to encourage her to regurgitate food for them.

PROBLEM LICKING

It's not only puppies that tend to lick. When they reach adulthood, dogs continue to lick both other dogs and humans. Some people can tolerate an occasional lick from their dog, but a constant stream of more and more licking is unacceptable. If you don't correct your dog, what starts as affection can become a subtle form of imposed rank. The more you resist by moving away, pushing him away and voicing your displeasure, the more pushy he may get.

AVOIDING THE PROBLEM

To avoid excessive licking, reassert your authority by correcting your dog whenever he performs this behavior. Put your dog's collar and leash on and, when he licks you, give him a strong verbal command of "No lick!" If he persists, give a short tug on the leash.

You can alter your dog's licking urge by substituting another activity that he prefers. Give him a new chew toy to occupy his mouth, play a game of fetch with him or take him for a long walk. Obedience training will also help assert your authority over him and decrease his tendency to lick.

GLAD TO SEE YOU Licking often signals submissive or solicitous behavior, and is the way dogs of all ages greet other dogs as well as humans.

Overprotectiveness

A protective dog makes you feel safe and loved. An overprotective

dog, however, can soon turn into an aggressive one.

It's comforting to have a dog who stays by your side, even sleeping on your bed or in your bedroom doorway. But when your dog starts to regard you as his personal property, becoming more and more possessive of you and guarding you against every little thing, it's not so great. When he starts growling because someone new has come to your house and is sitting on the sofa next to you, or he starts bullying the rest of the household with menacing barks and dominant behavior, your feeling of trust will soon turn to fear. Dogs that don't understand that you are the boss become a problem. And once he senses someone else is afraid of him, he'll protect you even more closely. If your dog is a herding breed, he may even try to nudge you into a corner away from the stranger, or nudge the other person away from you.

FAITHFUL PROTECTORS Dogs that were bred to guard, such as German Shepherds, tend to be particularly loyal to their owners and may be prone to overprotective behavior.

PREVENTING OVERPROTECTIVENESS

It isn't just big or status-seeking dogs that become overprotective of their owner—any size or breed of dog can develop this trait. To prevent overprotectiveness, avoid telling your dog "It's okay" when he growls at someone else. This just reinforces the behavior, because it gives him the message that growling is acceptable. Instead, tell him sternly "That's enough" or "No growl." Then command him to "Sit" or "Down;" this will give him something to do and lower his arousal when someone approaches.

To let your dog know that you're in charge, don't allow him to sleep on your bed or on the furniture. When he learns to behave more submissively, you can invite him back on.

To accustom your dog to other people being close to you, ask a friend to offer the dog a treat while he is on his leash. Stand close by and act in a relaxed manner; if he sees that you aren't nervous, he may be less inclined to protect you.

There are a number of reasons why your dog may become overprotective, but it's up to you to regain control over this potentially dangerous situation.

Possessiveness

Protecting possessions is an evolutionary trait from the time when dogs jealously guarded what little they had.

When a dog receives a new toy, his first reaction is to guard it so no one steals it. He'll take it to a secluded place, hold on to it tightly and lick or chew it. And when someone approaches, his immediate instinct is to protect his new possession by growling. Dogs are often possessive of their food bowls, too—even when they're empty.

LIVING IN HOPE Many dogs will even guard empty food bowls, possibly just in case someone comes along and puts something in them.

LEARNING TO SHARE TOYS

Some dogs can become so possessive that they will bare their teeth or snap if someone approaches them while they are eating or playing with their toys. Such behavior can be dangerous, especially around small children and other pets.

It's important to teach your dog not to be possessive with toys. To train him to share, put his leash and collar on. Give him a new toy, then immediately ask him to give it to you by saying "Drop it." The minute he releases it, even slightly, praise him. If he refuses, ignore the toy and give him a few "Sit" commands, with heaps of praise, especially whenever he shows an improvement. These drills will remind him that you are his leader and you control the toy. Repeat the drills several times, then end the session by taking away his toy. If he still fusses about giving it to you, then take it away after he has finished playing with it and get rid of it.

Another way to prevent possessiveness is to offer your dog another toy or a food treat in exchange for the item he is playing with. Tell your dog to "Drop it," and as soon as he releases the item, give him the new

MAKING A CHANGE Feeding your dog in different parts of the house may reduce his bowl-protecting tendencies.

PREVENTING FOOD WARS If you have more than one dog, feed each from his own bowl so that he is less likely to feel the need to compete with the others.

toy. A few minutes later, give your dog back the original toy, then repeat the exercise a few more times. By making a game of handing toys back and forth, you'll encourage your dog to expect that giving you his toys is worthwhile.

POSSESSIVENESS OF FOOD

Nothing affects survival as much as food. That's why dogs gobble up as much as they can as fast as they can, and also why they regard food bowls as worth protecting.

Dogs who have gone through lean times, such as rescued strays, may be particularly prone to this behavior. Dogs who live with other dogs will always regard them as competitors for food; no matter how well they get on at other times, each will resent the other if he or she approaches their food bowl—whether it is full or empty.

There are ways to reduce your dog's tendency to protect his bowl. In a multi-dog household, feed each dog separately from his own bowl, and preferably in a different part of the house or yard. If there are no competitors about, his protective instincts will decrease. Another tactic is simply to wash his bowl and put it away after each feed. If it's out of sight and not a permanent fixture, it may seem less important to him.

It's not only the bowl itself that your dog feels possessive about, it's the whole space. To reduce this tendency, vary the places where you feed him—on Monday, feed him in the kitchen; on Tuesday, in the yard; on Wednesday, in the bathroom, and so on. This way, no one part of the house will seem like his personal feeding station.

SOMETHING IN RETURN Dogs don't like to part with an interesting object and get nothing in return. The offer of a food treat makes this Irish Terrier more willing to give up his toy.

144

Separation Anxiety

Dogs are social animals, and don't like to be left alone. When they are, they may express their anxiety in undesirable ways.

Many dogs accept your comings and goings with equanimity, but many others might have a hard time understanding why you're there one moment and gone the next. Your dog may feel insecure and worry that you won't come back. And while you're gone, he may bark, whine or howl in fear. A worried dog may also become destructive, make messes inside the house, refuse to eat or attempt to escape from the yard or house.

MISSING YOU

There are several theories why a dog may be afraid of being away from his owner. Dogs that have been abandoned once before are the most likely sufferers of separation anxiety—perhaps they may assume they will be left again by their new owners.

Dramatic lifestyle changes, such as moving to a new house or sudden stress in the home, can bring on separation anxiety. And a dog who has had constant contact with his owner (because the owner is retired or works from home) will also find it difficult when his owner has to spend more time away from home for whatever reason.

WAYS TO OVERCOME ANXIETY

There are many things you can do to make your dog feel more secure when you go away. Start by crating him when you are away. Just like some small children who would rather be in their bedroom than wandering around a huge house, many anxious dogs prefer being in a small, confined space. Putting your dog in his crate will help to relax him and will prevent him from pacing about anxiously or trying to escape. He can't destroy the house, either, from inside his crate.

You should also try giving your dog more exercise. Even if you have to get up earlier in the morning, add a vigorous 20- to 30-minute running session every day prior to leaving him

GET THEM MOVING Extra exercise may help some dogs that suffer from separation-related distress.

LONELY DAYS Dogs who have been abandoned before—such as those rescued from shelters—may be particularly prone to separation anxiety.

alone. A dog who is tired is more likely to sleep than to worry about your absence.

Desensitizing your dog to your comings and goings also helps. Get him accustomed to seeing your routine of locking the door, lowering the drapes or putting on your coat every time you leave the house. At first, try leaving the house for very short periods of time. In the beginning, leave for just a few seconds then come right back. Don't rush to congratulate him the instant you come back in the door—you don't want your absences to seem like a big deal, just an everyday occurrence, so that he learns to take them for granted. If he's been quiet, praise him calmly a few minutes after you return.

Once he seems comfortable with this procedure, gradually add another minute to your absences, then five, and practice going out several times a day. It might take anywhere from a week to a couple of months before your dog feels calm about being apart from you, but once he's secure, he'll be less nervous about being alone. It also helps to desensitize a dog to being left inside the house before he is left outside.

A dog who has company or occupation will be less likely to fret when you're away. Getting another dog to visit during your periods of absence is one solution. If that's impractical, leave plenty of toys about for your dog to play with, especially ones that exercise his mind. A popular choice is a hollow plastic bone or a hollow Kong brand rubber toy into which you can put a small amount of some tasty food, such as peanut butter. Most dogs will happily spend hours trying to extract the treat inside.

NO STRESS You can gradually desensitize your dog to your absences so that he finds them less upsetting.

Stealing

Some dogs steal things to get your attention.

Others steal food simply because they can.

A dog who likes to steal can make off with things very quickly. A roast chicken, warm from the oven, one of your new leather shoes, your wallet or the bones from the trash were all there a minute ago, but now they're not. A clever canine thief waits until you're not looking, then jumps for the counter or dives into the trash to nab the treasure, and runs off with it as fast as he can.

If you catch your dog in the act, your instant reaction might be to yell at him to stop his antics. But if you shriek and start chasing him, you might frighten him or unwittingly buy into a game. Many dogs love a chase and will flaunt their prize to entice you.

When it comes to food, many dogs can't resist an unattended dinner plate. They're opportunists, programmed by evolution to eat pretty much whatever they can, whenever they can. It doesn't matter how well fed a dog is—he'll nearly always be tempted by the chance of a free meal.

EARLY PREVENTION

When your puppy first begins to take things, never chase him. Instead, try crouching down and gently asking the dog to come. If this doesn't work, try running away. If your pup chases you, you can then stop and praise the puppy for coming to you.

You should teach your pup a "Drop it" command from an early age. Offer him a toy and when he takes it, say "Good dog." Then grab the toy lightly, and say "Drop it." If the dog lets go, praise him. If your puppy won't drop the toy, try trading with him. Offer him a food treat or another prized toy while saying "Drop it." The same principle applies to things your pup picks up without your permission. If he drops it on command, lavish him with treats or toys. Once he drops the object, give him the treat or toy. Practice taking things from your dog, saying "Drop it," throughout the day. Quickly phase out the food reward so that it becomes unpredictable.

SCENE OF THE CRIME It takes only seconds for a dog such as this Rottweiler to take food from an unattended counter or table.

Always reward your dog with praise and, if the stolen item is not precious, give it back to him. That way he learns that although you take things, you also sometimes give them back.

Food stealing is a more difficult problem to stop. If there is food within reach, it is a rare dog that will not attempt to eat it, so it is really up to the owner to keep human food out of the dog's way. Sometimes the problem is that your puppy has too much freedom. Supervision is a vital part of early training.

THWARTING THE THIEF

The best preventative is to teach your dog to "Leave it." You can set up lures of food or things that he likes to steal. Watch him, and when he goes for the item, tell him "Leave it" and reward him when he backs off. It will take time and persistence for this approach to work.

To effectively correct a dog who continues to steal things, you must catch him in the act. The best way to do this is to booby-trap objects so they make a loud noise as he tries to steal them. Tie one end of a long piece of dental floss to a small piece of meat. Attach the other end to a soda can with a few pebbles inside. Place the meat on the edge of a table and leave the room. When your dog goes in for the grab, he'll get the shake can as an unexpected surprise, and it won't take long for him to come running out without his treat.

THE THRILL OF THE CHASE Chasing a canine thief is ineffective; it will simply make him think that you are joining in the fun and will excite him further.

(If your dog wises up to the sight of the shake can, you can cover it with a kitchen cloth).

This same method can be used on anything your dog loves to swipe. You can swap the shake can with a noisy bunch of keys and tie them to important papers left on the desk or to shoes in the closet. Sprinkling Tabasco sauce or commercial pet repellents on items your dog favors is another way to deter him from stealing. It's not foolproof, though— many dogs don't mind the extra flavor.

If you have a particular area in the house you want to protect from your dog's thieving, such as the den or kitchen, check out the gates made for toddlers, or ask your vet or other pet owners for advice. With persistence and patience, your dog will eventually come to the conclusion that crime doesn't pay.

As a last resort, there are a number of products that may help control some stealing behaviors, such as motion sensors that will go off when the dog breaks the field of the alarm. These can be used to alert the owner when the dog has gone into a certain room. Mats that produce a mild electrical charge will keep dogs out of certain rooms, but these are not recommended.

Submissive Urination

A dog who dribbles urine when stressed, nervous or frightened

has a problem with her confidence, not her bladder.

If your dog greets you happily but with a hint of shyness, while squatting or rolling on her back and dribbling several drops of urine, don't assume that you have a housebreaking problem. Instead, this is an anxiety problem, known as submissive urination.

Submissive behavior may be inherited, or it could have been caused by too frequent or too harsh correction, or even by abuse that your dog suffered before you got her.

Among wolves in the wild, such submissive urination is a kind of apology for anything the subordinate dog may have done to upset the pack leader. Though most common during a greeting, your pup may urinate in this way when you bend over to pick her up or when you chastise her. It's a conditioned reflex to assertive treatment and she isn't doing it on purpose. In fact, she's absolutely unaware of it.

Don't be upset with her because that will only make things worse. Instead, make your homecomings low-key. Silently toss a food treat for your pup as soon as you come in the door, then ignore her until she approaches you. (Coaxing her will tend to involve staring at her, which will be counter-productive.) When she does approach you, don't reach over her head to pet her.

A LIKELY CANDIDATE A very timid dog, such as this Stumpy-Tailed Cattle Dog, probably had a tendency to submissive urination as a pup.

A very submissive dog will read this as an intimidating gesture. Instead, kneel down and give her a chest rub.

Better still, teach your puppy a few easy commands so she learns how to please you and earn your approval. Use a command such as "Stand, stay" when she greets you, so she can express her devotion to you in a non-submissive posture and earn your praise. Put her in situations where you know she is likely to behave in a desirable way, so that you can praise her once she does. If she loves to be groomed and behaves nicely when you brush her, for example, groom her often—even if it's just for a few minutes at a time—so that you have plenty of chances to praise her.

Most young dogs naturally grow out of submissive urination once they're a few months old, by which time they have had the chance to learn more about the world and gain some confidence.

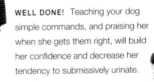

WELL DONE! Teaching your dog simple commands, and praising her when she gets them right, will build her confidence and decrease her tendency to submissively urinate.

Unwanted Sniffing

Sniffing is a normal part of canine communication, but should be discouraged around people, who usually don't appreciate it.

When two dogs meet, they inevitably spend the first few seconds sniffing each other's faces, before moving on to the genital region for a more prolonged sniff. Sniffing is a dog's way of learning information about a new animal. Because dogs have such a powerful sense of smell, they can detect such things as whether the other dog is male or female, friend or foe, as well as its state of health and whether it has been around other animals.

So when your dog meets new people, it's only natural that he greets them by sniffing. Your dog might even think there is nothing wrong in lifting a woman's skirt or nudging a man's crotch, but this behavior makes many people rather uncomfortable—especially if the sniffing gets out of hand—so it's up to you to teach your dog to greet your human friends in a manner that is more socially acceptable.

STOP THAT SNIFFING

To prevent your dog from getting too pushy in other people's private places, put his collar and leash on when you are expecting guests. Be ready to correct him with a "Leave it" command and a slight jerk on the leash if he tries to nose around where you don't want him to. Follow the "Leave it" command with a "Sit" or "Down" command so that you can praise your dog when he complies with your wishes. When he has calmed down, and if the guest is willing, allow your dog to satisfy his curiosity by sniffing the visitor's hand.

If your dog sniffs you in such a way, don't step backward or move out of his reach. Your dog may interpret this as submissive behavior and he'll begin to think that he's in charge. Instead, make him back away from you by moving forward into him and saying "No!" in a strong, clear voice. You can also offer him a substitute item to become interested in and reward him for leaving you alone.

A dog's desire to sniff can increase tenfold when you take him outdoors for his daily exercise sessions. If your dog is the kind who sniffs constantly while you're out walking, use the same "Leave it" command and a little leash correction. This way he'll know he doesn't have to investigate every odor he encounters.

HI THERE As an alternative to sniffing, this clever mixed breed has been taught to give a high-five when greeting people.

Whining

Whining is a leftover from puppyhood, when it was the way a dog got his mother's attention.

A whining dog, especially one who whines constantly, is bound to get on everyone's nerves. If your dog whines loudly and persistently, it may be a sign that he is stressed or overexcited. This may be because he wants something he can't do himself: to be let out of his crate, to be fed, to be given free rein to chase a cat or to go for a walk. Whining can also mean that your dog is so excited that he doesn't know how to calm himself down.

Steps to Stop Whining

If you don't correct this behavior, a strong-willed dog will soon learn he can get what he wants if he whines long enough. To stop the whining, don't coddle your dog with baby talk or pet him reassuringly. Try to ignore it. Only when he stops whining should you give him some attention. That way he learns that he gets rewarded when he doesn't whine, not the other way round.

Giving your dog something to do will also take his mind off whining. If he starts whining, lead him into another room or put him outside. When he is quiet, bring him in and tell him to "Sit" or "Lie down." After a few obedience drills, most dogs will quit whining.

You can also correct your dog's whining by telling him in a strong, low voice, "No whine!" Take care not to make your voice too harsh; an angry correction will just make some dogs more nervous or anxious. When he responds by being quiet, reward him and praise him. Once he understands "No whine!" you can even try giving him the command to whine. Being able to respond to commands, and receiving praise for it, will help boost the confidence of an anxious dog.

HOME ALONE In situations when dogs become anxious—such as when they are left alone—they may whine, sometimes for hours at a time.

Dog. A kind of additional or subsidiary Deity designed to catch the overflow and surplus of the World's worship.

AMBROSE BIERCE (1842–1914),
American journalist and writer

*If you get to thinking you're a person
of some influence, try ordering somebody
else's dog around.*

WILL ROGERS (1879–1935),
American actor and humorist

CHAPTER SEVEN

TRAINING YOUR DOG

Effective Training

Dogs need to know what they may and may not do so they can live harmoniously among humans and other pets.

Training is not unnatural, nor does it repress a dog's personality. In fact, dogs crave order and direction. Their pack-animal nature means that they expect one member of their social group to be the clear leader. This means that training your dog will be much easier once you have established yourself—and all other human members of the household—as the dog's superior.

Training has benefits for both dogs and humans. Well-behaved dogs are easy to live with; they bring pleasure to their family and to other people, so they get to spend plenty of time with humans. Being social animals, they find this an extremely potent reward.

It's never too early to start training a new puppy. Gentle training can begin as soon as you get your puppy home. House-training (see pp. 86–89) and learning to play gently with people (see p. 199) are two of the most important lessons for a new puppy.

ON THE ROAD If your dog will need to ride in the car, start getting her used to it from an early age.

Puppies also need to be socialized (see pp. 90–91). Puppy habituation classes will help your pup get used to other dogs and humans and to accepting your authority.

A good rule of thumb in early training is to think about the things you will expect of your pet when he is grown. Will he have to climb stairs or ride in the car frequently? Then teach him while he's young. Will you want to put a leash on him or keep him off furniture and out of certain rooms? Then teach your puppy these rules and tasks early on. Start off on the road to good behavior from the outset.

MAKING MISCHIEF

Dogs are not malicious; when they cause trouble, it is not because of bad intentions. Most behaviors that humans consider bad are simply things that dogs have always done, such as barking, chewing things, digging and chasing other animals. These only become problems when done in the wrong context. It is up to us, as dog owners, to teach dogs what is appropriate behavior in a human environment.

Over many generations, most breeds have been selected to show fewer of the aloof, independent ways of their wild ancestors.

ON HIS BEST BEHAVIOR Effective, humane training results in well-behaved, well-adjusted dogs that are a pleasure to have around.

PECKING ORDER Training is easier when dogs know that their place in the family is below all the human members, including children.

Selective breeding has promoted such traits as gentleness, eagerness to please, dependence, playfulness and soft features. Along with these appealing, puppylike qualities comes immature, puppylike behavior that often seems like mischief.

A dog's breed influences, but does not control entirely, the "mischief" that he is likely to get up to. Terriers love to dig; herding and retrieving breeds need a lot of exercise and may become restless and destructive if they don't get it; Basset Hounds tend to howl; sight hounds, such as Greyhounds and Whippets, have been bred to chase other animals. You can't completely eliminate a behavior that is natural to a particular breed, but you can nearly always reduce the intensity or frequency with which the behavior occurs.

How Dogs Learn

To teach your dog effectively, it is helpful to understand how animals learn. One of the primary ways learning occurs is through the relationship between a behavior and its consequence; that is, when an animal performs a certain behavior, something happens in return. The relationship between a behavior and its consequence can be either positive (reward) or negative (punishment). With repetition, a dog will eventually learn the connection and respond accordingly.

Reward

Positive reinforcement (or reward) increases the likelihood that a behavior will be repeated. Good behavior, therefore, will increase if it is immediately followed by a reward. This may be anything that sends the dog a clear message of approval, such as praise, a pat or a food treat. When done properly, positive reinforcement is an excellent way to shape a dog's behavior.

157

COLD SHOULDER Some dogs perform undesirable behaviors, such as jumping up, to get their owners' attention. Ignoring your dog when he behaves in this way denies him the desired reward, and if done consistently, should deter him from continuing the behavior.

Work out what your dog particularly likes—be it food, toys, praise, a pat, a game, or sticks to chase—and use his favorite things to motivate and reward good behavior. Rotate the rewards; this makes learning more fun for both of you and ensures that your dog doesn't get tired of them. If he starts seeming uninterested in a reward that normally generates enthusiasm, you'll know you've been overusing it.

Some rewards, such as food or praise, are obvious. In many cases, however, dogs and humans understand very different things to be rewards. For example, if your dog is barking to get your attention, you may yell at him to be quiet. You intend this as a chastisement, but your dog sees it differently. It will seem to him that he has achieved his aim; no matter how briefly, he has got your attention. Similarly, your dog may be nudging your hand while you read a book. If you push him away, he doesn't see this as the rejection that you intend it to be; instead, he

REPEAT PERFORMANCE Rewarding a dog, such as this Collie, for desirable behaviors—for example, fetching the newspaper—will encourage him to keep performing the same acts.

interprets it as a reward of both acknowledgment and physical contact, which was what he wanted in the first place. In both these situations, you have inadvertently rewarded an unwanted behavior.

Punishment

Punishment also involves a relationship between behavior and consequence. In this case, however, the consequence is undesirable. Each time your dog performs an unwanted behavior, the consequences are unpleasant and this should make the behavior decrease. For punishment to be effective, however, you must see evidence that the behavior has decreased or ceased. If it has not, then you are probably not punishing the relevant behavior.

Punishment is a difficult tool to use correctly. If it is too frequent or too harsh, it can result in fear and aggression, which are counterproductive to learning. On the other hand, punishment that is too mild will not stop the unwanted behavior. Either way, it is always easier to teach what you want, rather than punish what you do not want.

Punishment need not be in the form of a negative action; it can simply be the absence of the desired result. For example, if your dog is pestering you to get your attention, turn away and ignore him, or leave the room. Only when he stops should you pat or praise him or return to the room where he is. This will give him the message that his pestering tactics don't work, and that calm, passive behavior is what really gets your attention.

Punishment should never be harsh or physical. Hitting your dog or verbally abusing him will only teach him to fear you or provoke him to be aggressive; it will not stop his unwanted behavior. The most effective way to train a dog is to give him plenty of opportunities to do the right thing, and to reward him when he does.

Timing and Frequency

Of vital importance for learning is the timing and frequency of reward or punishment. As far as timing is concerned, reward or punishment must occur as soon as possible, and certainly within 15 seconds of the performance of the target behavior. Remember, behavior is something that occurs all the time, so the last thing the animal does before receiving the reward or punishment is what you affect. A delay of 30 seconds may mean that the dog is doing something else when the reward or punishment occurs.

For instance, perhaps your dog is chewing your shoe. You tell him "Drop it" then "Come." He does so, and when he does, you scold him for chewing the shoe. This confuses him, because in his mind he did what you asked; he came to you. He doesn't know that you are referring to his previous action because he doesn't understand your words. To train your dog effectively, you need to realise—and avoid— situations in which such misunderstandings might occur.

ACT QUICKLY A dog needs to be reprimanded immediately—that is, within 15 seconds of doing the wrong thing—to make any connection between the action and the punishment.

TABLE MANNERS If his owners relent and feed this terrier mix from the table, they will have rewarded an undesirable behavior and encouraged him to repeat it.

Behavior can be rewarded or punished continuously or intermittently, with differing results. Continuous reward means that every time the animal performs the behavior, it receives a reward. A problem with this rate of reinforcement is that when there are no longer rewards, the dog often ceases performing the behavior. Inter-mittent reward, on the other hand, means that not every performance of a action is rewarded. Instead, the reward may come after two times or five times, or after performing for a

159

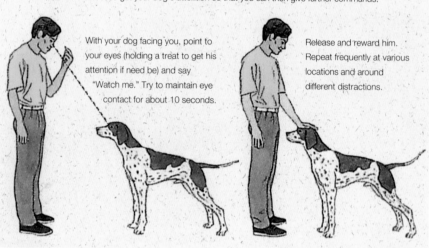

"WATCH ME"

One task that should be taught to any dog you train is a "Watch me" command. This serves to get your dog's attention so that you can then give further commands.

With your dog facing you, point to your eyes (holding a treat to get his attention if need be) and say "Watch me." Try to maintain eye contact for about 10 seconds.

Release and reward him. Repeat frequently at various locations and around different distractions.

certain period of time—the key is that the reward is not always given. This tends to increase the rate and persistence of behavior, because the dog never knows if this is the time it will be rewarded and so it keeps performing the behavior in the hope of a reward.

This is often the way bad behaviors are inadvertently reinforced and maintained. Consider a dog that begs at the table. If he is rewarded intermittently he will continue to beg, unless the rewards disappear completely. If he is never fed, he will stop begging.

A process of extinction takes place when a learned response—in this case, begging—is no longer followed by any reinforcer, or reward. The response will be performed progressively less frequently and less energetically.

Rules and Consistency

The two most important things you can do when training your dog are to set clear rules and to stick to them. Dogs like to know where they stand and what is expected of them, but they will only understand these rules if they are consistently enforced, not insisted upon one day then relaxed the next. All members of the household should know and abide by the same rules, or else the dog will become confused, and the result will be inadvertent bad behavior.

Set rules according to what matters to you; if your backyard is an unkempt jungle it may not bother to you if your dog digs it up, but it may drive you crazy if he climbs on the furniture. In

START THEM YOUNG It's easiest to teach a dog what you do and don't want him to do from a young age than to correct established behaviors in mature dogs.

this case, you can ignore his digging but you'll need to train him to keep off the furniture.

It is almost impossible to stop bad behavior if you're not consistent. Part of being consistent is using one command for one response. For example, if you alternate between "Come," "Come here" and "Come on, boy," your dog will almost certainly become confused and as a result may come unreliably or not at all. In this case the fault lies not with the dog but with the command he received.

Working for Rewards

Just as behavior occurs all the time, so does training, whether active or inadvertent. This means that training doesn't have to be concentrated into long sessions of obedience drills. Instead, all your dog's everyday actions and interactions can be used as training opportunities. An effective strategy is to teach your dog that nothing is for free. Whenever he wants something, he should earn it. If he wants his dinner, he can be made to sit before you put the bowl down, and then to await your command before he begins eating. If he wants a game, make him sit or lie down first. Constantly reinforcing your leadership in these small but powerful ways will mean that your dog always looks to you for instruction.

If you do obedience training in blocks, keep them short. Dogs can stay alert and focused for only about 20 minutes. It's better to do two or three sessions per day of ten minutes than one half-hour session. If your dog starts looking distracted, yawning, scratching, or performing similar "displacement behaviors" (see also p. 27), that's a sure sign that he needs a break.

Basic Commands

No matter how old or young your dog is, there are a few essential commands that he should know.

TEACHING "SIT"

The fact that a dog has a relatively inflexible spine means that if he tips his head up far enough, he will sit. You can use this to your advantage when teaching a dog to sit in response to a spoken command. Remember, your dog already knows how to sit; what you want to do is to produce the response on command.

By using a food treat, you can easily get your dog to sit. Repeat the process below six to eight times, praising him every time he performs the task. Then move onto another command.

Only say the word "sit" once as you maneuver the puppy into a sit. Be careful not to hold the food too high above his nose as he might jump up to reach it. Once your puppy gets used to the command, reward him with food only intermittently. You want to make sure your puppy will sit even if you do not have food.

RULES FOR TRAINING

- Keep training sessions short and interesting.
- Say the command one time, and wait for the puppy to perform the task.
- Use food initially to guide the puppy into the correct position. Once the puppy knows the task, give food rewards less frequently.
- Use praise every time your dog performs correctly.
- Try to end every session on a high note, when the dog has completed a task successfully.

1 With your dog facing you, hold a food reward between your fingers and thumb with your palm facing up, in front of his nose.

2 Then move it up and slightly back over his head. Say "Sit" once as you do this. As your dog follows the treat with his eyes and head, he will sit down.

3 Praise your dog, saying "Good sit," and give him the food reward.

TEACHING "DOWN"

To teach a dog to lie down, we again use food to help us guide the dog into position (below).

You may find that some dogs will not go into the down position when you push the food between their legs. For those dogs, it may be necessary to take the food and slowly pull it forward. The dog should follow it down. Once the dog's elbows have reached the floor, give the reward. Again, once the dog can associate the word with the action, begin to phase out the food rewards, but keep praising.

1 Place your dog in a sit. Take a food treat, say "Down" and quickly bring it from in front of the dog's nose down to the ground. See how his head follows.

2 Now take the treat and push it between the dog's front legs. As he tries to follow it, his front end will slide into a down position. Say "Good down" and give him the treat.

TEACHING "STAND"

Getting your dog to stand is easy; getting him to do so on command is a little harder.

1 To get your dog to stand, first place him in a sitting or down position.

2 Take a food treat and pull it forward, away from the dog, as you say "Stand." (If the dog is lying down, pull the treat upward.)

TRAINING TIPS

Try using these commands in different combinations. Vary the order of them, trying to get the puppy to do them with only one food treat or none at all.

Don't confine training to a set session. Employ these commands throughout the day as part of your dog's regular routine. Ask your puppy to sit before eating, going out or being petted. Make sure that your puppy will do these tasks whenever you ask and in any location. This will come in handy when you want him to sit for guests at the front door, for example, or to wait for a leash before a walk. By controlling your pet's behavior you establish yourself as the "leader."

3 As your dog gets up, say "Good stand" and give him the food reward.

TEACHING "COME"

Teaching a dog to come (or "the recall" as it is called in obedience training) is an extremely important and often difficult task. If your dog will reliably come when called, many disasters can be avoided. However, often owners don't manage to do this. Attention to a few details will make this command easier to instill in your dog.

First, never call your dog to you and punish or yell at him. If you call your dog and then punish him, why would he ever want to come in future? Another common pitfall is calling your dog away from something fun. Often we call our dogs to take them inside, to take away some object they're happily chewing or to put them in confinement because we are going out. It is important, then, to practice calling your dog under other circumstances. When he comes, give him a pat, or a hug or a food reward and send him back to play. This helps him learn that when he comes to you, it does not always signal the end of something good.

Plan for Success

At first, keep the distances short, but gradually make your dog come farther to reach you. You can also practice this task by calling your dog to you from across the room. If at first he will not come, crouch down, open your arms and make your voice very inviting. Remember to give him a good reason to come to you.

Once your puppy begins to come more reliably, add a "Sit" to the end of the come command. This will get your puppy used to being called and then sitting and waiting before charging off to have fun elsewhere.

1 Stand close to your dog with a food reward in your hand.

2 Back up a short distance, wiggle the treat and say "Come."

3 As your dog approaches, say "Good come" and give him a treat when he gets to you.

164

TEACHING "HEEL"

"Heel," or the follow command, is an extension of the "Watch me" command (see p. 161). Repeat this command several times and add the command "Heel." At first, move only short distances, but gradually move farther and for longer periods as the dog learns to stay with you.

1 With your dog in a sit by your side, say "Watch me" and make eye contact.

DIFFERENT LEARNING SPEEDS

Every breed of dog has been bred to perform different tasks, and this affects how quickly your dog will be able to learn. There are real differences in the breeds' anatomy, senses and natural levels of motivation. For quick results, match the breed to the task.

Sight hound breeds, such as Greyhounds or Salukis, are very fast and have excellent vision. They will have a hard time lying down and staying there for long, but if you ask them to run after an object, they will be able to do that in a flash. The more sedentary breeds, such as Bloodhounds or Newfoundlands, will probably be much better at learning how to lie down on command.

Retrievers have been bred to fetch game, so it's easy to teach them to bring back a ball or stick. Don't bother them with sled dog racing—leave that to Alaskan Malamutes and Huskies, but don't expect those breeds to be as skilled at fetching things. If a dog excels in one area, he may not be quite so good in another.

A dog's size also affects the speed at which he responds to commands. A small dog can respond very quickly to a command such as "Sit," for example. A giant breed, such as a Great Dane or Irish Wolfhound, might need a little longer to coordinate his large body and long limbs.

2 Take a couple of steps forward and say "Heel." If your dog is really watching and tries to maintain eye contact, he will move with you.

3 Stop, and when your dog also stops say "Good heel."

TEACHING "STAY"

Teaching a dog to stay on command may avoid a disaster, especially if you live in a busy urban area. Teaching "Stay" can be another difficult task, so it will be a lot easier if you try for small successes, rather than long stays.

Initially, reward your puppy with food and praise if he does not move for five seconds. Then gradually increase the duration of the stay. The same applies to the distance between you and the puppy. Do not go too far at first.

This will only result in your puppy breaking the stay and failing the task. Instead, you should always plan for success. If your puppy breaks the stay, the chances are you have gone too far or kept him waiting for too long. If he breaks the stay, don't scold him—promptly fetch him, place him back in position and try again, this time for a shorter distance and less time. When he holds the stay, praise profusely. Never call a puppy to you after telling him to "Stay" as this rewards him for breaking the stay.

1 With your puppy in a sit, place your hand, palm open, in front of his face.

2 Say "Stay" in a firm voice as you back away a few paces.

3 If your puppy does not move for five seconds, reward him with food and praise.

TRAINING PUPPIES

Puppies don't have great coordination or agility, so forget perfection and focus on play training. If your pup sees a leaf blowing in the breeze, he will naturally scamper after it. Tell him, "Fetch!" and when he catches it, say "Good dog!". You've given his chasing a name that you can use again later when you want to teach him to fetch. Or, when you set his food dish down, call his name over and over in an excited, happy voice. After a few times, he'll come flying to you when he hears your call.

Pups have short attention spans, so limit formal training sessions to five minutes, several times a day.

166

ur
uch
will

back.
ng items
because
in the

1 Toss a toy or ball a short distance. When the puppy looks to the toy, say "Fetch."

3 To get your puppy to drop the toy on command, hold up another toy and say "Drop it."

4 When your puppy drops the toy, praise him.

5 Now throw the new toy, and repeat the steps.

Showing

If you want an extra challenge for yourself and your dog, consider entering him in a conformation show or other competition.

While most people are happy simply for their dog to be a loving companion, some owners have higher aspirations. If you think your dog is a good enough representative of its breed to be a possible champion in the show ring, then conformation shows may interest you.

CONFORMATION SHOWS

Conformation simply means conforming to a breed standard (a description of the ideal example of a given breed). At formal conformation dog shows, purebred dogs are judged on how closely they measure up to their breed standard.

Dog shows are either restricted to one breed of dog (known as specialty shows) or are all-breed shows. At either show, the judges first examine and evaluate each dog for overall structure, fitness, coat color and quality, and temperament. The judges then evaluate each dog's movement, or gait, by watching it move around the ring.

In most countries, dogs of each breed are divided into classes, generally based on age, for the initial round of competition. The

ON SHOW In conformation shows, purebred dogs such as this Golden Retriever are judged against others of the same breed.

winners of each class then compete against each other as well as with dogs that are already champions. The judge then picks the "best of breed." If the competition is an all-breed show, the best of breed winners then compete against all the others in their group (for example, sporting or herding dogs). Finally, out of the winners of each group, the "best in show" is picked.

Most entrants at shows are competing for points that will eventually qualify them as champions (designated by the letters Ch. in front of the dog's name). The number of points that a dog can win at a show varies from one to five depending on a variety of factors, including the number of dogs at the show and the dog's breed and sex. For an animal to qualify as a champion, it must win 15 points under at least three

LABOR OF LOVE It takes considerable time, effort and expense to prepare a dog such as this Scottish Terrier for a show.

MEASURING UP

A breed standard is the ideal against which all members of the breed are judged. This Australian Terrier conforms closely to its standard.

SKULL
Long and strong with slight stop.

EARS
Small, erect; high on skull; well apart. Hair short.

OUTER COAT
Harsh, straight; blue and tan, red or sandy.

EYES
Small and dark.

BODY
Long in proportion to head.

NOSE
Black.

TOPLINE
Level and firm.

TAIL
High set, erect; docked to just under half its length.

LIPS
Tight, dark brown.

MUZZLE
Strong, powerful; same length as skull.

HINDQUARTERS
Strong, well-muscled thighs.

NECK
Long and strong, with ruff.

CHEST
Reaching slightly below the elbows.

FEET
Small, catlike; toes arched.

FORELEGS
Straight, set back, slightly feathered.

NAILS
Short, black and strong.

different judges, including at least two scores of three points or more (known as "majors").

Conformation shows are restricted to unneutered, purebred dogs, and for a dog to do well it must be an excellent representative of its breed. Some people choose to handle their dogs themselves at the shows, while others hire professional handlers.

OTHER COMPETITIONS

If formal dog shows seem a little out of your (or your dog's) league, there are other types of competition for which both neutered animals and mixed breeds are eligible. These include obedience trials, tracking tests, hunting trials, herding trials and agility competitions.

Obedience trials test both the dog's and handler's ability to perform a specific set of exercises, including such commands as sit, stay, down, heel and retrieve. Tracking tests require a dog to follow a trail by scent. Hunting trials test a dog's hunting ability in

the field (to point and retrieve, for example), while herding trials require a dog to control livestock in a variety of difficult situations. In agility competitions, dogs and handlers navigate an obstacle course consisting of tunnels, inclines, seesaws and hurdles, at high speeds. You may also be able to find a local dog show that gives prizes for the best trick, or even to the dog with the most spots or the biggest ears. Whatever your interest, a dog show can bring out the best in your dog and give you both a chance to show off.

BEAUTY CASE
Owners of show dogs travel with a well-stocked kit to keep their dogs looking their best.

A dog is the only thing on Earth that loves you more than you love yourself.

JOSH BILLINGS (1818–85),
American humorist and lecturer

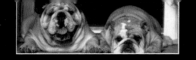

PART FOUR

THE BEST OF CARE

If you think dogs can't count, try putting three dog biscuits in your pocket and then giving Fido only two of them.

PHIL PASTORET

CHAPTER EIGHT

FEEDING

Your Dog's Nutritional Needs

Dogs need a supply of certain nutrients to aid growth and healing and keep the immune system in good working order.

A dog's individual nutritional requirements will vary depending on whether she is active or sedentary, young or old, a working dog that hunts, herds or races, is suffering from a chronic or temporary health condition, or is pregnant or nursing a litter of puppies.

The six basic nutrients that all animals need are clean water, proteins, carbohydrates, minerals, fats and vitamins. To balance their particular body needs, dogs must eat foods containing the right amounts of these six nutrients. Once eaten, the food will be broken down and processed into usable forms for the many cells of the dog's body. This, very simply explained, is dog nutrition.

THE SIX BASIC NUTRIENTS

Water

This building block of all life is one of your dog's most vital requirements. She can go for a while without food, but without water she would soon become dehydrated or suffer heatstroke and other serious conditions. An adult dog's body weight is 50 to 60 percent water; a puppy's is more than 80 percent. Have a bowl of fresh, clean water available for your dog at all times. A dog of medium size that eats a diet primarily of dry food could require upward of two quarts (2 l) of water each day.

ANY BOWL WILL DO When watching your dog's diet, remember that he won't eat only what you feed him— some of his meals may be gained by stealth or theft.

Clean the bowl and change the water every morning, then check it during the day. This is especially important in hot weather or if your dog spends a lot of time outside. Try to keep the bowl in a shady spot, too.

For a pregnant or lactating bitch, continual access to clean, fresh water is most important. Water carries nutrients to the developing fetuses and also helps flush wastes out of the mother's system. During lactation, she needs plenty of water to keep up her milk supply.

Your dog can drink as much as she likes, whenever she likes, except around serious exercise time.

Generally, you need never be concerned about giving your dog "too much" water.

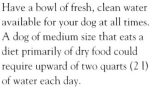

KEEP THE CHUB IN CHECK Dogs will become obese, like this Corgi, if their food contains too much fat, or if they are given too much food and too little exercise.

OFF TO A GOOD START Puppies need proportionally more protein than adult dogs, to fuel their rapid growth during the first few months of life.

Talk to your vet if you notice a marked increase in your dog's water consumption, however. Diabetes, kidney failure, Cushing's disease and other conditions are all characterized by increased thirst.

Proteins

Dogs don't actually require proteins as such; what they really need are the amino acids that make up proteins. Dogs manufacture some amino acids, known as the nonessential amino acids, within their bodies. They must get the rest—ten essential amino acids—from their food, specifically from animal or plant products that contain protein.

Proteins from animal sources, such as eggs, meat and fish, are high-quality, or complete, proteins. Incomplete proteins come from grains and vegetables, and contain only some of the essential amino acids. You might think that the more "high-quality" proteins your dog gets, the better, but it's not that simple. Dogs need both forms of protein, because they work together to ensure that the body's cell-building, blood-clotting, infection-fighting and other processes are working properly.

If your dog is a normally active and healthy dog, just a small amount of protein will get her by. The only exceptions are puppies, pregnant or nursing females and dogs that work hard. These dogs might need a greater ratio of protein in their food. Young and active dogs need more protein in their diets—young dogs for growth and active dogs because they are constantly breaking down more tissue, such as muscle tissue and red blood cells, which needs to be replaced. They need to get this protein from animal sources. See pp. 178–181 for more information on special diets.

Carbohydrates

There are simple carbohydrates, such as sugar, and complex carbohydrates, such as starches and fiber. They help provide dogs with energy and also keep the intestines functioning smoothly so that food waste passes through the system efficiently.

Fiber is often included in diets designed to help a dog lose or maintain weight, because it may make a dog feel full without sending the calorie count through the roof. High-fiber diets are traditionally prescribed for dogs that have weight problems.

The preferred source of carbohydrates in many commercially prepared dog foods is corn, followed by soybeans and wheat. Recently, rice

175

EATING FOR SEVERAL Pregnant and
lactating bitches need greater ratios
of protein than most other dogs.

has become a popular ingredient, particularly
in special formulations for dogs that have
developed an intolerance to other grains.
Carbohydrates are an important part of your
dog's nutritional needs, although they should
make up no more than about 50 percent of a
balanced canine diet.

Fats

Any diet too high in fatty foods will make
for an overweight dog, but that does not
mean that a fat-free diet is beneficial. Fats are
essential to a dog's health, and an important
source of energy. However, they must be
properly balanced with other nutrients.

Feeding your dog the
proper amount of a
complete and balanced dog
food should ensure that she
gets the right level of fat,
but beware of giving her
too many treats and snacks.
Too many calories (kilo-
joules) are often the result
of too much fat—usually
in the form of too many
biscuit treats or too many
table scraps.

Very active, hard-
working dogs may benefit
from a diet that is higher in
both fat and protein than
would be healthy for their
less active counterparts.
Sled dogs, for instance, can
eat up to 40 percent of the
dry matter of their diet as
fat—that would be enough
to make most dogs as wide
as they are long.

Minerals

Minerals either trigger chemical
reactions within the body or serve as building
blocks for specific bodily systems, such as
nerve tissue (magnesium), skin and enzymes
(zinc), or heart and kidneys (potassium).

Generally, dogs don't need a lot of
minerals. For instance, the amount of iron a
dog's body needs to affect her red blood cells is
measured in parts per million. Other minerals,
such as calcium and phosphorus, are needed in
relatively larger amounts to ensure she has
healthy bones. If a dog is fed a complete and
balanced diet, there is no need to supplement
her diet with minerals. At best, it has no value
whatsoever. At worst, it could be harmful.
Most commercial dog foods will provide your
dog with all the minerals that she needs.

Vitamins

Just as your dog's body needs minerals, it also
needs vitamins for vital chemical reactions
and normal metabolic functions. Dogs require
the same vitamins from
their food as we need from
ours, except for vitamin C,
which dogs' bodies are able
to manufacture.

Vitamins are divided into
two groups: those that are
soluble in water and those
that dissolve only in fat.
The B vitamins, which help
convert food into energy,
are water soluble, as is
vitamin C. This means that
they need to be replenished
every day, and any excess is
simply passed out again in
the dog's urine.

Fat-soluble vitamins,
such as vitamins A, E, K
and D, have more staying

THE RIGHT BALANCE Good
nutrition, along with regular
exercise and preventive health
care, will keep your dog healthy.

power in the body, which is fortunate, because
deficiencies can cause serious problems.
However, excess amounts of these vitamins,
especially vitamin A, can also lead to trouble.
For an older dog, supplements rich in vitamins
C and E (both antioxidants) can help combat
some of the deterioration that age can bring.

Achieving the right balance shouldn't
be a problem. There's really no reason to
supplement with vitamins as long as you
are feeding a complete and balanced diet.
Supplements are usually only necessary if you
are feeding your dog a homemade diet. Then
you need to make sure the food is nutritionally
balanced. If you choose to prepare your dog's

food at home, it is wise to review her diet with
your vet to check if any supplementation is
needed—your vet will advise you on this.

When to Feed

Most adult dogs can sustain their energy and
nutrient levels on one meal a day. You just
need to be sure that you give that meal at the
right time to suit your household. For a family
that's away at work and school most of the
day, it makes sense to feed your dog at night,
since someone will be home to let her out after
she eats. On the other hand, if there's always
someone at home during the day, a morning
feeding might suit you and your dog better.

KEEPING UP THE ENERGY Working dogs, such as
herding dogs, require diets containing more calories
(kilojoules) than their more sedentary counterparts.

Special Diets

*Your dog's food requirements will change throughout his life,
and should be evaluated and adjusted as needed.*

Adhering to a special diet may be as easy as buying food designed for puppies from the supermarket or carefully regulating when and how much you feed a diabetic dog. If you ever have a question as to whether your dog needs a special diet, talk it over with your vet.

PUPPIES

During his first year, a dog will undergo the greatest amount of growth of his whole life. Puppies grow astonishingly quickly and need energy and balanced nutrients at levels up to three times what they will need as adults. This decreases after about four months, but remains greater than adult needs until the pup is fully grown at ten months to two years, depending on when his breed matures.

Puppies also require more high-quality protein, which they can get from meat, eggs, milk or cottage cheese. These are tasty and also easily digested. Or you can opt for commercially prepared puppy food, which is formulated with the special requirements of puppies in mind.

Don't Overdo It

Most pups are weaned between six and eight weeks, so your pup will already be eating solid food by the time you bring him home. He may seem to want to eat all the time, but don't let him. He will have growth spurts, but should be fed only the amount he needs to maintain a steady, average rate of growth. A perfectly healthy puppy should not be roly-poly. Erring on the side of lean is better than overfeeding, especially with large breeds. If a dog eats too much, he'll grow too fast. Rapid, dispropor-tionate growth of bones and muscles could lead to hip dysplasia and other joint problems, especially in large breeds. Any large-breed pup is on a different, rapid growth curve that extends over a longer period of time, and he must be fed accordingly. Keeping such a puppy lean will reduce the likelihood that he will develop orthopedic problems.

FORGET THE PUPPY FAT It is healthier for a puppy to be lean rather than chubby, especially if he will grow to be large, like this German Shorthaired Pointer.

It is also vital to ensure the right balance of calcium and phosphorus in a large puppy's food. Too much calcium can interfere with normal bone and cartilage development. For large breeds, calcium should make up no more than 1.1 percent of the dry matter and must be balanced by at least the same amount of phosphorus. This information is not listed on pet food labels, but you can call the manufac-turer's toll-free line for a detailed nutritional analysis. This simple step could help prevent your dog from developing a painful condition.

Puppies from small breeds are not as prone to these types of orthopedic complaints. They are, however, particularly susceptible to low blood sugar levels and other problems.

Frequent Feeding

Puppy stomachs are small and can't hold enough food at one time to see them through an entire day. Until your puppy is about five months of age, feed him three meals a day (or four if he is a particularly small breed). If you feed dry puppy food, be sure to moisten it with warm water. Not only does this make it tastier, but it's also easier for him to eat with his puppy teeth until they fall out and are replaced by permanent teeth.

From five months until about nine months of age, feed the puppy twice a day. If he still enjoys his food moistened, indulge him for a while. But remember that crunching on dry food will be better for his teeth in the long run, since the chewing action cleans them.

By ten months, you can start feeding an adult diet once a day.

Introducing Adult Food

When a pup's rate of growth slows noticeably, that's a good time to introduce him to an adult maintenance diet. As a general rule, when a dog has reached 75 to 80 percent of his adult size, it is a good time to switch from puppy food to an adult diet. Generally, the smaller the dog, the earlier he will reach what is considered maturity. Your vet will be able to

ONE SQUARE MEAL Most adult dogs, such as these Vizslas, can get by on just one feed a day, but all dogs must have a constant supply of clean, fresh water.

advise you. Watch for changes in your dog's eating patterns and be aware of the average adult weight for his breed. With puppies of mixed breed, use the four-month rule of thumb: at four months, a puppy is roughly half his adult size. This is a fairly useful benchmark if you're uncertain just what exotic mix of breeds you're working with.

When you switch your pup to a maintenance diet, reduce the number of feeds. If you choose to feed him a different food, make the changeover gradually. This will be easier on his digestive system and taste buds. Over seven to ten days, substitute ever-increasing amounts of the new food for his customary fare.

PREGNANT OR LACTATING DOGS

Don't increase a pregnant dog's daily rations until about the third trimester, when she's seven weeks pregnant, and then only by 10 to 20 percent. The real eating starts after the pups are born. Don't overfeed your dog during pregnancy and underfeed during lactation. If she gains too much weight during gestation, she can have trouble whelping the puppies.

After a dog delivers her puppies, increase her daily ration by another 10 percent for the first day after she gives birth. Then let her eat to her heart's content (but dog food only; no chocolates or unhealthy treats). Feed by "free choice" rather than on a schedule during the first five weeks of lactation.

The puppies' demand for milk will increase daily for the first 20 to 30 days, so the mother must be allowed to eat what she needs to keep up with their demands. There's another advantage to having food

FOOD FOR ALL Lactating bitches need plenty of food to enable them to produce enough milk for their fast-growing puppies.

FOOD FOR ALL Lactating bitches need plenty of food to enable them to produce enough milk for their fast-growing puppies.

Older dogs require very good quality protein. Animal by-products, such as hair and hooves, are protein, but of low quality. By comparison, eggs provide the highest quality protein. Buy a premium food or ask your vet to recommend a food for your aging dog.

Be careful not to overfeed an older dog. Too much food combined with a low activity level could easily cause him to pack on the weight, which could lead to health problems. Some older dogs may be prone to obesity—the main nutritional disease among all dogs—if they eat the same amount as usual but do less exercise.

Some foods formulated for older dogs restrict protein to prevent kidney problems. However, such a cutback may be unnecessary, since renal disease is not common in older dogs. And if your dog doesn't actually have a problem, there is really no need to restrict the amount of protein he eats. If he's getting regular veterinary care and has a diet tailored to meet his state of health, that should be fine.

readily available during this time. At about three weeks, the puppies start sampling their mother's food and soon will be getting a good part of their nutritional requirements this way.

Lactating dogs have very high nutrient needs, as much as three to four times what's normal. They should be fed diets intended either for growth and reproduction or for "all life stages." Adult foods may be too low in calories (kilojoules) or nutrients. However, it's important to return your dog to pre-pregnancy levels of intake after the puppies are weaned so that she avoids any weight gain. Remember to make all dietary changes gradually.

OLDER DOGS

When feeding an older dog, it's not your dog's age that matters so much as his more sedentary way of life. However, while he may need only three-quarters of the calories (kilojoules) of his former diet, his need for the essential nutrients may be proportionately higher.

WORKING DOGS

True working dogs are those that herd sheep, cattle or other livestock, that run arduous sled races or spend hours in the field with their owners. They need a diet rich in high-quality protein and fat to maintain peak stamina and good body condition.

Physiologically, dogs differ from humans in several respects. They have more heart and muscle in comparison to their total body weight, and their cardio-respiratory system is superior to ours. Also, dogs do not sweat in the same way people do. Depending on the breed, dogs have greater stamina

SLOWING DOWN As they age, most dogs need fewer calories (kilojoules) because they are exercising less. Their diets may also need to be modified to ease certain medical conditions.

HIGH ENERGY When working, sled dogs need more than 10,000 calories (42,000 kilojoules) per day to maintain their body weight and energy levels.

and oxygen capacity than us, too. These differences become important when feeding a working dog in order to keep him at peak performance.

Working dogs thrive and work best when fed on animal proteins and animal fats. Cereals, vegetables and carbohydrates play less of an energy role. Make sure you buy a food with high-quality, animal-derived protein, not one that is high in corn or soy.

A hard-working dog might benefit from twice-a-day feeding, but be careful not to feed him immediately before or after a strenuous workout; this can result in vomiting, diarrhea or bloat. Similarly, don't let your dog resume strenuous activity until at least 30 minutes after he has had a drink.

Another factor to consider when feeding a working dog is how much time he spends out of doors in cold weather. Generally, dogs need to get 7.5 percent more calories (kilojoules) for each 10° F (18° C) drop in temperature.

Giving a hard-working dog small, light snacks in the field is an acceptable way to keep his energy up, if he'll take them. Many working dogs get too high strung and refuse to eat when they're working.

LONG-TERM CARE AND CONVALESCENCE

If your dog has been diagnosed with a health problem, you'll need to work with your vet to design the appropriate diet for him. The type of food he eats can often help in easing the condition. For instance, a diet for a dog with kidney disease would have decreased levels of protein, phosphorus and salt but increased caloric density—more power to the punch, since he may be receiving less food.

A convalescing dog could also benefit from a special diet. If he has lost weight due to an illness or surgery, you might increase the caloric density of his food until he reaches his pre-illness weight. If his normal diet is dry food and you want to encourage him to eat, try moistening it with a little warm water or even a little bit of stock or canned food.

There are prescription foods formulated for dogs with a wide range of health conditions. These are available only through your vet, who will work closely with you should your dog ever need to be put on this kind of diet.

How Much to Feed

Dogs aren't the best judges of when enough is enough, so it's up to you to decide how much your dog can eat.

The right amount of food varies with the individual dog. Even if they happen to weigh the same and be of the same breed, all dogs are unique. Their activity levels, ages, health and metabolisms differ, so their nutritional requirements differ as well. Every can or package of food has guidelines printed on it, but these should be used as starting points only, and adjusted to suit your dog.

THE SAME BUT DIFFERENT All dogs are individuals; even these Pug siblings may grow up to need quite different amounts of food and ratios of nutrients.

Helpful Guidelines

You can work out how much your dog needs to eat by evaluating her overall body condition, then adjusting her food accordingly. Many vets are now recommending that you use a five-point scale (see chart opposite) to assess her body condition and work out how much food she should be getting each day.

To determine your dog's body condition, take an objective look at her from the side and from above to see if she looks lean or heavy. Then put your hands over her ribcage to see if the ribs are prominent or heavily padded over with fat (see p. 273). Armed with this information, you can use the chart and the accompanying illustrations as guidelines to evaluate your dog's body, so you know to give more, less or the same amount of food.

Your aim is to feed your dog the right amount of food so that her body shape is "ideal." But if your check shows that she is on the overweight side, she's getting more food than she can use and you should either cut it back or give her more exercise. And if she's underweight, she's not eating enough, so feed her more food, or food of a better quality (see p. 185).

HOW TO WEIGH A DOG

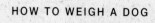

The best way to weigh a dog is to pick her up and step on the bathroom scales. Then you simply subtract your own weight from the total, leaving you with the weight of the dog. If you own a small dog or a puppy, this is a very simple procedure. However, if your dog is large, such as this English Setter, be sure to lift her correctly. Crouch down to gather up your dog (left) and rise slowly, using your legs, not your back (right).

HOW DOES YOUR DOG RATE?

This chart and illustrations will help you to determine whether your dog is very thin, underweight, ideal in size, overweight or obese. Then adjust how much you feed her until she is "ideal."

Score 1 Very Thin	Ribs	Easy to feel, with no fat cover.	
	Tail base	Prominent raised bony structure with no fat under the skin.	
	Abdomen	Severe abdominal tuck; accentuated hourglass shape.	
Score 2 Underweight	Ribs	Easy to feel, with minimal fat cover.	
	Tail base	Raised bony structure with little fat under the skin.	
	Abdomen	Abdominal tuck; marked hourglass shape.	
Score 3 Ideal	Ribs	Possible to feel, with slight fat cover.	
	Tail base	Either a smooth contour or some thickening; possible to feel bony structures under a thin layer of fat.	
	Abdomen	Abdominal tuck; well-proportioned lumbar "waist."	
Score 4 Overweight	Ribs	Difficult to feel, with moderate fat cover.	
	Tail base	Smooth contour or some thickening; still possible to feel the bony structures.	
	Abdomen	Little or no abdominal tuck or "waist;" back slightly broadened.	
Score 5 Obese	Ribs	Very difficult to feel, with thick fat cover.	
	Tail base	Appears thickened; difficult to feel the bony structures.	
	Abdomen	Pendulous, bulging belly, with no "waist;" back markedly broadened; a trough may form on either side of the spine when muscled areas in that region bulge outward.	

FOUR SIMPLE STEPS

Feeding your dog the correct amount is a very simple four-step process.

1. Choose the most complete and balanced dog food you can find.
2. Follow the feeding guidelines on the package.
3. Evaluate your dog every two weeks.
4. Adjust your dog's rations—always do this gradually—until she matches the ideal "score" on the chart above.

With this method, you can continually monitor your dog and adjust how much you feed her in response to the changes in her body and her lifestyle.

DIET WATCH Throughout your dog's life, you should monitor her food requirements to ensure that she always remains at a healthy weight.

Types of Food

A wide range of dog foods is commercially available to suit your dog's palate and your own convenience and budget.

Commercial dog foods come in three basic types (canned, semi-moist and dry), and three quality levels (premium, popular and generic).

Choose a nutritionally balanced food that meets your dog's needs. For instance, all-meat products are extremely palatable but will not provide all your dog's daily vitamin and mineral needs.

CANNED FOOD

Canned food is probably the favorite of most dogs. The palatability and digestibility of canned food make it a wise choice for small dogs that are sometimes finicky, for dogs that have trouble keeping weight on and for those whose teeth are no longer in peak condition.

Canned food contains about 75 percent water, plus a variety of meat, fish and cereal-based products. It is highly palatable and digestible, but its energy content is relatively low, so large dogs require more food to supply their needs. It also spoils quickly once it's opened, so you can't leave it out for your dog all day. If you don't use the full can, you can help keep the remainder appetizing by removing it from the can and wrapping it tightly in plastic, pressing out all the air. This will keep it as fresh as possible and prevent oxidation, which is what makes it unpalatable. Refrigerated in this way, the food will last for two or three days.

PLENTY OF CHOICE Commercial dog foods differ in convenience, cost, moisture content, ingredients, nutritional value and palatablity.

SEMI-MOIST FOOD

Semi-moist foods contain only about 15 to 30 percent water, as well as meat, cereals, vegetable proteins, fat, sugars and colorings. Their energy content is higher than that of canned foods, so smaller amounts can be fed. Semi-moist food also tastes good to dogs, but it's less messy than canned food and doesn't spoil as quickly. There's no need for refrigeration after opening, and packets often come in handy single-serving sizes.

Semi-moist foods have a long shelf life because they are high in sugar and preservatives, and that's their only potential drawback. For healthy dogs, these foods are fine. But dogs with certain diseases, such as diabetes, might do better on canned or dry food.

DRY FOOD

If you want to provide your dog with good nutrition on a budget, dry food is the way to go. Dry foods have the highest energy content and contain only about 10 percent water. Dry foods are crunchy, so they're less likely to accumulate on teeth and contribute to dental tartar and plaque. They're also every bit as nourishing as canned food. Canned dog food that looks like meat is no more nutritious than dry dog food that's made with meat meal or other sources of animal protein. And dry food can be left out all day without spoiling, so your dog can eat whenever he pleases.

If you prefer, you can mix a little canned food in with your dog's dry food. The cost won't be as high as feeding him canned food only, and he will enjoy the extra flavor.

PREMIUM QUALITY For a dog with special feeding requirements—a puppy, a pregnant or lactating dog, or one who has a health condition or is very active—it's probably better to opt for a higher-quality food.

WHAT QUALITY LEVEL?

Premium foods have been developed to give your dog optimal nutrition. They are available through vets and specialty feed and pet stores. Highly digestible, quality ingredients are used. Most such foods are made to fixed formulations, so the ingredients will not vary. They are more costly than popular brands, but less food needs to be fed on a per-weight basis, because of the higher-quality ingredients. This means the cost per serving is comparable to many popular brands. Another advantage of premium foods is that because your dog needs to eat less of them, he will produce less waste for you to clean up.

Popular pet foods are the brands available in grocery stores and supermarkets. Most are of reasonable quality, but the ingredients in a particular brand may vary from batch to batch, based on price and availability of ingredients.

Generic or private label pet foods, available in some grocery and discount stores, may contain only the bare minimum nutrients your dog needs, and the ingredients will vary as market prices change. While the labels on some generic foods say the contents are complete and balanced, the food's nutritional benefits have not necessarily been tested on dogs. While these foods seem low in price, their low nutritional value means that larger quantities must be fed, and any changes in formulation may upset your dog's stomach, causing diarrhea or vomiting. If you do buy a generic food, try to find one that meets the standards set by the organization governing the manufacture of pet food in your country.

HOMEMADE FOOD

For a dog with medical problems or special nutritional requirements, or with allergies to certain foods, colorings or preservatives, a homemade diet can be a good idea. These diets, such as boiled rice and chicken or ground (minced) lamb, can also be used for short-term problems such as upset stomachs that cause vomiting or diarrhea. The bland diet will soothe your dog's stomach.

To prepare your dog's food at home, you'll need lots of time and a recipe that is specially formulated to meet your dog's needs. Homemade food can also work out to be more expensive than commercial types—pet food manufacturers save by bulk purchasing.

Always get a recipe that's tried and true, preferably from a veterinarian or a veterinary technician. The ingredients in a homemade diet should be comparable to what you eat yourself—and everything must be fully cooked. This destroys some vitamins, which is why supplements are sprinkled onto cooked foods.

The greatest pleasure of a dog is that you may make a fool
of yourself with him and not only will he not scold you, but
he will make a fool of himself also.

SAMUEL BUTLER (1835–1902),
English writer

CHAPTER NINE

EXERCISE

The Importance of Exercise

Exercise is much more than just great fun for your dog;

it is also vital for her physical and emotional wellbeing.

As a species, dogs are naturally very active and playful. Their wild relatives spend most of their day hunting for food, defending their territory and playing with each other. Pet dogs, on the other hand, are given all the food they need—and often more—and are frequently confined for most of the day. As a result, many of them tend to become overweight, out of shape and lazy. Lack of exercise can also lead to frustration, which makes many dogs destructive. The key to a happy, healthy dog is exercise.

To create a safe exercise program for your dog, start off slowly, be consistent and patient, and gradually increase her level of activity. Take it especially easy if your dog is still young. Puppies aren't as coordinated as adult dogs. Their muscles aren't fully developed and their bones are softer. They are also more susceptible to heat and cold. Puppies do need some moderate exercise, but serious fitness training in most dogs shouldn't start until after they are about 14 months old That's when the last of the growth plates on their bones close. For giant breeds, such as Great Danes, the closure of growth plates may not occur until they are 22 months old. Increase your young dog's fitness program gradually, over a period of several months.

EXERCISE REQUIREMENTS

All dogs enjoy exercise and play, but the actual amount and type varies according to their age, breed and state of health. Before buying a new dog, get to know the different breeds and the amount of exercise they need. Many dogs, particularly the sporting, herding and working breeds, need regular vigorous exercise. If your work commitments or your health don't permit you to give a dog adequate exercise, it would be irresponsible to take on one of these breeds unless you can arrange for someone to exercise the dog. You would be better off with a toy dog or one of the less active breeds; these can get most of the exercise they need from a gentle walk or an indoor play session.

In general, you should try to give your dog some type of exercise every day, varying the type from time to time. If you have questions about your dog's fitness for exercise, see your veterinarian before starting an exercise program. He or she can check your dog for any health problems (such as heart and joint problems) that may be aggravated by exercise and give you suggestions for a safe exercise regimen. Those breeds that are prone to bloat (see p. 233) should not be exercised immediately before or after meals.

ON THE RUN Young dogs and those of athletic breeds are almost certain to enjoy jogging with you. Make sure they have had a chance to eliminate before you really hit your stride.

OLD FRIENDS Dogs of all ages need regular exercise. It keeps their bodies in condition as well as providing mental stimulation and social interaction.

FORMS OF EXERCISE

Walking is the best all-round form of exercise, providing cardiovascular conditioning and muscle toning. When walking a dog in public, always use a leash. An extendable leash allows your dog plenty of freedom to explore, but also enables you to reel the dog in when necessary.

If your dog is old, out of shape or has health problems, start with a gentle 15-minute walk on a leash each day and gradually increase the duration. Adding a few hills to your walk will further improve her strength and fitness. For young, healthy dogs, leash walks alone may not provide enough exercise. For these dogs, vigorous off-leash activities should be added. However, dogs should only be allowed off the leash if they obey commands and only in safe areas where regulations permit. If your dog enjoys playing with other dogs, organize for them to meet up and play together.

Jogging is another way to exercise energetic, healthy dogs, but use common sense when taking a dog for a run. Don't run with a dog until its skeleton is mature, and avoid running on very hot days. Try to stick to soft surfaces to protect your dog's footpads, especially in the early part of a fitness training program.

Many dogs, particularly the retrieving breeds, love to swim. Swimming is excellent exercise, being gentle on the joints while also building all-over stamina. It's also the best way to condition your dog during the hot summer months. A swim will exercise all her muscles, increase her heart rate and build up her stamina. And your dog will always remain cool—there's no risk of heatstroke when she's in the water. Because swimming doesn't stress the joints, it's especially good for dogs with hip dysplasia and other joint problems.

Be sure that the water is safe before you allow your dog to swim. Never encourage her to jump into an unfamiliar body of water in case she injures herself on hidden obstructions. Beware of undertows and fast currents, too.

GAMES AS EXERCISE

Playing games is one of the best ways to both stimulate your dog's mind and provide vigorous exercise. In addition, it allows you to establish your leadership in an enjoyable

NEW SENSATIONS When possible, take your dog to unusual places, such as a forest, to combine his exercise with the sensory stimulation that unfamiliar sights and sounds will provide.

way. Games of fetch with balls or flying disks are excellent ways to give your dog a good workout without getting yourself too sweaty. The sporting breeds, such as retrievers and spaniels, are naturals at fetch and easily give up objects. Other breeds, such as terriers, are more likely to hold onto things no matter what. All dogs, however, can be taught to drop an object on command.

When playing fetch, choose a toy that your dog likes to put in her mouth. Fleece toys, soft Frisbees, squeaky toys or soft balls are good choices. Avoid small or smooth balls that can be swallowed, and don't pick something edible, such as rawhide.

Tug-of-war games are enjoyed by most dogs and can be combined with a game of fetch as a reward for retrieving. Don't play tug, however, until your dog knows how to drop on command. Otherwise she may get overexcited and become aggressive. Some dogs have aggressive tendencies that can be aggravated by competitive games that have a win-or-lose outcome, such as tug-of-war. If your dog has these tendencies, avoid such games. On the other hand, the confidence of a timid dog may be improved by allowing her to win the occasional competitive game.

To prevent boredom for both of you, and to give your dog the best chance of an all-round workout, vary the types of exercise she does. Be guided by your dog's breed and preferences; if one type of sport or game doesn't seem to agree with her either mentally or physically, try something else. Always quit while your dog is having fun, and don't overtire her.

EXERCISE PRECAUTIONS

During most activities, your dog will run faster, work harder and cover more ground than you do. She may have so much enthusiasm that she keeps going past the point of exhaustion, just because she thinks you want her to. It's up to you to use common sense, practice moderation, and watch her for signs of fatigue or for difficulty in breathing. When in doubt, call a halt and give her time to recover. You should also make sure that she warms up and cools down correctly. Avoid fetch games on hot days as they compromise your dog's ability to pant.

Warming Up and Cooling Down

Before exercising, dogs, just like people, should always start with some gentle stretches. Doing a warm-up is the best way to protect against muscle strains and other pains. Begin all your dog's exercise sessions with a gentle warm-up, between five and ten minutes long. This helps prevent injury by stretching the tendons and ligaments, and getting the blood flowing to the muscles. Start with an unhurried walk for several minutes, then do some stretching exercises; for example, by bending and straightening each of your dog's legs a few times.

A leisurely saunter, followed by a few stretches, is the perfect way to bring another session of fun to an end and give your dog's body time to slow down again. Vigorous exercise should never stop suddenly. Cooling down is just as important as warming up.

Heatstroke

Dogs don't have a very efficient way of keeping cool, and can succumb all too easily to heatstroke during hot weather. Avoid exercising your dog too vigorously in the heat of the day, and in particularly hot weather,

THREE CAN PLAY If you have more than one dog, they will burn off some of their energy playing with each other, but will still need regular exercise from you.

INSIDE JOB Many toy dogs, such as Pomeranians, may be able to get much of their exercise running around an apartment.

be sure to keep her routine pretty relaxed. If she appears distressed and you suspect heatstroke—for example, her sides are heaving or she can hardly stand—stop immediately and follow the steps in "Heatstroke" on p. 292.

Pad Problems

While a dog's paws are strong and sturdy, they are also unprotected from things that you, in your socks and shoes, don't even notice. Exercise your dog during the coolest time of the day throughout the summer months, and consider the temperature of the pavement before you step out. Place your hand on it for several seconds to make sure it's okay. If it is still hot from the sun, it will burn her pads.

Winter brings different pad problems. Road salt, unlike ordinary salt, can burn your dog's feet. (It can also burn her mouth if she bites at her feet, and her belly if she kicks salt on herself while trotting along.) Road sand isn't any better. The chemicals it contains to melt ice can also burn her feet. To prevent pad

ALL IN A DAY'S WORK Working dogs, such as this Border Collie mix, will get all their exercise requirements from their daily tasks.

problems, towel off her chest, underbelly and feet when you get home. This will remove any snow and chemical residues between her toes.

When your dog plays in clean snow, take the normal precautions against frostbite, such as not letting her stay outside for too long on ice-encrusted snow or when there is a big wind-chill factor. Check for cracked pads or tiny cuts on her pads afterwards.

Dogs' pads sometimes become dry in the winter, just as our hands do, and a daily dab of Vaseline can be very soothing. For more information on preventing and treating treating sore or injured pads, see p. 262.

ORGANIZED ACTIVITIES

If you and your dog are bored with the same old walk around the neighborhood or if throwing a ball has lost its spark, organized dog activities may be exactly the inspiration the two of you need. Here are some things you might want to try.

Obedience

In novice obedience, dogs are judged on their ability to "Heel" at all speeds, "Come" when they're called, "Sit-stay," "Down-stay" and

EXERCISE ON THE FLY Most dogs love vigorous games, such as catching a flying disk.

stand for a judge's examination. Advanced obedience trials include retrieving over hurdles, obeying hand signals, scent discrimination and more.

Even if competitive events aren't your thing, attending obedience classes and practicing what you have learned exercises your dog's mind and body, gently reinforces your leadership and often turns problem pets into great companions.

Agility

Agility trials are one of the most enjoyable ways to exercise your dog. These timed events involve directing your dog through a course complete with a colorful variety of planks, jumps, tunnels and other obstacles. The training required practically guarantees that your dog will be in tip-top condition. Mixed breeds and purebreds can compete at events organized by various national or local canine organizations.

Lure Coursing

If your dog is a sight hound breed, such as a Saluki or Afghan Hound, she's a natural for the fast and physically demanding sport of lure coursing. When slipped, or released, by their owners at the hunter's command, three hounds will race off to chase the lure. The lure changes direction several times over the 800-yard (800-m) course and the dogs are judged on speed, agility, stamina, enthusiasm and ability to follow. To keep them in peak condition, most lure-coursing enthusiasts run their dogs nearly every day.

UP AND OVER Agility trials are a fun way to give your dog an exercise session with plenty of variety.

Herding Trials

In herding trials, dogs are evaluated on their ability to round up sheep, ducks or cattle and bring them through gates to a pen. This requires quickness, stamina and obedience, a combination to keep your dog in lean and hard condition.

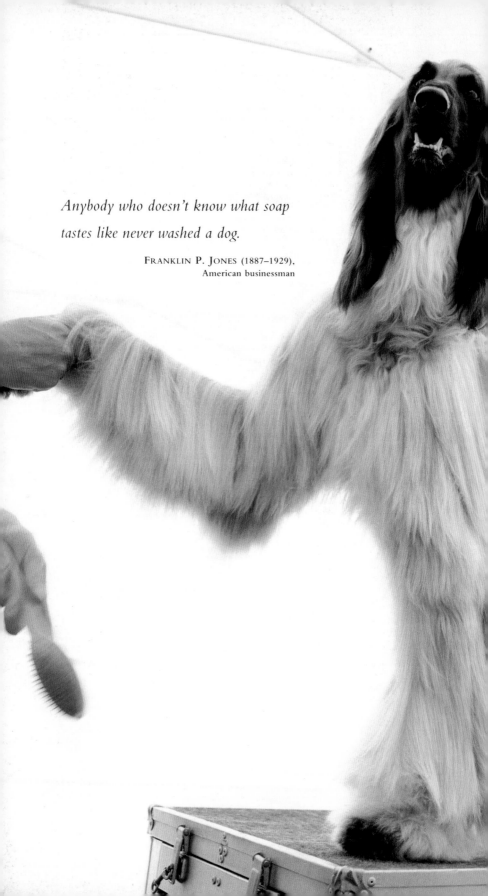

Anybody who doesn't know what soap tastes like never washed a dog.

FRANKLIN P. JONES (1887–1929),
American businessman

CHAPTER TEN

GROOMING

The Importance of Grooming

Grooming isn't just a matter of looking good;

it's vital for your dog's health and hygiene.

Regular grooming keeps your dog clean and looking her best. It also keeps shedding to a minimum and gives you the chance to inspect your dog to make sure her skin, teeth, ears, eyes and nails are healthy.

GROOMING TOOLS (From top) A combined bristle brush and pin brush; a fine-tooth comb; and blunt-ended scissors for trimming.

SHEDDING CYCLES

Most domestic dogs shed, or "blow," their coats at least once a year. Wild dogs usually do so twice a year, in spring and fall. It used to be thought that shedding was prompted by changes in temperature, but research has shown that shedding is more influenced by changes in surrounding light. The more they are exposed to light, the more dogs shed. This is why indoor dogs, exposed to long hours of artificial light, tend to shed all year round.

Other factors can influence shedding. Female dogs shed more after estrus, during pregnancy and especially while lactating.

Some dogs have double coats, consisting of a short undercoat of woolly hair and a longer outercoat of guard hair. Such breeds as Corgis, German Shepherds, Rottweilers and Labradors have short double coats; Chow Chows, Collies, Shetland Sheepdogs and Samoyeds have long double coats. When a dog with a double coat starts to shed, it may look as though it has a skin disease. This is because the undercoat is not shed uniformly but in patches, resulting in a moth-eaten look. This may seem alarming but is completely normal.

LOW MAINTENANCE Dogs with short, smooth coats, such as Dobermans, are among the easiest to groom. Just a few minutes a week will have their coats gleaming.

GETTING YOUR DOG USED TO GROOMING

Because grooming is so important, it's vital that you teach your dog to tolerate it as soon as you bring her home. Even if she's just a tiny puppy, spend time gently brushing her coat with a soft brush and handling her paws. An early start such as this will make your pup regard your grooming simply as a continuation of her mother's grooming. Talk to her all the while and give her the occasional treat so that her grooming sessions seem like enjoyable time spent with you, not a punishment. If she learns when she is young that grooming is a part of everyday life, she will be more cooperative when she's grown. If your new dog is already an adult, spend some time each day before meals teaching her how to be handled (see p. 130).

TOOLS OF THE TRADE

Buy the appropriate grooming equipment for your dog's coat type. Using the wrong tools will be ineffective and frustrating for you and possibly uncomfortable for your dog, making her reluctant to let you groom her in future.

If you bought your dog from a breeder, ask the breeder to give you a lesson in grooming. Most breeders are experienced in grooming dogs and their tips and expertise can be invaluable, especially if you want your dog to have the textbook look for her breed.

Bristle Brushes

These are good for stimulating your dog's skin and spreading the natural oils that help to keep her coat shiny and her skin healthy. They are best used on dogs with short coats, since they don't do a good job of penetrating longer coats.

Pin Brushes

The pin brush has long, straight metal pins attached to a rubber backing. Most pin brushes are oval-shaped and are used primarily on long-coated breeds. They are excellent for fluff-drying dogs with long hair.

Slicker Brush

This is the most versatile brush; it works with many different coat types. Its bent wire bristles grasp and remove a dog's loose undercoat. Dogs that are brushed regularly with a slicker brush seldom become matted.

Combs

Larger-toothed combs are used to remove undercoat in some of the heavier-coated breeds, while finer combs can be used to test the undercoat after grooming to see if there are still more loose hairs that need to be removed. The best combs for dogs are special canine combs with metal teeth that are rounded to avoid damage to the skin.

Stripping Combs

These are commonly used on terriers and other breeds with wiry coats to tidy them up. Proper use of a stripping comb requires considerable skill; this task is perhaps best left to a professional groomer.

Hound Gloves

Some people prefer to groom their dogs with a hound glove instead of a brush. These brushes fit over the hand like a glove and feature a cloth base with rubber nubs that capture grease and loose hair. A hound glove gives a dog's coat a polished look. Dogs usually enjoy being groomed with hound gloves because they like the feeling that they are being petted. The hair can be easily removed by hand, and the grease washed out with detergent.

MEDIUM LENGTH COAT A Border Collie's longish double coat will require a slicker brush or pin brush and a wide-tooth comb.

EXTENSIVE GROOMING Lhasa Apsos have long coarse coats that easily become tangled and matted.

Dematting Tools

These combs and splitters come in a variety of shapes and styles, all designed to saw through mats in your dog's coat without your having to cut them off. Some skill is required to use them properly, or your dog could end up looking rather shaggy.

DIFFERENT TECHNIQUES FOR DIFFERENT BREEDS

There is a basic technique for grooming each of the various coat types found in dogs. Even if you don't have a purebred, your dog will still benefit from the proper treatment of her coat.

There are three main aspects to grooming a dog's coat: brushing, combing and clipping. Your dog's breed will determine what technique you will need to use. For example, a Poodle will need an extensive workout with clippers, while a Labrador Retriever can happily get by with nothing more than a good brushing.

WORTH THE EFFORT Some dogs bred for cold climates, such as Samoyeds (right) and Rough Collies, have long double coats. These require extensive daily grooming, but the results are spectacular.

Of most importance in grooming is using the correct type of brushing technique and the right brush or comb for your dog's type of coat. All dog coats fit into one of the following categories. If your dog is a mixed breed, she will also fit into one of these categories, depending on the breed that is most dominant in her genetic makeup.

Short Smooth Coat

There is no undercoat to this type of coat. Pugs, Basenjis and Doberman Pinschers have short smooth coats.

These are probably the easiest coats to groom. Using a bristle brush or a hound glove, first brush against the direction your dog's hair lies, then brush again in the direction the coat lies. A once-a-week brushing will keep shedding under control, and an occasional wipe with a damp cloth or chamois will make the coat gleam.

Short Double Coat

This is a flat coat with straight, coarse hair over a soft, thin undercoat beneath. Labradors and Rottweilers have this type of coat.

These coats require more care, since the double coat underneath sheds constantly, with an even greater loss of hair in spring and fall. Using your hand, start by separating sections of your dog's coat so there is a parting where her skin is visible. Then use a slicker brush or pin brush to brush out the undercoat, brushing outward from the skin. The undercoat will be thickest at the front of the neck and the back of the hind legs.

Once you have finished doing the undercoat, use the same brush to go over the top coat, brushing in the direction that the coat lies. Brush your dog twice a week, increasing this to several times a week during the shedding season.

Short Wiry Coat

Dogs with short wiry coats have hair that is thick and hard, and somewhat bristly to the touch. Wirehaired Dachshunds, Schnauzers and many terriers have this type of coat.

A slicker brush, a medium-tooth metal comb and a stripping comb are needed to groom this type of coat. Start by running the stripping comb lightly along the back of the dog, going in the direction that the hair lies.

FINISHING TOUCHES Once you've brushed a short-haired dog such as this Kelpie mix, a wipe over with a damp cloth will remove stray hairs and add shine.

LONG AND LUSTROUS Silky Terriers have long silky coats that are not easy to groom. Most pet dogs with this coat type are clipped for ease of maintenance.

CURLY CLIP Bedlington Terriers do not shed, and need to be clipped every few weeks. In show dogs, the ears are shaved and a tassel left on the ends.

This thins out the overgrown wiry coat. Be sure not to thin it out too much. This thinning does not need to be done at every grooming session, only when the hairs on the very top of the dogs' coat (called the guard hairs) begin to protrude along her back. Overgrown guard hairs will curl up above the rest of the hair and give the dog an unkempt look.

After thinning out, brush the coat in layers, from the skin outward, with the slicker brush. You can then comb in layers in the same way with the metal comb, which will pick up any loose hairs.

A wiry coat will also need to be carded and hand-stripped regularly. Carding is a technique whereby loose hair is removed by "brushing" the coat with a blade or stripping stone. Hand-stripping is a technique in which the loose hairs are grasped between finger and thumb and tugged out. While you can eventually learn to do these procedures yourself, you should start by having them done by someone experienced— a poor carding or hand-stripping job can leave your dog looking and feeling terrible.

Curly Coat
This coat has close curls that are thick and soft. Poodles, Bichon Frises and Bedlington Terriers have curly coats.

The typical curly coat needs regular brushing to keep its neat, curly look.

Whether your dog is clipped in a modified show clip or a puppy clip (best done by a professional groomer; see p. 202), you will need to use a slicker brush to brush the coat against the way it grows to make it fluff up away from the body. If your dog's coat has started to look unruly, it may be time to go back to a professional groomer for another clip. Never attempt to do the job yourself unless you are experienced in this art.

Long Silky Coat
There is no undercoat with this kind of coat. Yorkshire, Maltese and Silky Terriers have long silky coats.

Long silky coats are difficult to care for because they form mats readily. In dogs that are not shown, these coats are usually clipped to keep grooming to a minimum. If you want to keep this coat long, you'll need to spend considerable time grooming it, at least two or three times a week.

LOOKING GOOD A Rottweilers' short double coat can be kept in good condition by grooming at least twice a week with a brush or hound glove.

The biggest challenge in grooming a long silky coat is dealing with the mats that often form around the legs, ears, side of the face or anywhere else where the hair is particularly long. To remove mats, use a dematting tool, then brush the entire coat with a slicker brush in the direction the hair lies.

Long Coarse Coat

Mixed into the long outer coat is a softer undercoat. Dogs with this coat include the Shih Tzu, Lhasa Apso and Tibetan Terrier.

This coat is one of the more time-consuming types to groom. It easily becomes tangled and matted, so most pet owners have it clipped regularly to minimise grooming. If you don't wish to clip, be prepared to make a big commitment in time and energy.

First, tell your dog to lie down on her side. Remove any mats that you find (see p. 201), being careful not to break the hairs as you do so. You can also sprinkle some cornstarch on the tangles to make them easier to separate. With a pin brush, brush the coat out gently in the direction that it grows. Once you have pinbrushed the entire coat, go over it again with a soft bristle brush.

If you want to trim the long hair that is sticking out of your dog's ears, do this before you bathe her. Don't clip it too close, and make sure to keep the cut hair from falling back into your dog's ear canal.

Long Double Coat

This combines a long, straight and coarse outer coat with a very thick undercoat all over the body. Samoyeds, Chow Chows and Collies have long double coats.

With a thick undercoat as their trademark, these coats are the ones that shed the most. You will need a slicker brush or pin brush and a large, wide-tooth comb for this coat type.

Brush your dog's entire body with the slicker or pin brush first, taking sections of her hair and separating it with your hand. Brush outward from the skin to remove loose hairs in the thick undercoat. After you have gone over her entire coat, take the wide-tooth comb and place it deep within the coat, parallel to the skin. Comb outward in this way to remove more loose undercoat. The undercoat is thickest on the back legs and around the neck, so if you have been inattentive to your dog's grooming needs, you may need to work through some mats here using a dematting tool.

AN ELEGANT COAT The Afghan Hound's luxuriant silky coat requires 15 to 20 minutes' combing and brushing a day.

SKIN DEEP If you have a hairless dog, such as a Chinese Crested, daily skin care is essential.

Hairless Coat

The Chinese Crested, Xoloitzcuintli (Mexican Hairless) and Inca Orchid are breeds of hairless dogs. Despite having little or no hair, their sensitive skins still need regular grooming.

Dogs with no hair obviously don't need regular brushing, but they do need to be bathed about once a month. Use a gentle shampoo, preferably one with an antibacterial agent, to help ward off the skin problems such as seborrhea that are common in these breeds.

About every week or so, it is beneficial to give hairless dogs a gentle scrub with a soft face puff while shampooing. This will help their circulation and get rid of dead skin cells. As with other dogs, great care should be taken to rinse hairless dogs thoroughly after a bath.

After their bath, and every day, hairless dogs should always be moisturized with an oil-free moisturizer. These breeds are also very prone to sunburn and you should apply an SPF (sun protection factor) 15 or higher sunblock all over, whenever they go outside.

Since not all hairless dogs are completely hairless, you can use a regular safety razor to remove any existing light body hair. On breeds where tufts of hair are found on the top of the head, legs and tail, such as the Chinese Crested, use a slicker brush to groom these areas. The Chinese Crested also comes in a Powderpuff variety, which has a long coarse coat that should be groomed frequently to avoid matting.

SILVER GHOST
The distinctive silvery coat of the Weimeraner is short, smooth and easy to groom.

REMOVING BURRS AND MATS

Sticky burrs and tangled mats are a problem for canine coats, especially for those dogs who love to play hard. If your dog swims, then she will have the biggest problem with mats because water causes a dog's fur to stick together. If your dog has a long coat, silky coat or thick double coat, burrs and mats will be a recurring problem, and you will need to know how to get rid of them.

Burrs and mats should be removed with a dematting tool and a slicker brush. The

dematting tool

burrs can usually be brushed out once the mats are broken up. The dematting tool will cut through the mats, separating them, and then a slicker brush can be used to brush the mat out. If the mats are too tight, use a mat-splitting tool. This cuts through the length of the hair instead of across it. Use a small slicker brush to brush a few hairs at a time gently from the tangle.

Some groomers recommend applying a chemical substance, such as a silicone-based mat spray, to a mat or burr before trying to remove it, and then patiently using old-fashioned elbow grease to work the

mat out. This manual method takes time, but causes the least trauma to your dog's coat and skin.

Whatever you do, don't bathe your dog until every mat has first been removed from her coat. Once a mat gets wet, it tightens and becomes harder to remove. Also, when a badly matted dog is bathed, the shampoo gets trapped in the mats and can't be rinsed out properly. This can result in skin irritation.

Sometimes dogs are so matted or covered in burrs that it's more practical to clip the coat and start over. If a mat is touching the skin, it is usually best to clip the dog.

Clipping

Many breeds of dogs can benefit from some tidying up with clippers, whether at home or at the salon.

Although the mastery of the art of clipping belongs to the professional groomer, you too can use these instruments to groom your dog and make him look good.

Most breeds never need clipping at all. If your dog does need to be clipped, the extent will depend on his breed and coat type.

NEED A CLIP?

The breed that requires the most clipping is the Poodle. This is because a Poodle's coat grows continuously and hardly sheds. The finely dolled-up Poodles you see at dog shows have their hair clipped down to the skin in places, and shaped and molded in others. This high-maintenance show clip (known as the lion clip) is not practical for most pet Poodles, but even the more informal "puppy" or "lamb" cut requires clipping.

Other breeds that are regularly clipped include the Bichon Frise, Bedlington Terrier, Kerry Blue Terrier, Bouvier des Flandres, Schnauzer and Airedale Terrier. While these breeds need less clipping than a Poodle, they do need shaping to keep them looking their best.

If your dog is of a breed that needs clipping, but you don't intend to show him, you will be better off keeping him in a simple clip that makes him look good but is relatively easy to maintain.

START THEM YOUNG If your dog is of a breed that will need to be clipped regularly, such as this West Highland White Terrier puppy, it's best to start getting him used to the procedure while he's still young.

Practice Makes Perfect

If you want to do the clipping yourself instead of taking your dog to a professional groomer, you will need plenty of practice—it takes considerable skill to clip a dog's coat properly. You may even decide to take a course on dog grooming; or, if you've been taking your dog to a professional groomer, you could ask her to teach you how to clip.

One of the most important things to be aware of is that you must always cut with the hair, not against it. Cutting against the grain of the hair can result in cuts and burns on your dog's skin.

Clippers and Blades

If you decide to invest in your own clippers, narrow your selection down to the two basic types that professional groomers use: standard clippers and small clippers. Standard clippers

CUTE AND CURLY To achieve the stylized look of the Bichon Frise, the puffy white coat is usually cut with scissors to follow the contours of the body, and is then brushed out to a soft cloud.

THE RIGHT EQUIPMENT Buy clippers from pet supply stores or pet supply catalogs; those from department stores can't cope with thick hair, such as that of Cocker Spaniels.

are used for all-around grooming. Small clippers, ones about the size of mustache clippers, are used on the face, ears and feet of some breeds.

Clippers are available from pet supply catalogs and at a few pet supply stores. The dog clippers that you find in department stores won't work on most dogs. They come with a blade that is designed to only cut clean Poodle hair. They will not cut any dog hair that is dirty, and will bind up on Cocker Spaniels or any other thick-haired dogs.

NEAT AND NATTY Schnauzers, as well as many other wire-haired breeds, should be clipped regularly. Their eyebrows and beards can be trimmed with scissors.

Ask your groomer to help you purchase some decent clippers and blades. Be sure to get a number 10 blade for the stomach, feet, face and genital area, and a number 7F blade for clipping the body. The number 7F is good for all coat types, from Poodles to Chow Chows. If your dog needs regular clipping, the clippers and blades may pay for themselves in a matter of months.

THE LION CLIP

The highly sculpted lion clip was developed to lighten a dog's coat for swimming while protecting the joints and major organs. It is now a popular show clip for certain breeds.

Toy Poodle

Lowchen

Bathing

If your dog looks, smells or feels dirty, he probably is,

and it's time to give him a bath.

A dog that spends a lot of time outside tends to get dirtier than an indoor dog, but most dogs are bathed at least two or three times a year. The skin is the largest organ on a dog's body and it's important to maintain cleanliness to keep the skin healthy.

Dogs with thick, double coats, such as Samoyeds and Chow Chows, rarely need washing. The main thing is to brush them regularly. This distributes the natural oils, gets rid of dirt and loose hair and prevents matting.

Most dogs have naturally waterproof coats. It's best not to bathe them too often because you could reduce the coat's ability to repel water—which is important in a dog that swims a great deal, lives in a cool climate or is kept outside.

In between baths, regular brushing will remove dead hair and any accumulated dirt, and wiping your dog's coat down with distilled water and a towel will help control allergy-inducing dander.

BATHING TECHNIQUES

Where you bath your dog—laundry tub, bathtub or outside—depends on his size and your own preference. The high sides of a laundry tub may deter any escape plans, and having the dog at this height is also easier on your back and knees. Or you may prefer to bathe him in the yard if the weather is warm.

Before bathing your dog, you need to brush him. This is useful for shorthaired dogs because it removes dead hair and loosens dirt, making it easier to wash away. For all other

dogs, especially those with double coats, brushing before bathing is essential to remove all mats, on both the face and the body.

If you try to bathe a dog that has mats in his coat, you will never get his hair clean. You will also hurt him, since the mats will pull tighter as they dry. You also risk trapping moisture against your dog's skin, which can cause skin problems.

If you've brushed and brushed and you can't get the mats out, even with a dematting tool (see p. 201), it's time to seek professional help from a groomer.

Soaping Up, Rinsing Off

Your dog's bath water should be about the temperature you'd use for a baby, or even a little cooler. Use a shampoo especially formulated for dogs, because the pH level of their skin differs from that of humans. Work the shampoo into your dog's coat with your fingers or a bathing mitt. Work it in all over his body, up onto his head—take care not to get any soap in his eyes—under his chin and neck, under his belly and bottom, right down to his toes.

If your dog is going through a spell of profuse shedding, a bath can be the best way to control the situation. After soaping him up, pull a slicker brush through his coat. Great clumps of hair will come out; keep at it until you're not getting any more.

Finally, rinse your dog thoroughly, and don't forget his feet. Any soap left on his skin or between his toes will irritate him.

After rinsing, some groomers recommend applying a conditioner to compensate for any loss of his coat's natural oils. There are various different kinds. The easiest ones are left in, while the others must be rinsed out.

PROFESSIONAL FINISH Blow-drying a long coat prevents matts. It will stop your dog from getting cold, too.

THE TASK IN HAND If the weather is warm, bathing your dog outside will minimize mess.

Drying Your Dog

Getting your dog completely dry is as important as getting him completely clean, especially if he has a long or double coat. If you let such a dog just dry naturally, the hair will often mat right up.

Shorthaired or hairless dogs won't mat, but they will still need to be thoroughly dried so they don't get cold. Usually a good toweling off and several hours inside a warm house is enough to do the job.

With an older dog, whatever his coat type, make sure you dry him as well as possible and keep him in a warm room for a few hours. You don't want him getting cold, and if he has an arthritic condition like hip or elbow dysplasia, a damp coat will only add to his discomfort.

Double-coated or longhaired dogs will also need a blow-dry, but a human hairdryer isn't suited to the task. Hair dryers for people get too hot and can burn a dog, plus they don't have sufficient power to get a dog dry.

You can get a good portable hair dryer, ideal for home use, for a reasonable price from a pet supply store, or check advertisements in dog magazines or mail-order catalogs. Or, you could take your dog to a groomer for his wash and blow-dry—although the cost of a year's grooming fees will probably be the same as the amount you'll pay for a canine hair dryer.

SNIFFING OUT PROBLEMS

If your dog starts smelling unpleasant, it may not be his coat that's causing the problem. Even if it is, a bath may not be the best solution. Give him a sniff test to discover the source of the smell first.

- Drop-eared dogs can start to smell simply because their ears are dirty. The warm, moist environment under the ear flap is perfect for fungal or bacterial growth. Cleaning his ears may be all you need do to quell the smell.
- A bad smell coming from your dog's mouth could signal canine dental disease, which will require a vet's attention.
- Not everything a dog eats comes out in his waste. Some of it is exuded through the skin, making his coat smelly. Feed your dog a high-quality food, and make sure he stays away from garbage in all its forms.
- Many longhaired breeds can get a doggy smell because of mats or dead hair trapped in their coats. Always be sure to remove all the mats out before washing your dog.
- The hair around your dog's rear end can trap a lot of dirt that will give off a bad odor. Many groomers suggest you clip the hair in this area if you don't plan to show your dog.
- A dog's anal sacs (see p. 230) can sometimes leak and release a very unpleasant fishy odor.

If your dog smells for no obvious reason, it's best to call your vet. Some odors can be symptoms of medical problems, and he may need a checkup.

Special Care Areas

Grooming isn't just about bathing and brushing—your dog's face,

eyes, ears, feet and teeth need regular attention, too.

Certain types of dogs require attention to certain areas, notably those with particularly hairy or creased faces, and those with weepy eyes. And whatever breed or mix your dog is, take good care of his ears and feet.

FACE FIRST

If you have a dog with lots of hair on his face, make sure that his face stays clean. Accumulated food or saliva will stain his hair and can cause skin irritations, so you may need to wash and dry your dog's beard and mustache after every meal.

For any dog with a wrinkled face, such as a Pug, Boxer or Shar-Pei, you will need to take extra precautions. The tight facial creases need to be thoroughly cleaned and dried at least once a week to prevent irritation or such conditions as eczema from developing inside the folds. To do this, dip a piece of paper towel or a cotton-tipped swab in hydrogen peroxide and wipe inside the folds. Then go back over with a clean, dry towel or swab to remove any moisture.

While you're dealing with your dog's face, have a quick look at his nose. It should be moist, not dry or cracked. A discharge or loss of pigmentation is not normal and should be checked out by your vet.

CLEAN EARS

Healthy ears are pink and fresh looking, without a noticeable smell. When the ears look dirty or inflamed, or there's an unpleasant smell coming from them, you can be pretty sure there's a problem.

EAR PATROL Remove excess wax and moisture from your dog's ears with a cotton ball or piece of gauze.

CHECKING FOR PROBLEMS Using a flashlight, look inside your dog's ears to check for any foreign objects, excess wax buildup or signs of infection.

The more hair in your dog's ears, the more chance there is of dampness and possible infection. Dogs that accumulate hair in the ear canal, such as Poodles and Lhasa Apsos, need to have that hair removed by grasping a few hairs at a time with either fingers or tweezers, and pulling gently. Gripping the hairs can be made easier by the use of commercial powders specially made for the purpose.

Alternatively, you can trim the ear hair with blunt-nosed scissors. Make sure you keep the cut strands from falling into your dog's ear, as it will cause irritation. If your dog won't sit still long enough for you to do this, take him to a professional groomer. You don't want to hurt him with the scissors while he is struggling.

Your dog's ears should be cleaned at least once a month, even if you don't bathe him that often. Dogs with floppy ears are especially prone to ear problems because the shape of their ear flaps prevents good air circulation. If you have such a dog, be especially diligent about checking and cleaning the insides of the ears. However, some wax needs to remain in the ears, so don't overdo it. If your dog's ears

POWDER HOUND After your dog has spent time in the snow, check her paws for damage or for clumps of ice between the pads.

seem particularly dirty, dampen a cloth with mineral oil or use a cotton ball and a commercial ear cleaner to wipe the inside of the earflap. If the dirty appearance returns in a week or so, your dog may have an ear infection and will need to see a vet.

If your dog has long, floppy ears, you may find that they hang in his food bowl when he eats. Some owners of long-eared dogs get around this problem by using bowls with narrow openings or by slipping a tube of stretchy or knitted fabric over the dog's head and neck while he feeds, to hold his ears out of the way. It should be just firm enough to restrain the ears—not uncomfortably tight.

CLEAN EYES

To keep your dog's eyes sparkling and clear, wipe them with a cotton ball dipped in lukewarm water (tap water is fine). This will get rid of any discharge that may have built up

WATCH THE WRINKLES Dogs with heavily creased faces, such as Boston Terriers (right), Pugs and Mastiffs, should have the creases cleaned regularly.

in the corners. If your dog has weepy eyes or a pale coat that stains easily, you may need to wash his eyes frequently, not just when you give him a bath.

Mostly, a wipe with water is all that is needed to remove debris from under your dog's eyes and on his cheeks. But to remove any matter that may have dried into his coat, use a baby's toothbrush. It is soft, so it will do no harm if you accidentally touch your dog's eye (although it will make him flinch), yet the bristles will remove more matter than a cloth, which will press the debris in deeper.

If your dog has hair that falls into his eyes, use a rubber band or a clip to pull it back. Or cut it with blunt-nosed scissors, taking care

examine the paws for blisters, cracks in the pads, redness on the webs between the toes, or objects such as burrs that may have become lodged there. If you find anything, remove it with a pair of tweezers.

If your dog is favoring one leg, there could be a paw injury. If the problem persists or your dog is in obvious pain, see your vet. The problem could be something as simple as a seed or burr caught between the toes, or it could be something more serious.

Nails are prone to injury, too. When a dog's nails get too long, they can crack, tear or become caught on things. Broken nails can be excruciatingly painful.

not to let the cut strands fall into the eyes. When you clean your dog's eyes, take a close look at them to check for anything unusual. If you see any redness, cloudiness, swelling or excess weepiness, take your dog to the vet.

NEAT FEET

Basic paw care is a vital part of your dog's health care routine. Your dog's feet probably take more of a pounding than any other part of his body—from hard concrete, hot pavement and jagged ice, to snow, rocks, sharp pieces of wood and other objects in his path.

Rubbing vitamin E and juice from an aloe plant onto the paws, both before and after taking him for a walk, will prevent some damage. Inspect the feet after each outing;

Clipping Between the Toes

With most medium- to longhaired dogs, it is important to keep the hair between the toes cut, because this space often hides dirt, burrs, fleas and tiny mats. Your dog may take to chewing on her feet, which soon becomes a habit that is hard to break.

TOOTH CARE A variety of chew toys will help reduce plaque buildup on your dog's teeth.

EXTRA CARE This Gordon Setter's long, hairy ears and furry paws will need special attention.

memory. Or look under the nail; you will see a groove running from the tip up toward the foot. The end of this groove is generally where the quick begins. If you cut no farther than that, you should not cut into the quick.

Be conservative in your cutting. Cut only a tiny amount at a time, and keep some styptic powder handy in case you cut into the quick. Sprinkling this over the cut area will quickly stop the bleeding.

CLEAN TEETH

An important, but often overlooked, part of your dog's daily grooming routine is the brushing of her teeth. Poor dental hygiene can lead to a number of diseases.

If you don't brush your dog's teeth regularly, plaque builds up on her teeth and under her gums. If this is not removed, a bacterial infection, called periodontal disease, can develop. If left untreated, the infection can enter the bloodstream and potentially spread to your dog's kidney, liver, heart or brain. Other problems, such as mouth abscesses and loose teeth, can also develop in dogs that don't have good dental hygiene. And dogs with dirty teeth and periodontal disease will have very bad breath. One way to avoid these problems is to brush your dog's teeth daily (see pp. 240–41). Your dog should also be examined once a year by your vet, who may recommend a professional cleaning.

Dogs also have hair between the foot pads. This is more difficult to cut, but it's a good idea to keep it trimmed also.

Use a small pair of blunt-ended baby fingernail scissors. Hold the foot up and separate the pads with one hand while carefully trimming the hair as close as possible to the pads.

Clipping the Nails

Nail-trimming is vital for a dog's health and comfort; it will be painful for her to walk with neglected nails. Cut the nail just at the point where it starts to curve downward. You want to avoid the quick, the area of the nail that contains nerves and blood vessels and that will be very painful if cut into.

If your dog has white nails, look for the pink line that extends from the base of the nail down toward the tip. When you trim, clip below this pink line so you don't cut into it. For dogs with dark nails, finding the quick is trickier. Hold a flashlight up to the nail to get an idea where the quick ends, then go by

DENTAL HYGIENE Regular home dental care keeps your dog's teeth clean, his gums healthy and his breath pleasant. This terrier mix's owner is using a piece of gauze to clean her dog's teeth.

In life the firmest friend,

The first to welcome, foremost to defend.

LORD BYRON (1788–1824),
English poet

CHAPTER ELEVEN

HEALTH

Health Basics

If your dog is to have a long and healthy life, she needs plenty of exercise, a well-balanced diet and preventive health care.

Puppies are susceptible to several life-threatening contagious diseases that are easily prevented through vaccination. After getting a puppy, you should take her to a vet as soon as possible. Ask your dog-owning friends to recommend a good veterinarian or call your local humane society or veterinary association for a referral. At the first visit, your vet will give your pup a thorough physical examination to make sure she is healthy, will probably check her feces for intestinal parasites and will certainly set up a vaccination schedule for you to follow.

VACCINATION

Most vaccines are given two or three times at three-to-four week intervals until the puppy is 12 to 16 weeks old (see chart, below). The vaccines are given several times because most puppies carry temporary protection (antibodies) from their mothers that may interfere with their ability to develop their own protection.

Most vaccines are boosted annually. Bear in mind that your puppy is not fully protected until she has received all of her puppy vaccines. Until she is fully immunized, don't

VACCINATION SCHEDULE

DISEASE	AGE AT FIRST SHOT	AGE AT SECOND SHOT	AGE AT THIRD SHOT	BOOSTER
Canine distemper A usually fatal viral disease that causes respiratory, gastrointestinal and nervous system problems	6–10 weeks	10–12 weeks	14–16 weeks	12 months
Infectious canine hepatitis (CAV-1 or CAV-2) A viral disease of the liver	6–8 weeks	10–12 weeks	14–16 weeks	12 months
Canine parvovirus A dangerous and sometimes deadly (especially in puppies) intestinal disease	6–8 weeks	10–12 weeks	14–16 weeks	12 months*
Bordetellosis A bacterial infection of the respiratory system that often follows any of a number of viral respiratory infections	6–8 weeks	10–12 weeks	14–16 weeks	12 months
Parainfluenza A virus that is part of the group of viruses and bacteria known to cause kennel cough, the canine equivalent of the human cold	6–8 weeks	10–12 weeks	14–16 weeks	12 months*
Leptospirosis A bacterial disease that affects the liver and kidneys	10–12 weeks	14–16 weeks	—	12 months
Rabies A deadly viral disease of the nervous system that affects all mammals, including humans. May be difficult to detect	12 weeks	64 weeks	—	12 or 36 months**
Coronavirus A contagious intestinal disease causing diarrhea	6–8 weeks	10–12 weeks	12–14 weeks	12 months

* Some veterinarians recommend a booster at 6 months of age for some breeds, such as Rottweilers
** Check with your veterinarian as to type of vaccine

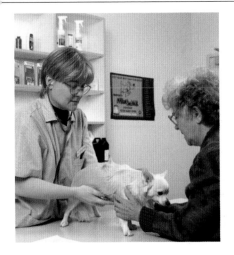

BETTER SAFE THAN SORRY Her annual check-up is a good time for your dog to have her annual booster vaccinations. Vaccines for many of the common canine diseases are given together in one injection.

YOUR DOG-CARE DIARY

Keeping a notebook of your dog's health can pay off when she gets sick. Your dog's health diary can help you to remember when she started having symptoms and what she was doing at the time, along with many other details that may help speed her recovery.

Many vets will give you a record book to keep track of her vaccinations. This information is important—you will need it if you want to board your dog at a kennel or enter her in a dog show. But don't stop there. Get yourself a notebook for each of your pets. It doesn't have to be fancy and it doesn't need to be big, since you'll probably use no more than a dozen pages.

Write your dog's name on the cover of the notebook. On page one, titled "Problem Master List," make a note of every medical problem your pet develops, followed by the date you noticed it and the date she started getting better. This is your pet's medical history in a capsule. It contains the important information that you must remember to pass on if, for example, you change vets, see a specialist or have to visit an emergency clinic, or your dog goes to live with another owner.

The remaining pages in your notebook will just be a log of veterinary visits and health comments. Don't underestimate the value of your own personal records. For example, if your dog is scratching and you see in your logbook that she was also itchy last year at the same time, there's an excellent chance that you have just helped confirm a pollen allergy.

take her to places where she will come into contact with unvaccinated dogs or their feces.

Depending on where you live and what your dog is likely to be exposed to, your veterinarian may also recommend vaccines for Lyme disease, a tick-transmitted disease that affects many body systems, and coronavirus, another intestinal viral disease that can be serious for puppies. An intranasal form of the kennel cough vaccine is often recommended for dogs who are going to be housed with other dogs (as at dog shows or in boarding kennels). Your veterinarian may also suggest an oral heartworm preventive, although this is not a vaccine.

VITAL SIGNS

Most dogs are not complainers and will hide their discomfort. It's up to you to observe your dog's behavior and vital signs and know when to seek help.

A dog's normal heart rate is between 80 and 140 beats per minute. The heartbeat can be felt by placing your hands around the chest just behind the elbows and gently pressing. To check for respiration, look for movement in the chest. If a dog is unconscious and appears lifeless, place a thread or hair in front of the nose. It will allow you to detect even the slightest flow of air.

The normal body temperature for a dog is between 100.5 and 102°F (38 and 39°C). To take your dog's temperature, just put a dab of lubricating jelly on the tip of a rectal or digital thermometer and carefully insert it about 2 inches (5 cm) into the rectum. Hold on to the thermometer throughout and read it after two minutes. Anything over 103°F (39.5°C) is a fever and calls for immediate attention.

Most feverish dogs have poor appetites, are inactive and have a "dull" look to their eyes. They tend to have warm, dry noses, but so do many healthy dogs, so your dog's nose is not a reliable indicator of fever. The only sure way to tell if your dog has a fever is to take her temperature as above (see also p. 250).

Medicinal Relief

There are a few things you should know when you need

to treat your dog's minor health problems at home.

From time to time, your dog may need some medication to treat a health problem. Although some drugs are administered as injections by your vet, most will be given at home, and you will be called on to do the honors. If she is going to get better, it's important that your dog takes the medications exactly as your vet has prescribed and that the entire prescription is used, even when it's obvious she's feeling a whole lot better after just a few doses. The medications won't do their job if you don't give them exactly as prescribed.

HOW TO ADMINISTER A PILL

Many common canine health problems respond readily to medication, which will often be supplied to you by your vet in the form of a pill. Dogs don't like being forced to swallow things, so be careful that you administer any pills carefully.

Hold the top jaw firmly open, making sure that the dog can't bite you. Then, with the other hand, place the pill as far back on the tongue as you can. Close the dog's mouth and wait for her to swallow. If she is having difficulty swallowing, stroking the throat may help the pill go down. If your dog still has an appetite, hiding the pill in cream cheese or peanut butter often works.

If your dog is in obvious distress and won't let you hold her muzzle, take her to a vet. It's not worth risking a bite on the hand.

GIVING LIQUID MEDICATION

When giving your dog liquid medicines, put the medicine in a dropper or syringe—most dogs won't like a spoon. It is also important to allow the dog to swallow the liquid in small volumes. Tip your dog's nose up toward the ceiling, with your hand steadying the snout. Insert the syringe or dropper into the lip fold at the side of her mouth and slowly squeeze in a little of the liquid, giving your dog plenty of time to swallow. You don't want to give the liquid too fast or too much at a time, because she may breathe it into her lungs.

ADMINISTERING EYE MEDICATION

Eye ointment is much easier to administer than eye drops, since it can be smeared on the rolled-out lower eyelid. If eye drops must be used, they often have to be given every three to four hours. This is usually a job for two people. One person sitting or crouching behind your dog can can sit her down and gently keep her head still, pointing her nose up. The second person can roll back your dog's upper eyelid and put the drops into her eye.

If you need to do this procedure alone, you will need gentle but firm control. Put your dog in a "Sit" position and, approaching from the front, use one hand to roll back the upper eyelid gently with your thumb and apply the drops to her eyes with your other hand. For a more skittish dog, put her in a "Sit" position and kneel beside her. Extend your arm gently around her neck as if you're going to apply a headlock. Cup her chin in your palm and tilt her head back until her nose is pointing right up. Use your other hand to apply the drops.

GIVING EAR DROPS

Always be very careful what you're putting into your dog's ears. Ear drops are not always safe—especially for dogs that may have other, undiagnosed problems, such as a perforated eardrum. Ingredients found in some ear drops sold freely over the counter can cause deafness if they trickle into the inner ear.

THE CANINE MEDICINE CHEST

Many veterinarians recommend that owners put together a first-aid kit or medicine chest that's specifically for dogs. You can certainly do this, but most of the time it's not necessary because many medicines that people use work just as well for dogs. Here are the basics you'll want to keep on hand.

- Activated charcoal for treating poisoning; your veterinarian will tell you how much to give
- Aloe vera lotion, or the whole plant, for treating minor burns
- Betadine or similar solution for cleaning wounds
- Buffered or coated aspirin for fever or miscellaneous aches and pains; give one-quarter of a 325-milligram tablet for every 10 lb (4.5 kg) of weight, once or twice a day

- Colloidal oatmeal (add it to bath water; will relieve itching caused by fleas or allergies)
- Epsom salts for cleaning and soaking wounds or sores
- Hydrogen peroxide (3 percent solution) to induce vomiting; give one tablespoon for every 15–20 lb (7–9 kg) of weight; or washing soda crystals or Ipecac
- Hydrocortisone cream for treating minor inflammation

- Pepto-Bismol for diarrhea and other digestive complaints; give one teaspoon for every 20 lb (9 kg) of weight every four hours
- Saline solution for flushing grit from the eyes and for soothing irritation
- Triple antibiotic ointment or cream
- Witch hazel for soothing minor inflammations as well as insect bites and stings

Check with your vet before putting anything stronger than a mild saltwater solution into the ears. Then, to put the drops in, gently grasp an ear flap and introduce the correct number of drops into the vertical canal. Keep hold of the flap and massage the ear gently. The longer the drops stay down the ear canal before she shakes her head, the better. Repeat for her other ear.

If there is a lot of debris in the canal, don't use drops. Instead, check with your vet about how to proceed, because no ear medication will get to where it will do the most good if the vertical ear canal isn't completely clear.

Also, be aware that some ear medicines contain alcohol, which will sting if there are open sores in the ear. This will make your dog "head shy" and she'll be unlikely to trust you with her ears again. Before administering any medicine to the ears, check for sensitive areas in the ear canal by gently massaging it.

LESS STRESS This Old English Sheepdog–Border Collie mix is more relaxed when treated by her owner.

FEEDING FOR RELIEF

A dog that has been vomiting or having diarrhea will need some time for her digestive tract to recover. In most cases, that means a rest from food for at least 12 hours. However, it's important to make sure she keeps up her water intake, unless she's vomiting. After that, stick to a bland diet, such as boiled chicken with rice, until signs of the stomach upset have been absent for at least three days. Then slowly reintroduce her regular diet.

Other, long-term conditions may require changes in diet. Dogs with heart disease may be put on a low-salt diet. Dogs with kidney disease are typically given a diet with small amounts of high-quality protein. Your vet will recommend a diet from more than a dozen prescription diets for such varied problems as obesity, gum disease and more serious health concerns, such as urinary tract "stones" and even cancer.

Neutering

Unless your dog is of breeding quality and you are a responsible breeder, neutering your dog at an early age is a sensible choice.

Neutering is the term for the permanent surgical sterilization of an animal. In females, the procedure is often referred to as spaying and it involves the removal of both the ovaries and uterus. In males, it is usually called castration or altering and involves the complete removal of the testicles. Because there are so many myths and fallacies about neutering, dog owners often fear the procedure. The following facts should ease your mind and convince you that neutering is the wise decision.

THE CASE FOR NEUTERING

Each year, thousands of dogs are put to sleep in animal shelters because no one wants them. Many of these dogs are the result of accidental breeding. The only way to halt this tragedy is to stop allowing our pets to breed, and the safest and most effective way to achieve this is to neuter. By not adding to the population of dogs, the chance that homeless pets will find homes is increased.

With current methods of veterinary surgery, both forms of neutering are quick and relatively safe and painless procedures. Furthermore, neutering brings various benefits in both health and behavior.

WHY NEUTER A MALE?

Castration has significant health benefits for a male dog. It prevents prostate disease, a serious problem for older male dogs, and eradicates the chances of testicular cancer or infection.

Neutering may also modify many behavioral problems. It eliminates the sex hormone testosterone, which is responsible for such "male behaviors" as mounting, urine marking (leg lifting), fighting and roaming. Not only

ONE THING ON HIS MIND It's difficult to confine an unneutered male dog when females are around.

is your dog less likely to fight with other male dogs, but he is also less likely to be picked on. Because neutered males have less desire to roam and search for females, they are also less likely to be hit by cars.

Contrary to popular belief, castration will not make a male dog calmer, but it will remove the cause of much of his frustration. Only maturity, exercise and good training will calm an active young dog.

WHY SPAY A FEMALE?

Spaying removes the primary source of the female sex hormones estrogen and progesterone. If you spay a female dog before her first heat, you radically decrease the chances of her developing breast cancer. Spaying also

NO DISTRACTIONS Most pets are even more loving and playful after neutering.

THE SAD TRUTH So many puppies are born that most have no chance of finding a good home. Neutering helps to reduce this tragic situation.

eliminates her chances of developing cancer or infection of the uterus. The latter condition is common and often life threatening.

Unlike castration, spaying has little effect on behavior. However, spaying does prevent the irritability and occasional aggression that females show during heat and the period of false pregnancy that often follows the heat.

Spaying also means that you won't have to contend with blood stains on your carpets from the discharge that occurs during heat. In addition, it will spare you the burden of persistent neighborhood males sitting outside your door waiting expectantly for your female.

MYTHS AND FACTS

A popular fallacy about neutering is that neutered pets become depressed. In fact, most are more loving and playful since they are no longer preoccupied with mating. Another myth is that neutered animals become fat and lazy. Neutered dogs do require fewer calories, but they will easily maintain a trim physique when placed on a proper diet and exercise program. Obesity is caused far more often by overfeeding and inactivity than by neutering. Some owners also worry that neutering will reduce their dog's basic instinct to defend his or her territory, turning their once-vigilant watchdog into a wimp. Again, this is untrue.

Neutering is best done before puberty, but it can be done at any age and will have the same effect on behavior and reproduction. There is no need to let your dog go through a heat cycle or have a litter before being neutered.

Neutering has the occasional undesirable consequence: for example, there is compelling evidence that Rottweilers neutered before 12 months of age have a one in four lifetime risk for bone sarcoma and are significantly more likely to develop bone sarcoma than dogs that are sexually intact. This is not to say that they should never be neutered; merely that it should be done at a later age in breeds prone to bone sarcoma. Your vet will tell you the best age at which to have your breed neutered.

There is really no reason not to neuter your dog. The procedures are affordable and readily available, with many humane societies offering low-cost neutering programs. The cost of the operation is certainly much less than the cost of raising an accidental litter of puppies or paying the medical bills for problems that neutering can easily prevent.

The Healthy Dog

Your dog's health and well-being are best maintained

by the person who loves and knows her best—you.

Use your regular grooming sessions to give your dog home health checks. Early detection of any physical health problems will help your veterinarian to treat them more successfully. Start the examination by giving your dog a whole body massage. Begin with the head and neck area and gently progress down to the tail and feet.

Run your hands through your dog's coat. Healthy fur is shiny and will not fall out excessively when you do this. Look for any bald spots.

Notice the skin under the fur. Normal skin is clean and has no flakes, scabs, odor or grease. Look around for any fleas, flea dirt (flea excrement, which looks like coarse black pepper) or ticks.

Examine your dog's tail end. The anal area should be clean, dry and free of lumps. Signs of irritation may mean that your dog has diarrhea or worms or that the anal sacs are blocked.

Check your dog's legs and paws. Feel for any lumps or painful areas.

Look for cuts on your dog's pads or damage to the nails. Do the nails need trimming?

WARNING SIGNS

Always consult your veterinarian if something in your home health check doesn't seem right or if you notice any of the signs below:

- Loss of appetite accompanied by changes in behavior for more than a day.
- Trouble eating or mouth pain.
- Sudden weight loss or weight gain.
- Prolonged gradual weight loss.
- Fever.
- Pain.
- Vomiting more than three times. Call the vet immediately if bloody or dark.
- Diarrhea for more than a day. Call the vet immediately if bloody.
- Change in bowel habits for more than a day.
- Sneezing, coughing or labored breathing for more than a day.
- Excessive drinking for more than a day.
- Increased urination, sudden accidents in the house, difficult urination, straining, bloody urine or decreased urination.
- Excessive salivation.
- Sluggishness or unwillingness to exercise for more than a day.
- Excessive scratching or itching, including ear rubbing or head shaking.
- Lameness for more than a day.
- Seizures or convulsions.
- Eye discharge for more than a day. If squinting or discomfort, call immediately.
- Chewing the skin for more than a day.

Look into your dog's eyes. They should be bright, clear and free of discharge. There should be no redness, squinting (a sign of pain) or cloudiness.

Your dog's teeth should be white. If they are yellow or brown, they probably need to be professionally cleaned.

Check inside your dog's ears. They should be pink, painless and free of discharge. Any odor, swelling, tenderness or discharge means trouble.

Normal canine noses are usually cold and wet, but they are free of discharge. A warm, dry nose may be normal if it is not accompanied by other signs of illness.

Find out if your dog is dehydrated by gently pulling up the skin on the neck. Normal skin is soft and rapidly falls back into place. Dehydrated skin is stiff and is slow to settle back in place.

Carefully check inside your dog's mouth. The gums and tongue should be pink (some dogs have black pigment spots, which are normal. Shar-peis and Chow Chows have totally blue-black tongues). Paleness or change of color to red, blue or yellow is a sign of disease. Any lumps in the mouth are abnormal.

Feel for your dog's ribs. If your dog is fit, you should be able to feel the ribs. Overweight dogs have an obvious fat layer. Underweight or ill dogs have very prominent ribs. A pot belly in an overweight animal may be normal, but not if the dog is thin over the rest of the body.

If your dog has "doggy breath," there is probably some gum or dental disease. But kidney and digestive problems are also a possibility. Notice your dog's breathing. It should be regular and comfortable. Dogs normally pant when they are hot, excited or stressed.

219

A Prevention Plan

Commonsense tells us that prevention is better than cure, so be aware of problems that can arise and have a plan to avoid trouble.

The modern dog's life brings some problems with it. Many vets believe that modern commercial foods and contemporary lifestyles, such as a lack of exercise, have led to an increase in a variety of health threats to your dog, including allergies, diabetes and arthritis.

It's not that dogs would be healthier if they went back to their wild ways. But they would do better if we all made an effort to combine the best parts of the new and old ways—good hygiene and regular checkups, as well as regular exercise and lots of interaction with fellow dogs. Preventive care is a whole lot cheaper than veterinary care after a problem has arisen and it doesn't take a lot of time.

EATING WELL

Dogs who eat wholesome, nutritious foods are much less likely to become overweight, so they're less likely to get diabetes and other digestive problems. A healthful diet may even reduce the risk of kidney stones.

Choosing the right food can be tricky. Most vets recommend avoiding generic foods. Even

VEGETARIAN SNACKS Lightly cooked crunchy vegetables make an excellent snack for your dog and will help in the prevention and treatment of constipation.

though they're often half the cost of name-brand foods, they're not made with top-quality ingredients. Premium foods, available from veterinarians and pet supply stores, are made from excellent ingredients, and are sometimes recommended for dogs with special needs, such as unusually active dogs. For most dogs, however, premium foods won't make a big difference in their health. Unless your vet has suggested otherwise, you can't go wrong buying the less expensive, name-brand foods at the supermarket, but always check the ingredients.

Always measure what goes in the bowl. Vets have found that when people guess how much they feed their dogs and then actually measure the amounts, they're amazed how much they're really giving. Not only will you be able to control more precisely how much your dog eats, you'll also notice when she's eating more or less than usual, which can provide extra clues about her health.

Keep track of treats—both the commercial and homemade varieties are generally high in fat and energy and can sabotage the best-planned diet. Replace some with bite-size pieces of fruit or vegetables. Many dogs also like popcorn (homemade and without sugar, salt or butter).

Overweight dogs are at higher risk for many different conditions, so weight control is essential. The easiest way to reduce calories (kilojoules) is to reduce the amount you feed your dog by 25 percent. Most

LOCK AWAY THE TRASH Your dog is much more likely to suffer stomach upsets if she has easy access to rubbish.

A REGULAR ROUTINE This Golden Retriever gets plenty of exercise, which, as well as keeping her muscles toned and her joints working well, stimulates her intestines and helps to reduce flatulence.

dogs start losing weight within a few weeks. If your dog doesn't start slimming down, talk to your vet about a different kind of plan.

Feed your dog at predictable times, for example, once in the morning and again in the evening. You can satisfy the cravings of a dog who's on a diet by adding a tablespoon or two of canned pumpkin to her food. It's high in fiber, low in calories and it's filling—most dogs love the taste, too.

Keep the trash out of your dog's way. Food-foraging can upset your dog's stomach in a big way, and it's not unheard of for dogs to eat large objects such as bones, or even paper or plastic, which can clog up the digestive tract.

Give your dog dry foods. Dry kibble helps keep the teeth clean by scouring them with each bite. Canned and semi-moist foods stick to the teeth, so bacteria are more likely to multiply and cause infections and inflammation. Store all dog foods in their own bags in a plastic container to maintain freshness and flavor without risk of contamination.

STAYING ACTIVE

Keeping dogs busy with regular exercise is among the most powerful strategies for keeping them trim, healthy and content. Exercise keeps the heart and lungs working well. It strengthens muscles and ligaments so that they are better able to protect the joints. It even makes pets less likely to misbehave. Many common behavior problems, such as digging holes or chewing on furniture, are caused by boredom, especially when dogs don't have other outlets for their energy.

The amount of exercsie dogs really need depends on the breed. Terriers, herding and sporting dogs are energy dynamos. They typically need an hour or more of

ENERGY TO BURN This energetic and bright-eyed Fox Terrier is the picture of good health.

KNOWING WHAT'S NORMAL

Every dog is different, physically and emotionally. The only way to know when your dog is getting sick is to know what she's like when she's healthy.

Vets refer to this as a dog's baseline. Any change from her baseline—meaning her habits, appearance, and moods—means something's going on.

Watch how much she eats. One of the first signs of illness is a change in appetite. Vets recommend measuring a dog's food every day, so you know when she's eating more or less than usual. Also notice if your dog is more reluctant to chew hard kibble, which may signal a problem in her mouth.

Watch how much she drinks. A dog's water intake normally fluctuates with the weather and how much exercise she's getting, but dramatic changes can be a sign of serious problems such as diabetes, kidney failure or adrenal gland problems.

Watch her bathroom habits. Take a quick look at your dog's urine and stools—they can provide a lot of information in a hurry. Any change in their usual appearance may be a warning sign.

Check her endurance and energy. A dog who has always been laid back and then is suddenly hyperenergized could have a hormonal problem. Similarly, when a dog who was always an energy powerhouse is suddenly tired all the time, you can be pretty sure something's wrong.

Look at her eyes. Your dog's eyes should always be clear and bright. A change in color or the appearance of more tears is worth noting and watching.

Look in her mouth. Take a look at your dog's teeth and gums regularly. The gums should be pink and firm, and the teeth relatively clean. Gums that look red or irritated, or breath that almost knocks you over, mean there's something wrong—either in

the mouth itself or elsewhere in your dog's body.

Feel her skin. It's normal to find a few lumps as dogs get older, but lumps can also be a warning sign of cancer. As a rule, lumps that feel soft and roll freely beneath the skin are less likely to be a worry than those that are hard and seem fixed in place.

See the vet. An annual checkup is a good idea. Older dogs need to see the vet more often, usually two or three times a year.

CHANGES IN APPETITE If your dog seems less hungry than usual, there may be something wrong.

vigorous exercise a day to stay happy and healthy. Dogs that are extra-large or extra-small tend to be more laid back and can get by with one or two fairly short walks a day. Generally, all dogs need at least 30 minutes of exercise a day—15 minutes in the morning and 15 more in the evening.

If your dog hasn't been getting much exercise lately, take it slowly at first. Take a couple of walks each day, preferably along a route without too many hills. Or play in the yard or the living room for a few minutes at a time. As she starts getting in better shape, you can increase the intensity—and explore other, more exciting ways of getting her moving.

One of the most effective fitness plans—and one that dogs love—is cross-training, in

which they do a variety of activities, such as swimming, walking, running, or chasing a ball. Swimming is particularly good for dogs who like the water, because it works all the muscles and is easy on the joints. Of course, it's important to supervise a dog in the water. This includes making sure that she can get out of the water, checking for underwater obstructions and avoiding rivers and the ocean, where fast-moving currents can pose hidden dangers. But if your dog simply doesn't like the water, you won't be able to force her to have a good time.

There is one caution about exercise: avoid doing hard exercise involving twists and turns on asphalt, paved surfaces or cement. These surfaces are too slippery for your dog's feet to

STRANGE SYMPTOMS

It's not always the case that physical symptoms are helpful warning signs. Dogs do a few very strange things, such as:

- The reverse sneeze. Dogs will periodically make a noise that sounds something like "whoosie," in which air rushes into the nose with a wheezing sound. Vets call it a reverse sneeze, and it doesn't mean much—although it may be caused by intermittent allergies.
- Eating dung. Nearly all dogs have sampled dung, either their own or that from other pets. Apart from increasing their risk of getting occasional parasites, it's not a serious problem.
- Sexual knot. After mating, the bitch's muscles contract and the male's penis swells. The resulting "tie" may keep them together for 30 minutes or more. This prolonged union allows nutrients to flow into the female's reproductive system and thus increase the odds of conception. It's a strange sight, but it's normal, and most dogs will unlock on their own.

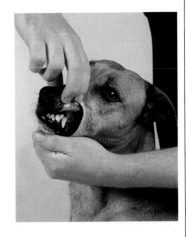

CHECK THE MOUTH The gums should be firm and pink and the teeth relatively clean. Inflamed gums and bad breath may both be signs that all is not well.

get a grip on, and the slipping and sliding are hard on her feet and joints.

SOCIALIZING

In years gone by, dogs kept busy hunting their prey and raising their young. Dogs today, on the other hand, often spend a lot of their time alone. Even if people are around, they don't have many opportunities to socialize with other dogs. This can lead to problems because dogs by nature are very social animals and they thrive on companionship. When they don't

THE HAPPINESS FACTOR Your dog loves to run, and enjoyable exercise is one of the most important preventive medicines available—and it's free.

have a lot to do, they may get bored and depressed—and they may cope with these emotions by barking, digging holes in the yard, ripping plants out of the garden or eating the furniture.

It's almost impossible to give dogs too many opportunities to socialize, and the improvements in their behavior and overall moods are often dramatic. Make an effort to play with your dog for a half-hour or an hour a day to help keep her happy and energized. Better yet, take her out of the house and away from the neighborhood now and then. New sights and new smells, and maybe a few other dogs to play with, are fun for her. And happy dogs are much less likely to be troublesome.

When to Call the Vet

*Dogs are often doing something—throwing up, having diarrhea
or leaving their food—that makes even calm people a bit nervous.*

Dogs are remarkably hardy animals and, in most cases, never have a serious illness. The key to keeping your dog healthy is to be alert to changes and to recognize problems early. This means that small problems can be taken care of before they turn into something worse. Some symptoms puzzle even your vet.

TRUST YOUR INSTINCTS

Dog owners see their dogs every day and usually realize quickly when things are not normal. Vets are trained observers, but they see their patients only once or twice a year, so they depend on owners' interpretations.

There are limits to instinct, of course. If you've seen a symptom before, you'll be more confident about deciding whether to call your vet. But some symptoms will not be familiar or will simply be too serious to take a chance with. Always call for help if you're worried.

SOME SERIOUS SYMPTOMS

If your dog shows any of the following symptoms, she will need veterinary help.

Breathing problems are among the easiest symptoms to recognize, and also the most dangerous. Dogs who pant heavily when they're resting or are struggling to breathe could have heart or lung problems. Even if the underlying cause of the symptom isn't serious, difficulty in breathing may reduce the flow of oxygen to the heart and other organs, possibly causing permanent damage. Get help quickly.

Pale gums indicate that tissues in the body aren't getting enough blood; blue gums signal insufficient oxygen. Except in dogs whose gums are naturally dark, such as Chow Chows, the gums should be bright pink. Many conditions, including internal bleeding and heart disease, can cause the gums to turn pale. Pale gums are nearly always an emergency.

Unusual fatigue that seems very severe, or lasts more than a day, warrants a call to your vet.

A swollen abdomen can signal a problem, especially in the big, deep-chested breeds, such as Irish Wolfhounds or Great Danes, who have a high risk of bloat. In this condition, the stomach suddenly becomes distended with gas.

Bloat can develop within hours and is always an emergency. Warning signs are restless behavior, swollen abdomen and labored breathing.

WATCHFUL WAITING

Some symptoms always need prompt treatment; many others do not. Don't ignore a problem, but watch your dog closely to make sure she's actually getting better. Here are some symptoms that warrant watchful waiting.

- Diarrhea. If your dog generally seems okay, it's fine to wait a day to see if the diarrhea improves. Keep her water bowl full, because she'll need to replace the fluids she's losing.
- Vomiting. A dog who throws up once is probably fine. A dog who keeps throwing up over a period of hours or days may have something seriously wrong.
- Bloody urine. Most of the time this means a urinary tract infection. Many go away on their own within a few days, but your vet should check that the infection isn't serious.
- Skipping meals. Dogs can safely go a day or so without food. If your dog keeps on refusing meals or has a fever or other symptoms, see your vet.
- Persistent scratching. The problem with persistent scratching is that dogs can damage the skin, causing hard-to-heal sores or infections. Consult your vet if the usual home treatments for itching (see p. 259) are not effective.

PROFESSIONAL HELP A discharge or bad smell from the ear, or any change in the appearance of the eyes, needs to be checked out by your vet.

Sudden injuries, such as being hit hard enough to be knocked down, perhaps by a car, don't necessarily show marks. But such accidents can cause internal injuries with no symptoms until hours or days later. No matter how well your dog looks after an accident, take her in for a checkup.

Chemical breath can be the result of your dog putting her nose into just about anything, including chemicals kept in the garage or under the sink. Even when what she's eaten isn't marked "poison," it may still be toxic. You could have less than an hour to start treatment. Unless you actually see your dog lapping at a puddle or pulling her nose out of a bag, poisoning can be hard to recognize. Pay attention if you see a tipped-over bottle or a bag that's been torn open. Dogs who have ingested poison may have a chemical smell to their breath, or be dizzy or vomiting.

Because of their adventurous appetites, some dogs have fairly regular digestive upsets. Severe digestive problems, such as occasional vomiting and diarrhea, aren't a problem for most adult dogs. In puppies, however, they can be serious. Puppies don't have very good reserves and can become dehydrated or develop low blood sugar quickly. Excessive

NATURAL DEFENSES

The body's inbuilt defense system, called the immune system, protects against thousands of hazards, including bacteria, viruses, allergens and even some snake and spider venoms. When an invader, called an antigen, enters the body, the immune system produces antibodies to fight it. Once this immune response has been activated, the antibodies remain in the body as a permanent defense against the antigen that triggered it.

Vaccination takes advantage of this defense mechanism by deliberately introducing a mild form of a disease, such as rabies or distemper, into a dog's body. This stimulates the immune system to produce antibodies that provide long-term protection against the severe form of the disease.

vomiting would be more than three times in an eight-hour period.

Straining to urinate could indicate kidney problems or a blockage in the urinary tract. Accumulations of urine can put pressure on the bladder, sometimes causing it to rupture.

Most eye changes, such as redness or excessive tears, are fairly minor and will clear up quickly, either on their own or with the help of antibiotics. But the same symptoms that indicate minor eye problems can also be caused by glaucoma, which may cause blindness if it's not treated quickly.

Spotting Common Health Problems

The best way to keep your dog healthy is to notice any tell-tale

signs and do what is necessary before problems develop.

If you give your dog a complete home examination every week, you will soon be able to pick up subtle changes that may indicate all is not as it should be with her. Do a physical check all over her body. You should also find out how her heart and lungs are functioning. This doesn't mean that you need a stethoscope around your neck. No fancy equipment is required to take your dog's pulse, check her weight, breathing and circulation, and make sure she's getting enough fluids. If you do these things regularly, you'll soon be able to recognize what is normal and what is not quite right.

CAPILLARY REFILL To tell if your dog has circulation problems, press on her gum, above the canine tooth, then release the pressure and note the time it takes the blood to flow back into the pressed spot. This is known as the capillary refill time; a slow time could indicate poor circulation.

BREATHING

Checking your dog's breathing is a great way to find out how she's doing. You can do this by putting your head close to her chest and listening, or by watching the rise and fall of her chest. Count the number of breaths she takes each minute. This is a seemingly simple task, but it can get a little tricky if your dog tends to pant, huff or wheeze. If it's too difficult, don't feel bad. Vets face the same problem. Far more important than the breathing rate is the clarity of your dog's respiration and the absence of coughing, wheezing and rattling.

Depending on her breed, your dog will probably breathe between 10 and 30 times a minute. If she seems breathless or the breathing is rapid when she's at rest, take her to the vet.

CIRCULATION

Your dog's heart may be beating, but it's only doing the whole job when the blood is getting around to all the tissues in her body. You can actually make sure the blood's going where it should by checking what vets call the capillary refill time. Lift the lip from the side of her mouth and press firmly (but gently) with your finger on the gum above the canine tooth. When you release the pressure, there should be a pale spot that becomes pink again within two seconds as blood quickly refills the capillaries. If it's pale for longer than two seconds, there may be a problem with your dog's circulation and you should see your vet.

DAILY HABITS: CONSISTENCY IS BEST

One of the best indicators of your dog's health is consistency. She should eat, drink and exercise about the same every day, and her bowel and urinary habits shouldn't change much, either. When any one of these elements suddenly changes, you'll know your dog isn't quite feeling herself and could be getting sick.

If your dog doesn't want to go outside to relieve herself, or if she can suddenly hardly wait to get out to her spot, or if she becomes incontinent, suspect a problem. Urinary problems crop up with age and are often signaled by changes in urination patterns. Similarly, bowel problems are usually signaled by changes in a dog's normal habits.

Keep an eye out for changes in your dog's energy level, as well. If she usually spends hours patrolling the backyard for squirrels, but one day entirely ignores the excitement, it's likely that something's wrong and you should take a second look. Dogs are creatures of habit, so take seriously any change you notice in your dog's daily routine.

FLUID LEVELS

A critical part of a home checkup is to make sure your dog has enough fluids in her body. Dogs that get dehydrated—from overheating, for example, or from an internal problem such as kidney disease—can go into shock, which is an emergency. To check for dehydration, gently grab some skin over your dog's shoulder, then carefully pull and twist it before releasing. If your dog has enough fluids, her skin will be very elastic and will snap back into position in a second or two. If she is dehydrated, the twist will persist, creating a "tent" in her skin that takes longer to slip back into place.

TAKING HER PULSE

Your dog's pulse tells you how her heart is doing. If the pulse is normal, then she's doing just fine. If it's unusually fast or slow, that's a sign that she may not be feeling

well. To take her pulse, try to find the femoral artery, which is where the pulse is strongest. It's on the inside of the upper thigh (on the rear legs), and you'll be able to feel it either when your pet is standing or when she's lying on her back. The artery is usually fairly prominent. Put one or two fingers on it and count the number of beats in 15 seconds. Multiply that number by four to get the beats per minute. If you're having trouble finding the femoral artery, put your hand on your dog's chest just behind her left elbow. The heart gives a double beat, so what you should feel is a dub-dub rhythm.

A dog's normal pulse can vary significantly, depending on her breed, size and age. Larger dogs tend to have slower heart rates than smaller dogs, but the normal heartbeat for average-size dogs ranges from between 60 and 150 beats per minute. Ask your vet what heartbeat rate you should expect for your dog, and remember that the beats should always be strong and regular, never weak or erratic.

LOSING OR GAINING WEIGHT

It's important to notice if your dog is losing or gaining weight. This is not as easy as it sounds. Changes in bodyweight typically occur gradually over an extended period, so you may not notice them. Often it is the occasional visitor who will first draw your attention to the change in your dog's bodyweight. That's why you should weigh your dog regularly—say, once a month—and to write the result down.

WHAT'S NORMAL FOR YOUR DOG This Collie–cattle dog mix sits quietly while her owner listens to her breathing. Rattles and wheezes may signal a problem.

Allergies

Dogs who lick, scratch and bite themselves may not be bothered
by the obvious culprit, fleas. Instead, they may have allergies.

Allergies are one of the most common conditions in dogs. In fact, in some parts of the world they even rival fleas as the main cause of canine itching and scratching. Check your dog for fleas first, and if you can't find any, her problem may be an allergy. But don't expect your dog to sneeze constantly and blow her nose. The telltale signs that your dog has an allergy are:

- She starts licking and chewing at her paws.
- There is redness around her armpits and groin area.
- She rubs her face.
- She generally scratches and itches all over.

It's unusual for a puppy to get an allergy. Most dogs are at least six months and usually more than one year old when they first develop an allergic reaction to a substance, called an allergen. It could be pollens, molds, house dust, a type of grass—all the same things to which humans have allergies.

Depending on what the allergen is, her allergy may be seasonal, or she may be itchy all year long. For example, if it's ragweed that she's allergic to, the itchiness will be worse in the autumn; if the problem is house dust, the itchiness will probably be a year-round thing.

EASING THE SYMPTOMS

The good news for your dog is that there is a great deal you can do to lessen her need for a good scratch. There are products such as antihistamines and marine oils that will relieve her symptoms and make her feel a whole lot more comfortable.

Some antihistamines designed for relief of allergies in humans are effective in about one-third of canine cases, and you can purchase most from a pharmacy without a prescription. Diphenhydramine (Benadryl), chlorpheniramine (Chlor-Trimeton) and clemastine (Tavist) have all been used successfully with dogs. Ask your vet to recommend an antihistamine that will suit your pet and the dosage that you will need to give her.

Marine oils are also very useful for treating allergies. These oils, derived from certain cold-water fish, contain anti-inflammatory agents. Given daily, they will curb the symptoms in about 20 percent of dogs with allergies. When they are used with antihistamines, the overall success rate jumps to more than 50 percent. So there's a good chance that you will be able to help alleviate your dog's symptoms, but if not, your vet will be able to investigate further and advise you of possible treatments.

AVOIDING ALLERGENS

As a general rule, trees produce pollens in spring, grasses in summer and weeds in the autumn. So if your dog's allergic season is a particular time of year, then this is one clue to tracking down what she's allergic to.

House dust and mold allergies occur year-round, although molds tend to be worse during damp periods. A dust-mite allergy gets worse when humidity is high. But to be really clear about what your pet is allergic to, you will need to have her allergy-tested by your vet.

AVOIDANCE THERAPY If you know your dog is allergic to a particular plant or pollen, try keeping her indoors as much as possible during its flowering season.

WASHING HER CARES AWAY A cool bath soothes irritated skin, as well as rinsing away allergy-causing particles that may be caught in your dog's coat.

OUTDOOR PROBLEMS

Keep your dog away from newly mown lawns, as these tend to be rich in pollens and molds. And if you know it's a particular plant or weed that gets her going, at least remove all traces of it from your yard and try to ensure that she doesn't come into contact with it when out and about. Putting clothes on her may help prevent allergens coming in contact with her skin. Put her head through the head hole of a T-shirt, then put her two front legs through the sleeves. With the clothing pulled down over her body, she's ready to get out among the grasses. For a dog with very sensitive feet, you could also try getting her to wear booties.

INSTANT RELIEF

For immediate, short-term relief for a dog who can't stop scratching, give her a bath. This will help remove pollens, molds and dust from her coat, and the water will soothe her skin. Bathing also reduces some of the odor characteristic of dogs with skin disorders.

Run the water cool; warm or hot water will only increase her itchiness. Add something soothing, such as colloidal oatmeal, to the bath water, or rinse her off with medicated rinses containing antihistamines, 1-percent hydrocortisone or topical anesthetics. Your vet can also prescribe a rinse for you to apply after her bath. Don't wash it off—leave it on so that it can keep working. You can't always be giving your dog baths, of course, so in between times, use one of the sprays that are available that have the same itch-relieving properties as those listed above. She will certainly thank you for the relief that these little attentions bring.

Don't let your house-dust-allergic dog sleep in your bedroom. This room has one of the highest dust mite populations in your home, so keeping her out at night could be doing her a favor. If that's impossible, try using special covers to control allergies. These encase your mattress, box spring and even pillows to contain the mite population. Contact your local dermatologist (either veterinary or human) to find out about suppliers near you.

Washing your own sheets, blankets and comforters in hot water every seven to ten days is a good way of removing potentially allergy-causing particles. And washing your dog's bedding will get rid of flea eggs and larvae as well.

Getting a high-efficiency particulate air (HEPA) filter can also dramatically reduce house mites, molds and pollens in a home. Try to keep the humidity in your home to 50 percent or less, and clean areas where molds can accumulate, such as in air filters and dehumidifiers.

PROTECTIVE CLOTHING If you can't keep your dog indoors, try putting her in a T-shirt before she goes outside. This might help to limit allergens coming into direct contact with her skin.

Anal Sac Problems

If your dog is dragging her backside along the ground,
chances are she's got an anal sac problem.

The anal sacs are two pouches on either side of the anus. A foul-smelling liquid accumulates in them—this is the scent marker that dogs use to communicate. The anal sacs usually empty when a dog has a bowel movement. But sometimes they don't fully empty and enlarge like tiny balloons, causing pain. Your dog will respond either by "scooting"—dragging her backside across the floor trying to unload the sacs—or she will bite and chew at the area beneath her tail. Both actions cause damage.

You may also notice signs of pain when grooming or petting the dog around the tail area. The first time you observe this, take her to your vet. He or she will examine the area to determine if the problem is one of simple impaction or whether something else, such as an infection, is going on.

DRAINING THE PAIN

The most direct method of relief is to squeeze the sacs and force the contents out. This unpleasant task is referred to professionally as "expressing" the anal sacs—it isn't a job for the uninitiated or the faint of heart.

Your dog will not thank you while you are performing this service and the smell of the liquid you collect will bring tears to your eyes. You can take your dog to the vet whenever she seems to be suffering and get him or her

LOCATION The anal sacs are easy to find. They are on either side of the anus at the five and seven o'clock positions.

to do the expressing. But an anal sac problem can recur, because although it is easy to remedy, it can be hard to cure. You could be seeing a lot of your vet if you can't face up to this unpleasant task. You may prefer to ask the vet to show you how expressing is done. Always try it for the first time at your vet's office.

You will always need a helper for the task, someone to keep firm control of your dog. You may also want to muzzle your dog, because even a gentle dog can bite when in pain, and expressing the anal sacs can be painful.

Wearing either surgical or latex gloves, grasp and raise your dog's tail firmly so that the anus is puckered. You should now be able to feel the anal sacs at the five and seven o'clock positions of the anus. Put your index finger on the side of one sac and the thumb on the side of the other and gently press thumb and forefinger together, forcing the anal sac contents out of the openings. It is important to use a touch that is firm enough to force the contents out of the sacs but not so firm as to damage the walls of the sacs and cause them to rupture and become infected. Have a gauze or tissue in your gloved hand to collect the smelly material.

OTHER CARE

Get your dog to sit in some water to which Epsom salts or an antiseptic has been added to relieve pain or itching. If the area is infected, your vet will prescribe antibiotics. You should also discuss your dog's diet with your vet. Soft or poorly formed bowel movements may be passed without causing the sacs to empty, so a gradual change in dietary fiber to create more bulk might prevent a recurring problem.

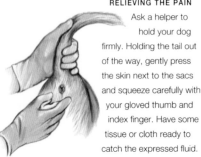

RELIEVING THE PAIN
Ask a helper to hold your dog firmly. Holding the tail out of the way, gently press the skin next to the sacs and squeeze carefully with your gloved thumb and index finger. Have some tissue or cloth ready to catch the expressed fluid.

Arthritis

Veterinary surveys suggest that 20 percent of adult dogs will develop osteoarthritis, also known as degenerative joint disease.

The most common form of arthritis is osteoarthritis, a painful inflammation of the vulnerable joint areas. It's usually a part of the normal aging process. Occasionally, rheumatoid arthritis affects dogs, too, and, while it can't be cured, relief is possible.

You can't predict when arthritis will start or, indeed, if your dog will develop it, but some circumstances make it more likely. If your dog has a history of hip dysplasia, elbow dysplasia or osteochondrosis (a condition in which bone and cartilage in the joints break down), there's a higher risk of osteoarthritis.

Apart from these instances, arthritic changes tend to appear when a dog has reached about 75 percent of her estimated life span—around 7 years old for a large dog and up to 11 or 12 years for a small dog.

See your vet if you notice that your dog's joints seem stiff and sore or she shows signs of lameness. She may also have difficulty getting up, especially after she's been resting or sleeping for a while. Or you may hear her whimpering while she tries to get about.

GIVING RELIEF
There's no cure for arthritis, but there's a lot you can do at home to relieve the pain and improve joint mobility.
- Keep out the cold by giving her an extra blanket or layer of bedding on cold, wet days.
- Keep her weight down. Extra weight just puts stress on joints

that are already overloaded. Reducing the burden on joints can sometimes postpone the onset of arthritis by many years.
- Get her moving. Dogs with arthritis are often quite sedentary, simply because their owners are nervous about causing more pain. But exercise is very important because it keeps the joints working, which improves mobility. Plus, exercise makes the muscles stronger, which will help keep her joints stable. The key is regular, gentle exercise.
- Give some hands-on care. You know how good a massage feels. Well, your dog will enjoy a brisk massage to her achy bits almost as much as you do, especially after a walk.

EASING THE PAIN
There are dozens of drugs to choose from to ease the pain, but one of the most effective is also the oldest and least expensive: aspirin. It relieves the pain, but also reduces the joint inflammation that often goes with arthritis.

When the arthritic aches are flaring, vets usually recommend that you give about a quarter of a 325-milligram tablet for every 10 lb (4.5 kg) of your dog's bodyweight. Always check with your vet before giving aspirin (or any medication, for that matter) to your dog.

EASING STIFFNESS Use your thumbs and fingertips to massage gently in small circular movements around the sore spots.

Bad Breath

Whether you call it "doggy breath" or halitosis, bad breath can make being close to your dog the last thing you want to do.

Unfortunately, bad breath in dogs is all too common. As with people, bad breath often occurs when bacteria-laden plaque collects on the teeth. Unlike humans, dogs don't brush their own teeth. This means the plaque, along with the smell, won't go away without your help. Worse, the bacteria can lead to gum disease, which gives off additional pungent odors.

There's really no reason to put up with your dog's bad breath. By making a few changes in her diet and practicing basic oral hygiene, you'll soon have her breath smelling sweet again—and you'll help to protect her teeth and gums at the same time.

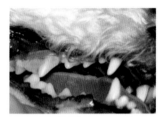

SIGNS OF TROUBLE Badly discolored teeth indicate dental problems. Take your dog to the vet for a thorough clean, then aim to maintain the teeth at home.

If your dog's breath is truly overpowering or the teeth are distinctly discolored, you will need to take her to your vet or veterinary dentist to have her teeth professionally cleaned and polished before you start with home care. Not only will you notice a big improvement in her breath, but once her teeth are clean they'll be easier to maintain.

KEEP HER TEETH CLEAN

The easiest way to take the edge off doggy breath is to brush your dog's teeth regularly. Pet supply stores sell special brushes and tasty, meat-flavored toothpastes designed with canine tastebuds in mind. At the very least, wrap a piece of gauze around your finger and quickly rub the surface of each tooth to remove food particles and plaque. For more information, see "Clean Teeth" on p. 209.

FREQUENT FEEDING

Crunchy snacks may help reduce plaque, but other types may make it easier for plaque to accumulate. What's more, the steady supply of food particles on the teeth allows bacteria to thrive. If you leave food available for your dog, make sure it's the crunchy kind.

BREATH-FRIENDLY TREATS

Carrots, rawhide chews or nylon bones—especially the kind with raised "dental tips"—are better treats than table scraps or too many biscuits because they remove plaque without adding calories. Before you know it, her "doggy breath" will be a breath of fresh air.

SUSPICIOUS SMELLS

While bad breath usually just means that your dog needs her teeth cleaned, it can sometimes be a sign that something else is wrong. Diabetes can change the smell of your pet's breath, as can kidney disease. With both these illnesses, she is also likely to drink and urinate more than usual and may lose weight. So if you notice her breath smells a little different than usual, get your vet to check her out.

A TRASH SNACK Your dog's breath is not likely to smell sweet if she's allowed to eat rubbish.

Bloat

Discomfort, panting and dry heaving are all signs that your dog may have gulped in enough air to painfully distend her stomach.

Dogs tend to eat with gusto, gobbling a bowl of food and slurping a dish of water as though it's the last meal they'll get. This can cause a life-threatening problem. Dogs that swallow a lot of air while eating or during vigorous exercise, or who ferment food in their stomachs, can develop a dangerous digestive condition known as bloat. Bloat causes the stomach to expand like a balloon, which can be very uncomfortable. But worse still, in some cases, the stomach will actually become twisted, cutting off the flow of blood to the stomach and possibly to other organs, too.

A dog with bloat will often seem restless and uncomfortable. You may notice that the abdomen is swollen and puffing out behind the rib cage. If you lightly flick the area with your finger, it may make a sound like a taut drum.

Bloat is always an emergency. It also comes on very quickly, so if you even suspect there's a problem, you must take your dog to see the vet immediately.

PREVENTING BLOAT

Once bloating occurs, there is no home remedy; the only thing you can do is rush your dog to the vet. However, there are several steps you can take to prevent bloat. Here's what vets usually recommend.

Watch what and when she eats. Because bloat often occurs when dogs have gobbled large amounts of food, it's best to feed your dog several small meals a day rather than give her one or two large meals or to have food available all day long.

If your pet normally eats dry kibble, moisten it with some water before giving it to her. This will let the food expand before it is in her stomach. Also, when gulping down dry food, your dog will tend to swallow more air; with moist food, she'll swallow less—which is why canned food is considered less likely to cause bloat than dry kibble. If your dog is fed dry kibble, don't give her anything to drink during mealtimes.

PREVENTIVE MEASURES You can reduce the chance of your dog becoming bloated simply by raising her food bowl off the ground so that she doesn't have to stretch her neck to reach the food.

233

SLOWLY DOES IT You can slow your dog's eating by putting something too large to swallow—maybe a smooth stone or a rubber ball—in her bowl, so that she has to eat around it. Or use a puzzle feeder, such as a Buster cube or Kong toy, to supply food at a trickle.

By stopping the gulping and gobbling, you can help to reduce the amount of air your dog swallows along with her food. To do this, make some simple alterations to the way she eats. Raise her food bowl off the ground so that she doesn't have to stretch her neck to reach the food. This will help reduce the amount of air she takes in. Pet supply stores sell elevated food stands. Or you can simply put her bowl up on a chair or step stool at about her head height. You can also try putting a large object, such as a smooth stone or a rubber ball, in the bowl of food. Your dog will have to pick around the object to get to her food, and that should slow down her eating.

Don't Exercise Her Close to Mealtimes

Avoid exercise immediately after feeding as this seems to increase the fermentation of gases in the stomach. Whether you feed your dog before or after an exercise session, allow at least an hour between the two activities for her body to settle back to normal first.

Watch Out for Stress

It's no easier to prevent stress in your dog's life than it is in your own. But it's worth making the effort when there are lots of changes going on at home—such as refurbishment or family tensions—because it is believed that dogs who are stressed can swallow large amounts of air, which can lead to bloat.

This is particularly likely to be a problem if your dog is going to be spending time in a kennel. Not only is this naturally stressful, but she'll be getting less supervision than when she's at home with you. Let the staff at the kennel know that you're worried about bloat, and they will be sure to keep an extra close eye on her.

MOST SUSCEPTIBLE BREEDS
Bloat most commonly occurs in the larger breeds with deep chests, such as Irish Setters (left), Great Danes, Golden and Labrador Retrievers, Saint Bernards and Weimaraners.

Coat Changes

If your dog's coat seems to have lost its usual bounce and shine,

be on the lookout for other signs of a problem.

Although there are many distinctive types of coats among dogs, the hair in them all consists of a tough, fibrous protein called keratin. The hairs are protected and lubricated by oils produced in tiny glands in the skin. Not every dog's coat looks and feels the same. Some breeds have hair that's silky and shiny; some coats are naturally coarse; some are short, others long. But in general, the coat should look healthy and be odor free. A change in the coat's usual appearance—if it becomes dull, dry, greasy, matted or smelly—is a sign that there's a problem with your dog's health.

BALD PATCHES

Occasionally, your dog may shed a little more than is usual for her. During pregnancy, for example, hormonal changes can cause dogs to lose tremendous amounts of hair. And some perfectly normal dogs may shed a lot one week and almost nothing the next.

There's a big difference, however, between the occasional bout of heavy shedding and shedding that's so severe your dog develops bare patches. Patchy hair loss that doesn't grow back could be a sign of mange (see pp. 266–267). Don't wait for heavy hair loss to get better by itself. See your vet right away.

Bald patches that are the result of excessive licking by your dog also call for immediate attention from your vet. Dogs that focus all their licking energy on one spot of skin will sometimes develop serious, raised sores called lick granulomas, which can take a long time to heal. Lick granulomas usually appear on the upper surface of the lower legs. It is essential to keep your dog from

chewing at the spot so the sore can heal. You may need to bandage the area or fit your dog with an Elizabethan collar (see p. 236). This will keep her from licking and give the sore a chance to heal. Lick granulomas can become quite deep and will often get infected.

DULL, DRY COAT

This may indicate a problem with the diet. Your dog may not be getting enough of a substance called cis-linoleic acid in her diet. Most good-quality commercial dog foods provide plenty of this substance, but it can be lost when kibble is stored for too long. Always check the use-by date on pet food.

Giving your pet too many baths can also result in a dry, dull coat by stripping it of its

INSTANT CLEAN AND SHINE
For a quick spruce up, rub warmed oat bran or a mixture of cornstarch and talcum powder well into your dog's coat, then brush it out thoroughly.

natural oils. Dogs' coats are naturally self-cleaning and the oils that are on them are there for a very good reason—to waterproof the coat—so keep bathing to a minimum. Most indoor dogs can get by with a bath once a year. Vets recommend using shampoos that are made for dogs because many human shampoos are too harsh. Baby shampoos work well, as do mild dishwashing liquids.

A lack-luster coat can also indicate the presence of internal parasites, so a visit to the vet to rule this out is a good idea.

MATS AND TANGLES

Regular grooming does more than make dogs look good. It removes hairs as they're shed, preventing them from accumulating next to the skin. In dogs that are not brushed, this hair essentially forms a thick blanket that prevents air from reaching the skin and reduces the efficiency of the oil glands. It also makes the surface of the skin hot and humid, leading to hot spots and other skin infections.

If you encounter a mat in your dog's coat while grooming, take the time to try to remove it by gently untangling it with your fingers and then combing through it. If you can't untangle it, use scissors or a mat splitter to cut into the center of the mat. Put a comb or your fingers between the mat and your dog's skin to avoid cutting the skin. Always remove mats before wetting your dog because water makes the mats tighten up and become even more difficult to deal with.

SEBORRHEA

It takes about three weeks for skin cells to mature, travel from the inner layer of skin to the surface, and die and flake off. In dogs with a condition called seborrhea, however, this process is accelerated. Dead cells quickly accumulate, making the skin and coat look flaky. The combination of oils and skin "debris" provides a fertile breeding ground for bacteria, so dogs with seborrhea often get skin

MAKING AN ELIZABETHAN COLLAR

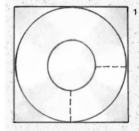

1 In the center of a sheet of stiff plastic or cardboard, mark a circle with a circumference 3 inches (7 cm) larger than your dog's neck. Outside this circle, mark another with a diameter 6 inches (15 cm) larger than the first. Cut out the circles and remove a wedge, as shown.

2 Cut ½-inch (1 cm) slashes around the inside circle and bend back the margin to form a rim. Punch out the lacing holes on each end of the collar.

3 Insert a lace into the holes and pull together—the circle will become a cone. Put the collar over your dog's head and tie the lace securely to the dog's collar.

infections, making them itchy and smelly. The coat will be greasy, and there may be oily, brownish scales on the elbows, hocks and ears.

LACK OF SHINE

A quick way to put shine in your dog's coat is to rub it well with a mixture of cornstarch and talcum powder, or with dry oat bran that's been slightly warmed. Then brush the coat out thoroughly. The bran or cornstarch will soak up grime and excess oil, leaving your dog's coat gleaming.

OLD AGE

The entire body slows down as dogs get older. Oils and nutrients take longer to reach the skin, which is why older dogs often have coats that are somewhat dry and tired-looking. Regular brushing will help to stimulate the oil glands and keep the natural oils flowing.

Constipation

Dogs get constipated, just like people—and when

things aren't moving, it can cause discomfort.

Constipation usually occurs when a dog has had to wait longer than usual to relieve herself—she may have had to spend a long day indoors while her human family was away at work and school. This allows the stool to get dry and hard. Not getting enough water and fiber in her diet and not getting enough exercise can also lead to constipation.

CURING CONSTIPATION

Many of the same things that relieve (or prevent) the problem in people will help keep your dog regular, too.

Increase the Exercise

One of the simplest remedies is to take your dog for regular walks. Not only will this give her plenty of opportunities to relieve herself, but exercise helps to stimulate the intestines naturally to move things along a little faster.

You may notice that exercise in novel new areas is particularly helpful because some dogs, especially entire males, generate feces to mark territory.

PLENTY OF FIBER Adding extra fiber to your dog's diet should help.

Make Some Dietary Changes

For dogs that are often constipated, vets usually recommend increasing the amount of fiber in their diets. Dietary fiber absorbs water in the intestine, making stools larger, softer and easier to pass. A sprinkle of bran cereal on her food will add a healthy amount of dietary fiber. Canned pumpkin is also good.

Keep the Water Bowl Full

One cause of constipation is not getting enough water. Fluids are essential for keeping the stool moist and the digestive tract working well. And with all that extra fiber she'll be eating, she'll need even more water. So make sure her water bowl is always full.

Don't Bother with Laxatives

Laxatives might work for humans, but they're not good for dogs. Over-the-counter laxatives may well cause diarrhea and thus do more harm than good.

LONG-TERM PROBLEMS

In most cases, constipation won't last more than a day or two. If it goes on for longer than that, however, there could be a more serious underlying problem, such as an intestinal obstruction, and you should contact your vet.

Incidentally, don't assume that straining is always caused by constipation. Dogs will also strain when they have diarrhea or even when they're trying to pass a bladder stone. If your dog is straining for a long time or seems very uncomfortable, play it safe and see your vet.

REGULAR EXERCISE This is the best way to keep your dog's system working well.

Coughing

Coughs—and whatever is causing them—will often clear up in a few days, but if they persist, your dog needs a checkup.

Coughing is a natural reflex in humans, but in dogs it usually points to a viral infection, sometimes with a secondary bacterial infection. Dogs are especially prone to canine cough, or kennel cough. This occurs when viruses invade the upper airways, making them ticklish and sore. The dog develops a hacking cough that can hang around for weeks.

Canine cough isn't serious and usually goes away on its own. In some cases, however, it can make your dog more susceptible to other more serious infections. It is also very contagious, which is why vets usually recommend vaccinations against canine cough conditions such as parainfluenza and bordatellosis.

Because coughing can also be a sign of more serious illnesses, such as bronchitis and pneumonia, or even heart disease, it's important to see your vet if the cough persists for more than a day or two, or if your dog is coughing constantly.

Your vet can treat some of the underlying causes of coughs, but here are a few tips to help you to relieve your dog's discomfort.

BREATHING PROBLEMS Dogs with pushed-in faces, such as Pugs, often have narrow (or folded) nasal passages. The soft palate also extends back a long way, which makes it difficult for them to breathe, especially when they are excited or stressed.

MOISTEN THE AIR
Dry air makes the mucus in the throat and airways dry and sticky, and that makes your dog want to cough. Plug in a vaporizer near where your dog sleeps. (Just be sure the cord is out of reach.) Or take your dog into the bathroom when you're bathing or showering. The warm, moist air will lubricate the throat and airways and reduce the urge to cough.

OVER-THE-COUNTER MEDICINE
In mild cases, cough suppressants such as Robitussin DM can be given to dogs ("DM" stands for dextromethorphan—the active ingredient in many cough suppressants). Your vet will advise you on the dose. For more severe coughs, he or she may prescribe a stronger cough suppressant.

EXERCISE AND DIET
You won't need to cut out your dog's exercise regime completely, but you should take it easy—a race around the park might have her hacking the whole way home. If she starts coughing from the exertion, immediately back off on the exercise.

Be especially gentle when using a collar, as these can be uncomfortable for sensitive throats. Until the cough is better, try using a harness that goes around her chest.

If your dog eats dried food, moisten her kibble with a little water in case her throat is sore. It's also a good idea to add a little tasty beef or chicken broth to her drinking water. This will encourage her to drink plenty of fluids, which will help keep her throat moist and reduce the urge to cough.

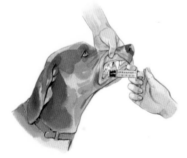

SUPPRESS THE URGE TO COUGH Cough medicines made for humans can help relieve your dog's cough. Use a needleless syringe to administer the medicine into the side of her mouth.

Dandruff

Dogs have dandruff as often as people do—and for similar reasons.

Most dandruff is merely dead skin cells that are being shed.

Dandruff tends to be worse in winter when the air is drier, but in some cases it is caused by skin mites or mild infections. If you notice scabs, crusting or itching, see your vet.

DANDRUFF CONTROL

All dogs get dandruff, but it tends to be most visible in short-coated dogs, such as Doberman Pinschers and Vizslas. You may not prevent it entirely, but there are ways to control the problem and make it a little less obvious.

One solution is to give your dog more frequent baths, say, twice a week, to help wash away dandruff before it gets a chance to build up. It is important to use a special dog shampoo with good cleansing ingredients, such as sulfur, salicylic acid or selenium disulfide.

If your dog's problem is caused by yeast—and your vet will be able to tell you if it is—you may need a shampoo that includes anti-fungal ingredients. Lather her up well and massage it into her coat. You can leave it on for a few minutes, so the active ingredients can do their job. Then rinse thoroughly with cool water to soothe any itchiness.

It might take a month or two of this regimen to bring the dandruff under control, but once it is, you can ease off a little. Bathing your dog every two to four weeks will keep her coat looking and feeling good. Take care to dry her thoroughly to avoid the development of wet eczema (also known as "hot spots").

All this frequent soaping and rinsing could actually dry out your dog's skin, but this can be prevented with regular grooming; this stimulates the production of sebum, a natural lubricant made by the body, and spreads it through your dog's coat, keeping the skin well lubricated and healthy.

Pet supply stores also stock a range of moisturizing sprays to protect her skin between baths. Follow the manufacturer's directions as to how often to use them.

DIET AWAY DANDRUFF

Dandruff can occasionally be caused by a fatty acid deficiency. If you feed your dog a balanced commercial diet, this is unlikely. It might be best to upgrade your dog's diet if she is normally fed a generic type of dog food—it might not be giving her all the nutrients her skin needs. A dog food of better quality could be all the help she needs to stop the dandruff.

Your veterinarian may recommend supplementing your dog's diet with fatty acids, from a half teaspoon to one tablespoon of vegetable oil to each meal, depending on the size of the dog. The vital ingredient in these is linoleic acid, found in sunflower and safflower seed oils and, in lesser quantities, in corn oil. If you already add vegetable oil to your dog's diet, ask your vet about extra vitamin E to keep the balance right between fatty acids and vitamin E. Evening primrose oil also gives good results.

GOOD GROOMING A thorough daily brushing distributes the natural oils through the coat of this mixed breed dog.

Dental Problems

With regular care, your dog can avoid most of the dental problems that are common in dogs.

Cavities aren't common in dogs. Their dental problems are different. The most common reason for a dog to be seeing a dentist is periodontal disease. This causes damage around the teeth and can develop into gingivitis, which damages the gums. And these canine dental problems are common—85 percent of dogs older than four years of age suffer from periodontal disease.

If your dog is more than a few years old, she probably has a coating of hard, brown material on her teeth. It's called tartar, or calculus, and although it does make her teeth look less than attractive, it's not the cause of all the tooth trouble. The main culprit is the stuff you don't see: plaque, a thin, sticky, bacteria-laden substance that forms on the teeth. If your dog has developed plaque, she will have to have her teeth cleaned professionally.

The best way to avoid plaque building up is to keep your dog's teeth, gums and mouth—and her breath—in mint condition. And you can do that by taking care of her teeth with a regular dental hygiene routine.

CRUNCHY FRUITS AND VEGETABLES Foods such as carrots and apples will help keep your dog's teeth clean and her breath sweet.

PREVENTING DENTAL PROBLEMS

With a simple prevention program at home, you can definitely stop dental problems before they even get started.

Do a Daily Plaque Patrol

Brushing your dog's teeth every day is vital to maintain ongoing dental and periodontal health. You might find having to do this once a day a bit daunting, but plaque accumulates quickly and you have to brush often to keep it under control. And because tartar develops from plaque, if you stop the plaque from settling, the tartar doesn't stand a chance. This is a good thing, because once tartar accumulates, it takes more than just a toothbrush to get rid of it.

Use Dog Products

Your dog's teeth-cleaning accessories should include a toothbrush and toothpaste. Human toothpaste is designed to be spat out, not swallowed. It has a higher level of fluoride and it can contain sodium or detergents. Your dog will no doubt swallow, so it's best to use a product designed for dogs. Dog toothpastes come in poultry, beef and other flavors, so she'll like the taste of them, too.

Start Off Slowly

Your oral hygiene program will have most success if you start slowly and patiently. You want your pet to regard teeth-brushing

REGULAR, ROUTINE CARE This Dachshund is having the outer surfaces of her teeth and the gumline brushed with a gentle circular motion.

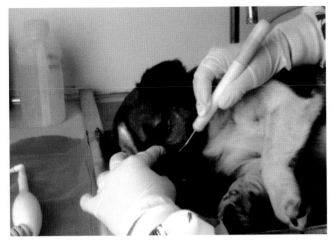

DENTAL CHECKS If your dog's teeth have a buildup of tartar on them, the vet will need to remove it. You can then begin regular maintenance at home.

sessions as enjoyable time spent with you, not as punishment. Start by getting her used to having her mouth touched.

For about a minute each day, lift her lips and rub around her teeth with your fingers. Try putting some good-tasting substance, such as a little garlic powder, on your fingers if she resists, and always pile on the praise. After about a week, she should feel okay about this and you can move on to a toothbrush and a little bit of paste—just let her lick the brush.

When she's comfortable with this development, start wiping the brush downward on the front teeth. Use gentle, circular motions and slowly increase the area you cover until all her teeth are being cleaned. Brushing doesn't need to last more than a minute, and always praise her to let her know what a good dog she's been. For a detailed guide to how it's done, see "Clean Teeth" on p. 209.

There are gels, rinse solutions and other anti-plaque products available, as well as a prescription dog food designed to reduce tartar buildup. Your vet will prescribe one of these products if he thinks your teeth-brushing efforts need extra help. Most rinses are squirted on the gumline, while the gels are rubbed on the teeth.

Crunchy Snacks

Hard, crunchy snacks and kibble will help keep your dog's teeth clean if she takes the time to chew them rather than gulping them whole. A better tartar-control treat is a compressed biscuit coated with anti-plaque and anti-tartar ingredients. A hard rubber chew toy, especially one with grooves, is a

great way for your dog to have some fun and do her teeth some good, too. The rubber will scrape under the gum tissue and dislodge the material that can accumulate there. Steer clear of soft rubber chews because they can be chewed into lumps and swallowed. Choose products with specially designed dental ridges, which are available from pet supply stores.

Dogs love gnawing and chomping on big bones, too, but not all bones are fully safe. Occasionally, hard bone can damage your dog's teeth but, more importantly, a bone shard could get lodged in her mouth or even cause choking or vomiting. So always select bones that have to be gnawed rather than those that can be shattered.

THE IMPORTANCE OF REGULAR CHECKUPS

Regular checkups are the best way to ensure that problems are caught early. Puppies should have their first dental checkup at 8 to 16 weeks of age and again when they are six months old. (Dogs have 30 puppy teeth, then 42 adult teeth, comprising 4 canines, 12 incisors, 16 premolars and 10 molars.)

After that, most veterinary dentists recommend that your dog's teeth be checked once a year. You can have it done at the same time as her annual vaccinations. Your vet may recommend giving her teeth a professional cleaning, known as a prophy, to clean out the plaque underneath the gums. Then her teeth will be a clean slate for your ongoing home health care.

CHEW TOYS Choose hard toys with grooves and ridges designed to dislodge particles from under your dog's gums.

Diarrhea

Diarrhea usually gets better on its own within a day or two, but there's always a risk that it's a sign of something more serious.

There's nothing unusual about your dog having the occasional bout of diarrhea. After all, no matter how vigilant you are, she will still manage the odd dawn raid on the trash or pick up an intestinal virus from one of her canine friends at the park.

The most common cause of diarrhea is diet. Overeating, or eating foods that the intestines aren't used to, may cause diarrhea. Other causes include intestinal parasites, viral diseases (parvovirus), food allergies, digestive disorders, kidney and liver disease and cancer. Most cases of simple diarrhea can be handled at home, but diarrhea from parvovirus, for example, can cause profound dehydration and intestinal damage in a short time.

In most cases, all you have to do is cut out food for a while—but not water—and whatever is causing the problem will be passed out of your dog's system. Occasionally, the diarrhea can be a symptom of something more serious and your vet will tell you to bring her in. Check your dog carefully to see if she has fever, vomiting, abdominal pain or if she seems depressed. If you notice any of these symptoms, or if the diarrhea contains mucus or blood, call your vet. Be prepared to describe the problem before you telephone for advice.

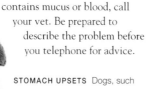

STOMACH UPSETS Dogs, such as this Husky, love routine and can be stressed by change. A little extra attention can help in maintaining a calm stomach.

SIGN OF DEHYDRATION If your dog's normally moist gums have become dry and tacky, she has lost precious fluids and you must encourage her to drink and take her to your vet.

DEALING WITH DIARRHEA

Diarrhea is one way your dog has of getting bad bugs out of her body—and fast. In a weird kind of way, it's actually doing her good. But that doesn't mean that either of you wants it around for too long. So here are some tactics your vet may suggest to slow the flow.

- Vets recommend that dogs with diarrhea skip a meal or two so their upset stomachs have a chance to rest. When there's nothing going in, there won't be anything there to come out again.
- After she's missed a couple of meals, you can start her back on food again, but her tender gut or bowel will appreciate something that's easy to digest. Bland foods, such as rice or farina, with just a little cooked, skinless white chicken meat mixed in are good.
- Your dog's body can lose its essential fluids very quickly during a bout of diarrhea, so it's important that you ensure she doesn't become dehydrated. Keep her water bowl full and check that she is drinking regularly.

- If she doesn't seem interested in her bowl of water, give her ice cubes to lick or chew to keep her liquid levels high
- Try an over-the-counter medicine. In simple cases of diarrhea, a quarter to a half of the dose recommended for a child of a home remedy such as Pepto-Bismol or Kaolin can be given once or twice. But sometimes it's best to let nature take its course, so use medications only on your vet's advice.

WHEN IT WON'T GO AWAY

Even if your dog seems to be fine, diarrhea that continues for more than two days, or is bloody, explosive, or seems painful, could be a problem and you should call your vet. Conditions that can result in chronic diarrhea, such as a food allergy, colitis or pancreatic problems, will not get better without your vet's help.

ONCE THE DIARRHEA STOPS

Continue to feed her bland foods for one to four days, depending on your vet's advice. Once the diarrhea has finished, you can slowly reintroduce her regular food by gradually substituting it for the blander food over the next three to four days.

LOCK TEMPTATION AWAY
Like most dogs, this mixed breed can't resist a trash can, so keep it out of reach.

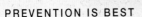

PREVENTION IS BEST

You can't prevent diarrhea entirely, but there are ways to keep your dog's insides calm. Here are a few things you may want to try.

- Maintain a steady diet. People get tired of eating the same food all the time, and they assume their dogs do, too. But most dogs are perfectly content to eat the same thing every day—and it's good for their digestive tracts. A sudden switch to a new diet is a common cause of diarrhea. If you do decide to change your dog's diet, do it slowly. Over a week or so, gradually begin swapping a little bit of the old food for some of the new. Keep adding more of the new food until you've made a complete switch.
- Be careful what you cook. Some people are giving up commercial dog foods and replacing them with home-cooked meals. Dogs love human foods, but these foods don't always agree with them. Milk, cheese and other dairy foods are a common cause of diarrhea in dogs.
- Skip the eggs. Many people slip the occasional raw egg into their dog's food because eggs are said to improve their coats. But this increases the risk of salmonellosis, a type of food poisoning that can cause a bout of diarrhea.
- Don't give your dog leftovers or "refrigerator rejects." Such foods represent a sudden change of diet and will often cause diarrhea.
- Keep cans refrigerated. If you feed your dog canned food, don't leave open cans on the counter. If she eats less than a can of food at one meal, cover the remainder securely with plastic wrap, pressing out as much air as possible. Then store the food in the fridge.
- Avoid garbage gut. Almost every dog makes an occasional raid on the trash—and usually pays the price the next day. You can't change your dog's unfortunate appetite, but you can put temptation out of reach. Keep trash cans—including the one in the kitchen, which most dogs can easily open—tightly closed and in cupboards or behind barriers.
- Watch the water. Clean your dog's water bowl every day, since bacteria from her mouth may accumulate in it and trigger diarrhea. And watch to see where your dog is drinking outside. Dogs can get viral or bacterial infections from outside water sources, such as mud puddles and stagnant water trapped in old containers lying about the backyard. Of special concern is Giardia, protozoal organisms that often occur in slow-moving springs or in stagnant groundwater.

Drooling

There's nothing quite like having a beloved pet rest her head in your lap … and finding a puddle of spittle there when she leaves.

Your dog probably drools because she is one of those breeds whose lips are designed in a way that allows saliva to pool, collect and then overflow out of her mouth. It's not that she produces more saliva than other dogs—though that's often hard to believe. It's just that she doesn't swallow it all. Among chronic droolers, the worst offenders are Basset Hounds, Newfoundlands and Saint Bernards.

MEALTIMES ARE WORST Even dogs who don't usually have a problem will drool when there's food around.

AVOIDING INFECTION

Certain other breeds have a lip design that can increase the likelihood of infection. Although these dogs do not actually drool, they have extra lip skin that creates a fold in the lower lip, just behind the canine teeth. This is particularly prominent in most spaniel breeds, including Cocker Spaniels, Springer Spaniels and Brittanies, and it provides a moist haven where bacteria can thrive. The lip folds can be altered surgically so bacteria don't build up, but most owners prefer to simply clean the area once a day.

Use a cotton-tipped swab to get down into the fold and get rid of any accumulated gunk. Then dip another cotton-tipped swab in peroxide, chlorhexidine or alcohol—only use alcohol if there are no cuts around your dog's mouth—and gently cleanse the area.

DEALING WITH DROOLING

Saliva flows in all dogs when there's food around or they get excited. It's completely natural. But if your dog isn't a regular drooler and she suddenly starts producing excess amounts for no apparent reason, it could mean anything from a broken tooth to insecticide poisoning; take her to your vet right away. There aren't any magic potions or solutions to make your dog drool less, but there are ways to limit the effects of the big wet.

Veteran owners of droolers always carry a towel. It's easy to wipe around your dog's mouth when things start looking a little too moist. Or make a stylish and functional bandanna out of an absorbent fabric; fold it in half and tie it so the triangle part hangs down over your dog's chest.

A mat, or just some newspaper, under her food dish will help keep the floor dry and make cleaning up after meals as simple as whisking the mat or paper away. If she's a die-hard drooler, a mat should be mandatory, unless you're not bothered by the puddles.

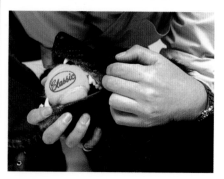

AVOID A BITE If you need to look in your dog's mouth, prop it open with a tennis ball or similar object.

Ear Problems

If you dog is scratching a lot at her ears, chances are she's trying to get relief from some kind of problem that's bothering her there.

Itchy ears can send your dog into a frenzy of scratching. It could be a colony of ear mites that has taken up residence, or it could be a sign of some other type of irritating ailment.

Ear Mites

Ear mites are one of the most common causes of canine ear troubles. The tiny, crablike mites are passed from dog to dog, or cat, or any other furry pet you might have. They munch on ear wax and other debris and secretions in the ear canal, and although they rarely bite, sting or otherwise hurt, they can lead to intensely itchy allergic reactions, causing dogs to scratch their ears raw. But they're easy for your vet to diagnose and easy for you to treat at home, even if they can be a little persistent at times.

If you suspect your dog has ear mites, lift up the ear flap and look inside. Even though ear mites are difficult to see, the debris they leave behind—a brownish-black discharge that resembles used coffee grounds—is quite visible. Get your vet to confirm that this is indeed the cause of the ear scratching, and to advise what type of ear drops you should use. It can take four to six weeks of using the drops to evict the mites.

You'll also need to go after traveling mites. Ear mite products go directly into your dog's ear canal, but ear mites have eight legs and they do what parasites do when you squirt insect-icide into their home: they move to a new place, usually at the base of the tail. When the medication in the ear canal wears off, they head home as if nothing has happened.

SUSPECT A PROBLEM? This Shar-Pei's owner uses a flashlight to check for foreign objects.

The way to avoid this trap is to treat not only the ears but also to use a flea powder or spray over your dog's whole body. Most common flea treatments, including pyrethrins, permethrin, rotenone, carbaryl and organophosphates, will kill ear mites on the body surface.

Treat all your pets—don't stop at the dog with the obvious problem. Ear mites are passed readily from pet to pet. If you have more than one pet, remember to treat every animal on the premises (dogs, cats, ferrets and rabbits included). Otherwise, you might find your pets are just playing "pass the mites."

You'll need to be persistent; mites can be difficult to eradicate. Treat your dog (and all other pets) for up to a month—that will cover the entire life cycle of the mites from egg to adult. If you stop too soon, you won't get rid of every last one of them.

As a last resort, your vet may recommend stronger medications, possibly even injections, to kill the mites on board. However, if your dog is still in contact with the mite carrier, she will still be susceptible to new infestations.

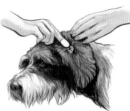

CLEANING To prevent infections, flush out your dog's ear canals and dry gently and thoroughly with a scrap of gauze wrapped around your finger.

Ear Infections

Dogs often get bacterial or yeast infections in the ear canal, not from other dogs, but because there is an underlying reason why they are susceptible to infections. It could be:

- Your dog's ear shape; floppy ears or small ear canals, in particular.
- Humid conditions or a fondness for swimming.
- Overdoing the ear care; excessive hair plucking or cleaning efforts, or irritating cleansers or drops.
- Health problems such as allergies, food intolerance or a hormonal imbalance.

If you notice debris in your dog's ear canal or on her ear flaps, or if her ears are red, hot or tender, she could have an infection and you should take her to the vet for treatment. If she constantly tilts or shakes her head, she could have inner ear problems. Your vet will be able to diagnose the underlying cause of her trouble and set about fixing the problem. Regular checks for foreign objects, such as grass seeds, should also be routine.

Preventive Ear Care

The best way to keep your dog's ears healthy is to follow a regular ear-care program. Here's what vets recommend.

Check her ears weekly. Good ear care begins by regularly inspecting the insides of the ears as part of the regular grooming regimen. Ear canals should be clean, with no signs of inflammation, no nasty odors and no redness around the ear flaps. While you're at it, check carefully for ticks, and don't forget those ear mites. There's no need to explore the ear canal too deeply; just check the external area, then lift the flap to find out what you can smell and see.

If your dog is prone to waxy accumulations, do a regular cleaning. Make keeping your dog's ear canals clean and free of parasites part of your regular bathing or grooming routine. But before you put any solutions in your dog's ear canals, make sure you discuss it with your vet. The ears are very sensitive and many antiseptics and antibiotics can cause deafness if they get down to the inner ear—which they may do, for example, if the ear drum happens to be ruptured.

After making sure the ear is clear of debris, dip a cotton-tipped swab into ear-cleaning solution. Gently clean around and between the ridges of the ear flap—but be careful not to push the swab too far into the ear canal. As long as you can always see the cotton end, you can use the swab safely.

Be careful not to push debris farther down into the canal when using the swab. If there is any excess fluid and debris in the ear opening, use a cotton ball to remove it carefully. For more information on how to clean your dog's ears, see p. 206.

Routinely plucking the hair from the ear canals of dogs who otherwise have healthy ears is not recommended. The exceptions are woolly breeds, such as Poodles and Bedlington Terriers, where the hair may stop medication from getting into the problem area or where infected material is blocked from draining out of the ear. Light plucking only is needed. Never use depilatory creams on a dog; they are not designed for dogs and the chemicals they contain are far too harsh for canine skin.

ADMINISTERING EAR DROPS Hold the ear flap firmly to prevent your dog from shaking her head, and squeeze in the required number of drops.

Maintaining your firm grip on the ear flap, cover the opening and massage the base of the ear gently to work the drops into all the nooks and crannies that can harbor the problem.

246

Elbow Dysplasia

The elbow joint holds the bones tightly together, yet allows enough
flexibility so your dog can run and jump with grace and agility.

Your dog's elbows are designed to be strong, yet mobile. In some dogs, however, the elbow joints don't fit together as tightly as they should. There is a certain amount of "wobble," which can lead to pain and stiffness, especially after playing hard. This problem, called elbow dysplasia, is thought to be hereditary, and tends to set in even before a dog reaches her first birthday.

LIKELY CANDIDATES Chow Chows are among the breeds most susceptible to elbow dysplasia (see box).

If you suspect your dog either has elbow dysplasia or is at risk of getting it because her parents had it, your vet will probably recommend X-rays. Diagnosing the problem early will allow you to take preventive measures to protect the elbows from further damage. If the joints haven't already deteriorated, your vet may suggest surgery.

EASING THE ACHES

One way of reducing the discomfort of elbow dysplasia is simply to keep your dog's weight in check. By keeping her light and lean, you will ensure that she has less weight to carry around, which will reduce pressure on those vulnerable joints.

Giving calcium supplements to dogs with this condition is not recommended. Instead of strengthening your dog's bones, calcium supplements can actually interfere with the normal growth of both bones and cartilage, and that can make things even worse.

Make sure your dog gets regular and gentle exercise. This helps strengthen the muscles, ligaments and tendons around the elbow joints, while at the same time increasing lubrication that helps the joints to move more easily. Don't overdo it, but a 20-minute walk twice a day will do her good. Or try a swim, as long as the water isn't cold and she can get warm and dry after it. For more information on easing sore joints, see p. 231.

Your vet may recommend medications to help control any pain and swelling. Applying heat or cold several times a day can also be soothing. In addition, your vet may prescribe a cartilage-protecting agent, such as Adequan and Hylartin V, and nutrient combinations that will help repair her cartilage.

Since elbow dysplasia is often inherited, your vet will probably recommend having your dog spayed or neutered. If you are buying a breed prone to this condition, get a pup only from a breeder who will guarantee the dog's family has been free of the clinical signs of elbow dysplasia for at least three generations. In some countries, such as the United States, certification is available to show that your prospective pup is "clear."

CHECK THE PARENTS Breeds such as this Bullmastiff may be genetically more susceptible to joint problems.

MOST SUSCEPTIBLE BREEDS

Some dogs get elbow dysplasia and some don't, for reasons that aren't fully understood, but genetics clearly plays a role. Most susceptible are:

- Bearded Collies
- Bernese Mountain Dogs
- Bloodhounds
- Bullmastiffs
- Chow Chows
- German Shepherds
- Golden Retrievers
- Labrador Retrievers
- Mastiffs
- Newfoundlands
- Rottweilers

Eye Problems

The canine eye is very much like the human eye, and every part

can be affected with problems that affect your dog's ability to see.

Although you won't see dogs running around in spectacles, they have problems with failing eyesight and eye infections, just as people do. Cloudiness in the eyes is one of those bothersome things that often happens to a dog as she gets older. It's called nuclear lenticular sclerosis and it can look a lot like cataracts but it's nowhere near so serious. It can reduce close vision, but this is not nearly as important for dogs as it is for people.

You might not realize at first that your dog has a vision problem, because dogs are extremely adaptable and she will possibly compensate well with her other senses. Some of the signs you might notice are that she negotiates obstacles poorly, stumbles on steps or curbs and makes more such errors at dusk or night. If you notice that her eyesight is failing, take her to the vet for a diagnosis to make sure it's nothing serious.

Another common problem is discharge and debris in the corner of your dog's eyes. These are natural secretions that accumulate, and a good wash is often all that's needed.

Conjunctivitis, an inflammation usually caused by allergies or infections, is another common ailment that will make a dog's eyes red and itchy.

SUN VISORS Your dog can't really wear sunglasses, but her eyes need protection as much as yours do. A snappy sun visor might be just the thing.

HELPING FAILING EYES

Although impaired vision, even blindness, is a handicap, dogs often cope much better than people do, and there's a lot you can do to make life easier for your pet.

Start by leaving things where she'll remember them. With her eyesight not all that it once was, your dog will use her memory of the way things were to negotiate her way around the house. So don't suddenly move the sofa to a new position, because she's bound to walk into it rather than around it. Leave her bed and food and water bowls where they've always been, so she'll be able to find them.

If you must redecorate or rearrange the furniture, take your pet on a gentle guided tour so she can work out the new layout. Use lots of verbal encouragement to help her find her way around objects and get where she wants to go.

Protect her from trouble spots by taking extra precautions around stairways or other potentially dangerous areas, such as the kitchen. Put a childproof gate in front of any doorway or opening that you don't want your dog to have access to except when she's with you. If you use the same keep-out strategies you would for a new puppy or a toddler, your pet should do just fine.

Just because your dog can't enjoy the scenery doesn't mean that she won't like the fresh air and interesting smells that a nice walk offers. She still needs to get adequate exercise and stay fit, although you must now keep your eyes open for the both of you.

CATARACTS These are a common problem, especially in older dogs. The center of the eye appears white or opaque. If severe, cataracts may require surgery.

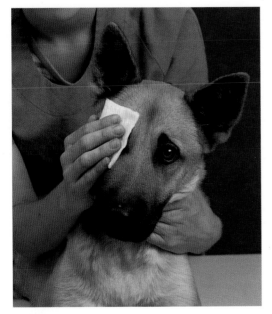

WARM COMPRESS A wad of gauze soaked in warm saline solution may help reduce the pain of a sore eye.

Progressive retinal atrophy (PRA) is another inherited disease. It involves a loss of function of the retina in the back of the eye, which typically results in blindness. The vision is slowly but progressively impaired, so you may be unaware of the problem at first. While there is no effective treatment, most dogs will adapt to it with your help.

CORNEAL DAMAGE

Cats' claws and tree branches often cause corneal injury in dogs. A dog with a corneal injury will hold her eye closed and produce excessive tears. If left untreated, the damaged area may become infected and ulcerated, resulting in blindness.

Inherited abnormalities of the eyelids can also lead to corneal damage. Some dogs have eyelids that roll abnormally in or out or have eyelashes that grow in the wrong direction, toward the eye, causing irritation. Most of these problems can be corrected with surgery.

You will now find it much better to attach her leash to a harness rather than to a collar, because you will need to have greater control over her and rein her in more often. The harness will give you a much more gentle means of control than a leash will.

EASING IRRITATED EYES

Wash away the muck from an eye discharge once a day with warm water, cold black tea or an over-the-counter eye wash. Wipe firmly toward the center of her nose. There are all kinds of cleaning products available from pet supply stores to tackle the stains that may be left on her fur by an eye discharge. Dogs with hay fever often get sore, red eyes in spring and summer, when pollen counts are high. In cooler weather, dust and mold spores can produce allergies and red eyes in susceptible dogs. If your dog has conjunctivitis or some other eye infection, there will often be a watery discharge along with the redness. See your vet for advice on treatment.

GENETIC PROBLEMS

There are a number of eye diseases caused by genetic problems in certain breeds. For example, most cataracts are seen in particular breeds of dogs, including the American Cocker Spaniel and Doberman Pinscher, and younger dogs are affected. Surgery will almost always resolve the problem.

APPLYING EYE OINTMENT If there is any debris in the corner of the eye, flush it out or wipe it away first with a moistened cotton ball—always wipe from the outside of the eye toward the nose. Holding the eye open, squeeze a little ointment into the corner of the eye nearest the nose.

To spread the ointment over the eye, allow the dog to close the eye, then gently massage the lids together.

Fever

*If your dog is off her food, is less active than usual and has
a "dull" look about her eyes, she probably has a fever.*

If your dog seems a little out of sorts, it's time
to reach for a thermometer—see the box
below for the different types available and tips
on how to take her temperature.

The most common causes of fever include
a viral or bacterial infection or a reaction to
medication. Occasionally, a fever indicates
something more serious, such as an immune-
system problem or even cancer, but in most
cases it is just a temporary reminder that your
dog isn't feeling well and needs to take things
easy. A temperature of more than 103°F
(39.5°C) is classified as a fever; if it persists
for more than a day, take your dog to the vet
without delay.

TAKING YOUR DOG'S TEMPERATURE

If you think your dog is looking or feeling a little
low, taking her temperature may give you some
answers. But forget about under her armpit or her
tongue. The way to take your dog's temperature is
by using a rectal thermometer—so she'll need one
all her own.

Taking your dog's temperature is easy.
Lubricate the tip of the thermometer with some
petroleum jelly, then stand or kneel alongside your
dog, facing her rear. Lift the tail and gently twirl the
thermometer into the rectum, going in about an
inch or so (about 3 cm). Praise your dog and keep
her standing for the two minutes it will take to get
an accurate reading.

If you've bought a high-tech digital
thermometer, you won't have to wait even
that long. The normal temperature for a
dog is 99.5° to 102.5°F (37.5° to
39.1°C). If it goes above 103°F
(39.5°C), it is considered a fever.

If you'd rather not get this intimate
with your dog, you could spend a little
extra on an aural thermometer, which
will take the temperature reading from
inside her ear almost instantly.

EASING A FEVER

There's no cause for panic when your pet has a
fever. Just do what you would normally do if it
were you that was running the temperature.

- Ease off on the activity. A dog with a fever
  doesn't need vigorous exercise or play. Let
  her rest or sleep in a quiet spot.
- Give her lots of liquids. Keep her water bowl
  full or, if she doesn't seem very interested in
  drinking, give her ice cubes to chew or lick.
  Beef broth may tempt her to drink more.
- Do nice things for her. Your pet will like to
  feel pampered when she's not feeling well.
  Sit with her and watch a movie or give her
  a gentle massage to help her relax. If she
  enjoys a bath, a soak in cool to lukewarm
  water is comforting and will also help bring
  her temperature down.
- Try some over-the-counter relief. Aspirin
  can be very effective for lowering your dog's
  temperature. Vets usually recommend giving
  one-quarter of a 325-milligram tablet of
  buffered aspirin for every 10 lb (4.5 kg) of
  body weight once or twice a day. But always
  check with your vet before giving human
  medications to pets.
- Monitor her progress. Recheck your dog's
  temperature every six hours or so, to see
  how she is doing and if the fever is
  coming down. If it persists for
  more than a day, see your vet.

EXTRA ATTENTION While the
fever persists, encourage your
dog to drink plenty of water
or to lick ice cubes so she
doesn't become dehydrated.

Flatulence

Gas is a normal product of digestion, but some dogs produce more than others. The problem usually responds well to home remedies.

SEPARATE BOWLS If there's more than one pet in the family, feed them separately. Dogs often gobble food to make sure they get their full share.

Flatulence usually occurs when food isn't completely broken down, allowing a build-up of gases in the intestine. Much of this gas is absorbed into the blood stream, but not all. Here's what experts recommend.

- Overhaul her diet. Certain foods—especially those containing soybeans—are notorious gas producers. Changing to a food with little or no soy may be all it takes to stop your dog being so gassy. You may have to try several foods over a few months to find one your dog can tolerate. To avoid unpleasant side effects such as diarrhea, be sure to switch foods gradually, substituting ever-increasing amounts of the new food for the old over a period of seven days.
- Certain foods, including broccoli, cauliflower, milk and cheese, will cause flatulence in just about any dog. Cut them out for a few days and see if things improve.
- Change the protein. If her current food gets most of its protein from beef, for example, try a food with a lamb-based protein.
- Give more fiber. Adding fiber to your dog's diet will cause food to move more quickly through the intestines, giving gas less time to develop. High-fiber Metamucil (or a generic counterpart) is readily available. It can be mixed into your dog's food with every meal: use one teaspoon for every 10–20 lb (4.5–9 kg) of body weight. Canned pumpkin or green beans are also worth trying.
- Bring her insides into balance. The intestines normally contain large amounts of beneficial bacteria to aid digestion. If dogs don't have enough of these bacteria, flatulence can result. Give your dog acidophilus—the ingredient in live-culture yogurt—to bring the beneficial bacteria back to healthy levels. Dogs don't like the sour taste of liquid acidophilus, but will readily take it in the form of chewable tablets. You can give your dog the human dose listed on the label. It usually takes a few days for acidophilus to be effective. Or add some plain yogurt (with active acidophilus culture) to your dog's meal, if she'll eat it. Activated charcoal biscuits will also reduce gas.
- Slow things down. If dogs gobble their food, they swallow a lot of air while eating, causing gas to accumulate in their intestines. Vets sometimes recommend placing a large object—one that's too large to swallow—in the middle of your dog's food bowl. She will have to pick around the obstacle in order to get at her food, and this will slow her down.
- Head outdoors. Exercise stimulates the intestines and helps dogs to have a bowel movement, both of which remove excess gas from your dog's system.

Fleas

They can make your dog's life a misery. Fortunately, in the battle for control, the odds are shifting against these persistent little pests.

Most dog owners have a problem with fleas at some stage, but new developments now allow superior flea control without any exposure to harmful insecticides. Fleas are not pushovers. It will take persistence to achieve control. But in the past decade or so, researchers have been focusing on flea remedies that effectively break the life cycle.

Fleas are not just biting pests, they also transmit a number of diseases to dogs, including tapeworm infection, typhus and tularemia. They can also cause intense itching and discomfort for your dog. And they're not always easy to see. Don't think that all is well if you part the fur of your scratching dog and don't see fleas. She might have only a few fleas, which are going to be difficult for you to find. But her problem could be that she is allergic to the flea saliva—and it only takes a few bites from a few fleas to send a dog with that kind of allergy into a mad scratching frenzy. If your dog is scratching and you can't find an obvious culprit, do her a favor and get her checked out by your vet.

GROOMING AIDS Stiff brushes and fine-toothed flea combs are very effective for removing adult fleas and their larvae from your dog's coat.

FIGHTING FLEAS

There's no product or strategy that will wipe out fleas in one hit. But you can achieve complete control in three to four weeks, the duration of the flea life cycle. With persistence,

REGULAR FLEA CHECK Fleas are hard to find, but if you brush your dog over paper, you can easily see the gritty reddish-brown dirt they leave behind.

your reward will be a flea-free pet and a flea-free household.

Tackle the adult fleas first by treating your dog's coat with a flea spray once a month. There is a wide range of insecticide sprays to choose from. Pyrethrins, made from chrysanthemums, are very safe but don't last very long. Some synthetic pyrethrins, such as permethrin, do slightly better for dogs, but seem to be toxic for other species, especially cats.

Some products now offer safety to people and pets, effectiveness against adult fleas and once-a-month convenience. Products such as Advantage, containing imidacloprid, kill almost all the fleas on your dog within 24 hours. Then there are products such as Frontline, containing fipronil, which work against both fleas and ticks and are safe to use even on puppies and dogs that are pregnant. With these new products, you need to spray only the fur on your dog's back once a month to have the dog fleas dying in droves.

Remember, too, that to break the fleas' life cycle, treating the environment is just as important as treating the dog (see box).

COLLAR THE FLEA PROBLEM

Insecticides will certainly put adult fleas out of action, but not the eggs, larvae and pupae in and around your house. So as soon as you let down your guard for a minute, there will be a whole new crop of adult fleas.

One option is to put a special kind of flea collar on your dog, one containing an insect growth regulator (IGR) such as pyriproxyfen, methoprene or fenoxycarb. These are fake flea hormones that trick the flea eggs and larvae into drying out and dying. In fact, an IGR-laced collar is a bit like birth control for fleas.

IN THE HOUSE AND GARDEN

Once you've treated your dog, turn your attention to the flea population in the house.

- Vacuum once a week, especially around all pets' beds.
- Spray indoors with a safe, nontoxic insecticide spray, such as pyrethrin, to target adult fleas in the house.
- Get a pest-control professional to apply Polyborate (a cousin of borax). This powder gives flea control for up to a year (depending on your floor surface).
- Launder your dog's bedding once a week. Use the warmest temperature the fabric can stand—and the fleas can't.
- Spray shady areas around the garden edges, doghouse and patio with chemicals such as diazinon, which aren't broken down by sunlight.
- Or you could water your yard with worms. You can now purchase microscopic worms called nematodes from pet supply and garden stores. These attack flea larvae and cocoons without harming other beneficial insects. Apply them to your lawns, gardens and even sand, following the instructions that come with them.

The collars are very safe and work well for as long as the label says. Choose a collar carefully. Some kill adult fleas, but have no effect on the larvae or eggs.

OTHER TACTICS

Ask your vet about Program, a compound containing lufenuron, which stops the fleas' hard shells from developing. Without that protective coating, the fleas die. This product is given orally just once a month. Lufenuron has also been combined with a heartworm preventive medicine in a product called Sentinel, so if you live in an area that's bad for heartworm, you might want to consider this optional extra.

To control fleas, it's important to go after the adults, eggs and larvae at the same time. Only the adults live on the dog; the eggs and larvae do not. So whichever product you choose for killing the eggs, be sure also to use another product to deal with the adults and larvae.

FLEA PATROL Regular combing keeps this Maltese's coat flea free. Dip the comb into hot water or rubbing alcohol after each stroke to kill fleas that are picked up.

A SURE SIGN Use a damp cotton ball to wipe up debris after brushing your dog's coat. Any flea dirt will dissolve, leaving a brownish stain.

By combing your pet regularly with a flea comb, you can stop a possible flea infestation in its tracks. This type of comb is not expensive. Just comb through the coat carefully for five minutes every day and you'll have the fleas leaping out of their hiding places. Their favorite dens are the middle of the back, the base of the tail, the back of the neck, the armpits and the groin region.

Dip the comb in a small jar of rubbing alcohol and the fleas will drown instantly. (Even if you don't get any fleas, you might see little comma-shaped pieces of dirt on the skin, which are actually flea feces.) Always do this job outside—if you don't catch the fleas as they jump ship, it's better that they end up in the grass, not in your carpet.

253

Food Allergies and Intolerances

While both food allergies and food intolerances cause your dog

an adverse reaction, they're not quite the same.

A dog has a food allergy when her immune system reacts to certain ingredients in her food, such as soy protein. A food intolerance, on the other hand, doesn't affect the immune system at all. It occurs when certain ingredients in the food (lactose is a common offender) upset the dog's stomach or intestines.

While the underlying causes are different, food allergies and food intolerances are similar in that they can make your dog feel miserable. Occasionally, it's as simple as a dog vomiting soon after eating, but usually, the link isn't quite so obvious. The food could cause rashes, digestive difficulties, asthma-like symptoms, lots of itching and scratching or abnormal behavior, or all sorts of other problems that may seem to have nothing to do with meals.

Suppose, for example, your dog has a history of recurrent ear infections. There's a possibility that a food allergy could be playing a role in her discomfort. An adverse reaction to food isn't an easy thing to detect, but it will be worth the effort, for your dog's health and happiness, if you can find out for certain, then change her diet so that it suits her better.

TRACKING DOWN THE CULPRIT

To find out what food disagrees with your dog, you'll need the advice and guidance of your vet and the cooperation of your pet—the latter should not be too difficult, since her main role will be eating. You'll also need time and patience—it can take weeks or months to make the diagnosis.

HOLD THE DAIRY
Lactose—a component of dairy products such as cheese and milk—is a common cause of food intolerance in dogs.

ITCHY SYMPTOMS
A dog who constantly scratches, like this Miniature Schnauzer, could be suffering from a food allergy or intolerance.

The first step is to put your dog on an elimination diet in which you give her a food, available from veterinarians, that contains ingredients with a protein source she's never had before, such as venison, turkey, lamb or duck. You must stop giving her snacks and even chewable medicines, as well. If she really does suffer from food allergies, the itching will usually subside within about 12 weeks. This method is based on a simple rule about allergies: you can't be allergic to something you've never eaten before, because allergies build up over time.

If your dog improves dramatically on her elimination diet, the next step is to reintroduce other common foods, one at a time, to pinpoint which ingredient is the culprit. (Your vet will provide you with the "test" foods.) For example, if she's allergic to beef, it doesn't matter if it's a sirloin steak or a fast-food hamburger—they'll both set her symptoms going again. It could be chicken, soy or corn, so test for all of these individually, one every five to seven days. The food that makes her symptoms come back is the food that she has the allergy or intolerance to, and that's the food you'll need to ban from her bowl from now on.

You can now fix her problem 100 percent, and no drugs are needed. If it turns out that your dog is allergic to soy, for example, just buy a dog food that is soy-free. If she has a problem with lactose, give her a food that contains no dairy products, which are high in lactose. Or at least give her lactase supplements, which will help her digest the lactose found in dairy foods. There are plenty of dog

she improves on her special trial food, you'll know for certain that it is food that is contributing to her problems. If she doesn't improve, at least you know that food isn't the cause of her recurring symptoms. With your mind set at rest on that score, you and your vet can set about tracking down clues and looking for other potential causes.

HOME-COOKED DIETS

Be careful about continuing with a home-cooked diet. If you want to feed your dog home-cooked meals (minus the food she reacts to, of course), make sure you ask your vet for a good recipe that is properly balanced to meet your dog's nutritional needs. A test diet isn't well balanced and will cause deficiencies if she stays on it for too long.

foods on the market, so once you know which ingredients you need to avoid, finding the right food for your dog should be no problem.

A HOME-MADE ELIMINATION DIET

The advantage of feeding a home-made elimination diet is that it gives you total control over what goes into your dog's stomach. Your vet will advise you on a recipe. Your dog must be fed this for at least a month, preferably three, before you can be certain of the results.

Conducting an elimination diet can be hard work. The up side is that your dog will really benefit from your efforts. If

There is no cure for food allergies, which can escalate to severe diarrhea or bad skin reactions. So you'll have to monitor your dog's diet closely to make sure unauthorized foods don't slip in and start the problems all over again. You'll also need to make sure that she doesn't scavenge any forbidden foods out of the trash or go begging from the neighbors.

GOOD RESULTS The pay-off for persisting with an elimination diet is a healthier, happier dog who is free of allergy symptoms.

Heartworm

This dangerous parasite is transmitted by that annoying little pest,

the mosquito, but fortunately, you can protect your dog.

Mosquitoes are certainly not a dog's best friend. They can transmit heartworms, dangerous parasites that can literally clog a dog's heart and lungs like strands of spaghetti, making it very difficult for blood to circulate. It's impossible to protect your dog totally from mosquitoes, but there are ways to keep their numbers under control. Here's what vets recommend.

Start by giving early protection. When you live in an area where heartworm exists, it's essential to give your dog preventive medicine. Then, even if she is bitten by an infected mosquito, the medication will kill the heartworms before they can mature and cause problems. The chewable heartworm medication is safe and inexpensive and is usually given monthly. Before prescribing preventive medication in adult dogs, your veterinarian will do a simple blood test to determine whether your dog already has heartworm.

There are additional benefits to giving your dog the medicine. Some heartworm drugs also protect against intestinal parasites. Depending on which heartworm medication you give your dog, it may also help to control roundworms, hookworms and whipworms.

Keeping mosquitoes out is also important. No one wants to keep the windows shut in hot, humid weather, but that's precisely when mosquitoes are thriving. Tight-fitting window and door screens will keep them out of the house. And be sure to repair tears in the screens right away. Even the smallest hole makes it easy for mosquitoes to enter.

Don't forget the yard or garden. Use an outdoor insecticide regularly to keep your dog's yard, kennel or doghouse mosquito-free. Keep things dry, too, because mosquitoes

PROTECTIVE MEASURES Heartworm prevention tablets can be fed to your dog like a chewy treat. This Boxer has no idea he's taking medicine that will keep him safe from a potentially fatal disease.

breed in stagnant water—anything from ponds and large puddles to a small amount of water in a tin can. It's worth doing everything possible to keep your yard dry—by removing objects that can trap water, for example, or changing the landscaping to prevent water from collecting. It's also helpful to sweep away small puddles of water before mosquitoes have a chance to move in and start breeding.

Mosquitoes are most active in the late afternoons and early evenings, when they're looking for food. To minimize the risk of bites, try to keep your dog indoors at these times, especially on still evenings.

Even if heartworm rates are low where you live and there aren't many mosquitoes, your dog may be at risk when you travel to areas where heartworm is a problem. If she isn't currently taking heartworm medication, discuss preventive measures with your vet before you set out on vacation.

Hip Dysplasia

*Certain dogs have hips that don't fit together as snugly as they
should. This painful inherited condition is called hip dysplasia.*

Although puppies aren't born
with the clinical signs of
hip dysplasia, they may be born
with a tendency to develop it.
Your dog's hind legs will become
sore and stiff, but the changes
can happen so gradually that
sometimes they aren't evident
until she is one to two years of
age. Over time, the "loose" hip
joints can cause the bones to
wear, leading to a painful form
of arthritis.

GENTLE EXERCISE Swimming is particularly beneficial
as the weight normally borne by the hip joints is gone.

Any dog can develop hip dysplasia, and
not just the large breeds, as is often thought—
many medium-sized dogs get it, too. Vets often
treat it with drugs or even surgery. But there
are a number of preventive strategies, as well
as some effective home-care treatments.

HELPING THE HIPS

If your dog is one of those breeds that is
particularly prone to hip dysplasia, it's
important to do everything you can to prevent
it. You can improve the situation dramatically
if you do as vets recommend here.

Keep her light on her feet. You want to feed
your fast-growing pup well so she does not get
hungry, but be very careful not to overdo it.
A pup that is at risk for hip dysplasia will do
much better if she is lean rather than plump.
You don't want her to be carrying extra weight
around, because that will
put extra stress and
strain on her hips.

Feed your pup small
amounts of food several
times a day. And don't
leave the bowl on the floor
for longer than 15 minutes,
as this will just encourage
her to overeat.

If your dog is at risk for
developing hip dysplasia,
a low-mineral diet will be

best for her because it will contain less calcium
and may also have a better balance of electrolytes than other diets. There are several such
diets available by prescription. Your vet will
typically recommend this type of food until
your dog has finished all her growing.

Stay away from calcium supplements, too.
Children need calcium for growing bones,
so it's a good thing if they drink lots of milk.
Puppies need calcium for their growing bones,
too, but not calcium supplements. In fact,
these should never be given to young, rapidly
growing, large breeds such as Great Danes,
Doberman Pinschers and retrievers, as they
actually interfere with cartilage and bones
developing normally in large dogs. Puppy
foods already contain lots of calcium and
phosphorus in the right ratios, and additional
supplementation only causes problems.

If your dog is susceptible to
hip dysplasia, go easy on the
exercise. It is important that

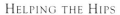

LIKELY SUFFERERS
Dalmatians are on the
list of susceptible breeds, which
also includes Golden Retrievers,
German Shepherds, Standard
Poodles and Siberian Huskies.

257

NO ACROBATICS While it's best to keep your dog moving, avoid having her jumping and twisting to catch balls or flying disks. Walking her on a leash at the beach or in a park is far better for her vulnerable joints.

In addition, make sure that her bed is in a warm, dry place. Give her a gentle massage around the hip joints to relax the area and give her some pleasant relief. To learn more about ways to relieve the pain of sore hips, see p. 231.

Avoiding Hip Dysplasia

Since hip dysplasia is an inherited problem, certain breeds of dogs are much more prone to it than others. Both large breeds and many medium-sized dogs can be affected. Before you fall in love with a pup, make sure she comes from a family with no clinical history of hip dysplasia for at least three generations.

Good breeders will be able to provide certification proving that the radiographic measures of hip dysplasia are low in your pup's family. Get advice from your vet on what scores are considered low in that particular breed. This is the best insurance you can get that your pup won't ever be affected.

your growing dog remains active, as this strengthens the muscles around the hip joints, which helps keep them stable. But don't overdo it because that could stress the already abnormal hip joints and make matters worse.

Make her exercise sessions regular and aerobic, but not haphazard. Opt for a two-mile walk on a leash rather than catching Frisbees in the park. Swimming, too, is a great way of keeping her toned—the water supports her weight and reduces wear and tear on joints.

Easing the Aches

If your pet has already developed signs of hip dysplasia, then some of the same things that help prevent it can also help relieve the aches. For a start, make sure you keep her lean, which will lighten the load on her hip joints. And do keep her moving, gently. A 20-minute walk twice a day will do her a lot of good. If she's actually hurting, take a day off. Rest as well as exercise can help the hips feel better.

Your vet may also recommend giving your dog over-the-counter medications to relieve pain and inflammation; he or she will advise you on the dosage.

HANDLE WITH CARE Holding the stifle (knee) joint in place allows you to move the hip joint in isolation. Dogs with hip dysplasia may show their discomfort when this procedure is performed.

Itching

The cause may be tricky to pin down, but you can't let your dog
continue to suffer with a persistent itch.

There are more than 500 different reasons for a dog to itch. When your dog is scratching all the time, it's important to find out what's bothering her, which is not always so easy. While there are some very common causes of canine scratching, it can sometimes take a lot of detective work to pin down the particular culprit.

A FRENZY OF DISCOMFORT An itchy spot can drive your dog to distraction and, if she keeps chewing at the same place, she can damage the skin and quickly make the problem much more difficult to deal with.

EASING THE ITCH

Your dog doesn't really care what's causing the itching. All she wants is relief. Here's what the experts recommend you do.

- Bathe her regularly. It may be a little labor-intensive, but frequent baths are the fastest way to give your itchy dog some relief when she needs it. Always use cool water—warm water will only make the itch worse. Add some Epsom salts, colloidal oatmeal (such as Aveeno) or baking soda to the water to increase the soothing effects. Soaking your dog for five to ten minutes can provide temporary relief that will last from a few hours to a few days. After bathing and rinsing thoroughly, pat your dog dry with a fluffy towel. Don't use a hair dryer unless it has a cool setting.
- Give her fatty acids. Research has shown that special fatty acids found in either marine oils or evening primrose oil can be very effective for easing itching. These supplements, available at pet supply stores, will usually need to be given for several weeks before your dog will start to feel the benefits. This means they are more useful for easing long-term problems than for on-again, off-again irritations.
- Stop bugs from biting. Like people, dogs can get very itchy from insect bites and stings. When you're visiting insect-infested areas, vets often recommend applying mosquito repellents containing DEET. Just be sure to follow your vet's instructions exactly because these products can be dangerous if not used in the correct way.

- Take fast action. Dogs will occasionally get itchy after contact with something that irritates the skin, such as poison ivy. This often affects the skin on their bellies, where there isn't a lot of fur to protect them. Wash the area thoroughly with a gentle skin cleanser, then apply a mild, over-the-counter cortisone ointment, such as Cortaid, with 1 percent hydrocortisone.
- Try an antihistamine. Vets sometimes recommend giving itchy dogs an over-the-counter antihistamine. These are most effective for easing short-term itches—such as from an insect bite or a flare-up of hay fever. Oral antihistamines that will do the job include chlorpheniramine (Chlor-Trimeton), clemastine (Tavist) and diphenhydramine (Benadryl). Your vet will advise you on the appropriate dose.
- Try a soothing bath or spray. Treat bites by bathing them with cool water, following up with a soothing spray of witch hazel. In fact, witch hazel will make any kind of itch feel better. Also try hydrocortisone ointment or oral antihistamines to give your dog some immediate relief.

Nasal Discharges

Dogs get drippy noses almost as often as people do, and for some of the same reasons—including allergies, colds and sinus problems.

You won't see dogs wiping their noses, but they do get drippy noses as a result of colds and allergies. They also use their noses almost like vacuum cleaners to sniff the exciting things around them, sometimes sniffing up irritants, such as grass seeds or pollen, which can cause the nose to run.

Many dogs get a nasal discharge from time to time, but it tends to be a problem only in breeds with short, squashed noses, such as Staffordshire Bull Terriers, Boxers, Pekingese and Pugs, and long-nosed dogs with narrow airways, such as Collies. Such breeds are also susceptible to breathing difficulties.

Most nasal discharges aren't serious, but they can make it hard for dogs to breathe. The constant flow of moisture also dries and irritates the nose, and the mucous membranes can become very sore.

COMMON PROBLEMS

It's not uncommon for dogs to get mild viral infections, and these will often cause a clear nasal discharge. Most viral infections will clear up on their own in a few days. In the meantime, however, your dog could be contagious and infect other dogs, so keep her away from them until the problem is fixed.

While viral respiratory infections usually aren't serious, those caused by bacteria or fungi can be a real problem because they'll usually get worse unless dogs are treated with medications. If the discharge is bloody, thick, milky or green, it's time to take your dog to your veterinarian.

Dogs can also develop allergies to various substances. Dogs with allergies are more likely to be itchy than sniffly, but occasionally their noses will start running, too. Any type of allergy can cause a nasal discharge, but usually it's an inhalant allergy—one that's caused by breathing airborne pollen, molds or dust. As with discharges caused by viral infections, an allergy-related discharge is usually clear and watery.

The blood vessels that line the nasal passages are very small and delicate, and an energetic sneeze or two can sometimes cause them to break. A nasal discharge that's tinged

SOOTHE A SORE NOSE This Collie–cattle dog mix is having her nose soothed with moist baby wipes impregnated with aloe vera.

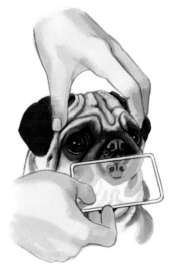

MIRROR TEST If you suspect that there is a foreign object in your dog's nose, hold a small mirror close to her nostrils. If the misting is uneven, there is probably something in there and you should take a closer look.

with blood usually isn't serious and goes away in a day or two. If it doesn't, see your vet in case there's substantial nasal damage, or something more serious, such as a tumor, that's causing the bleeding.

KEEP YOUR DOG COMFORTABLE

To turn off the drip and keep your dog's nose from getting sore, here's what veterinarians advise. Dogs with allergies or colds can secrete tremendous amounts of mucus in a day. If you don't remove it right away, it will dry on the nostrils, possibly clogging them and making the nose raw and sore. It's worth taking a few moments from time to time to gently wipe the nose with a warm, damp cloth, then dab on a little moisturizer to keep the nose lubricated.

Since dogs with a nasal discharge usually have irritated mucous membranes, you can give them quick relief by taking them into the bathroom with you when you bathe or shower. The steam will instantly soothe the inside of the nose, which will help to reduce the drip later on.

If your dog has a nasal discharge, her ability to breathe is compromised, so keep her exercise light. It's best to avoid other dogs, too, so that any infection is not spread far and wide among the canine friends she usually meets while out walking.

GIVE AN ANTIHISTAMINE

Over-the-counter medications such as Benadryl are very effective for easing allergies that can cause a drippy nose. Vets usually advise giving dogs one to three milligrams for every 1 lb (500 g) of your dog's bodyweight. Individual dogs respond differently to medications, however, so it's a good idea to check with your vet for the precise dose.

DO THE MIRROR TEST

It's common for dogs to get small objects stuck in their nostrils, and these can cause a copious nasal discharge and a veritable frenzy of head-pawing or nose-rubbing. The easiest way to check for an obstruction is to hold a small mirror under the nose. If you don't get equal fogging from both nostrils, it's likely that there is a foreign body in the nostril.

Take a flashlight and try to see what's stuck inside. If you can see the object, you may be able to remove it with your fingers or blunt-nosed tweezers. Most dogs won't hold still for this, however, so ask a friend to hold your dog steady while you probe inside. On no account push the object further in. If your dog keeps squirming or the object is difficult to remove, ask your vet to take a look. Vets have specialized instruments with which to remove the object easily and with minimum pain.

Paw and Nail Problems

*Paw problems can be extremely painful, but they are usually
fairly easy to treat at home.*

The paw pads act as shock absorbers every
time a dog's feet hit the ground. The pads
are covered with thick skin that is designed
to be resilient, but in dogs who do a great deal
of running on hard surfaces, the skin can
thicken, forming a hard callus. Calluses are
tough, but they aren't very flexible and they
easily dry out, causing painful cracks. Most of
the time, the leathery surface of your dog's
paws takes whatever nature dishes out. But
unlike a pair of sturdy work boots, paw pads
can become scraped, cracked or sore.

It's not only pads that are vulnerable.
Other potential problem spots are the nails.
A dog's nails grow quickly, and when they get
too long, they can crack or tear. Regular
checks and a few minutes a week spent on
basic paw care will keep your dog's feet
healthy and strong all year round.

KEEPING THE PADS HEALTHY

The pads' tough, rough
surface is not very thick
and is easily cut. And your
dog's hairy feet are perfect
traps for burrs, irritating
moisture or even jagged spurs of ice.
More than any other part of your dog's body,
the feet need regular attention—not only to
prevent injuries, but to treat them quickly
once they occur.

Unlike human feet, which dry quickly
when exposed to air, a dog's furry paws can
stay damp for hours. This can soften and
damage the skin. Take a few seconds to dry
the feet thoroughly whenever they get damp.
Pay particular attention to the area between
the toes, where moisture is most likely to
accumulate. A dusting of unscented talcum
powder will help dry residual moisture.

Dogs that spend a lot of time outside often
develop brittle nails and tiny cracks in the
pads. In winter, especially, apply a little
moisturizer, such as Alpha Keri lotion or

TORN NAILS

Injured nails are painful and bloody. Regular nail
trimming greatly reduces the risks, but even well-
trimmed nails get torn from time to time.

To stop the bleeding, apply firm pressure with
gauze pads or a clean rag. Once the bleeding has
stopped, wash the paw well with warm water and
soap and examine the injury.

If the nail is not dangling but has simply torn, it
probably won't have to be removed. A torn nail that
has come away slightly from the paw on the inner
side of the nail needs to be trimmed. If you usually
do this for your dog, trim it and dress the wound so
it can heal. If you're not familiar with nail-trimming,
apply ointment and clean, dry gauze pads, taping
them firmly in place, and take your dog to the vet.

If the nail is dangling, concentrate on
stopping the bleeding. Wash the wound
and bind it with sterile bandages, then
see your vet right away.

A CHANCE TO HEAL Apply moisturizer to
cracked paw pads and put socks
on your dog's feet to stop
her from licking it off. This
will soothe the soreness
and allow the pads to heal.

petroleum jelly, for a few days until the pads
are back to normal. Don't do this too often,
though, because it will make the pads too soft
to provide adequate protection.

The combination of moisture and wear and
tear can make your dog's feet very susceptible
to infections, causing the pads to become
puffy, red and sore. A quick way to ease the
pain and ward off any potential problems is
to soak your dog's feet for five to 10 minutes in
a solution of 10 parts cool water and one part
of an antiseptic such as Betadine (to about the
color of weak tea).

If your dog will cooperate, put some of the
antiseptic solution in a bucket and let her

stand with one leg inside. If she won't hold still long enough to soak, wet a washcloth in the solution and thoroughly clean the pads and between the toes. Dry the foot well.

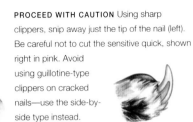

PROCEED WITH CAUTION Using sharp clippers, snip away just the tip of the nail (left). Be careful not to cut the sensitive quick, shown right in pink. Avoid using guillotine-type clippers on cracked nails—use the side-by-side type instead.

Mud can cause paw problems, too. Wet mud isn't an issue, but when it dries, the rough edges will irritate the paws. Diaper wipes do a good job of removing mud from the paws. And simply washing your dog's feet in warm, soapy water—or, in summer, splashing them with the garden hose—will easily remove the mud before it dries and hardens.

Winter is especially tough on your dog's paws, not only because the dry air robs them of moisture, but because snow, ice and road salt abrade and irritate the pads. It's inconvenient to wash your dog's feet after every walk, but it's the only way to protect them. One way to make it a little easier is to keep a bowl or bucket of water near the front door. This way you can give her feet a quick dip whenever she comes inside. Remember to dry them, too.

Even though your dog's coat provides protection from the elements, hair on the feet traps moisture and prevents air from circulating. Trim the hair between the toes to keep the feet drier and healthier, especially in long-haired breeds like Golden Retrievers, Maltese or many of the spaniels. Lift one foot at a time and spread the toes with your fingers. Using blunt-nosed scissors, and

following the line of the toe, trim the hair by cutting straight down rather than across.

Do a daily foot check to head off problems. Dogs step on nails, and pick up thistles and thorns in their wanderings, so remove these before they cause further injury or an infection. When you remove an object from the paw, be sure to clean the area thoroughly and dab on a little antibiotic ointment.

Immune system problems and autoimmune disorders, such as lupus, may cause the body to begin attacking the skin, causing painful cracks. These illnesses can come on fairly quickly, so if your dog suddenly starts to develop pad cracks even when she hasn't been active, see your vet promptly. Hardened areas on the pads used to be much more common because of the viral condition distemper (also known as hardpad).

Also, give sore feet some time off. Pad cracks are often slow to heal because of the pressure and friction caused by walking. Reduce paw stress by walking your dog only on grass or other soft surfaces until the cracks on her feet have healed.

DAILY FOOT CHECKS
Watch for soreness or damage to your dog's feet, especially if she has access to rough or wild areas. Remove foreign objects before they cause further injury or an infection.

Prostate Problems

Dogs with prostate problems may walk a little stiffly because of pain caused by the swollen gland, and urination is often frequent.

Located at the base of the bladder, the prostate gland is essential for reproduction—it produces a liquid constituent of the semen. As dogs age, however, the prostate gland often enlarges and may press on the urethra or the rectum. Urination is often frequent and distressing. The prostate gland is also prone to infection.

What You Can Do

The best way to prevent and treat prostate problems is to have your dog neutered. But there are also things you can do at home to keep him a little more comfortable.

If the prostate gland is swollen and obstructing the flow of urine through the urethra, your dog will take a lot more time to urinate. He will also need more opportunities to urinate, since it's difficult for him to finish all at once. This means you should plan on taking your pet outside much more often, and be prepared to wait for him to finish.

If the swollen gland is pressing against the large intestine, your dog may have trouble passing a bowel movement. Give him a little oat bran or canned pumpkin, both of which are high in fiber, to soften his stools and make them easier to pass. Or add a little Metamucil to his food. If he's still constipated, your vet may prescribe a stool softener to make him regular.

Prostate problems sometimes cause urinary tract infections because urine trapped in the bladder provides a breeding ground for bacteria.

ENCOURAGE HIM TO DRINK
Drinking more water will help flush away any bacteria in your dog's bladder before they cause problems.

EARLY SIGNS

The prostate gland typically enlarges very slowly, so most dogs won't have problems until middle age or beyond. But prostate infections can come on very suddenly and, once started, they can quickly cause whole-body problems. Call your vet at the first sign of trouble.

Dogs with a prostate infection, prostatitis, will urinate more frequently, although relatively little urine will come out, and there may be blood in the urine. Most prostate problems occur in intact dogs, so it makes sense to neuter your male dog if you don't have plans to show or breed him.

Encourage your dog to drink more so that the urine will be less concentrated and infections less likely to take hold. Bacteria will be flushed away before they cause problems.

If your dog is reluctant to get up to go for a drink, put the bowl where it's easy for him to reach. It's also helpful to encourage him to drink before and after a walk. Dogs don't need gallons of water, but sometimes a gentle reminder that it's there will entice them to lap up a little more.

Keep the walks gentle and slow until he's feeling better. Prostate problems can be painful and most dogs won't want to run around too much. While some exercise is good and can help to ease constipation, too much may be uncomfortable. To ease prostate pain, your vet may prescribe a painkiller such as Rimadyl. He may also prescribe hormone tablets that will reduce the prostatic enlargement.

Shedding

Do you sometimes feel as if your dog is shedding so much you could knit yourself a sweater with her hair?

When it comes to hair loss, most dogs have a lot of hair to get rid of, but there's usually nothing abnormal about it. Shedding is a normal part of the cycle of your dog's hair growth. The amount of normal shedding that an animal does is very much dependent on the type of coat she has, genetics and the environment in which she lives. Most outdoor dogs have a shedding season in the spring as their "winter" coats are lost. However, if your dog is an indoor pet, she possibly won't be outside long enough for her body to register the change in seasons, so she will shed all year round.

All dogs shed, some more than others—unless they're one of the few hairless breeds with absolutely nothing to lose. Long-haired dogs might seem to shed more, but it's just the length of their hair that gives that illusion. Dogs that really do shed the most include Collies, Dalmatians, German Shepherds and Samoyeds. If you want a dog that loses hair lightly, consider a Poodle, Bichon Frise or maybe an Old English Sheepdog.

Even though shedding is completely normal, dogs will occasionally begin to lose much more hair than usual. If bald patches begin showing through the fur, there's probably something wrong and you need to visit your vet right away. There are physical problems that can cause dogs to lose abnormal

GROOMING TOOLS (From left) Use the pincushion side of this soft bristle brush on short- or wire-haired dogs. After brushing, use a wide-toothed comb or a shedding glove to remove excess loose hair on most coat types.

amounts of hair, including mange, ringworm, skin infections, stress and even cancer. But your pet shouldn't be losing her hair just because she is getting older. It isn't normal for the coat to thin out as a dog ages.

HELP FOR HAIR LOSS

Nature intended for your dog to shed and there isn't anything you can do to stop it. But if your dog is a big shedder, you can make it less of a problem. Forget drugs or nutritional supplements. The best way to handle excessive shedding is simply to remove dead hair before it lands on your clothes, carpets and furniture.

It's best to brush your dog once a day, especially during the shedding season. There are a variety of grooming tools you can use, from slicker brushes to combs specially designed to remove loose hair.

Your groomer or your vet will recommend the tools and techniques that will work best with your dog's coat. For more information about particular coats and their requirements, see "How to Groom" on p. 196. Don't be surprised if you fill a garbage bag with hair on your first serious brushing session. You may well think there's more hair in the bag than there is left on your dog. But remember, if the hair loss is abnormal, she will have bald spots. Otherwise, keep brushing until her coat feels soft and clean.

PARTICULAR CASES

Some Arctic breeds, such as Siberian Huskies and Alaskan Malamutes (right), have a genetic tendency to absorb too little zinc. This can cause hair loss along with scaly, crusty patches on the skin. When these dogs are given zinc supplements, however, their coats quickly return to normal.

Skin Irritations

Your dog's skin performs a great many important duties, but it is also vulnerable to attack from many pests and infections.

Mange can make a dog look as if moths have been eating her. There might be hairless patches, open red sores or what looks like dandruff. Or it could be extremely itchy, depending on the type of mange it is. Mange comes in many different forms—the most common are scabies, cheyletiellosis and demodectic mange. Ear mites cause another form of mange. In fact, each type of mange is caused by different kinds of mites that dwell on or in the skin. Your vet will first diagnose the type of mange that your dog has, and then prescribe appropriate treatment.

SCABIES

This is the itchiest condition known in dogs and is caused by minuscule scabies mites that burrow into the skin and lay their eggs. Dogs often develop a skin sensitivity to the mites, which makes the itching even worse. The mites are easily passed from dog to dog.

While highly contagious, scabies is quite easy to treat. Most dogs will be mite free within four weeks and the itching will have eased after 10 to 14 days, regardless of which treatment you opt for. Medicated dips are one easy solution. Washing your dog with lime and sulfur medications diluted with water not only kills the mites but also eases the itch.

However, your vet will probably give your dog a series of injections, as this is the most efficient treatment. When the mites go, the

itch goes. While not licensed for the purpose, some flea-control products, such as Frontline, also seem to be effective against scabies.

Even when you successfully treat scabies, your dog can pick up a new infestation the next time she comes into contact with a dog with scabies on board. It pays to keep her away from any balding or scratchy dogs. It also pays to treat all your pets, not just the one with the infestation, because chances are if one pet has it, the others will also get it.

Be careful how close you get to your dog while she has scabies because it can be contagious to people, too. The mites can bite, especially if they come in direct contact with

SPEED UP THE HEALING A hot spot will heal more quickly if it's exposed to the air. Use electric clippers to trim away the hair over and around the hot spot.

HOT SPOTS

Hot spots, or pyotraumatic dermatitis, are painful sores that appear suddenly on a dog's body, mostly behind the ears and around the tail. Usually, it's when a dog has been scratching, biting or licking because she's itchy from an allergy or other irritation. Although hot spots look scary, only the top layers of skin are affected and they heal without leaving scars. They are rarely anything to worry about and, with the following simple treatments, most hot spots will heal within a week.

- Trim or shave off the fur around the spot. It will dry up and heal more quickly if exposed to air.
- Clean the hot spot gently with an antiseptic, such as chlorhexidine or povidone-iodine. Don't use isopropyl alcohol—it is excruciatingly painful on an open wound. Rinse well and pat dry.
- Give cool baths with some Epsom salts or Burow's solution dissolved in the water to relieve the pain and soothe the itchiness.
- It may help to use an Elizabethan collar (p. 236) to stop her from biting the spot.
- Don't use any kind of ointment or moisturizer.

TOO HOT Dogs bred for hot climates, such as Huskies, are particularly prone to skin irritations in hot weather.

house and your dog's bedding with a flea-control spray that kills mites.

your skin. You might notice itchy patches between your fingers or around the belt line, but fortunately, biting is about all they can do to you. The mites that cause scabies in dogs can't live and reproduce on people, so once your dog is successfully treated, the mites will go from you, too—no treatment necessary.

CHEYLETIELLOSIS

This type of mange is courtesy of a white, crablike mite that goes by the name of Cheyletiella. It looks like "walking dandruff." Although not as itch-provoking as scabies, cheyletiellosis will make most dogs scratch. And, like scabies, it is passed from pet to pet—your dog will even share these pests with you if you don't keep a safe distance.

Treatment options are the same as for scabies, so see your vet. The problem is usually resolved within four weeks, but these mites can survive in the environment for a few days. Clean the house thoroughly and wash your dog's bedding in hot water to stop late-comers from settling in. To be doubly sure, spray the

DEMODECTIC MANGE

Demodectic mange, or demodicosis, is caused by a microscopic, cigar-shaped mite that lives in the hair follicles. These mites normally live on a dog's skin—they live on people's skin, too, and are not contagious. The mites cause no problems for the dog while her immune system is functioning okay. But if she becomes run down or her immune system gets over-loaded or develops some kind of defect, there may be a sudden explosion in the mite population. The mites crowd the hair follicles and eventually rupture them, causing her hair to fall out and her skin to become infected.

The good news is that once your dog's immune system is restored to health, the mite problem will disappear. In about 90 percent of cases, if you just give it time, the mange will cure itself. But in 10 percent of cases, the immune system doesn't recover unaided. So if the mange does not improve after a month or if it is getting worse, see your vet for treatment to kill the mites and control the infections.

PROBLEM LICKING

Sometimes dogs will lick at the same spot until they create a large, open wound—a condition called acral lick dermatitis or lick granuloma. These wounds can be very serious and often become infected, so see your vet promptly.

Some vets believe this is a skin problem, others that it is behavioral, and still others that a problem with the nerve endings causes dogs to experience "phantom" pain. Vets occasionally recommend that dogs wear an Elizabethan collar (see p. 236) to prevent them from worrying the wound, but when the wound heals and you take the collar off, the dog often goes right back to licking. Bitter-tasting sprays aren't even a mild deterrent when it comes to a lick granuloma.

A number of medications can help. Different drugs seem to work for different dogs. Some respond to long-term antibiotic therapy, some to cortisone and some to anti-anxiety medications. Before resorting to medication, though, try increasing your dog's exercise quota and avoiding the stress caused by separation anxiety.

Sunburn

Dogs are less likely than humans to suffer sunburn because their insulating fur protects them, but they do have sparsely haired areas.

Take a good look at your dog and you can probably guess where she is most vulnerable to sunburn: the nose, the tips of the ears (especially if she has upright ears) and the belly. Also, those dogs with fair skin and short hair will need extra protection, especially Dalmatians, white Bull Terriers and American Staffordshire Terriers, German Shorthaired Pointers, white Boxers, Whippets and Beagles.

PROTECT THEIR NOSES Australian Shepherds, such as these puppies, have a tendency to get sunburned on their pale noses.

Sun-damaged skin is not a trifling matter. It's not just the pain, there's also a possibility of skin cancer, and some diseases, such as lupus erythematosus, are aggravated by too much exposure to the sun. You don't need to go crazy with sun protection, but it pays to be safe, particularly if the furry sun worshipper in your household is a pale-skinned one.

DEALING WITH SUNBURN

Vets advise various ways to soothe your pet's heated skin and to protect her from sunburn. The simplest relief for a sunburnt dog is to spray her with a squirt bottle of water to cool down her burnt bits. Mix in some witch hazel to give her extra help. Or let her soak in a cool, soothing bath. Some baking soda dissolved in the water will give extra relief.

There are also over-the-counter sprays, such as Solarcaine and Lanacane, which contain a local anesthetic to reduce pain. And don't forget the healing qualities of aloe vera. Buy a cream or lotion from your pharmacy and gently apply this, or if you have an aloe vera plant handy, simply break off a leaf and squeeze the gel out onto the affected area.

For a dog who'll be out in the sun, sunscreens are a definite plus, especially the kinds that don't wear off in the water—or get licked off. Even if your dog isn't fair-skinned, if she is going to spend a lot of time in the sun, give her ears and nose a little extra help.

Look for a sunscreen with an SPF (sun-protection factor) of at least 15—the higher the SPF, the more protection it provides. Also, it mustn't contain an ingredient called PABA, because if your dog licks the sunscreen off—and chances are she will—the PABA can be dangerous. Human sunscreens are fine, but canine products are available, too.

A child's white T-shirt could be the answer for dogs with pale skin or those that like to expose their sensitive bellies. So, if your dog will allow it, pop the neck opening over her head, put her front legs through the armholes and pull the T-shirt down over her body.

Avoid prolonged summer sun exposure between about 10 a.m and 3 p.m.—the hottest time of day. And always provide shade.

VULNERABLE AREAS Short-haired white dogs, such as this Fox Terrier, need sunscreen on bare parts.

Ticks

Tick control and tick patrol are a must if you live in or visit a part of the country where ticks are common.

Ticks latch on to whatever skin is passing and start sucking up blood—their food of choice. During feeding, they can swell up to 50 times their normal size. But they also carry diseases, such as Lyme disease, tick fever, encephalitis, Rocky Mountain spotted fever, tick paralysis and a new, potentially fatal, illness called hepatozoonosis. It takes 24 to 72 hours for ticks to transfer their diseases.

TACKLING TICKS

There are many kinds of ticks and not all of them spread the same diseases, but if there's a tick on your dog, you can be sure it's up to no good. Here's how to get rid of them.

Do a tick check. Ticks like humid wooded or grassy areas, so when you have encountered this type of vegetation, take the time to do a head-to-toe search through your dog's fur. Ticks tend to congregate in and around a dog's head and neck, especially around the ears, and also between the toes. But check all over.

Collar the problem. A tick collar that contains amitraz (Preventic) will cause embedded ticks to leave. It will also discourage new ticks from moving in. It can be relied upon to give protection for about four months. But because it doesn't totally deter ticks, it's still a good idea to check your dog over after you've been in tick country. Other types of flea and tick collars are not as effective.

Use spray-on protection. Vets often recommend treating dogs with products such as Frontline, which contains fipronil and kills ticks within 24 hours of them attaching to your dog. Spray it on as directed on the label for control of ticks (and fleas). It is very safe and can be used on puppies and pregnant females. Repellents such as DEET and perma-none are also effective, but the chemicals they contain may be hazardous for certain pets.

Patrol the yard. Most ticks are found on vegetation, so mowing the lawn and removing damp underbrush, leaf litter and extra foliage gets rid of their hiding places in your yard.

REMOVING TICKS

It's best to get rid of ticks quickly. Here's what to do if they're embedded and feeding on your pet.

1. Wear surgical gloves or cover your hands with plastic wrap. You risk being exposed to diseases ticks carry, so be very careful not to squeeze, crush or puncture the body. Hand-to-eye contact after handling ticks can also cause infection.

2. Soak the tick with alcohol. (Don't use kerosene or gasoline because they will hurt your pet's skin.) Stunned by the alcohol, the tick will loosen its grip and won't start trying to dig back in the minute you apply some pressure. This will make it much easier for you to pull out the entire tick, body and head.

3. Grasp the tick's body near its head with forceps, a tick-removing tool or tweezers. Pull gently until you feel the tick pull away. Try your best not to leave the head in the skin. If you just get the tick's body but leave the head in, there's a risk of an abscess forming. In that case, your vet will need to take a look at it.

4. Dispose of the tick in a jar of alcohol.

5. Disinfect the area with cleansers such as povidone-iodine or chlorhexidine. Alcohol may be too irritating on the small wound.

6. Wash your hands well with soap and water. If you don't feel up to removing a tick, spray it with fipronil (Frontline), which will kill it within 24 hours.

Urination Problems

Just like humans, dogs sometimes have problems with urination—
urinary tract infections, urinary "stones" and even incontinence.

Any urinary tract problem is potentially serious and should be treated by a vet. Blood in the urine should never be ignored. But there are things you can do at home to ease urinary tract discomfort and help prevent a recurrence of some problems.

INFECTIONS

A urinary tract infection is likely if your dog used to be able to wait all day between toilet trips, but lately is standing at the door every five minutes. Another indication is the ability to pass only small amounts of urine. Such infections can be painful and give a dog an urgent, frequent need to pass urine.

Give your dog lots of opportunities to relieve himself. And make sure he drinks plenty of water, because this will help flush out his system, though it won't cure the infection. Apart from frequent toilet trips, there's not a lot you can do at home. Your vet will probably prescribe oral antibiotics and urinary antiseptics.

BLADDER STONES

People get stones in their kidneys. With dogs, most urinary stones are found in the bladder. Veterinarians typically call them uroliths, and the condition is known as urolithiasis. Suspect this problem if your dog is straining to urinate, but having little success.

Your vet will help you to implement a two-pronged care program. The first objective is to stop any crystals in your dog's bladder from developing into stones. To do this, make sure he drinks lots of fluids and has plenty of opportunities to urinate. All this liquid in his system will flush out any crystals before they have a chance to evolve into stones. Your vet may also recommend a special diet that makes the crystals less likely to form into stones.

The other goal is to dissolve stones that have already formed. There are different types of stones, and before you can help your dog out, your vet must run a test to determine which type he has. Some stones are more soluble in acidic urine; some in alkaline urine.

Once your vet has diagnosed the type of stone, he may recommend special diets or additives to change the pH of your dog's urine to help dissolve and eliminate the stones.

INCONTINENCE

It's normal for puppies to leave puddles, but when an older dog urinates when (and where) he shouldn't and doesn't know he's doing it, there's almost certainly something wrong. This condition, called incontinence, is most common in older, neutered females, probably because they have low levels of the hormone estrogen, which the body needs to keep muscles in the urinary tract strong. It also tends to occur in pets that are carrying excess weight,

ENDLESS SUPPLY It may seem like frequent urination, but this dog is just leaving signals that he's been here. He sprays as high up as possible to indicate that he's a big dog.

TAKING CARE OF BUSINESS Just like this Boxer, your dog needs lots of opportunities to go outside.

where it's easier to clean up later (see "Caring for Older Dogs," p. 298).

SUBMISSIVE URINATION

When a dog wants to show another dog the ultimate form of respect, he'll roll over on his back and urinate on the spot. Among dogs, this type of behavior, called submissive urination, is usually practiced by puppies and adult dogs who are particularly shy or submissive. Dogs who do it in the human family are generally insecure about something—either because something has frightened them or because they're naturally a little that way. It pays to ignore dogs that roll over in greeting,

which causes extra pressure on the bladder, and sometimes in dogs that are excited or under stress. It isn't the same as the occasional accident. With incontinence, the dog doesn't know it's happening.

Incontinence can often be controlled, but you'll probably need help from your vet. One standard treatment is to give hormone supplements, along with other medications that improve the tone of the bladder muscle. And at home, the most important thing you can do is not to blame your dog for accidents—he can't help it. The last thing you want to do is to make him feel more anxious or stressed.

Instead, try to reduce stress in his life and spend more time with him outdoors, where a little dribbling doesn't matter. Also, the more chances he has to relieve himself, the less urine there'll be causing pressure on the bladder, and the less likelihood of accidents.

If you are going out and are afraid of what you might find on the carpet when you return, consider putting a diaper on your dog or confining him to the bathroom or laundry

because the submissive urination that sometimes follows can become a learned ritual.

For many dogs, all that's necessary to stop messes in the house is to let them out more often. It's important to let them out first thing in the morning and after meals, when the urges are strongest. You should also let them out before you go to bed, because the eight to nine hours from night to morning is longer than some dogs can wait. Puppies need to go outside more often—at least every two hours during the day and every four hours at night.

Dogs who are suddenly making messes often need a refresher course in basic training. Keep an eye on your dog whenever he is in the house. Your goal is to catch him before he squats on the carpet, since it's more effective to praise good behavior when he goes in the right place than to punish him for making a mistake. You don't have to wait until he's almost in the act before heading for the door. Letting him out more often and the praise you give will help him to understand what he is supposed to do in the future.

Vomiting

Dogs vomit much more readily than people and, most of the time, there's a simple reason for it.

Few things are less pleasant than coming home and finding the remains of your dog's breakfast on the living room carpet. But for your dog, it's just another day. A lot of the time, there's a simple reason for it, like a raid on the trash can or eating too much too quickly. But if you're still unsure about the cause, give your dog a quick physical examination and take her temperature before calling your vet for more specific instructions.

If your dog appears physically ill or the vomiting won't stop, you should call your vet immediately. Your dog may have swallowed something poisonous or toxic, in which case every second counts. Also, if she has been vomiting a lot, she may need intravenous fluids to replace the water and electrolytes she has lost.

TRASH IS TEMPTING A determined dog, like this Australian Shepherd, will get into the trash if she possibly can and the result will be an upset stomach.

SOOTHING UPSET STOMACHS

Most cases of vomiting will turn around within 24 hours. In the meantime, there are things you can do at home to help your dog feel better again.

Your dog will benefit from missing at least one meal after she's vomited. This will give her stomach a chance to rest and get back to normal again. If the problem is trash-raiding or a bout of the flu, things should settle down within a day. Until then, try to limit her food intake—this is not the time to worry that your pet is going hungry.

However, make sure your dog always has access to small amounts of water—just don't fill her bowl. Or, give her

WHAT'S THE HURRY?
A dog will have to eat more slowly with less gulping if you spread her food out on a flat tray.

ice cubes to lick. It's important that she doesn't become dehydrated, but at the same time you don't want her gulping down huge quantities of water, which will only make her feel queasy again.

If your dog has fasted for 24 hours and the vomiting has stopped, you can get her back onto solid food again. Start by slowly reintroducing bland foods, such as boiled chicken, cottage cheese, rice or beef bouillon, until you're sure that her stomach has settled down and is able to cope with food again. Then gradually start giving your dog her regular food mixed with the bland foods until she's eating normally again.

A stomach soother may help. Pepto-Bismol coats the stomach and will give your dog some temporary relief. But always check with your vet first so you know it's safe and you get the right information on the dosage and frequency for her size.

Weight Problems

It's natural for dogs to eat whenever there's food around—that's what their ancestors did—but obesity is becoming a huge problem.

Perhaps we're pampering our animals too much, but obesity is a real problem in the canine population. In one study, more than 25 percent of dogs were found to be more than 15 percent above their optimal body weight. Sometimes it's because of a medical problem, but usually it's a case of too much food and not enough exercise. Regardless of the cause, being overweight can lead to diminished quality of life as well as a shortened lifespan for your pet.

Dogs love to eat—and food is a very convenient, and popular, reward to give them. It's not that dogs don't get signals from their intestines to tell them when they're full or when they've put on enough fat. The problem is that the canine body's idea of enough fat may be very different from ours. Since you control the feed bag, you have the ultimate power—and responsibility—when it comes to controlling your dog's food calories (kilojoules). He will probably eat whatever you give him. So you are really the only one who can help him to lose that extra weight.

Putting your dog on a weight-loss program is an act of love and caring. And you'll find most dogs don't mind a sensible program at all—it just takes some physical and behavioral planning on your part to accomplish it.

much is to find out what his ideal weight is. If he is a purebred, you will be able to get this information from a book about his breed. Compare this with his weight and you'll know whether dieting is in order. An even better alternative, especially if your dog is a one-of-a-kind mixed breed, is to do a rib test. Feel his sides; if you can't find his ribs, it's diet time.

The next step is to try a change in diet. It's important that you evaluate your current feeding practices. Your vet can help calculate how many calories (kilojoules) a day your dog should be consuming compared to how many you're actually feeding him. It may simply be a question of changing the amount or type of food he eats to reach the lower energy target.

For example, if you are feeding your dog a premium or performance dog food, it is probably providing far too much energy, especially if he is sedentary a lot of the time. Such diets are typically high in meat protein and fat and provide more calories (kilojoules) than a sedentary dog can use.

If he's a working dog or he gets plenty of exercise, that's another matter—and he probably won't have a weight problem anyway. In most such cases, you can safely switch your dog to a wholesome product with moderate

LOSING WEIGHT

A canine weight-loss regime is not difficult or expensive. Follow the suggestions outlined here and your dog will soon be healthier and happier.

First of all, recognize when he has a problem. Maybe your dog is solid but not overweight. Or maybe he's a shade more than solid—he really is overweight. One way to tell if a dog truly does weigh too

THE RIB TEST At a healthy weight, your dog will have a distinct waist and you will be able to feel just a slight amount of padding over the ribs.

TIME FOR A DIET This Rottweiler's excess weight is likely to cause other serious health problems.

amounts of protein and less fat and more fiber than he was previously getting. Most of the time, you won't even need to reduce the amount you feed him.

If your dog is on a diet, feed him several small meals a day rather than one large meal at the beginning or end of the day. This will help keep hunger pangs at bay and convince him that his tummy is feeling okay. Just because you're feeding him more often, this doesn't mean you feed him a larger quantity—simply divide the amount of food he is fed in one day into two to four servings and serve them up at more frequent intervals.

Keep in mind that snacking is the downfall of every dieter who finds it hard to resist those tempting between-meals moments. But you don't have to stop giving your dog snacks and treats completely, you just need to change his habits. Cereal biscuits tend to be very high in

calories, so swap to something healthier. Try carrots, fruit or popcorn—without the salt, sugar or butter, of course.

When your dog earns a treat and you want to reward him, don't automatically reach into your pocket for a bit of food. Consider a social reward instead, such as playing fetch or tug-of-war or going for a swim. You might be surprised to learn that your dog prefers social rewards to food in many instances. Sure, dogs love to eat, but substitute play and exercise for food and most will think it's a fair trade.

You may need to think again about high-fiber diets. Traditionally, such diets have been prescribed for dogs with weight problems. These slimming diets have plenty of roughage that will fill up your dog's stomach. This produces one of the signals the brain uses to determine whether enough food has been eaten. However, recent research has suggested that fiber may not leave a pet feeling "full." Fiber can also interfere with the absorption of such nutrients as selenium and zinc, so discuss the benefits of high-fiber diets with your vet before deciding to put your plump pet on one.

A regular exercise program is a great way for your dog to shed weight and start feeling and looking better. This doesn't mean you need to start him on exhausting exercise sessions or marathon runs. A good long walk or relaxing jog twice a day is the way to get the heart pumping and burn off some calories. If exercise is new to him, start with short walks and build up to more vigorous workouts.

Keep an eye on the results. You don't want the weight to suddenly

BREEDS MOST LIKELY...

Some dogs are more likely to pile on the pounds, and keep them on, than others—it's in the genes. If your dog is one of the following breeds, you're going to have to pay extra special attention to his weight and feeding needs:

- Basset Hound (right)
- Beagle
- Cocker Spaniel
- Dachshund
- Labrador Retriever

SUDDEN WEIGHT LOSS

The combination of easy living and an abundance of food means that dogs gain weight almost as easily as people do. It's a lot less common, however, for them to lose weight. Except for dogs on diets, weight loss is usually a sign that a dog is ill.

Dental problems. Veterinarians have found that more than 85 percent of dogs over the age of three have some degree of periodontal disease, a condition in which bacteria and a variety of irritating substances work their way beneath the gums, causing painful infections or inflammation. Periodontal disease that isn't treated can make eating very painful, and many dogs will simply quit. Other dental problems, such as a fractured tooth or an abscess, may also cause dogs to stop eating.

Competition. Even easygoing dogs can get very aggressive about food. In households with a number of dogs, it's common for one dog to be both greedy and assertive and to steal the other dogs' suppers. Most dogs will protect their food, but some are so timid about confrontations that they'll just walk away. Eventually, they may start losing weight.

Pain. Your dog might lose his appetite when he's not feeling well. This is especially common in older dogs who may have arthritis or problems with their hips or other joints. The discomfort takes away their appetites, and even when they're hungry, they may have difficulty getting up and walking to the food bowl.

Stress. The fast pace of modern life can be very stressful for dogs, who don't respond to changes very well. Dogs who are anxious or nervous—because their owners are away from home more than usual, for example—may stop eating. This type of weight loss is rarely serious, however, because they'll start eating properly again once things calm down.

High-energy living. Modern dog foods contain an abundance of nutrients, and most dogs get all the calories (kilojoules) they need. Dogs who burn a lot of energy, however, such as working dogs or mothers who are nursing puppies, may lose weight because they're getting less food than they need. In this case, your vet will advise you on an eating plan that will help your dog.

Diabetes. The hormone insulin is responsible for transporting the sugars in foods into the body's cells. Dogs with diabetes don't have enough insulin, which means that no matter how much they eat, they aren't getting all the calories they need.

Since weight loss may accompany dozens of internal illnesses, from parasites to cancer, see your veterinarian as soon as you notice that your dog is looking thinner than usual. Even though the problem may turn out to be a simple one, some of the conditions that cause dogs to lose weight will get worse very quickly unless they're treated.

drop off your dog—that's not good for him. Your aim is for him to lose the extra weight over a safe period of about 12 weeks. Keep in regular contact with your vet during this time, and if your dog hasn't reached his target by then, it's time for another veterinary visit.

FOOD STEALING Your dog may not like being on a diet, but if he's to reach his ideal weight, you must see that he doesn't resort to grabbing whatever extras he can.

Worms

The good news is that there are now more ways than ever before to eliminate internal parasites from your pet.

Nobody likes to hear that their dog has worms, but they are a common canine problem. The most common worms are roundworms, hookworms, whipworms and tapeworms. Most puppies are either born with them or become infected soon after birth by inadvertently consuming infected eggs or infected fleas during close contact with their mother. The roundworms and tapeworms are the ones you can see in a dog's stool. They look ugly, but they don't do a great deal of harm—usually nothing worse than a little diarrhea, vomiting or anal itching.

Hookworms and whipworms tend to keep a lower profile and do more damage, sometimes causing anemia, dehydration or nutritional deficiencies. But the bottom line is that no worm is a good worm, because they all put stresses on your dog as his immune system tries to cope with their presence. And they can all be spread to people, with the same unpleasant and sometimes dangerous consequences. So these parasites are an important human as well as canine health concern.

CONTROLLING WORMS

Fortunately, controlling worms in your dog is not a difficult task so long as you treat the parasites, treat the premises, and also prevent new worms from developing.

Worming products today are safer as well as more effective than their

predecessors. If you suspect your dog has worms, a trip to the vet is in order. Once he knows which worms your dog has, he will recommend prescription or over-the-counter medications that will eradicate the parasites. Always use a product recommended by your vet. Don't buy over-the-counter wormers unless your vet recommends them, because some such wormers contain toluene or dichlorphen, which can be toxic to some dogs.

If you have a puppy, you probably want to start treatment at two to three weeks of age and continue every two weeks until the pup is several months old. Most pups are infected, but they won't actually have worm eggs turning up in their stool for a few weeks or months. The idea is to begin treating your pup before he starts showing signs of infection. That way, not only do you eradicate the worms from his system, you also make sure his toilet deposits don't become a source of infection for others.

Treat your dog for fleas, too. The most common form of tapeworm is carried by fleas—a dog swallows an infected flea and the tapeworms form inside the dog. For further information on ridding your pet of these pests, see "Fleas," on p. 252.

The best way to control worms in your dog's environment is to clean up after him. Removing stools promptly will help to prevent reinfection. If there are no infected feces hanging around, no soil

WELL ROUNDED It's normal for puppies to be plump, like this Staffordshire puppy, but if they are really potbellied, they probably have worms of some kind.

THE MOST COMMON WORMS

Worms aren't all the same, although they all cause the same shudder when you (or your vet) discover them in your dog's stool. Here are the most common offenders.

Roundworms. Adult roundworms live in the intestines after a dog has become infected by consuming something contaminated with larvae. You may see eggs in the stool, although in some cases you may actually see what look like wriggly strands of spaghetti. The worms can grow up to 7 inches (18 cm) in length.

Roundworms

Hookworms. These latch onto the intestinal wall and consume large amounts of blood. Typically, the worms are less than 1 inch (2.5 cm) long, with a bend in one end—hence the name hookworm.

The bodies are sometimes red from ingested blood. Dogs may ingest hookworm larvae or larvae may penetrate the dog's skin.

Whipworms

Whipworms. These worms will take up residence in your dog's colon after he has swallowed the eggs. They can cause the colon to become inflamed. He won't start shedding new whipworm eggs into his stool until three months after being infected, which can make diagnosis quite difficult. The worms themselves, which can reach 3 inches (7.5 cm) or more in length, do not show up in the stool. They get their name because they look a bit like a whip; most of the body is slender and threadlike, while the end is thick, like the handle of a whip.

Tapeworms. Dogs are susceptible to several different tapeworms. The most common type is transmitted by infected fleas, which your dog accidentally swallows when he is licking himself clean. This kind of worm is long, flat and made up of rectangular segments that each contain eggs. It can grow up to 32 inches (80 cm) in length. Individual segments are passed into the stool, and you may notice them on the skin and fur around the anus. They look innocuous enough, rather like grains of rice.

Tapeworm

will become contaminated with eggs, so the cycle of reinfection can be kept to a minimum.

Take advantage of extra protection—some of the newer medicines that prevent heartworm have the added bonus of preventing intestinal worms, too. Heartworm medications that include pyrantel (Heartgard-30 Plus) control roundworms and hookworms in addition to heartworm. The ingredient milbemycin oxime (Interceptor) prevents hookworms from developing and controls roundworms and whipworms, as well as stopping heartworm. No one product directly kills tapeworms, but a combination of milbemycin oxime and lufenuron (Sentinel) controls roundworms, hookworms and whipworms as well as helping to control fleas,

which are carriers of the tapeworm. So, as your dog will probably be taking heartworm medications anyway, it makes sense to give him a product that also protects him against other types of worms.

START THEM YOUNG Like these wirehaired Dachshund puppies, your puppy should be on a prevention program. Your vet will recommend worming products that are safe, effective and easy to administer.

First Aid

*After an injury, your dog will need special care and handling
to keep her from further harm.*

When your dog is in pain and doesn't understand what's going on, she will be scared. No matter how gentle she normally is, the fear that accompanies an injury can turn any dog into an out-of-control biter.

Get your injured dog to a vet, a shelter or an emergency treatment center as quickly as possible so she can receive expert attention. It may never happen, but just in case it does, you should be prepared, because the quicker you act, the better. Keep a first-aid box handy at home as well as the one in the car (see p. 291). Also, think ahead of time about how you can move your dog safely and how you can keep her still and prevent her from biting.

A GENTLE RESTRAINT

Your dog won't be able to understand that you are trying to help her. If you look at it from her viewpoint, she's only trying to stop you and the pain she thinks you are causing her. The surefire way for her to do this is to give you a good bite. And the best way to avoid being bitten is to put a muzzle on her. Use one bought from the store, or improvise (see box, opposite).

Depending on where you live, there may be another good reason for preventing a dog from using her teeth. Once a dog bites someone—even if that person is her owner—United States law, for example, requires that the dog be impounded (whether she's hurt or not) by a local animal control officer so she can be monitored for rabies. This is necessary in all dog-bite cases, just to be sure the dog doesn't have rabies. A dog that has been vaccinated against rabies must be confined and observed for ten days; an unvaccinated dog will be

EXPERT ATTENTION Immediately after a bad accident, your dog should be examined by a vet to check for possible serious internal injuries. He will also advise you on ongoing care if your dog is injured.

quarantined for six months. Local authorities decide whether the pet is observed at home or an animal control center.

The only times you shouldn't muzzle your dog are if she has facial injuries, if she is having difficulty breathing, or if she is vomiting. And if she is very distressed, and is both vomiting and trying to bite you, don't attempt to either muzzle or move her. Instead, call an animal control officer, who will help you move your dog safely, without further damage to her or any injury to yourself.

AN IMPROVISED MUZZLE

When your dog is injured, or you are trying to help someone else's injured dog, the first thing to do is to muzzle her. You can fashion a makeshift version using your dog's leash, a pair of pantyhose, a necktie or a long strip of stretchable gauze. If none of these is handy, a dishcloth or a T-shirt will also work well.

A homemade muzzle is entirely safe, but make sure to leave your dog's nostrils free so that she can breathe easily. Fabric with a bit of stretch works better than a stiff leash. While it can be upsetting to see your dog trying to free herself from the muzzle, remember that the muzzle is there to help you both, not hinder you.

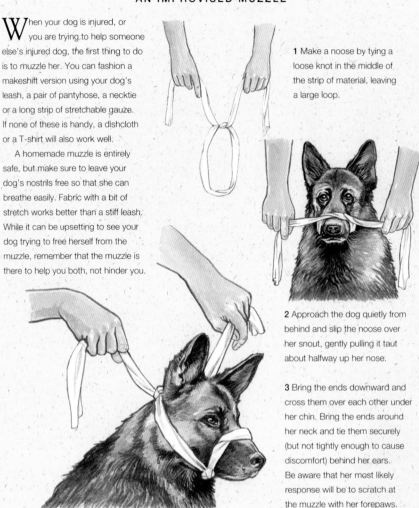

1 Make a noose by tying a loose knot in the middle of the strip of material, leaving a large loop.

2 Approach the dog quietly from behind and slip the noose over her snout, gently pulling it taut about halfway up her nose.

3 Bring the ends downward and cross them over each other under her chin. Bring the ends around her neck and tie them securely (but not tightly enough to cause discomfort) behind her ears. Be aware that her most likely response will be to scratch at the muzzle with her forepaws.

MOVING A DOG SAFELY

An injured dog must be transported to the vet quickly, but in your urgency, don't forget that the move involves more than speed. If your dog has been hurt in a car accident, she may have broken bones or internal injuries that you probably won't know about. Moving her in the wrong way could worsen a fracture or cause the broken bones to push through the skin. Even gentle movements may aggravate unsuspected internal bleeding.

Your goal should be to try to move your dog as one unit, without twisting her body. For a small dog, once she is muzzled, you can simply scoop her up in your arms. Another way to transport a small or medium-size dog is in a cardboard box. Simply lift her into the box with one swift, careful movement, then carry the box to the car. For a larger dog, use a coat, blanket or towel to make a sling in which to carry or drag your dog. To make up for the lack of a firm surface underneath her, try to find a second person to help you hold the sling as if it were a firm stretcher. If you can, get the second person to drive you to the vet's office so that you can sit in the back of the car with your dog to watch her progress and keep her calm.

Bites and Wounds

Chances are, at one time or another, your dog will come home with a wound and you'll have to make a dash for the first-aid kit.

Your dog's natural curiosity will lead her to investigate anything that moves or smells, and this can be a painful experience if the object of interest has a stinger, fangs or quills. She may even decide to stand her ground against a larger dog or other animal, regardless of personal danger.

BANDAGING A WOUND

Many wounds heal just fine unbandaged, but others do better covered. Wounds that should be bandaged include cuts on the foot pads and other areas that are likely to get dirty, large gashes and scrapes, and any wound that your dog licks excessively. If the wound is deep, embedded with dirt or debris, or continues to bleed, take your dog to the vet immediately. Don't attempt to dress these wounds yourself.

Before dressing a wound, it must be cleaned thoroughly by washing it with gauze pads soaked in warm, salty water. Rinse with warm water, then pat dry the wound with gauze

pads. Don't use cotton balls, as the fibers may stick in the wound. Dry the surrounding fur with a clean cloth, then apply an antibiotic ointment. If the wound needs bandaging, cover it with a sterile gauze pad. How you bandage the wound depends on its location.

LEG AND PAW WOUNDS

No matter where the wound is on the paw or leg, you'll need to wrap the entire leg to prevent swelling and speed healing. Hold the gauze covering the wound in place with one hand and use the other to wrap the leg. Start at the paw and wrap the entire leg firmly but not too tightly, right up to the top. Tape the end of the gauze to the layer below. Finally, cover the entire paw and leg with bandaging tape, again taping from the paw up.

Change all bandages at least every other day, sooner if they get wet or dirty, or come loose. Each time you change the bandage, gently clean, rinse and dry the wound, then apply antibiotic ointment. Watch for signs of infection, redness, swelling, foul odor or discharge. These require a vet's attention.

BACK WOUNDS

Because they are easiest to keep clean, back wounds rarely need bandaging. To prevent infection and give better access to the wound, you may have to clip some fur away. Sterilize a pair of blunt-tipped scissors by dipping them in rubbing alcohol, then use them to gently clip hair from around the wound. Monitor the wound regularly, cleansing it and applying antibiotic ointment twice daily.

If the wound is large or your dog won't leave it alone, cover it with a sterile gauze pad and keep the gauze in place with a large bandage. Find a piece of large, rectangular cloth the width of your dog's belly (from armpit to groin). It should be long enough

MINOR OR MAJOR? Minor wounds can be dealt with at home; more severe ones will need a vet's attention.

THAT HURTS! Wounds from the sharp, narrow teeth of cats or other dogs are often deeper than they look.

to tie around her body. At each end, cut two slits into the material to create three tails. Place the center of the cloth over her back to hold the gauze pad in place, then bring the ends down under her belly. Tie each pair of tails firmly but comfortably together under her belly. This bandage, reversed, will also work for chest and abdominal wounds.

Ear Wounds

Wounds on the outside of the ears are rarely bandaged. Wounds on the inside of the ears, though, may need a special kind of bandage—to keep the wound area open to air. This is very important if your dog has long floppy ears that lie close to her head, creating a warm, moist environment where infection can occur. Fold the ears over the top of the head and secure them with a strip of cloth wrapped under your dog's chin and tied in a double bow on top of her head. Make sure the ear canals are open and your dog's vision is not blocked.

Dog and Cat Bites

Because of the way dogs defend themselves, they tend to be bitten on the neck, face, ears and chest. Although it may not look too bad, a bite from long, sharp teeth damages the tissues under the skin and is often much deeper than it looks. Clip the hair from around the area, wash the wound well with soap and warm water and pat dry. Apply an antibiotic ointment and cover with gauze. See your vet if there are puncture wounds, or if the bite seems unusually deep.

If you see your dog in a fight, the first task is to separate the animals. Don't step into the scuffle because you might get injured yourself. Instead, use either a hose or bucket to douse the fight with cold water. Once your dog has settled down, take a good look at any wounds.

Cat bites tend to be worse than dog bites because a cat's saliva is packed with bacteria and the wounds are deep and exceedingly narrow. Dogs with serious cat bites should always be treated by a vet.

Snake Bites

Suspect a snake bite if your dog comes back from a jaunt with a swollen, bleeding wound, especially on her head or legs. She may already be trembling, drooling, vomiting, have dilated pupils or be collapsing. If you can't identify the snake with absolute certainty, always treat for a poisonous bite. Your goal is to slow the entrance of venom into your dog's system, and to get her to emergency care promptly.

Keep your dog still and calm. If you can, carry or drive her to the vet, rather than walking her, as this will slow her blood flow. Talk to her quietly—the calmer she stays, the slower her heart rate is and the slower the venom enters her system. Cover your dog with a blanket or coat to help delay shock.

REMOVING PORCUPINE QUILLS

If your dog has an encounter with a porcupine, use a pair of pliers to remove the quills. Grasp each quill as close to the flesh as possible, working it out steadily but slowly. The ends of porcupine quills are barbed, which makes removing them a challenge. If you can extract the quills successfully, wash the wounds with warm, soapy water, rinse with fresh warm water and apply an antibiotic ointment. If any quills break as you try to pull them out, or if any swelling, redness, weeping or other signs of infection develop, see your vet right away.

Bleeding

*The sight of blood might make you feel woozy, but when your dog
is hurt and bleeding, you are her only lifeline.*

Take charge of the situation by talking to your dog in a soothing voice she knows and trusts—doing this will help you to stay calm as well.

Always act quickly if your dog is bleeding, but with even greater speed if the blood is pumping rhythmically from a cut. Spurting blood generally indicates a cut artery, which bleeds more rapidly and causes heavier blood loss than a cut vein. Blood from a cut vein will ooze more slowly and evenly.

First, remember to muzzle the dog if she is in pain. Then, to stop the bleeding, use three methods in the following order of preference: apply direct pressure to the wound; apply pressure on pressure points; and as a last resort, apply a tourniquet. Take the dog to the vet whether or not you manage to stem the flow.

Apply Direct Pressure

Place a sterile gauze pad directly over the bleeding area and press down firmly. If you don't have sterile gauze, use a clean rag, cloth

KEEP THE WOUND CLEAN
Bandage the foot and wrist firmly, but not too tightly, to keep the wound clean. Leave the toes free so you can check for swelling.

or your fingers until someone can get you bandages. If possible, smear the gauze or cloth with some petroleum jelly, such as Vaseline, to stop it sticking to the wound later. If blood soaks through the material, don't remove it. Just add layers of additional material to the pile. This way, if clots have started to form, you won't break them apart.

Once the bleeding has stopped, remove the bandage and pile of cloths, then use clean material to bandage the wound. If the bleeding hasn't stopped after five minutes of applying direct pressure, bind the gauze pads in place with bandage tape so your hands are free to attempt the second strategy, putting pressure on pressure points (see box, opposite).

Applying a Tourniquet

If your dog is still bleeding heavily after you have applied pressure to her pressure points for more than ten minutes, apply a tourniquet. This will constrict the blood vessels between the cut and the heart and stops the flow of blood. Vets stress that a tourniquet should be used only as a last resort. It should be used only for injuries to a dog's leg and tail, never

BLOOD TYPES IN DOGS

Just as dogs have different kinds of coats, they also have different blood types, which they have inherited from their parents. There are eight common blood types in dogs. But most of the time your vet won't test your dog's blood to determine what type it is since most dogs won't ever need to have a blood transfusion.

In the rare event that they do, however, they have one big advantage over people. Almost every dog can receive a first transfusion of any blood type. For the second transfusion, they need to receive the correct type. While vets always prefer to give dogs the correct blood type, it's faster to give whatever they have on hand—and in an emergency situation, time is of the essence.

APPLY PRESSURE
Press a pad of clean cloth firmly against the wound and hold it there until the bleeding stops.

PRESSURE POINTS

The second technique to reduce bleeding is to clamp down on the artery that supplies blood to that area. There are five main pressure points on your dog's body and, depending on where the cut is, you should apply firm pressure to whichever one of these areas is between the wound and the heart. Always choose the one closest to the wound (see illustration, below). Even if the bleeding continues, let up on the pressure slightly for a few seconds every few minutes. While you want to stop the bleeding, you must allow some blood flow to the surrounding area so that healthy tissues aren't damaged by being deprived of their blood supply.

- If the cut is on your dog's front leg, press your middle three fingers firmly and deeply into her armpit.
- If the cut is on her rear leg, place your middle three fingers deeply into the middle of the groin (the area inside the thigh where it meets the body) and press firmly.
- If the cut is on her tail, reach under it and place your three middle fingers where it joins the body. Keep your thumb on the top of the tail and apply gentle pressure.
- For a cut on the neck, feel for the round, hard windpipe just below her throat. Slide your middle three fingers to the side

of it where the cut is until you find the soft groove next to her windpipe, and press firmly, but gently. If you suspect your dog has a head injury—perhaps he's dazed or disoriented—don't use this pressure point. Reducing blood flow to the brain could worsen a head injury. It's better to apply firm, direct pressure to the cut while you hurry her to the veterinarian.

- If your dog has a cut to her head, find the spot where her lower jaw curves up just below the ear, and press firmly with your middle three fingers. (This is also the spot where dogs love to be scratched.)

Upper inside of both front legs (armpit)

Upper inside of both rear legs (groin)

Underside of tail

PRESSURE POINTS
Apply firm pressure to whichever one of these points is between the wound and the heart.

to her body or neck. A tourniquet isn't really a home remedy and you should use it only when you are on your way to the vet. Tourniquets are also uncomfortable, and most conscious dogs won't tolerate them.

Find a broad strip of material—such as a necktie, gauze strip or panty hose—and wrap it twice around the limb or tail above the cut, but don't knot it. Put a stick, pencil or other long and thin, sturdy object on top of the second layer of the material. Tie the stick in place with the two loose ends of material, then twist it so as to tighten the tourniquet just enough to stop the bleeding. It is extremely important to loosen the tourniquet every five to ten minutes for a couple of seconds to allow some blood flow to sustain the healthy tissues

in the area. Even with intermittent releases, however, permanent damage can occur, so immediate veterinary attention is vital.

A BLEEDING NOSE

If your dog has a nose bleed, examine the nose in good light to see if you can find the cause. If you can see a cut, apply pressure with your fingers. If there is no visible cause, keep the dog still, and if she will let you, apply cold compresses or ice cubes to the bridge of the nose. Never try to pack the nostrils; you may damage the delicate nasal lining. Take the dog to the vet for a complete examination. A nose bleed could indicate a foreign body in the nose, a nasal tumor or generalized bleeding, such as that caused by Warfarin poisoning.

Broken Bones and Tail

All fractures will need veterinary care at some stage and most should be considered emergencies, in need of immediate attention.

The most common cause of a broken bone is a car accident. Other possible causes of fractures include falls, being trodden on or kicked by another animal, or gunshot wounds. Even everyday movements may be sufficient to fracture bones that are weakened by other conditions, such as cancer.

The bones of the legs and feet are most commonly affected, but any of a dog's bones may be fractured, including those of the jaw, skull, rib cage, shoulder blades and spine. Dogs with weak bones, such as very young pups or those with diseases affecting the bones, may be more at risk of fractures than healthy adults.

If you know that your dog has been involved in an accident of any kind, take him to the vet immediately, even if he doesn't seem to be seriously injured. He may have broken bones or internal injuries that are not obvious.

Broken Legs

Sometimes it's hard to know that your dog's leg is broken because dogs are quite stoic. Fortunately, they are also pretty smart about lessening the pain. They tend not to put any weight on a broken leg. Other telltale signs to look out for include a leg that has a lump in it, a paw that is facing in a slightly different direction, or one leg looking slightly deformed in comparison to the others.

Fractures that have broken through the skin, called compound fractures, warrant an immediate trip to the vet. These open wounds may be bleeding and they can easily become infected. Fractures that don't break through the skin, called simple fractures, can wait overnight for treatment, if necessary. But even simple fractures can be painful, and your dog will feel better after the vet has set his leg with proper splinting material. The vet may use a plaster cast, or stainless steel bone plates, pins and screws. Modern veterinary methods now allow most fractures to be to treated with minimum discomfort to the dog and a rapid return to normal use.

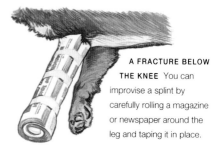

A FRACTURE BELOW THE KNEE You can improvise a splint by carefully rolling a magazine or newspaper around the leg and taping it in place.

How you treat a break will depend on whether it is above or below the stifle or the carpal joint. The stifle in dogs is the equivalent of the human knee. It occurs in the hindleg. The carpal joint in dogs is the equivalent of the human wrist. It occurs in the foreleg.

Immobilizing a Broken Leg

In all cases, the immediate aim is to prevent further injury to the fractured area. Depending on the type of break, you can do this either by applying a splint to the injured leg or by completely immobilizing your dog. The next step is to take him to the vet. If another adult is available to help you, ease your dog onto a blanket and carry him by holding the corners like a sling, then put him in the car and drive to the vet immediately.

A Fracture of the Lower Leg

A break below the carpal joint or the stifle is relatively easy to splint, because the joint above the break is easily accessible. Choose a splinting material that suits the size of your dog. In most cases, an effective splint can be made by rolling a magazine or several sheets of newspaper around the fractured area and taping it in place. Depending on the size of your dog, sticks, pencils and yardsticks (broken in half and the sharp ends taped with masking tape) also make good splints.

Make sure the splint extends above the stifle or carpal joint and below the end of the paw. Before you try to move your dog, secure the splint in place by tying several strips of

PAINFUL INJURIES While broken tails are not all that common, a dog that travels a lot by car is at particular risk of having her tail caught in a closing door.

cloth or gauze around it, or binding it with some bandage tape. Don't tie the splint too tightly as you could stop the blood supply to the leg.

A Fracture of the Upper Leg

A fracture above the stifle or the carpal joint is difficult to splint because the hip area (above the rear legs) or shoulder area (above the front legs) is difficult to immobilize. This is best not attempted at home. Instead, muzzle your dog (see p. 279), put him in the car and take him to the vet.

Protruding Bones

When a broken bone pushes through the skin, dress the wound. If possible, soak sterile gauze in contact lens solution or plain water, and apply the moist material to the open wound. If this is not possible, wrap a thick, clean cloth around the wound to protect it. The broken leg is now ready to be splinted.

BROKEN TAIL

Unfortunately, a dog's excitably wagging tail can get him into trouble. At some time or other, many dogs have their tail accidentally slammed in the car or house door. You can tell if your dog's tail is broken because he'll only

COMMON SYMPTOMS

Symptoms will depend on the affected bone and the type of fracture, but may include:
- An obvious skin wound (the ends of the broken bone may be visible).
- Swelling of the tissues around the fracture.
- Unusual behavior resulting from pain, such as whining or aggression, especially when the dog is handled.
- Abnormal appearance of the affected body part.
- Inability to use the affected body part. A broken leg will be held off the ground; a fracture of the spine or pelvis may cause paralysis; a fractured jaw may cause the mouth to hang open.

have half a wag and won't be able to move it beyond the break. Until the fracture heals, he'll probably wag away as if nothing has happened, but he will need a little help. If the skin is broken, the tail will bleed heavily, and even more when your dog wags it.

TREATMENT

First of all, you'll need to stop the bleeding. Gently grasp the tail where it's bleeding with a couple of gauze pads, or a clean rag or cloth. Remember, your dog's tail still hurts, even if he acts as if it doesn't, and grabbing at the point where it's broken may cause even the most stoic of dogs to let out a yelp. Press down on the area gently, but firmly, to stop the bleeding, then tape sterile gauze pads over the wound.

If your dog's tail is broken at the base, you will need to see your vet immediately. With a break at the base, your dog may not be able to go to the toilet on his own, simply because he can no longer lift his tail. In addition, your dog may have suffered nerve damage and only your vet will be able to tell for sure. Just keep him calm and comfortable until you get there.

Your vet will splint the break properly. The fracture will take three to four weeks to heal. Your dog should then be able to wag his whole tail and move it as he did before the fracture.

Dogs sometimes appear to have a broken tail the day after they have been swimming a lot. The tail is limp, but is not actually broken. This condition, called "limber tail," is transient and requires no treatment other than rest.

Burns

Quick action is called for if your dog suffers a severe burn. If you do the right thing immediately, recovery will be faster.

Ever hopeful that you'll share or drop a morsel of what you're cooking, dogs are often underfoot in the kitchen. While most kitchen beggars manage to stay out of trouble, some get a little too close to the action. As a result, they may suffer burns, especially from spattering grease or scalding water.

Dogs may also suffer chemical burns from splashed yard or household chemicals, and curious puppies who bite into electrical cords often get the inside of their mouths burned. Whatever the cause, quick, calm action can help your dog to recover faster.

HEAT BURNS

Quickly put ice on a burn or hold it under cold running water to help ease the pain and stop further damage. The coldness stops the heat of the burn from penetrating and damaging the deeper tissues. The easiest way to cool a burn is with the garden hose, provided you don't turn the faucet on full force. Your dog may not cooperate if you turn the hose on too strongly. Worse, too much water pressure could also damage tissue if the burns are deep and have broken the skin. Help your dog to remain calm by talking to her continuously in a soft, soothing voice and by stroking her with one hand as you wet her down with the other.

Alternatively, hold your dog in a gentle hug as you apply an ice pack to the burned area. You should apply cold water or an ice pack for a full 20 minutes.

The next step depends on how badly your dog is burned. Burns are divided into three categories: first, second and third degree. With a first-degree burn, the skin is red, tender to the touch and possibly swollen. Deeper burns that blister and swell are second-degree burns. The most serious, third-degree burns, are easy to recognize because the skin is white, charred or burned away.

For first- and second-degree burns, apply a triple-strength antibiotic ointment twice daily. Each time you apply the ointment,

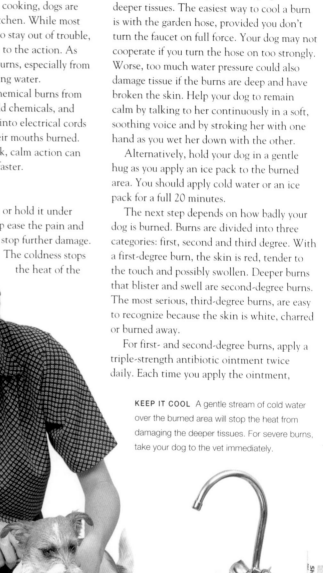

KEEP IT COOL A gentle stream of cold water over the burned area will stop the heat from damaging the deeper tissues. For severe burns, take your dog to the vet immediately.

APPLY AN ICE PACK Put some crushed ice in a plastic bag and wrap the bag in a kitchen towel. To ease the pain, hold the ice pack against the burned area. A packet of frozen peas makes an excellent ice pack.

check the skin carefully to make sure it's getting better, not worse. If the burned area starts to weep, increase in size or become more tender to touch, take your dog to the vet to make sure the burn has not become infected.

Third-degree burns require immediate professional care. Before you take your dog to the vet, place sterile gauze pads over the burned area, then apply an ice pack. Even if you don't have sterile gauze pads, still use an ice pack. Crushed ice in a plastic bag will work fine. At the same time, keep your dog warm to prevent shock.

Severe burns can send a dog into shock, a condition in which her circulatory system slows right down. To conserve her body heat and prevent shock, wrap your dog in a blanket, sweater, coat or towel as you take her to the vet. As with all serious injuries, try to find someone to drive while you attend to your dog. On the way, keep her warm and continue to hold the ice pack on the burn.

ELECTRICAL BURNS

Puppies will chew through just about anything they can sink their teeth into, including electrical cords. If she's lucky, your puppy will just get a nasty burn in or around her mouth. Fortunately, most dogs recover well on their own from such burns, but in some cases tissues in the mouth will flake off after a few days.

If you haven't seen your dog eat a wire cord, you can suspect an electrical burn if she doesn't eat anything, despite appearing to be hungry. Her mouth will be sore and tender,

KEEP OUT OF REACH

Some household products can cause burns to your dog. Things to watch out for include:

- Cleaning detergents
- Drain cleaners
- Weed killers and other garden sprays
- Paints
- Paint strippers
- Turpentine
- Battery acid
- Petroleum-based products

so feed her on a diet of liquid or soft foods until the tissues in her mouth recover.

Chewing an electrical cord can cause more serious injuries, damaging lung tissue or even halting your dog's breathing. If she stops breathing, start CPR immediately (see p. 290). Lung injuries will cause drooling, coughing and breathing difficulties. If you notice any of these signs, even a day or two after your dog bites an electrical cord, call the vet at once.

CHEMICAL BURNS

There are a number of common household chemicals that can cause burns to your dog's body. If your dog suffers a chemical burn, dilute the substance by flooding the area with water. Even though the skin may break open right away, flush the area with copious amounts of water to wash away any remaining chemical on the skin and to stop further burns. Then take your dog to the vet immediately.

Car Accidents

It can happen so quickly. An open gate or a dropped leash,
followed by an innocent dash into the road by your dog.

Even when you are careful, accidents still happen. If your dog is hit by a car, immediately protect yourself and your dog from oncoming traffic. Ideally, you should assess and possibly bandage the dog before moving her. But if she is lying on a busy street, you don't have that option. In heavy traffic, wave a white or brightly colored cloth to alert approaching cars, and enlist someone's help to move your dog to a safer spot.

Although normally your dog would never bite you, she may try to if she is in pain or shock. If your dog is conscious, protect yourself from her frightened bite by muzzling her (see p. 279). Then, grasp the fur along her backbone with both hands and drag her out of harm's way. Pull her evenly and keep her body flat on the ground. Remember, talking to your dog in a soothing voice will help her through this difficult situation. This will also give you something to focus on and help to keep you calm.

THE THREE-POINT CHECK
After moving the dog out of the traffic, or if you have the luxury of leaving her where she is for a few moments, you should check three

things in the following order. First, check if your dog is breathing. Look for the rise and fall of her chest or place your hand near her nose to feel for any expirations. If there is no sign of breathing, you will need to perform CPR (see p. 290).

Next, check whether your dog has a pulse. The easiest place to check for her pulse is her inner thigh. This is where a major blood vessel, called the femoral artery, runs very close to the surface of the skin. To feel for the pulse, place your index and middle fingers on the middle of the inside of her rear leg, where it meets the body. If you can't feel your dog's pulse, you will need to perform CPR.

Finally, check for bleeding. If a gash is bleeding profusely, try to stop the bleeding by applying direct pressure to the wound or pressure to the pressure point between the wound and the heart.

KEEP HER COVERED
Dogs can go into shock after an accident, especially if there's heavy loss of blood. Keep your dog warm by covering her with a coat, sweater, blanket, towel or rug.

Even if there's little sign of blood, there may be internal bleeding, which is extremely serious. Any dog hit by a car should be checked over as soon as possible by a vet.

TRAFFIC SENSE Some dogs love to chase cars, so it's no surprise that they are sometimes injured. But most responsible owners keep their pet within a fenced area and on a leash near traffic. By all means teach your dog to stop, look and listen, but in spite of all your training and vigilance, your dog may still be involved in an accident, so it's important that you know what to do.

Choking

*Whatever the cause of choking, your calm and efficient actions
can quickly restore the breath of life in your best friend.*

Choking may occur because your dog forgot to chew a large piece of food. (Remember, dogs once lived in packs where the fastest eater got the most food.) Or perhaps a toy slipped too far back in her mouth. Choking is always an emergency, but whatever caused the problem, you need to act calmly and efficiently. A choking dog may breathe very loudly, cough, become anxious or gasp for air. To stop her choking, you will need to get the lodged object out of her mouth immediately.

If she's light enough for you to lift totally off the ground, put your arms under your dog's belly and slide them back until they catch her at the groin, just in front of the hind legs. Lift her into the air upside down and give her a gentle shake to try and dislodge the item. For heavier dogs, grasp them in the same manner, but let the front legs rest on the ground like a wheelbarrow. With your dog's head down, give her back legs a good shake.

Because she's not getting enough air, a choking dog may eventually faint. Fortunately, though, that makes helping her easier because you won't have to worry about her resisting your efforts. If she does faint, open her mouth and pull her tongue out as far as you can. While a bare hand works, you can get a better grip on the tongue if you grasp it with a cloth. With the other hand, reach into her throat and fish out whatever is blocking her airway.

COMMON CHOKING HAZARDS

Dogs most commonly choke on toys, especially on balls that are small enough to disappear over the back of the tongue. They usually begin to panic and immediately start to scratch at their mouths. They may also gag and retch. This is also what happens when a bone or stick becomes lodged across the roof of a dog's mouth.

STRING, COINS, PEBBLES AND NAILS
Although these objects are unlikely to result in choking, they are typical of the kind of foreign bodies that your dog may swallow. Such objects can cause intestinal obstructions.

You can sometimes dislodge foreign bodies that have become jammed in your dog's throat with a pair of strong pliers. Barbecue tongs may also prove useful when you have to reach in for the object. The important thing is to act quickly.

NOT CHOKING, BUT COUGHING

Sometimes a dog with kennel cough may appear to be choking. This condition begins as a dry cough and may develop into a deep, hacking cough. Affected dogs may seem to be in considerable distress and may act as though they have something stuck in the throat. They may put their heads forward, cough, gag and even vomit.

A dog with pharyngitis (an inflammation of the throat) may also cough and gag as though her throat is obstructed, but on examination the throat will be red and inflamed and no foreign object will be present.

PLAYTIME DANGER
A common cause of choking is a small ball or toy that becomes lodged in a dog's throat, or a piece that has been chomped off a larger rawhide chew toy. Although dogs love rawhides, hard rubber chew toys are a safer option.

CPR

*If you can perform CPR, there's a good chance you can breathe
life into your dog and restart her heart after a serious accident.*

We all know that cardiopulmonary resuscitation (CPR) can bring a person back to life. It can also work for your dog. You have only about five minutes before there will be irreversible brain damage, so it's always worth trying. Remember the simple ABC of CPR: Airway, Breathing and Circulation.

BLOW AIR IN With your dog's mouth held closed, blow air into her nostrils strongly enough to inflate her chest.

A. OPEN HER AIRWAY

A dog that's been hit by a car may not be able to breathe because something is blocking her airway, perhaps blood, vomit or saliva. Make sure that her nostrils are not obstructed and use your index and middle finger to swipe the back of the throat clear.

In other cases, your dog might not be breathing because of the position of her neck. Place her on her side, extend her head back and pull the tongue forward to make breathing easier. That may be all your dog needs to start breathing spontaneously.

B. BLOW AIR IN

Hold your dog's mouth shut, place your mouth over her nostrils and blow into her nose four times. Blow with enough force to make your dog's chest rise. You should feel some resistance as the air enters the lungs.

C. CIRCULATE BLOOD

Position your dog on her right side on a hard surface. Place the heel of one of your hands on

the ribs over the heart, where her left elbow would touch her chest when bent. Place the heel of your other hand on top of the first and press down. Use enough force so that you press the chest about halfway to the ground or floor. Compress 15 times, then blow into your dog's nose twice. Repeat the process.

Ideally, you should be compressing the heart 80 to 100 times in one minute, so 15 compressions should take no more than ten seconds. If you can enlist the help of someone else, one person can blow twice into your dog's nose after the other does each of the 15 compressions.

Continue to give CPR while someone else drives you to the vet. If you're not able to reach a vet, continue to do CPR until your dog is breathing on her own, or for at least 20 minutes.

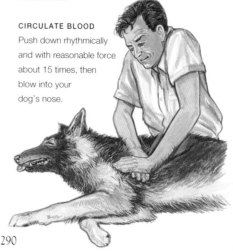

CIRCULATE BLOOD
Push down rhythmically and with reasonable force about 15 times, then blow into your dog's nose.

OPEN THE AIRWAY Taking care not to get bitten, swipe the back of your dog's throat with your index and middle fingers to clear it.

Drowning

Just like small children, dogs can drown quickly and often silently.

The key to prevention is constant vigilance.

Although most dogs are naturally good swimmers, some aren't. Dogs can get into trouble if they fall into a swimming pool, lake or river, or perhaps fall through ice and are unable to get a footing to pull themselves out. And sometimes even great swimmers can get caught in a strong current and not be able to make it back to shore.

If you find your dog floating unconscious in the water, pull her out, then suspend her in the air by her rear legs. Gently swing her back and forth to drain the water from her lungs. If she's heavy, rest her front legs on the ground as you swing her, or find some way of elevating her pelvis as high as possible if you can't hold her.

Then, lay your dog on her side and place a towel, rug or pillow under her haunches so that her head is lower than the rest of her

DRAINING WATER FROM A DOG'S LUNGS If the dog is motionless, first clear any discharge from the nose and mouth and gently pull the tongue forward. To drain the water from the dog's lungs, hold the animal by its hind legs and gently swing it back and forth (left), resting the front feet on the ground if necessary.

body. This will allow any additional water to drain from her lungs while you check for respiration and a pulse. If your dog is not breathing or there is no pulse, administer CPR (see p. 290). Then get her to a vet as quickly as possible.

Better safe than sorry—even dogs that are strong swimmers should wear a life jacket when they are going out in a boat.

FIRST-AID KIT

A first-aid kit for your pet can literally spell the difference between life and death. So don't wait until after an accident has happened to prepare a first-aid kit for your dog. Here's what you should include:

- Vital Information Card. This should list the name and phone number of your vet; the phone number, address and travel directions to the nearest emergency pet clinic; and the phone number of the local poison control office or your local animal control center.
- First-aid manual (in the United States, *Pet First Aid* can be ordered through the American Animal Hospital Association).
- Pantyhose, a long strip of stretchable gauze (to make a muzzle) and a spare leash.
- Blunt-tipped scissors.
- Tweezers.
- Eyewash (such as sterile contact lens solution or an eye rinse for dry eyes).
- Antibiotic ointment or powder.

- Hydrogen peroxide.
- Milk of magnesia.
- Rectal thermometer.
- Lubricant, such as K-Y jelly.
- Bandaging materials:
  – 1- to 2-inch (2.5–5 cm) stretchable and nonstretchable gauze rolls;
  – gauze pads in varying sizes, depending on your dog's size;
  – bandage tape.
- Cotton balls.
- Strong packaging tape (for splinting a broken leg).
- Soap.
- Needle-nose pliers.
- Beach towel or blanket (for a stretcher).

Heatstroke

While your dog's furry coat is good at preserving body heat in cold weather, it is less efficient at keeping her cool when it's hot.

Although dogs have sweat glands on their feet, these are almost useless and a dog must rely exclusively on panting to breathe off excess heat. This cooling system isn't very efficient, which means that all dogs are prone to heatstroke.

PREPARED FOR A HEATWAVE
A child's wading pool filled with water provides your dog with an extra-large drinking bowl as well as a source of entertainment on a hot day.

single coats, such as Poodles and terriers.

Leaving a dog in a parked car is the leading cause of heatstroke. Contrary to what many people think, heatstroke can strike a dog in just minutes even on relatively mild days. On a 75° to 80°F (24° to 27°C) day, the temperature inside a parked car—even with a window cracked open—quickly climbs to more than 100°F (38°C). Not surprisingly, this drives up your dog's body temperature very quickly.

Dogs can also suffer heatstroke if they are exercised too heavily on a hot, humid day, or if they live outdoors and don't have shelter from the sun. If they are overweight or have heart or lung ailments, they are also more susceptible. An older dog is less tolerant of heat and will suffer heatstroke more rapidly than a younger dog.

WHICH DOGS SUFFER MOST

Certain breeds, however, are more susceptible to heatstroke than others. These include short-nosed breeds such as Pugs, Bulldogs and Boxers, who have small airways and therefore reduced ability to blow out hot air.

Dogs with double coats, such as German Shepherds and Old English Sheepdogs, are particularly prone to suffer from heatstroke because they retain more heat than dogs with

PREVENTING HEATSTROKE

Nearly every case of heatstroke is preventable. Here's what you can do:

- Don't take your dog with you on errands if you will have to leave her in the car. The five minutes you spend finding what you need and standing in line at the checkout can spell disaster.
- Make sure she has unlimited access to cold water, especially during hot weather.
- If you're an avid exerciser, don't push your dog to keep pace with you on exceptionally hot and humid days. If she drops behind, let her take a rest break.
- Keep older dogs and those with heart or lung conditions inside on hot days. If you don't have air conditioning, turn on a room fan.
- For dogs living outside, provide all-day shade, such as a doghouse, overhang or a large beach umbrella. Remember, as the sun shifts, so does the shade; trees may not offer protection for your dog all day long.

HOW TO HANDLE HEATSTROKE

The first sign of heatstroke is rapid, heavy panting, often with excessive salivation. Shortly after this, your dog will start gasping for air. Her eyes will become glassy, her gums and tongue may turn bright red, and she'll become weak and unable to stand. If heatstroke progresses, your dog may develop bloody diarrhea, vomiting or seizures.

As soon as you suspect heatstroke, cool down your dog as quickly as possible. The easiest ways to lower your dog's body temperature is to immerse her in cool water in the bathtub, kitchen sink, a bucket or a child's swimming pool. Avoid icy water, because a sudden or dramatic change in temperature can be dangerous.

COOL AND FRESH Most dogs love to drink from the hose. Just make sure the water is running through cool before you allow her to drink.

You can also use the garden hose to cool her down. If the hose has been turned off for a while, let it run until the water becomes cool. Alternatively, place towels soaked in cool water on her head, neck, chest and abdomen. Take the towels off and re-dip them in cool water every five minutes because they will heat up fast. In addition to using cool water, you can park your dog in front of an air conditioner or fan. If your dog is conscious and can drink, offer her cold or even ice water.

Heatstroke sometimes leads to serious problems that only a vet can detect. For example, high body temperatures can damage kidneys, brain, heart or lungs. After cooling her down, take your dog to the vet.

TO CHECK FOR DEHYDRATION
A simple home check is to gently pinch and pull up the skin on your dog's back near the neck. Release it and see how quickly it snaps back—it should be firm and spring back into place

within seconds. When your dog is dehydrated, the skin will creep back slowly or not all. This means that her body is very low on water and she needs to see a vet at once.

WELCOME RELIEF If you dog seems to be affected by the heat, keep wetting a towel in cold water and gently wiping over her body, especially sparsely haired areas, such as the stomach, to cool her down.

293

Poisoning

Dogs will gulp down bitter-tasting household chemicals without a second thought and seem to love the taste of slug and snail poison.

Dogs often eat before they think—and not just dog food. They may steal a plate of brownies or chew up a packet of medicine. Suspect poisoning if your dog has seizures, has trouble breathing, has a slow or fast heartbeat, drools or foams at the mouth, has burns around her mouth and lips, or is bleeding from the anus, mouth or nose. Other symptoms of poisoning include drowsiness, unconsciousness or your dog acting as if she is out of control. If you notice any of these symptoms, quickly check the house, garage and yard for the shredded remains of bottles or packages that may have held something poisonous. Also check the bathroom and your purse to see if any medications are missing.

To help your dog, you should know how to make her vomit and when it's safe to do so (see chart at right). If you don't think it's safe to make her vomit, or you don't know what she's eaten, call your vet for advice right away. Any dog that has ingested something poisonous should be checked by a vet, even if you've already made her vomit. Take the poison or pill container and a sample of the vomit with you and get to the vet right away.

INDUCING VOMITING

The best way to help your dog vomit is to give her hydrogen peroxide. Trickle one teaspoon of hydrogen peroxide for each 10 lb (5 kg) of body weight into her mouth. If it doesn't work the first time, give her the same amount again after 15 or 20 minutes. You should also be making your way to the vet. If you don't have any hydrogen peroxide, take a cup of cold water and stir in one tablespoon of dry mustard or one tablespoon of washing soda

DANGEROUS SUBSTANCES Your purse may contain potentially harmful items, from chocolate to medications, all irresistible temptations to inquisitive dogs such as this Hungarian Vizsla.

HOW MUCH CHOCOLATE IS DANGEROUS?

For a dog, the smell of chocolate is almost as tempting as the smell of a big juicy steak. But although she may love it, chocolate doesn't agree with your dog's system. That's because it contains caffeine and a related chemical called theobromine. Both of these are stimulants that raise your dog's heart rate—occasionally to the point of being fatal. Fortunately,

most dogs who overdose on chocolate just get an upset stomach, which may be accompanied by vomiting and diarrhea.

The amount of chocolate that can cause death depends on your dog's size and the kind of chocolate she has stolen. With baking chocolate—the worst type for dogs—as little as 1/2 oz (15 g) can cause death in small dogs such as Chihuahuas and Toy Poodles. In

medium-sized dogs, such as Cocker Spaniels and Dachshunds, the amount is 2–3 oz (55–85 g). In large dogs, such as German Shepherds, Collies and Labrador Retrievers, the amount is 4–8 oz (110–225 g).

With milk chocolate, death can occur after a small dog has eaten from as little as 4 oz (110 g), a medium-size dog from 1 lb (450 g) and a large dog from 2lb (1 kg).

WHEN TO INDUCE VOMITING

Poisoning is an emergency that requires fast action. Often the best remedy is to get your dog to vomit, which will remove the harmful substances from her system. However, if she has swallowed caustic substances, such as drain cleaner, vomiting will make things worse. The following guide will help you know whether or not to induce vomiting as an emergency measure.

Poison	Induce Vomiting?	Poison	Induce Vomiting?
Antifreeze	Yes	Nail polish	No
Arsenic (ant, rat and mouse poison)	Yes	Paint thinner	No
Aspirin	Yes	Paintbrush cleaner	No
Battery acid	No	Paste (glue)	No
Bleach	No	Pesticides (see arsenic, strychnine, warfarin)	
Carbolic acid (phenol)	No	Phenol (see carbolic acid)	No
Crayons	Yes	Pine-oil cleaners	No
Drain cleaner	No	Plaster	No
Fertilizer	No	Putty	No
Furniture polish	No	Roach traps	Yes
Glue	No	Shampoo	Yes
Household cleaners	No	Shoe polish	Yes
Insecticides (including flea and tick dips)	Yes	Sidewalk salt	No
Kerosene	No	Slug and snail bait	Yes (if bait has organo-phosphate carbamate, induce vomiting only if just eaten)
Kitchen matches	Yes		
Laundry detergent	No	Strychnine (rat and mouse poisons)	Yes
Lead (found in old linoleum, old paint, old plaster or old putty)	Only in first half hour after ingestion	Toilet bowl cleaners	No
		Turpentine	No
Medications (antihistamines, tranquilizers, barbiturates, amphetamines, heart pills, vitamins)	Yes	Warfarin (rat poisons and medications)	Yes, but only if just eaten
Motor oil	No	Weed killers	Yes

crystals. Although it's vital to get the substance out of your dog before it gets into her system, making her vomit is not always safe. Such substances as petroleum-based products and drain cleaners are caustic, so they can burn twice: once on the way down and again when they come back up. The poison still needs to be removed from her stomach quickly, but only the vet can do so safely.

That's why it's so important to know what your dog has eaten before you take any action. If you don't know, assume it's something that might hurt her on the way back up, and get her to the vet. Never induce vomiting if your dog is having trouble breathing, is having seizures, has a slow heart rate, is unconscious, has a bloated abdomen or the product label says not to.

ANTIDOTES
Depending on the substance your dog has consumed, your vet can sometimes administer an antidote to dilute the poison in her body or reduce its absorption. Sometimes an antidote to a poison is simply milk or water, but you should always ask your vet to administer it as he will know the correct amount to give and the correct way to give it.

Emergency Quick-Reference Chart

If an emergency happens,

consult this chart for advice

on what to do.

Emergency	Symptoms	What to Do
Bleeding		• Gently but firmly press sterile gauze or clean cloth over wound • Keep dog warm to prevent shock • If wound bleeds through pad, apply more cloth on top; do not remove soaked gauze or cloth • If bleeding continues beyond five minutes, apply pressure to pressure point between wound and heart (groin, armpit, neck, jaw or tail base) and take dog to vet • If bleeding continues another ten minutes, apply a tourniquet on the way to the vet—loosen it for a few seconds at five-minute intervals
Broken leg	Dog won't walk on leg; leg is deformed	• If bone protrudes through skin, cover wound with sterile bandage or clean cloth • For breaks below knee, splint with firm material (magazine, ruler), bind in place with cloth strips and take dog to vet • For breaks above knee, place dog on flat surface, secure him in place and take to vet
Broken tail	Tail doesn't move below fracture	• For tail breaks not at base, clean and dress open wound then tape entire tail, starting from tip and working toward body, with cloth bandage tape • For tail breaks at base, take to vet
Burns First and second degree	Red, swollen, blistered skin	• Apply cold water or ice immediately for ten minutes • Apply antibiotic ointment. Dress and monitor wound
Third degree	Red, swollen, blistered and charred skin	• Cover and take dog to vet immediately • Apply ice to burn at once. Keep dog warm to prevent shock
Car accidents		• Protect yourself from bites by muzzling dog • Check dog is breathing and has heartbeat. Move dog to safety • Start CPR as necessary • Stop bleeding • Put dog on flat surface and take to vet immediately

Emergency	Symptoms	What to Do
Choking	Dog gasping for air, coughing or unconscious	• Reach in and clear mouth of foreign objects • Pull tongue forward and extend head back to open airway • Grab dog by legs, suspend him in midair to shake foreign object from airway (with a large dog, rest front legs on ground) • Grasp dog from behind, around his belly just before front legs, and squeeze firmly to expel foreign object from lungs • Take to vet, administering CPR as necessary
Drowning		• Clear mouth of any material • Pull tongue forward and extend neck back to open airway • Suspend dog by hind legs, swing gently to drain lungs • Start CPR as necessary as you take dog to vet
Heatstroke	Dog panting excessively, drooling, glassy-eyed, vomiting, unconscious	• Immerse in cool (not icy) water • Offer cold water to drink if dog is conscious • Place in front of fan or air conditioner • After cooling down, take to vet for examination
Poisoning	Dog has seizures; burns around mouth; low or fast heartbeat; trouble breathing; is drooling; foaming at mouth; bleeding from anus, mouth or nose; is unconscious; or behaving erratically	• Induce vomiting only if you are certain what the dog has eaten and if vomiting is appropriate for that poison (see p. 295) • Take to vet, taking the container of poisonous substance and/or a sample of the vomit along
Shock	Dog is weak, cold to the touch, has pale or gray gums and is breathing rapidly	• Keep dog warm • Try to control bleeding if this is the cause of shock • Take dog to vet immediately
Snake bite	Bleeding wound on head or legs, dilated pupils, trembling, drooling, vomiting, collapse	• Keep dog calm and still • Take to vet immediately • Don't lance bite or suck out venom
Unconscious dog	Motionless, but has a heartbeat	• Make sure dog is breathing. If not, clear mouth of foreign objects, pull tongue forward, perform mouth-to-nose resuscitation (hold mouth shut) • Put dog on a flat surface to protect any broken bones, and take to vet
Wound Superficial	Bleeding, scrape or cut	• Stop bleeding with pressure direct to the wound • Wash with soap and water and apply antibiotic ointment
Deep	Bleeding, deep gash	• Try to stop bleeding • Monitor for signs of shock and take dog to vet

Caring for Older Dogs

With the help of your vet, you can do a lot to ensure that your dog's final years are happy and comfortable.

You may start to notice little changes in your pet as she grows older. It's subtle, but you know her so well, you feel sure something is going on. When she gets up from her nap, her joints seem a little bit stiffer. You go for your daily walk in the park and it's clear she's not going to win any races with the squirrels. And you don't remember her ever asking to be let out so often before.

The changes you're seeing are brought on by old age. And in dogs, much the same as in humans, changes caused by aging can affect what they get out of life. Certain conditions your dog will be prone to can be treated by your vet. Then there are the things that you can do. By making some simple adjustments to her environment and daily routine, you can provide her with a lifestyle that is low on stress and big on ease and enjoyment.

THE SIGNS OF AGE

That distinguished touch of gray around her muzzle is a real giveaway. Your dog is entering her senior years. There are a few other obvious signs to look out for, such as slowing down and weight gain, rather like the way humans age.

BEDDING DOWN Older dogs such as this Labrador mix often have joint problems and will appreciate a soft, supportive bed.

There's also one sign that dogs don't share with us. Many older dogs get a cloudiness in their eyes called "nuclear sclerosis," and this represents a hardening of the lens protein. This makes the dog's eyes cloudy, a bit like cataracts, though it's quite different. With cataracts, the dog's vision is affected and she'll need medical attention. With nuclear sclerosis, her eyesight is okay. If you notice that your dog's eyes are getting cloudy, ask your vet to check her over.

COMMON COMPLAINTS

As the years pass, your old friend's body will begin to slow down, and some illnesses become more likely. We tend to think of health problems such as arthritis and bad breath as being what old age is all about. But many of the problems we think of as conventional "signs of aging" are illnesses that can be successfully treated. Age is not a disease. An owner should not see a dog slowing down and say "Oh, she's just old." Often, what's going on is a treatable disease.

With all the recent advances in veterinary medicine, animal doctors can now cure or greatly relieve many ailments of the more mature dog. Vets see the care of older animals as an important facet of dog health care, so dogs are living longer and healthier lives. It's a good idea to take your older dog to the vet whenever she's not looking or feeling up to par. Talk to the vet about the physical signs and changes in behavior you've noticed since your last visit.

CLOUDY AND BLUE Check your older dog's eyes regularly. Any signs of cloudiness warrant a visit to your vet.

DON'T STARTLE HER When an old dog is sleeping peacefully, don't assume that she is aware of your presence. Gently call her name as you approach.

Vets rely on owners for clues to diagnose medical problems in older dogs.

ARTHRITIS

That stiff-legged walk she's developed looks painful, and it is. Arthritis, also called "degenerative joint disease," is one of the more common and potentially crippling effects of old age. It's the result of years of use, of running, walking, sitting, jumping and generally doing all the doggy things she's always done. The affected joints lose their lubrication, or cartilage gets damaged, or there's some other bone problem. It can happen after a dog has been walking on an imperfectly formed joint for many years.

But there are new medications to help the older dog deal with the pain of arthritis. As well as reducing the pain, many of the new drugs introduced in the past few years seem to slow the degeneration down. So, if your dog seems to have developed a few aches, creaks and groans in her bones, take her to

the vet for evaluation and treatment. It is best to head off the problem before it really sets in.

It's important to keep up the exercise. For dogs that like the water, swimming is good because it moves the joints and muscles through their full range of motion, and the water greatly reduces pressure on the joints.

CANINE DENTAL DISEASE

Once upon a time, your dog would flash you a "grin" and her teeth would be white. Now, they're yellow or even brown, and her breath may be quite malodorous. Dogs that are up in years tend to have this combination of bad teeth and bad breath. It's not from all the dog food they've eaten over the years—it's the start of canine dental disease.

As well as giving her smelly breath and a gappy grin, dental disease can cause more serious problems for your dog. Dental disease is a major contributing factor to heart and kidney problems in older dogs because of the harmful bacteria that accumulate in unhealthy gums. An important part of prevention of such problems is to keep the teeth clean. Like people, dogs need to have their teeth cleaned on a routine basis. If this is not done,

GENTLER PLEASURES This Bassett Hound still enjoys a visit to the park, even if the pace is a little slower.

bacteria, plaque and tartar build up, which can lead to the loss of teeth.

COUGHING

This can be a real problem, especially for very small dogs, whose tiny airways are easily blocked. Coughing can happen to all dogs in old age, but is seen most in smaller breeds. Airways in aged lungs begin producing too much mucus and bronchitis develops. If your dog develops a cough, take her to the vet right away. There are medications that will stop, or at least soothe, the problem.

DIABETES

Diabetes occurs when the pancreas either produces too little insulin or the insulin it produces doesn't work as well as it should. Insulin is a hormone that takes sugar from the bloodstream and delivers it to cells throughout the body, where it's used as fuel. Dogs experience many of the same symptoms of diabetes as people—including increased thirst and frequent urination. When the balance of insulin is right, dogs receive the necessary amount of sugar. When insulin levels fall, they aren't able to maintain the proper sugar balance and become weak and tired. In addition, dogs with diabetes will burn fat to make up for the missing sugar energy, causing them to lose weight.

INSULIN TREATMENT

While giving the right amount of insulin helps control high levels of glucose in the bloodstream, giving too much can make blood sugars drop to dangerous levels, causing a life-threatening condition called hypoglycemia. This usually occurs within several hours of your dog being given an insulin injection. Symptoms to watch for include:

- Lethargy or weakness
- Staggering and disorientation
- Seizures
- Lack of responsiveness

Although you can treat hypoglycemia by quickly giving your dog a little honey or syrup, it's always an emergency and you should see your vet.

HEART PROBLEMS

Heart problems can come on fairly quickly and they're not always easy to recognize. In small dogs one of the heart valves may not close properly, a condition called mitral regurgitation. Large dogs are more likely to get a heart condition called dilated cardiomyopathy, in which the heart muscle enlarges and doesn't beat as vigorously as it should. About 90 percent of dogs with dilated cardiomyopathy belong to one of the following breeds: Boxers, Doberman Pinschers, Golden Retrievers, Great Danes, Irish Wolfhounds, Cocker Spaniels, Saint Bernards and German Shepherds.

Dogs with heart problems always need to be under veterinary care. They usually need medication, in some cases, right away. The sooner you know what's going on and get your dog to the vet, the more likely she is to recover. Here's what to look for:

- She's having trouble breathing
- She coughs, especially when she wakes up or gets excited
- She seems lethargic or weaker than usual
- She faints

Even though dogs with diabetes should always be under a veterinarian's care, it's fairly easy to control the symptoms by giving twice daily injections of insulin, which replenish the body's natural supply. In addition, your vet will advise you about some very effective things you can do to improve your dog's blood-sugar balance and even reduce her need for medication. Dogs that have a higher than usual risk of developing diabetes include Dachshunds, Doberman Pinschers, German Shepherds, Golden and Labrador Retrievers, Samoyeds, Rottweilers, Miniature Poodles, Cocker Spaniels and Pomeranians.

EYES AND EARS

Some older dogs can slowly lose their vision or their hearing. There's no reason to worry, but if you think your dog isn't as keen eyed or sharp eared as she once was, see your vet. He may be able to reverse or arrest the condition. Even if that's not possible, your dog can still live a comfortable life. With the love and emotional support of a caring owner, a dog can adapt to many kinds of physical handicaps better than you might expect.

INCONTINENCE

The last time you found a puddle in the house, she was ankle-high. Now you're cleaning up after her again. It's quite frustrating, but incontinence affects many senior dogs. As they get on in years, they can have trouble containing their urine or feces. And sometimes, accidents happen.

If your dog has a mild case of the leaks, taking her for more toilet trips outside may do the trick. Contact your vet, too. Medication can help if it's a case of lost muscle tone. The vet will first check to make sure there is no underlying cause. There is usually an answer and a drug that can help, but you must rule out urinary tract infection or another internal disease or metabolic problem first.

If medication doesn't help, take special care so that her incontinence doesn't lead to other health difficulties. Keeping her dry and clean is very important. Urine can burn the skin, and feces can attract parasites, so your pet's bedding must be changed frequently.

LIVER AND KIDNEY PROBLEMS

Every day your dog's body produces vast amounts of wastes—not merely the kind you see when you're patrolling the yard or when she stops at every post to leave her calling card, but also other byproducts of digestion and metabolism, such as mineral compounds. Many of these wastes are altered, broken down, or trapped in the kidneys and liver, which are the body's main filters. One of their key jobs is to remove toxins from the blood before they accumulate in the body.

The functions of the kidneys and liver are extraordinarily complex, and it's not

DOGGIE DIAPERS For dogs with bladder-control problems, these products will keep both fur and carpets dry.

MANY PROBLEMS CAN STILL BE TREATED

Changes are natural in older dogs, but don't assume every change is caused by old age. Your dog could be suffering from something that's easily treated. With proper care there's a good chance she'll soon be feeling fine. See your vet if you notice any of the following symptoms:

- Loss of energy or appetite
- Increased water consumption
- Increased urination
- Discharges
- Sores that don't heal
- Changes in weight
- Abnormal odors
- Lumps or bumps on the skin
- Color changes in the skin or eyes
- Coughing or sneezing

uncommon for them to work a little less efficiently as dogs get older. In some cases this is a normal part of the aging process. More often, kidney or liver problems occur when something—a viral or bacterial infection, for example, or exposure to harmful toxins in the environment—has caused internal damage.

The kidneys and liver are tough organs, which is why they can withstand a lifetime's exposure to harmful compounds. But this also means that they keep working even when they're damaged. Many dogs won't show any symptoms at all until the damage is well advanced—and, consequently, harder to treat. The kidneys in particular have a great ability to compensate for damage—up to three-quarters of kidney function may be gone before your dog shows any sign of illness.

Dogs with advanced liver disease will usually have abdominal tenderness on the right side of their bodies. The eyes and

gums may look yellow, and there may be some abdominal swelling. Dogs with advanced kidney disease will usually urinate much more than usual. The urine will be almost clear because the kidneys aren't conserving water the way they should. As a result, most dogs with advanced kidney disease will drink tremendous amounts of water. They may also have bad breath and some muscle weakness.

WEIGHT GAIN

Weight problems are often seen in elderly dogs. As your dog gets on in years, her body and metabolism both slow down. So it is far easier for her to put on weight than it used to be. Obesity is perhaps one of the most common and easily preventable health problems in older dogs. Old dogs have different nutritional requirements from their younger counterparts, so they need a different diet. Ask your vet to advise you. Older dogs also need to keep up their exercise.

OTHER THINGS TO LOOK FOR

There are other problems an old dog may face, including endocrine disorders and cancer. This may sound frightening, but between you and your vet, you should be able to keep such problems under control.

ON THE MOVE An older dog will not be as fast or as nimble as she once was, but she will still need regular exercise to keep her mind and body healthy.

When to Let Go

As dogs age, they become susceptible to a number of health

problems. It's a hard decision, but sometimes you just have to let go.

We love our dogs so much that we want them to live forever. Sadly, this isn't how nature works. So when the time comes, it's important for you to be there for her, to make her passing as easy for her as possible.

Euthanasia is something we don't like to have to think about, but it's best to be prepared before the time actually comes. It is a simple and painless procedure that your vet will perform when you've decided it's time. It results in a peaceful and dignified death. Some pet lovers view euthanasia as one of the greatest gifts we can give to a suffering pet. But it's understandable that most people find, when it comes to the time, that letting go is very hard to do.

QUALITY OF LIFE

The key question every pet owner has to ask of themselves is whether their beloved pet still has dignity, is free of pain and has a good quality of life. Before you begin trying to make any decisions, talk to your vet. Have a consultation either by phone or in person to discuss the issues.

It's important to have this discussion before going through the process of deciding, since you may find that the problem your dog is

SIZE MAKES A DIFFERENCE Small dogs, such as this West Highland White Terrier, can live for 15 years or more.

having isn't so bad after all, and it may even be curable. Euthanasia is unquestionably the most difficult decision any pet owner will ever have to make. Unfortunately, our pets don't usually pass away in their sleep, so we have to face up to the issue. More often, the dog's quality of life deteriorates, and the owner starts to see that the dog is having more bad days than good. When this happens, it's time to discuss euthanasia with your vet.

There is support available for people who lose their pets, and also for those who are trying to decide about euthanasia. Today, pet loss and pet grieving are recognized by the human medical community. In some countries, there are support groups and specialists who can help you deal with this most difficult time, both before and after losing your pet. Do what feels right to you, and is best for your dog.

HOW LONG IS A DOG'S LIFE?

When you look at a Chihuahua and a Newfoundland, it's hard to believe that they are members of the same species. That's one of the most amazing things about dogs—how different the breeds can be. They vary not only in appearance, but also in personality, style and, of course, longevity. Some breeds live a lot longer than others, and the distinctions seem to be all about size. Age goes up as size goes down. The giant breeds have the shortest lifespans, between seven and ten years. Smaller dogs, such as the West Highland White Terrier, Beagle and Dachshund, can live for more than 15 years.

But these are mere generalizations. There are many reasons an individual dog may live a longer, or indeed a shorter, life than expected. It's a lot harder to predict the lifespan of a mixed breed, but the dog's size will give you a rough idea.

Buy a pup and your money will buy
Love unflinching that cannot lie.

RUDYARD KIPLING (1865–1936),
Indian-born English novelist and poet

CHAPTER TWELVE

BREEDING

Breeding Your Dog

Breeding puppies should always be done responsibly. Thousands of
dogs are abandoned each year because of unwanted pregnancies.

If you are going to bring new dogs into the world, aim to improve the standard of the breed. Every dog that is bred should represent an improvement over its parents. In general, it is best to avoid breeding mixed-breed dogs. Dog overpopulation is a huge problem and shelters are already full of unwanted mixed breeds, as well as purebred dogs. Unless you can guarantee a good home for each and every puppy you breed, you will only be contributing to the problem.

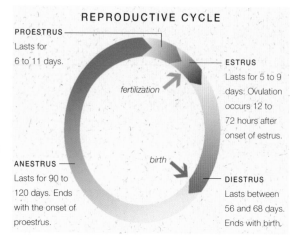

REPRODUCTIVE CYCLE

PROESTRUS
Lasts for
6 to 11 days.

fertilization

ESTRUS
Lasts for 5 to 9
days: Ovulation
occurs 12 to
72 hours after
onset of estrus.

ANESTRUS
Lasts for 90 to
120 days. Ends
with the onset of
proestrus.

birth

DIESTRUS
Lasts between
56 and 68 days.
Ends with birth.

CHOOSING A MATE

To ensure that the pups you breed will be of the best quality, choose a mate from an experienced and reputable dealer. Don't pick a neighborhood dog that will perform for free! Make sure the dog is registered with a national kennel club. However, registration alone does not vouch for the quality of a dog, so check out any potential suitor carefully.

Pay particular attention to the dog's temperament. Although dogs were once bred for specific tasks, most are now kept as companions. Choose a mate who has

the qualities of a good companion. Never breed with a dog who is aggressive, very timid or has hereditary diseases.

Ideally, a bitch that you choose to breed will be at least two years old, in good health and with her vaccinations up to date. A healthy bitch is more likely to have a trouble-free pregnancy and to produce sound pups.

THE BREEDING CYCLE

Unlike human beings, dogs breed only during certain times of the year. Although males may attempt to breed at any time, females will only accept them when they are ovulating. At this time, the bitch is described as being "in heat" or "in season." The technical term is estrus. Most bitches come into heat twice a year (wolves and Basenjis have only one heat cycle per year). Depending on a bitch's breed and size, she will have her first heat

BEFORE YOU BREED YOUR DOG

- Arrange good homes for all potential puppies.
- Investigate any hereditary disorders that are common in your breed.
- Choose a mate carefully.
- Check that both dogs are registered with a national kennel club.
- Have both dogs examined by a veterinarian, including a check for parasites and brucellosis (a sexually transmitted disease that causes sterility).
- Read up on canine reproduction, pregnancy, birth and postnatal care.

NEW GENERATION Puppies, like these young English Setters, are delightful, but should not be bred randomly. Your aim should be to improve the breed, not to contribute to dog overpopulation.

WHAT TO LOOK FOR IN A MATE

- Choose a good representative of your breed from a reputable and responsible breeder.
- Make sure the dog is registered with a national kennel club.
- Make sure he is healthy and doesn't have any hereditary diseases. This may require blood tests, X-rays and eye exams by a specialist.
- Look for a dog of sound temperament who would make a good companion.

between 6 and 24 months of age. Smaller dogs come into heat sooner. Wait until your bitch's third or fourth estrus before breeding. This way you can be sure that she is both physically and emotionally mature.

Males go through puberty, begin to produce fertile sperm and are therefore capable of producing puppies generally between seven and nine months of age. They are eager to breed any time afterward.

Phases of the Cycle

There are four phases of the canine reproductive cycle. The beginning of the heat period is known as proestrus. The most reliable indicator of the beginning of this stage is a bloody vaginal discharge. Other signs are a swollen vulva and frequent urination and licking. Male dogs are attracted to the bitch during this phase, but she will not permit mating. Proestrus lasts for six to eleven days.

Estrus begins when the bitch begins to permit mating. To indicate this, she often crouches, elevates her vulva toward the male

and moves her tail to the side. Her vulva becomes soft, tense and hot and the discharge becomes less and less bloody.

Ovulation takes place during estrus, which usually lasts for five to nine days. Great care must be taken at this time to prevent unwanted pregnancies. Any female in season is best confined to the house and taken out only for short, supervised leash walks.

The next stage, diestrus, is characterized by a steady reduction in vulvar swelling and a loss of attractiveness to male dogs.

If mating has taken place, this stage is the beginning of pregnancy. Even if a bitch is not pregnant, many show signs of pregnancy, a stage known as false pregnancy. Diestrus lasts between 56 and 68 days in pregnant bitches and 60 to 80 days in an unfertilized bitch.

The final stage of the cycle is called anestrus. In the pregnant bitch, it begins with the birth of puppies and ends with proestrus. In a non-pregnant animal, its onset is less obvious. Basically, a female dog in anestrus is hard to tell apart from one who has been spayed.

Mating and Pregnancy

*Your pregnant dog requires some special care, but to a large extent
she should be allowed to follow her usual routine.*

Once a bitch is in season, dogs generally
have no problems mating. Some first-
timers, however, do experience anxiety and
may be reluctant to mate. If you anticipate
this being a problem, there are a number of
ways you can prepare in advance (see box).

MATING

In dogs, courtship begins with the male
sniffing at the female's nose, ear, neck, side
and vulva. The bitch sniffs the male in return
and may want to play, but will not tolerate
mounting until fully receptive. When ready,
the bitch typically presents her hindquarters
to the male and stands still with her tail to
the side. The male then clasps the sides of the
female with his forelegs, inserts his penis into
the vagina and begins to thrust.

While inside, the erectile tissue in his penis
swells, resulting in the so-called "coital tie."
With the penis firmly in place, ejaculation
begins. Then with their genitalia still locked,
the dog dismounts and swings to the side so
that he and the bitch are facing in opposite
directions. This position is required for full
ejaculation and may last anywhere from 5 to
60 minutes. Don't try to separate two dogs
in a tie as injury could result.

THE PREGNANCY

Fertilization occurs about 72 hours after
mating and the gestation period lasts 56 to
68 days, or eight to nine weeks, the average
being 63 days. It's hard to tell that a dog is
pregnant until at least
the fifth week, although
pups can be felt by an
experienced person after
about 20 days of pregnancy.
If you can't stand not knowing
whether your dog is pregnant,

MOTHER-TO-BE This Chihuahua
mix is in a late stage of pregnancy,
carrying four puppies.

HINTS FOR NERVOUS COUPLES

- Choose an experienced male.
- Take the bitch to the dog's place for mating.
- Arrange for the dogs to meet prior to mating.
- Allow them plenty of time to get
  used to each other.
- If it is not possible for
  the dogs to meet prior
  to mating, provide
  each dog with an
  object that smells
  of the other.

you may want her to have an ultrasound. This
is expensive, but will give confirmation at
about 24 days. It might also be worthwhile if
you need to plan time off from work for the
birth, or if she has any health problems.

After you have confirmed that your bitch
is pregnant, go over the basics of prenatal care,
the whelping process and emergency procedures with your veterinarian. If your dog is on
medication, discuss this with your vet also.
There are some medications, such as cortico-
steroids, that should be avoided during
pregnancy because they can affect the litter.

A bigger belly doesn't always occur in first-
time mothers, but the breasts and nipples do
tend to enlarge. Your dog might also be a little
more cranky and demanding than usual.

Feeding, Exercise and Grooming

A pregnant female requires more food to
support the growth of the puppies inside her
and to produce the
milk that they will
live on after birth. A
good regime to follow
is to feed her the same
amount she normally eats for
the first six weeks. Increase
her intake during the final
three weeks until she is eating

about 50 percent more at the time of whelping than when she was bred. At this time, feed her three or four small meals a day. Because the puppies take up so much room, her stomach won't be able to fill as much as normal. Let her have as much as she can eat in 15 minutes. Feed a premium dog food that is specifically designed for all life stages or for pregnancy and lactation. Now is not the time to economize on your dog's food.

Supplements aren't necessary and may even be detrimental. They can cause abnormalities in the developing puppies, or a severe depletion of calcium is the blood when your dog tries to nurse.

Exercise is especially important for a pregnant dog. It keeps her muscles toned, and that helps during labor. Do what you usually do. Take her on her regular walks and let her continue her other activities until she gets too big and ungainly to enjoy them.

If she's used to jumping in field trials, it's okay until she's uncomfortable. She shouldn't just laze around. Even at the end of the pregnancy, be sure your dog has a turn or two around the yard once or twice a day.

Groom a pregnant dog as usual, and give her baths when necessary. Make sure you keep her out of drafts until she's totally dry, though. And if she needs a bath in the last two or three weeks, be extra gentle so the unborn pups aren't harmed or disturbed.

THE PUPS' FIRST HOME A well-prepared whelping box will provide a comfortable nest for your bitch and her new family.

The Whelping Box

In the final seven to ten days, your dog will display nesting behavior. This is the time to introduce her to her whelping box, which should be big enough to comfortably accommodate both her and her pups. Keep one side low to permit the bitch to easily enter and exit. Place it in a warm, quiet and secluded area. Line the box initially with newspaper; she will probably circle in it and shred it until she's satisfied with her nest. For the actual birth, line the bottom of the box with soft towels, and have plenty of fresh ones on hand to replace those soiled during whelping.

Try to include a guard rail, about 3 inches (7.5 cm) from the floor and 3 inches from the sides of the box, to prevent the bitch from crushing any puppies against the sides.

Several days before whelping, you will notice a marked enlargement of your bitch's mammary glands. Milk is likely to appear on the nipples at this time. About 24 hours before whelping, she will begin digging and nesting in her whelping box. At this time, carefully clip the hair around her nipples so that the pups won't have any trouble finding them. Also clip the hair around her vulva if necessary.

Two or three days before delivery, your dog may lose her appetite and have a slight discharge of thick, clear mucus from her vagina. During the last week of pregnancy, you may want to take her temperature twice a day. You'll know that birth is imminent when her temperature drops below 100°F (38° C). Once this happens, the pups will probably start appearing within 24 hours or so.

The Birth and After

Most bitches do not need help to give birth.

You should interfere only in an emergency.

Make sure you have arranged for someone to be with you for the delivery, just in case there is a problem and you need to help deliver the pups. No matter how gentle your dog normally is, if she's in pain she may bite, so another pair of hands can help to hold her. Make sure an assistant is available for you, but only help with the birth if you really need to. Too much interference may cause a bitch to become nervous and prevent her from adequately caring for her newborns.

THE DELIVERY

Signs that a bitch has entered the first stage of labor are panting, shivering and restlessness. She may also vomit. As the pups move into position for delivery, the bitch's belly will begin to sag. She may walk around, unable to get comfortable, and she may come to you often, so give her lots of reassurance. This stage can last from 6 to 24 hours.

As labor continues, your dog will finally settle down to the serious business of pushing. She may lie on her side as the contractions increase, sometimes panting, whining and groaning. Stay calm, speak softly, and stroke her slowly to help her feel better. It's best not to have the whole family watching. Your dog doesn't want to be distracted or disturbed. You'll know she's about to give birth when you see a sac emerging.

Your dog may give birth lying down or standing up. If she prefers to stand, you'll need to be there to catch the pups. As a pup is delivered, the bitch tears the placental membranes in which the puppy is wrapped and eats them. The puppy then takes his first breath. The mother bites off the umbilical cord and may eat the afterbirth, which usually appears a few minutes after the pup. She'll then lick the puppy dry, which will keep him warm and stimulate his breathing.

Keep a tally of the afterbirths: if there isn't one for each puppy, it means that a placenta has remained in the uterus, and your vet will need to remove it to make sure that your dog doesn't develop an infection.

If your bitch doesn't remove the placental membranes from a pup's nose and mouth within two minutes of birth, you should do so. Then, keeping the pup's head down, use a small bulb syringe to suction out any mucus in the mouth. Rub the puppy vigorously with a clean hand towel. Your aim is to hear him cry. After you have done this, clamp off the umbilical cord with your fingers, then cut it with blunt-nosed scissors. Tie the cord off

A FINE FAMILY Larger breeds, such as Weimaraners (below), tend to have larger litters. Litter size can also depend on the bitch's level of experience—first-time mothers may have fewer puppies.

NEWBORNS Puppies, such as these Chihuahuas, are born blind and deaf, and are entirely dependent on their mother for food and protection.

with unwaxed dental floss or thread, and dab the area with iodine to disinfect it.

The pups may appear every few minutes, or your dog may rest for an hour or two between each delivery. After all the pups are born, you will probably see a green, dark red or brown discharge. This odorless fluid is a natural part of her body's cleansing process and may last several weeks. There's no need to worry about it unless an odor develops or the dog's thirst increases; this could indicate an infection, and you should see the vet.

WHEN TO HELP

As the birth proceeds, watch the time and jot down when things start and stop. If your dog seems to be having hard contractions, is panting and pushing, and seems stressed, one of the puppies may have become lodged across the birth canal instead of heading downward. If a pup doesn't appear within 20 minutes of continual strong contractions, call your vet for advice. He may talk you through turning the pup or recommend that you bring your dog in.

FIRST WEEK OF LIFE At one week of age, puppies such as these Labradors still have their eyes closed, and spend most of their time sleeping.

This is probably the most common problem during delivery. The first puppy dilates the cervix, but not enough. As there may not be time to get to a vet, you will have to help with the delivery. To do this, reach up to the cervix with your thumb and at least one finger (make sure your hands are clean and your nails trimmed) to see how the puppy is positioned. Most pups come out nose first, stomach down, but it's also fine if they're born rear first. Hold the pup's body—not his legs or head—firmly but gently, and let the contractions push the pup out. Your bitch is likely to be scared and in pain, so have somebody hold her head to prevent her biting you.

AFTER-BIRTH CARE

Check that the puppies are all nursing strongly and that everyone has found a nipple. It's vital

WHELPING EMERGENCIES

From time to time, a whelping bitch may get into difficulties. If you notice any of the following, don't delay in calling your veterinarian.

- If the normal discharge that occurs a few days before the birth is greenish rather than clear. This indicates the separation of the placenta and probably means that at least one of the placentas has detached.
- If the birth hasn't begun within 24 hours of her temperature dropping.
- If a puppy hasn't appeared after about 20 minutes of strong contractions. Your dog's inability to get the pups out can be life-threatening not only to the puppies but also to your dog.
- If your dog pants and acts as if she's going into labor but doesn't, or she goes into labor and then stops for more than three hours. These are signs that contractions are not taking place and your dog may need a cesarean section.

for them to get milk from their mother during the first three days of life. That first milk contains colostrum, which provides antibodies that protect the puppies from disease until they can be vaccinated.

Weigh each pup and write down its weight. You'll need to weigh them on a gram or ounce scale every 12 hours for at least the first week, to make sure they are gaining weight and thriving. If they're not, you may need to supplement their feeding with formula.

It's also a good idea to have both mother and pups checked by your veterinarian in the first 24 hours. He can make sure there aren't any other pups still inside the uterus, or any retained placentas, and he can examine the

pups for umbilical hernias, cleft palates or any other problems.

Once the pups are safely delivered and nursing, they need warmth and quiet. For the first week of life, pups are unable to shiver or control their own body temperature. They depend on their mother and other pups to keep warm. An external source of heat which keeps the temperature in the whelping box at around 86°F (30°C), such as an electric heating bulb or a hot water bottle covered with a towel, will help keep the pups warm. If necessary, secure an electric heating bulb about 4 feet (1.2 m) above the center of the box to keep everyone comfortable. Just don't have the heat source too close to the puppies in case they get too hot or become dehydrated.

For the bitch's comfort and the pups' safety, keep noisy kids and curious neighbors away. After the first few days, start picking the pups up and handling them for a couple of minutes a few times a day so they become used to the presence and scent of people. Make sure anybody who handles the pups has clean hands. Although the bitch will do her best to keep the pups and the whelping box clean, you should clean any parts of the box or the living area that she has missed. Gently wipe the pups' eyes, ears and mouth when necessary.

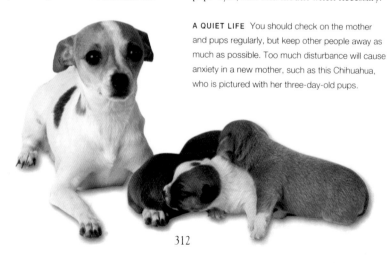

A QUIET LIFE You should check on the mother and pups regularly, but keep other people away as much as possible. Too much disturbance will cause anxiety in a new mother, such as this Chihuahua, who is pictured with her three-day-old pups.

Feeding and Weaning

Make sure that each puppy has access to a nipple and is able to suckle. If a pup is not receiving adequate milk, try holding her up to a nipple several times a day so she does not have to compete with the other pups. If she is still not getting enough milk, you may need to supplement her feeding with puppy formula from your vet. Use a small bottle with a hole in the nipple just large enough for a drop of milk to ooze out.

FEEDING TIME Most bitches wean their pups after about six or seven weeks. By this time, the puppies should be able to eat enough solid food to meet all their nutritional requirements.

Once the pups start to walk, give them a papered bathroom area a short distance from where they sleep. They will naturally urinate and defecate away from their sleeping area.

At three or four weeks of age, most puppies will begin to eat food. To make it easier for them, prepare a gruel of puppy weaning diet and water. Offer this in a large bowl to all the puppies three to four times a day. Over the next few weeks, reduce the water in the gruel until it is omitted altogether.

CARING FOR NEW MOTHERS

Your dog may not feel like eating solid food for a day or so after the birth. In this case, you can give her puppy milk replacer formula. Feed it to her three times a day until her appetite returns—this keeps her nutrients and fluids up.

Keep a close eye on your dog in the days after the birth. If she seems shaky or weak, or suddenly collapses, go to the vet immediately. She may need a calcium injection if she's lactating heavily and not getting enough nutrients. Check her temperature daily; if it reaches 103°F (39.5° C), she needs a vet check. A fever may indicate a uterine infection, which must be treated quickly. Also examine her mammary glands to make sure they feel full and warm. If they seem hot or hard, you need to take her to the vet.

When the pups stop nursing, the bitch will probably feel pretty uncomfortable. Your vet may advise giving her a mild diuretic for a day or two to help to relieve the pressure. And once the puppies are weaned, cut back on the amount of food you give her.

OFF TO A GOOD START Pups should be weighed frequently to ensure they are making satisfactory progress. These six-week-old Corgi–Beagle mixes are doing fine.

If you can't decide between a Shepherd, a Setter or a Poodle, get them all … adopt a mutt!

AMERICAN SOCIETY FOR THE PROTECTION OF ANIMALS

PART FIVE

A GUIDE TO BREEDS

A History of the Domestic Dog

*From scavengers on the outskirts of the earliest human settlements
to the treasured pets of today, dogs have evolved with us.*

Domestic dogs, coyotes, jackals, wolves and dingoes make up the genus Canis. Although the fossil record is limited, the first members of this genus probably appeared about one million years ago, but the domestic dog developed much later.

THE DOMESTICATION OF THE DOG

The domestication of the dog probably began around the time our ancestors became hunters and gatherers. Packs of wild dogs would have scavenged on the outskirts of temporary camps and the hunters would have appreciated the warnings they gave of approaching danger. As settlements became more permanent, dogs would have become increasingly useful as guard dogs, and later hunting and eventually herding dogs.

From these early times, the evolution of the dog was largely dictated by humans. Dogs were selectively bred to perform specific tasks by breeding together those dogs that exhibited particular traits, such as size, hunting ability and docility. Gradually, through this process of interbreeding, distinct types of dogs were developed and maintained.

Greyhounds and Mastiff-type dogs are the oldest recognizable breeds of which there are historical records. Depictions of Greyhounds have been found on 8,000-year-old fragments of Mesopotamian pottery, and there are records of Mastiffs that are nearly as old as this. In ancient times, Greyhounds were used primarily as hunting dogs, while the large, aggressive Mastiffs were used in battle and as guard dogs.

AGE OLD Some breeds have changed little over centuries. The dogs in this first-century Roman sculpture bear a striking resemblance to today's Whippets.

MEDIEVAL HUNTERS Dogs have been selectively bred for thousands of years. The dogs in this fifteenth-century hunt scene appear quite similar to today's Greyhounds and terriers.

DIVERSIFICATION

Over thousands of years (possibly as many as 150,000), dogs developed and diversified as human needs changed. The evolution of hunting dogs is a good example of this process. The Greyhound was an exemplary hunting dog; swift, powerful, possessing acute eyesight and great stamina, it could chase and kill a variety of prey. However, over the centuries, as hunting methods became more refined and the kinds of prey hunted became more varied, new breeds of hunting dog were developed. Dogs were now bred not only to chase game but also to sniff it out (scent hounds), to point to it in the field (pointers and setters), to flush it out so hunters could shoot it (spaniels), to retrieve it (retrievers) and to chase it down burrows or dig it out of them (terriers).

Breeding for Looks

In early times, dogs were bred to perform specific tasks, and their appearance was largely irrelevant. However, even in ancient times this was not always the case. In Asia, there is a long and rich tradition of breeding dogs for their looks. As long as 5,000 years ago, Chinese emperors were breeding tiny "lap dogs" to carry around their palaces. This process of miniaturization led to the development of the toy dogs, many of which became favorites with royalty over the centuries. Toy dogs remain popular pets to this day.

The Industrial Revolution

The greatest influence on the domestication of the dog since wolves and humans first made contact was the Industrial Revolution. During the eighteenth and nineteenth centuries, urbanization and changes in the nature of employment meant that people had more leisure time to devote to hobbies. By the late nineteenth century, breeding and showing of dogs were popular pastimes. As a result, the focus of breeding shifted to the appearance of the dog and the variety of recognized dog breeds grew enormously.

CLOSE RELATIONS Due to a number of similarities, both genetic and behavioral, it is believed that the domestic dog evolved from the wolf. Once the bond was established in ancient times between humans and wolves, the domestic dog emerged as a process of selective breeding.

Breed Standards

The basic dog types remained remarkably consistent over thousands of years due to careful breeding. However, no one attempted to define a breed in any official sense until 1867, when *The Dogs of the British Islands* was published, setting out for the first time the defining characteristics of 35 breeds. This introduced the concept of a breed "standard"—a written description against which a breed could be judged.

Then, in 1873, the world's first kennel club was established in Britain. Known as The Kennel Club, this organization published its own set of standards for 40 breeds. In addition, it stipulated that for a breed to be officially recognized it had to be registered with the club. From this point on, kennel club recognition became the defining feature of a breed.

BEST OF BREED At conformation shows, dogs such as this Doberman are judged against a written standard.

The Ethics of Breeding

The American Kennel Club (A.K.C) was set up in 1883 and the Fédération Cynologique Internationale (F.C.I.), representing European countries, in 1911. The number of dog breeds grew rapidly, but with each kennel club acting in isolation, recognition of specific breeds varied from country to country. Today, the A.K.C. recognizes 150 breeds, The Kennel Club recognizes 196 breeds and the F.C.I. 331. Worldwide, there may be as many as 500 breeds and the number is growing every year.

While any breed must breed true to a consistent set of standards over time, there remains no absolute definition of a dog breed. For example, in Britain the Belgian Shepherd is considered to be one breed consisting of four distinct types, the Malinois, Tervuren, Laekenois and Groenendael. However, in the U.S. the Laekenois is not officially recognized at all, while the other three varieties are considered to be distinct breeds. Furthermore, the same breed may differ slightly from one country to another due to local variations in the breed standard.

The proliferation of dog breeds and the drive to conform to written breed standards over the last hundred or so years have meant that domestic dogs have changed appearance dramatically. Many breeds have become rather stylized, or in some cases have been bred to show extreme traits. While human intervention of some sort has probably always influenced the evolution of the domestic dog, the performance and health of dogs bred for specific tasks were rarely compromised. However, when dogs are bred chiefly for appearance, traits that actually hinder a dog's performance may be inadvertently selected. The Bulldog, for example, has developed to the point where its large head, wide-set legs, soft palate and sagging facial skin may jeopardize its health and longevity. Indeed, since the Bulldog standard calls for a narrow pelvis and a large head, pups of this breed regularly struggle to pass through the birth canal. This accounts for the prevalence of cesarean sections in this breed.

WIDE WORLD OF DOGS Thousands of years of selective breeding have resulted in as many as 500 breeds of dog, greatly differing in size, appearance and the purpose for which they were designed.

HYBRID VIGOR A first cross, such as this Maltese–Shih Tzu, has a lower risk of inherited diseases than a purebred dog.

Even with hardy working breeds, inbreeding for show purposes has left a common legacy of genetic diseases, such as hip dysplasia. Today, kennel clubs and responsible breeders go to great lengths to avoid breeding dogs with genetic defects or traits that may compromise their well being.

The Development of New Breeds

From time to time, a group of enthusiasts approaches their country's kennel club and puts a case for the establishment of a new breed. This includes an argument that it is morphologically distinct from similar breeds and that it "breeds true"; that is, the parent dogs within the gene pool no longer produce litters of disparate type. This is perhaps where the notion of breed purity came from. Unfortunately, it is also an invitation to inbreed.

If a breed meets with kennel club approval, it may be first granted provisional recognition, and later receive full recognition.

"Designer Crosses"

Contrary to popular belief, first crosses between pairs of purebreds are as predictable as purebreds in terms of their shape and behavior. However, such hybrids will have a far lower chance of exhibiting the disorders that are common within the parental breeds, so their genetic health tends to be substantially higher. The critical point here when selecting two breeds for crossing is that the genetic flaws of one parent should not appear in the other. Consider a "Labradoodle." Since hip dysplasia is not reported in the Miniature Poodle, the flaws in this part of the Labrador's genetic make-up are less likely to surface in any of the pups than if the other parent had been a Standard Poodle, another breed in which hip dysplasia is recognized.

With so many breeds to choose from as parents when cross breeding, it should be possible to find combinations that suit just about every owner's need, and match just about every type of modern environment in which dogs are likely to be kept. Once particularly favorable combinations have been determined, breeders of the parental breeds have a large market for the sale of pets.

There are already examples of the way in which first crosses combine favorable traits from both parental breeds. For example, the Labrador Retriever x Miniature Poodle (Mini Labradoodle) has received attention from guide dog associations in Australia because it combines the "tolerance" of the Labrador with the hypoallergenic coat of the Poodle. It is worth noting that the advantages of crossing are seen only in first crosses, so it is not appropriate to use first crosses as breeding stock.

Classifying Breeds

Although most dogs are now kept only as companions, dogs remain largely classified by the work for which they were developed.

The classification of dogs into groups varies from country to country. The Tibetan Spaniel, for example, is classified in the non-sporting group by the American Kennel Club (A.K.C.), the utility group by the Kennel Club (U.K.) and the companion and toy group by the Fédération Cynologique Internationale (F.C.I.). The Chow Chow is considered a working breed in the U.K. but a non-sporting breed in the U.S.

This guide to breeds uses the A.K.C. system, which recognizes seven groups. The U.K. also recognizes seven groups and the F.C.I. ten.

ON THE HUNT Terriers, such as this Norwich Terrier, were bred to hunt small game and rodents.

SPORTING DOGS

Sporting dogs, also known as gundogs, were bred to work with hunters in the field. Pointers were bred to sniff out game birds, and once located, to point toward them with an upraised leg. Setters also located game, and then indicated its presence by standing still, or "setting". The smaller, faster spaniels were bred to flush out game from the undergrowth for hunters to net or shoot, while retrievers were bred to retrieve game from land or water once it was shot.

Today, sporting dogs are popular pets. They retain a liveliness and love of exercise as well as intense loyalty to their owners.

HOUNDS

Dogs from this group are among the most ancient; Greyhounds were the first hunting dogs for which there are historical records. Developed to chase and kill large prey, many hounds are capable of great speed and possess enormous stamina.

Hounds are divided into sight hounds and scent hounds, depending on how they locate their prey. Some scent hounds are not particularly fast, choosing instead to corner their prey. These days, hounds are often used for racing or in police work. They make good pets but are not always easy to train.

WORKING DOGS

This is another ancient group, and includes breeds that date back to times when dogs were used to guard settlements, carry loads and engage in battle, as well as to hunt. There have been depictions of large Mastiff-type dogs for many thousands of years.

LOOK HERE This German Short-Haired Pointer displays the behavior for which pointers were bred.

Working dogs are generally large, strong and obedient. Some of them, such as the Doberman Pinscher, still make exemplary guard dogs. Others, such as the Saint Bernard, have been used in rescue work. While some dogs within this group can be aggressive, they are unflinchingly loyal to their owners.

TERRIERS

These dogs were developed mainly in the British Isles over the past few hundred years, although there are records of small hunting dogs from earlier times. Generally small, short-legged, determined dogs with powerful jaws, they were bred to hunt small game, often digging them out of burrows. Long-legged terriers, such as the Airedale, were bred to hunt larger game. Much of their aggression has been bred out of them, but terriers remain playful and exuberant, although many are incorrigible diggers.

TOY DOGS

Miniature dogs were developed by ancient Chinese Emperors as palace companions and lap dogs, and they remained popular with royalty through the ages. These days,

LITTLE LAPDOGS Maltese, like most other toy dogs, were developed simply as pets and companions.

UP TO SPEED Greyhounds, like other sight hound breeds, are capable of great speed and stamina.

they are popular pets, particularly in cities, where their size and gentle temperament suit them to apartment living.

NON-SPORTING DOGS

This group contains breeds that don't fit neatly into any of the other categories. Some belong in this group because the task for which they were developed no longer exists. The Bulldog, for example, was bred for bull-baiting and fighting, pastimes that are now outlawed.

While dogs in this group have little in common, they are some of the most beautiful, intelligent and popular dogs today.

HERDING DOGS

Although not as ancient as some hound breeds, herding dogs have been used for thousands of years to protect livestock from predators and to keep them from straying. They tend to be nimble and intelligent and to have great stamina.

Today, many of these dogs are still employed in their traditional roles, although they also make wonderful pets if given sufficient exercise and attention.

How to Use the Guide

If you are interested in becoming the proud owner of a purebred dog, this is the place to start. This guide provides details of more than 100 of the most popular dog breeds to help you decide which dog is best suited to your needs.

NAME OF BREED
The name of the breed as used by the American Kennel Club. Breeds are arranged in approximate order of height within their respective groups.

INTRODUCTION
This provides a succinct and lively overview of the breed.

MAIN TEXT
The running text provides a detailed description of the breed, including its history, distinguishing characteristics and temperament. It also details the grooming, feeding and exercise requirements for the breed, as well as alerting prospective owners to common health problems that may afflict these dogs.

MAIN IMAGE
A representative of the breed, shown in profile. Some are breed-standard quality, others are pet quality.

SIZE AND WEIGHT
Average size for males and females of the breed. Height is measured from the ground to the withers.

A GUIDE TO BREEDS

Japanese Chin

The lovely little Japanese Chin is truly a dog to dote on and will gladly return the love that is unfailingly lavished upon it. It is a superlative lapdog with few, if any, flaws or vices.

small living spaces. With its gentle ways and charming manners, it is perhaps best suited to homes in which there are no small children.

GROOMING
Although the coat looks as though it might be difficult, a few minutes each day will keep it looking beautiful. Comb out tangles and brush lightly, lifting the hair to leave it standing out a little. A professional dog groomer can show you the correct technique. Dry shampoo occasionally and bathe only when necessary. Clean the eyes every day and check the ears regularly for any signs of infection.

HISTORY
These gorgeous little dogs have been known in Western countries for only about 150 years. However, they were the pampered pooches of wealthy Japanese, including royalty, for many centuries, having been introduced to Japan from China in ancient times. They are probably distantly related to the Pekingese.

DESCRIPTION
The Japanese Chin looks like a tiny toy. The profuse, straight, longhaired coat comes in white with markings either of black or shades of red. The gait is graceful with the feet lifted high off the ground.

TEMPERAMENT
The engaging little Chin is a lively, happy, sweet-tempered animal, the perfect size for

EXERCISE & FEEDING
While they don't require a great deal of exercise, Chins love a daily walk and an opportunity to play in the

open. There are no special feeding requirements, but they prefer to "graze" on small meals and tidbits.

HEALTH PROBLEMS
The large and prominent eyes are vulnerable to damage and subject to cataracts and progressive retinal atrophy.

PET FACTS	
Intelligent, lively, gentle	Daily brushing
Regular, gentle	Ideal for apartment living
Poor watchdog	

🐾 **BE AWARE**
• Matted hair must be clipped off the feet

Male: 7–11 in (18–28 cm)
Up to 9 lb (4 kg)
Female: 7–11 in (18–28 cm)
Up to 9 lb (4 kg)

398

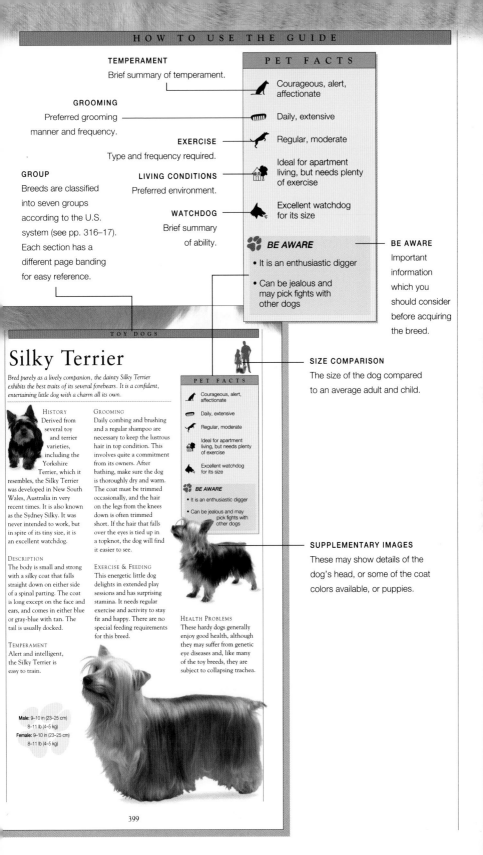

TEMPERAMENT
Brief summary of temperament.

GROOMING
Preferred grooming
manner and frequency.

EXERCISE
Type and frequency required.

GROUP
Breeds are classified
into seven groups
according to the U.S.
system (see pp. 316–17).
Each section has a
different page banding
for easy reference.

LIVING CONDITIONS
Preferred environment.

WATCHDOG
Brief summary
of ability.

PET FACTS

Courageous, alert,
affectionate

Daily, extensive

Regular, moderate

Ideal for apartment
living, but needs plenty
of exercise

Excellent watchdog
for its size

BE AWARE

- It is an enthusiastic digger

- Can be jealous and
may pick fights with
other dogs

BE AWARE
Important
information
which you
should consider
before acquiring
the breed.

TOY DOGS

Silky Terrier

Bred purely as a lively companion, the dainty Silky Terrier exhibits the best traits of its several forebears. It is a confident, entertaining little dog with a charm all its own.

SIZE COMPARISON
The size of the dog compared
to an average adult and child.

HISTORY
Derived from
several toy
and terrier
varieties,
including the
Yorkshire
Terrier, which it
resembles, the Silky Terrier
was developed in New South
Wales, Australia in very
recent times. It is also known
as the Sydney Silky. It was
never intended to work, but
in spite of its tiny size, it is
an excellent watchdog.

GROOMING
Daily combing and brushing
and a regular shampoo are
necessary to keep the lustrous
hair in top condition. This
involves quite a commitment
from its owners. After
bathing, make sure the dog
is thoroughly dry and warm.
The coat must be trimmed
occasionally, and the hair
on the legs from the knees
down is often trimmed
short. If the hair that falls
over the eyes is tied up in
a topknot, the dog will find
it easier to see.

PET FACTS

Courageous, alert,
affectionate

Daily, extensive

Regular, moderate

Ideal for apartment
living, but needs plenty
of exercise

Excellent watchdog
for its size

BE AWARE

- It is an enthusiastic digger

- Can be jealous and may
pick fights with
other dogs

DESCRIPTION
The body is small and strong
with a silky coat that falls
straight down on either side
of a spinal parting. The coat
is long except on the face and
ears, and comes in either blue
or gray-blue with tan. The
tail is usually docked.

TEMPERAMENT
Alert and intelligent,
the Silky Terrier is
easy to train.

EXERCISE & FEEDING
This energetic little dog
delights in extended play
sessions and has surprising
stamina. It needs regular
exercise and activity to stay
fit and happy. There are no
special feeding requirements
for this breed.

HEALTH PROBLEMS
These hardy dogs generally
enjoy good health, although
they may suffer from genetic
eye diseases and, like many
of the toy breeds, they are
subject to collapsing trachea.

SUPPLEMENTARY IMAGES
These may show details of the
dog's head, or some of the coat
colors available, or puppies.

Male: 9–10 in (23–25 cm)
8–11 lb (4–5 kg)
Female: 9–10 in (23–25 cm)
8–11 lb (4–5 kg)

399

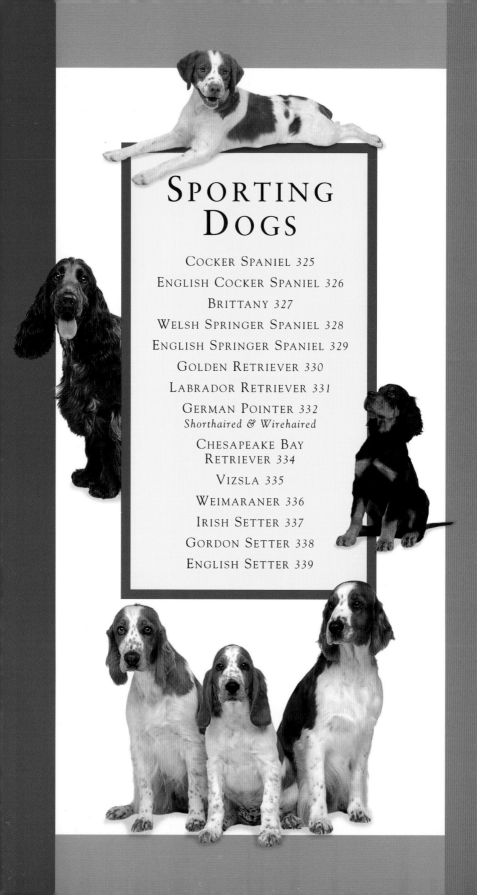

Sporting Dogs

Cocker Spaniel

This attractive dog is smaller than its English cousin but retains the lively, friendly personality for which spaniels are known. The Cocker Spaniel is a most appealing pet.

HISTORY

Although derived from the same stock as the English Cocker Spaniel (see p. 326), the Cocker Spaniel had become so different by the 1930s that it was recognized in the U.S. as a separate breed. British recognition followed about 35 years later.

DESCRIPTION

This is a strong dog with a sturdy, compact body. The fine, silky coat is short on the head and longer on the body—it may even be ground length. It comes in black and tan, any solid color, parti-colors, tricolors and roans. The ears are long and set low on the head and the tail is usually docked.

TEMPERAMENT

Intelligent and responsive, the Cocker Spaniel is generally friendly and good natured. However, some dogs may display aggression toward their owners, a condition similar to Rage Syndrome in English Springer Spaniels (see p. 329).

GROOMING

Some owners prefer to leave the coat long, brushing daily and shampooing frequently. Others clip the coat to medium length to be more functional. Either way, the dog will need regular trimming. When brushing, be careful not to pull out the silky hair.

EXERCISE & FEEDING

These dogs have plenty of stamina and need regular exercise. When walking, avoid brushy thickets that can tangle the coat. There are no special feeding requirements.

HEALTH PROBLEMS

These dogs are subject to ear infections, skin problems (such as seborrhea), heart problems, inherited eye diseases (such as glaucoma and progressive retinal atrophy) and spinal problems.

PET FACTS	
	Lively, happy, friendly
	Daily brushing
	Regular, moderate
	Adapts well to urban living, but needs plenty of space
	Good watchdog

☙ BE AWARE
• Some dogs may display unprovoked aggression

Male: 13–16 in (33–41 cm)
25–35 lb (11–16 kg)
Female: 12–15 in (30–38 cm)
20–30 lb (9–14 kg)

English Cocker Spaniel

An absolute charmer, the joyous English Cocker Spaniel is one of the most popular house pets in its adoptive country. For sheer good looks and personality, it's the leader of the pack.

PET FACTS

 Joyful, affectionate, intelligent

Regular brushing

 Regular, moderate to vigorous

Adapts well to urban living, but needs plenty of exercise

 Good watchdog

🐾 BE AWARE

• Prone to ear infections so check ears regularly

HISTORY

The spaniel family originated in Spain—the word may be a corruption of *espaignol*, French for Spanish dog—and various types became popular gundogs all over the world. In Britain, two kinds of spaniel developed along similar lines, the Springer and the Cocker. The Cocker is named for its ability to flush woodcock from the undergrowth.

DESCRIPTION

This strong dog has a sturdy, compact body covered in silky, medium-length, flat-lying hair. The coat comes in solid reds, black, golden and liver, as well as particolors and roans, in which the color is broken up with white. The tails are usually docked short.

TEMPERAMENT

The Cocker is energetic, playful and eager to please, and is sure to alert you to the presence of strangers on your property. However, this breed was the first known for Rage Syndrome (see p. 329), an inherited behavioral disorder occurring mostly in solid-colored dogs.

GROOMING

Regular combing and brushing of the coat are important. Bathe or dry shampoo as necessary. Check the ears for grass seeds and signs of infection. Brush the hair on the feet down over the toes and trim it level with the base of the feet. Trim the hair around the pads, but not that between the toes.

EXERCISE & FEEDING

This breed enjoys as much exercise as you can give it. Brush out burrs and tangles after the dog has been playing in grassy fields or woods. There are no special feeding requirements.

HEALTH PROBLEMS

Prone to inherited eye and heart diseases and ear infections due to poor ventilation of the ear canals.

Male: 15–17 in (38–43 cm)
28–34 lb (13–16 kg)
Female: 14–16 in (36–41 cm)
26–32 lb (12–15 kg)

Brittany

An agile and vigorous hunter, the Brittany is admired for its abilities in the field and for its grace and charming personality. Although a companionable pet, it prefers an outdoor life.

HISTORY

The Brittany, or Breton, Spaniel has a long history in its native France, with records of these dogs going back for hundreds of years. Today, it has a growing following in the U.S., where it was officially recognized as the Brittany in 1982. As well as being an excellent tracker and retriever, this dog is also a natural pointer, a trait possibly acquired through interbreeding with setters in the past. In the field, the Brittany tends to work close to its master.

DESCRIPTION

The smallest of the French spaniels, the Brittany is graceful, active and rugged, well muscled and has long-legged, elegant lines. The medium-length coat is dense and feathered on the ears, chest, underbody and upper parts of the legs. It comes in white with orange, black, brown or liver, as well as tricolors and roans. The tail is usually docked to have an adult length of no more than 4 inches (10 cm).

TEMPERAMENT

Easy to train and handle, the Brittany is a loving and gentle animal, obedient and always eager to please.

GROOMING

Regular brushing of the medium-length, flat coat is really all that is needed to keep it in good condition. Bathe or dry shampoo when necessary. Check the ears carefully, especially when the dog has been out in rough or brushy terrain.

EXERCISE & FEEDING

These dogs need vigorous activity to stay in peak condition. There are no special feeding requirements.

PET FACTS

- Gentle, friendly, energetic
- Regular brushing
- Regular, vigorous
- Adapts well to urban living, but needs plenty of exercise
- Good watchdog

BE AWARE

- These dogs love exercise and have great stamina

HEALTH PROBLEMS

While generally a healthy breed, Brittanys are prone to ear infections due to poor ventilation of the ear canals. They also get cataracts and progressive retinal atrophy.

Male: 17–21 in (43–53 cm)
35–40 lb (16–18 kg)
Female: 18–20 in (46–51 cm)
30–40 lb (14–18 kg)

Welsh Springer Spaniel

Sociable and very intelligent, the Welsh Springer Spaniel adapts well to any environment but is in its element with space to run and, if you can manage it, access to somewhere it can swim.

HISTORY

Less common than the English Springer Spaniel, to which it is closely related, the Welsh Springer Spaniel is from similar ancient stock. Springer Spaniels were used to "spring" forward at game to flush it out for the net, falcon or hound and, later, the gun. The tail wags faster as the dog nears its quarry.

DESCRIPTION

A hard worker with amazing stamina and endurance, the Welsh Springer is smaller overall than its English cousin, with much smaller and less feathered ears. The thick, silky coat is straight and always pearly white and rich red. The tail is usually docked.

TEMPERAMENT

Its gentle, patient nature and love of children makes the Welsh Springer an easily trained and attractive family pet.

GROOMING

The coat is fairly easy to maintain and regular brushing with a stiff bristle brush will suffice. Extra attention is required, however, when the animal is shedding. Bathe or dry shampoo only when necessary. Check the ears regularly for grass seeds and any signs of infection. Trim the hair between the toes and keep the nails clipped.

EXERCISE & FEEDING

This energetic and lively dog needs plenty of regular exercise, as much of it as possible off the leash. There are no special feeding requirements, but do not overfeed.

HEALTH PROBLEMS

A generally hardy breed, but like other dogs with large, heavy ears, it is prone to ear infections. Some Welsh Springers also suffer from hip dysplasia and eye problems.

PET FACTS

Sensible, energetic, friendly

Regular brushing

Regular, moderate

Adapts well to urban living, but needs plenty of space

Good watchdog

BE AWARE

- Without enough exercise, these dogs become bored, fat and lazy

Male: 17–19 in (43–48 cm)
40–45 lb (18–20 kg)
Female: 16–18 in (41–46 cm)
35–45 lb (16–20 kg)

English Spaniel
English Springer Spaniel

The handsome robust English Springer Spaniel excels in the field at flushing out game, but also makes a delightful pet in the home. It is a spirited and loyal companion.

PET FACTS

 Alert, friendly, loyal

 Regular brushing

Regular, moderate

 Adapts well to urban living, but needs plenty of exercise

Good watchdog

BE AWARE
• Susceptible to Rage Syndrome, a behavioral disorder

HISTORY
One of the largest of the spaniels, the popular English Springer Spaniel descends from the oldest spaniel stock and its blood probably runs in the veins of most modern spaniels. Once known as the Norfolk Spaniel, it is an all-weather retriever and loves the water.

DESCRIPTION
This strong dog has a sturdy, compact body. The soft, medium-length, flat-lying coat comes in all spaniel colors but mainly white with liver or black, with or without tan markings. The tail is usually docked.

TEMPERAMENT
A quick learner, the Springer enjoys company, is patient with the family and makes a good watchdog. Sadly, the breed is susceptible to an inherited behavioral disorder, Rage Syndrome, which can cause aggression. Before buying a pup, check whether any of its relatives are afflicted.

GROOMING
The coat is fairly easy to maintain and regular brushing with a stiff bristle brush will keep it looking good. Take extra care when the animal is shedding. Bathe or dry shampoo only when necessary but check the ears regularly for signs of infection.

EXERCISE & FEEDING
The Springer enjoys as much exercise as you can give it. There are no special feeding requirements, but avoid overfeeding these dogs.

HEALTH PROBLEMS
A generally hardy breed, but like other dogs with large, heavy ears, it is susceptible to ear infections. It may also develop epilepsy, allergic skin problems, eye problems and elbow and hip dysplasia.

Male: 19–21 in (48–53 cm)
45–55 lb (20–25 kg)
Female: 18–20 in (46–51 cm)
40–50 lb (18–23 kg)

Golden Retriever

This dog gets the seal of approval from everyone who has ever owned one. Visualize a happy family around a fire—a Golden Retriever asleep on the hearth completes the picture to perfection.

HISTORY

The ancestry of this breed is difficult to prove, but Golden Retrievers have some of the characteristics of retrievers, Bloodhounds and Water Spaniels, which make them very useful gundogs—they are renowned for their tracking abilities. They are thought to have been developed in the United Kingdom by Lord Tweedmouth, 150 years ago.

DESCRIPTION

This is a graceful and elegant dog. The lustrous coat comes in any shade of gold or cream with the hair lying flat or gently waved around the neck, shoulders and hips. There is abundant feathering.

TEMPERAMENT

These are well-mannered, biddable dogs with great charm. They are easily trained, always patient and are gentle with children. As a result, they make great companions or family pets. While unlikely to attack, Golden Retrievers make good watchdogs, loudly signaling a stranger's approach.

GROOMING

The smooth, medium-haired double coat is easy to groom. Comb and brush with a firm bristle brush, paying particular attention to the dense undercoat. Dry shampoo regularly, but bathe only when necessary.

EXERCISE & FEEDING

Golden Retrievers like nothing better than to work—if they have regular strenuous duties, so much the better. At the very least they need a long daily walk and preferably an opportunity to run freely. Golden Retrievers love to swim and should be allowed to do so whenever possible. There are no special feeding requirements.

HEALTH PROBLEMS

Skin allergies are common in Golden Retrievers and require immediate veterinary attention. These dogs are also prone to hip dysplasia and genetic eye diseases.

PET FACTS

 Calm, affectionate, gentle

 Regular brushing

 Regular, vigorous

 Adapts well to urban living, but needs plenty of space

Good watchdog

BE AWARE

- These dogs shed a fair amount of hair, but regular grooming will help

Male: 22–24 in (56–61 cm)
60–80 lb (27–36 kg)
Female: 20–22 in (51–56 cm)
55–70 lb (25–32 kg)

Labrador Retriever

Courageous, loyal and hard working, the Labrador Retriever has earned worldwide respect for its dedication to duty. However, it is also one of the most popular and loving of family pets.

HISTORY

Originally used by fishermen in Newfoundland, rather than Labrador as the name suggests, Labrador Retrievers became indispensable as sled dogs, message-carriers and general working dogs. Once known as St John's Dogs, they were part of every fishing crew. They carry on this tradition of service still, being widely used as guide dogs for the blind and as sniffer dogs for the police.

DESCRIPTION

This strong, active dog with its solid, powerful frame is a very good swimmer. The tail, described as an "otter" tail, is thick at the base, round and tapered. The coat is dense and waterproof with no feathering, and comes in solid black, yellow, fawn, cream, gold or chocolate, occasionally with white markings on the chest.

TEMPERAMENT

Reliable, obedient and easily trained, Labrador Retrievers are friendly and very good with children. They crave human attention and need to feel as though they are part of the family.

GROOMING

The smooth, shorthaired, double coat is easy to groom. Comb and brush regularly with a firm bristle brush, paying attention to the undercoat. Bathe or dry shampoo only when necessary.

PET FACTS

- Reliable, loving, loyal
- Regular brushing
- Regular, vigorous
- Adapts well to urban living, but needs plenty of exercise
- Good watchdog

BE AWARE
- If allowed, these dogs quickly become obese

EXERCISE & FEEDING

Labrador Retrievers are energetic dogs, delighted to work and play hard. There are no special feeding requirements, but beware of overfeeding as they easily become obese and lazy.

HEALTH PROBLEMS

Like other large breeds, these dogs are prone to hip and elbow dysplasia. They also suffer from eye diseases, such as cataracts and PRA.

Male: 22–24 in (56–61 cm)
60–75 lb (27–34 kg)
Female: 21–23 in (53–58 cm)
55–70 lb (25–32 kg)

German Pointer

These versatile, athletic dogs are excellent all-rounders, able to track wounded game, point and retrieve. The German Shorthaired Pointer is the older type, but the Wirehaired has the advantage of a durable, hard-wearing coat. Both varieties make good pets.

HISTORY

The ancestors of the German Shorthaired Pointer include Spanish and English Pointers, the Bloodhound, French hounds and Scandinavian breeds. The modern dog has such a formidable array of talents that it was, and is, highly prized by hunters. In the continuing search for perfection, they were bred with terriers and Poodles in the late nineteenth century. The result was the German Wirehaired Pointer, which has all of the skills and has gained a tough, rugged coat in the bargain.

DESCRIPTION

These superlative hunting dogs are used for fur and feathered game in all types of terrain and are excellent swimmers. Their lean, muscular bodies and powerful loins give them a useful turn of speed on land, and their strong jaws enable them to carry quite heavy kills. The short, dense, water-resistant coat of the Shorthaired comes in solid black or liver, or these colors with white spots or flecks, or as roans. The Wirehaired has a thick, medium-length, wiry coat, also water-resistant, that comes in solid liver, liver and white, and black and white. The tails of both are usually docked to two-fifths the length.

PET FACTS

Intelligent, reliable, keen; the Wirehaired can be slightly aggressive

Regular brushing; Wire more than Smooth

Regular, vigorous

Adapts to urban living, but needs plenty of space and exercise

Good watchdog

BE AWARE

- With insufficient work, these dogs can become frustrated and hard to manage

TEMPERAMENT

German Pointers make obedient and affectionate pets and are clean and well behaved in the house, but they are better off and far

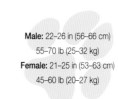

Male: 22–26 in (56–66 cm)
55–70 lb (25–32 kg)
Female: 21–25 in (53–63 cm)
45–60 lb (20–27 kg)

happier with an outdoor life and plenty of work to do. Intelligent and reasonably easy to train, the German Pointer has a mind of its own and should never be allowed to get the upper hand. Although both types are generally good with people and reliable with children, the Wirehaired has acquired a slightly aggressive trait along with its wiry coat, probably from its terrier genes, and so may be argumentative with other dogs.

GROOMING

The smooth coat of the Shorthaired is very easy to groom. Just brush regularly with a firm bristle brush, and bathe only when necessary. A rub with a piece of toweling or chamois will leave the coat gleaming.

The Wirehaired's short wiry coat needs a little more attention. You will need to brush it about twice a week with a firm bristle brush and thin it in spring and fall. Bathe only when necessary. Check the ears of both varieties regularly for any discharge or foreign bodies. Check the feet also, especially after the dog has been exercising or working.

EXERCISE & FEEDING

Exercise is of paramount importance for these tireless, energetic animals. They are more than a match for even the most active family and they should not be taken on as family pets unless they can be guaranteed plenty of vigorous exercise. There are no special feeding requirements for these dogs, but always try to measure the amount of food given against the dog's level of activity.

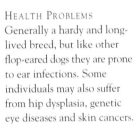

HEALTH PROBLEMS

Generally a hardy and long-lived breed, but like other flop-eared dogs they are prone to ear infections. Some individuals may also suffer from hip dysplasia, genetic eye diseases and skin cancers.

Chesapeake Bay Retriever

A hardy outdoor type, the Chesapeake Bay Retriever is considered a duck dog without peer, with an extraordinary ability to remember where each bird falls and retrieve them all efficiently.

PET FACTS

 Keen worker, can be aggressive

 Regular brushing

 Regular, vigorous; loves to swim

 Adapts to urban living, but best with access to the country

Good watchdog

BE AWARE

- These are strong dogs and they have a tendency to be territorial, so they require firm training and good management

HISTORY

The Chesapeake Bay Retriever was developed entirely in the U.S., in the Maryland area, from a pair of shipwrecked puppies that were crossed with various dogs used as retrievers. The result was an intrepid dog, highly valued for its prowess in the field.

DESCRIPTION

Although not universally considered handsome, this medium-sized dog is athletic and strong. The coat is tight, dense, wavy and totally water resistant; the soft undercoat is quite oily and the feet are webbed. It is a strong swimmer and can swim even in heavy, icy seas. Water is shed completely with a quick shake, so the dog stays warm and dry.

The coat color varies from dark tan to dark brown, the colors of dead grass, so it is well camouflaged for its work.

TEMPERAMENT

These dogs are courageous and intelligent, but can be tricky to train. They also have a tendency to be aggressive with other dogs.

GROOMING

The dense, harsh, shorthaired coat is easy to groom. Brush with a firm bristle brush and bathe only if necessary. Bathing destroys the natural waterproofing of the coat.

EXERCISE & FEEDING

These dogs need a great deal of vigorous activity, including swimming, to stay in peak condition. There are no special feeding requirements but measure the quantity of food given against the dog's current level of activity.

HEALTH PROBLEMS

While this breed is generally very healthy, some dogs may suffer from hip dysplasia and hereditary eye diseases.

Male: 23–26 in (58–66 cm)
65–80 lb (29–36 kg)
Female: 21–24 in (53–61 cm)
55–70 lb (25–32 kg)

Vizsla

Hungary's national dog, the agile Vizsla was little known elsewhere until after World War II. This excellent gundog is now becoming increasingly popular outside its country of origin.

HISTORY

Also known as the Hungarian Pointer, the Vizsla was bred for hunting, pointing and retrieving. It is possibly descended from the Turkish Yellow Dog and the Transylvanian Hound, but it is more likely to be the result of crosses with the Weimaraner. A good swimmer, it originally worked the plains, woodlands and marshes, retrieving just as well on land as in water. It is an excellent tracker.

DESCRIPTION

This is a handsome, lean, well-muscled dog that moves gracefully either at a lively trotting gait or in a swift, ground-covering gallop. The coat is short and close, rusty gold to sandy yellow in color and greasy to the touch. The last one-third of the tail is usually removed.

TEMPERAMENT

Although good natured, intelligent and easy to train, the Vizsla is somewhat sensitive and needs to be handled gently. It is reliable with children and quickly adapts to family life.

GROOMING

The smooth, shorthaired coat is easy to keep in peak condition. Brush with a firm bristle brush, and dry shampoo occasionally. Bathe with mild soap only when necessary. The nails should be kept trimmed.

EXERCISE & FEEDING

This is an energetic working dog with enormous stamina. It needs plenty of opportunity to run, preferably off the leash, and a lot of regular exercise. If these dogs are allowed to get bored, they can become destructive. There are no special feeding requirements.

HEALTH PROBLEMS

Vizslas are reasonably healthy dogs, but some suffer from epilepsy and blood clotting disorders.

PET FACTS

- Intelligent, affectionate, willing
- Regular brushing
- Regular, vigorous
- Adapts to urban living, but needs plenty of space
- Good watchdog

BE AWARE

- Vizslas are great jumpers and, if bored, will escape from a yard that does not have a sufficiently high fence

Male: 22–26 in (56–66 cm)
45–60 lb (20–27 kg)
Female: 20–24 in (51–61 cm)
40–55 lb (18–25 kg)

Weimaraner

Given firm handling by a strong adult, the confident and assertive Weimaraner makes a wonderful companion and working dog, but you will need boundless energy to keep up with it.

HISTORY

Once widely used in Germany to hunt large prey, such as bears and wild pigs, the Weimaraner became prized in more recent times as a gundog and retriever of small game, such as waterfowl. It is sometimes referred to as the silver ghost.

DESCRIPTION

This superb hunting dog has a well-proportioned, athletic body. The sleek, close-fitting coat comes in silver-gray to mouse shades, often lighter on the head and ears. The striking eyes are blue-gray or amber. The tail is usually docked to be approximately 6 inches (15 cm) in adults.

TEMPERAMENT

Alert, intelligent and strong-willed, the Weimaraner is a versatile breed that is happiest when it is fully occupied with work or tasks that engage its mind. It requires firm and thorough training, makes an excellent watchdog and is good with children.

GROOMING

The smooth, shorthaired coat is easy to keep in peak condition. Brush with a firm bristle brush, and dry shampoo occasionally. Bathe with mild soap only when necessary. A rub over with a chamois will make the coat gleam. Inspect feet and mouth for damage after work or exercise sessions. Keep the nails trimmed.

EXERCISE & FEEDING

These are powerful working dogs with great stamina. They need plenty of opportunities to run free and lots of regular exercise. As they are prone to bloat, it is better to feed them two or three small meals a day rather than one large meal. Do not exercise straight after a meal.

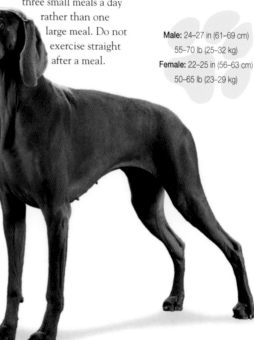

PET FACTS

🐕 Intelligent, obedient, friendly

〰️ Regular brushing

🐕 Regular, vigorous

🏡 Adapts to urban living, but needs plenty of space

🐕 Excellent watchdog

🐾 **BE AWARE**

- This powerful dog requires plenty of exercise to stop it from getting bored

- Prone to bloat, which can be fatal

HEALTH PROBLEMS

In general, Weimaraners are a hardy breed of dog. However, like many large breeds, they sometimes suffer from bloat and hip dysplasia.

Male: 24–27 in (61–69 cm)
55–70 lb (25–32 kg)
Female: 22–25 in (56–63 cm)
50–65 lb (23–29 kg)

Irish Setter

This elegant and graceful dog is much admired for its lustrous chestnut coat with profuse feathering. It is a little lighter and speedier than other setters, having been bred to cope with Ireland's marshy terrain.

HISTORY

The Irish Setter, also known as the Red Setter, evolved in the British Isles over the past 200 years from a variety of setters, spaniels and pointers. Like all setters, these dogs were bred to "set," or locate, game birds and then to remain still while the hunter shot or netted the birds.

DESCRIPTION

The Irish Setter's profusely feathered silky coat comes in rich shades of chestnut to mahogany, sometimes with splashes of white on the chest and feet. The ears are long and low-set and the legs are long and muscular.

TEMPERAMENT

Like most sporting dogs, Irish Setters are full of energy and high spirits. They are also very affectionate, sometimes overwhelmingly so. Although they can be difficult to train, being easily distracted, the effort will be rewarding for both owner and dog. Training must never be strict.

GROOMING

Daily combing and brushing of the soft, flat, medium-length coat is all that is required to keep it in excellent condition.

Keep it free of burrs and tangles, and give a little extra care when the dog is molting. Bathe or dry shampoo only when necessary.

EXERCISE & FEEDING

All setters need plenty of exercise, if possible, running free. If they don't get a long, brisk walk at least daily, they will be restless and difficult to manage. Feed two or three small meals a day rather than one large meal.

HEALTH PROBLEMS

The breed is particularly prone to epilepsy and severe skin allergies. They also suffer from bloat, eye problems and elbow and hip dysplasia.

PET FACTS

- Lively and affectionate
- Daily combing
- Regular, extensive and vigorous
- Needs plenty of space to run free. Unsuited to apartment living
- Not a good watchdog

BE AWARE

- Lack of exercise can make this dog restless and difficult to train
- Prone to skin problems

Male: 26–28 in (66–71 cm)
65–75 lb (29–34 kg)
Female: 24–26 in (61–66 cm)
55–65 lb (25–29 kg)

Gordon Setter

Larger, heavier and more powerful than its cousins, the Gordon Setter was once known as the Black and Tan Setter of Scotland. A natural pointer and retriever, it also makes a delightful pet.

HISTORY

Bred in Scotland as a gundog by the fourth Duke of Gordon in the late eighteenth century, this dog has setter, Collie and possibly Bloodhound genes. It easily handles tough terrain.

DESCRIPTION

This breed has great stamina. The silky coat is generously feathered and is always a gleaming black with tan to reddish mahogany markings. On the face, the markings are clearly defined and include a spot over each eye.

TEMPERAMENT

Calmer than other setters and more reserved with strangers, the Gordon Setter is an excellent, affectionate companion. It is reliable with children and fairly easily trained, but training must never be harsh or heavy-handed, because it is important not to break the dog's spirit.

GROOMING

Regular combing and brushing of the soft, flat, medium-length coat is all that is required to keep it in excellent condition. It is important to check for burrs and tangles, and to give extra care when the dog is shedding. Bathe or dry shampoo only when necessary. Trim the hair on the bottom of the feet and clip the nails.

PET FACTS

- Intelligent, friendly, loyal
- Regular combing and brushing
- Regular, vigorous
- Needs plenty of space to run free; unsuited to apartment living
- Adequate watchdog

BE AWARE
- These dogs are inclined to drool

EXERCISE & FEEDING

All setters need plenty of exercise, if possible, running free. If they don't get a long, brisk, daily walk, they will be difficult to manage. As these dogs are prone to bloat, it is a good idea to feed them two or three small meals a day.

HEALTH PROBLEMS

The breed is prone to bloat, hip dysplasia and eye diseases, such as progressive retinal atrophy and cataracts.

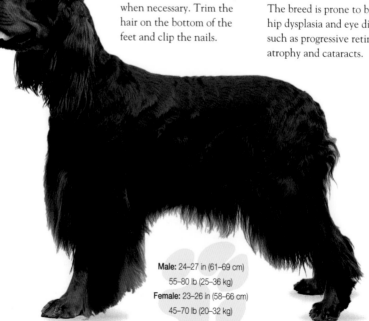

Male: 24–27 in (61–69 cm)
55–80 lb (25–36 kg)
Female: 23–26 in (58–66 cm)
45–70 lb (20–32 kg)

English Setter

Reliable and hard-working, this beautiful dog has strength, stamina and grace. It also seems to have an innate sense of what is expected of a gundog, responding intelligently to each new situation.

HISTORY
Descended from a variety of Spanish spaniels, this breed was also known as the Laverack Setter, after Edward Laverack, who played a major role in its development.

DESCRIPTION
This elegant dog has a finely chiselled head and large nostrils. Its flat, straight coat is of medium length and comes in white, flecked with combinations of black, lemon, liver, and black and tan. There is feathering along the underbody and on the ears.

TEMPERAMENT
Gentle and high-spirited, these dogs take their duties seriously, and when one becomes part of a family, it is quiet and very loyal. They are friendly, intelligent and adept at anticipating their owner's wishes.

GROOMING
Daily combing and brushing of the medium-length, silky coat is important, with extra care when the dog is shedding. Bathe or dry shampoo only when necessary. Trim the hair on the feet and tail and check the long ears for any signs of infection.

EXERCISE & FEEDING
Like all setters, these dogs require a long daily walk. As they are prone to bloat, feed two or three small meals a day instead of one large one.

HEALTH PROBLEMS
These dogs may suffer from elbow and hip dysplasia, deafness, bloat and progressive retinal atrophy.

PET FACTS

- Intelligent, friendly
- Daily combing and brushing
- Regular, vigorous
- Needs plenty of space to run free; unsuited to apartment living
- Adequate watchdog

BE AWARE

- Will become restless if not given sufficient exercise
- Likely to roam if its yard is not securely enclosed

Male: 24–26 in (61–66 cm)
60–75 lb (27–34 kg)
Female: 23–25 in (58–63 cm)
55–65 lb (25–29 kg)

HOUNDS

Beagle

It's not only its manageable size that makes the Beagle so popular. It is an endearing and engaging creature, eager to romp and play and demanding little of an owner's time for grooming or exercise.

Alert, joyful, even-tempered

Regular brushing

Regular, moderate

Adapts well to urban living

Not a good watchdog

BE AWARE

- Beagles bay when they bark, which can be irritating
- They are prone to wander

HISTORY

Packs of Beagles were traditionally used to hunt hares by scent. The name may come from the Celtic word for small, *beag*, or the French for gape throat, *begueule*. The modern dog is considerably larger than those of earlier times, which were often carried in pockets or saddlebags.

DESCRIPTION

This muscular little dog is the smallest of the pack hounds. Its dense waterproof coat comes in combinations of white, black, tan, red, lemon and blue mottle. The US recognises two size ranges, under 13 inches (33 cm) and 13–15 inches (33–38 cm).

TEMPERAMENT

This strong-willed breed needs firm handling, as it is not always easy to train. When Beagles pick up an interesting smell, it can be hard to get their attention. Alert and good tempered, they are rarely aggressive and love children. Indeed, they crave companionship.

GROOMING

The Beagle's smooth, shorthaired coat is easy to look after. Brush with a firm bristle brush, and dry shampoo occasionally. Bathe with mild soap only when necessary. Be sure to check the ears carefully for signs of infection and keep the nails trimmed.

EXERCISE & FEEDING

Energetic and possessing great stamina, the Beagle needs plenty of exercise, but a yard of reasonable size will take care of most of its requirements. A brisk daily walk will cover the rest. There are no special feeding requirements, but if you use food as a motivator when

training, be careful that the dog does not become obese and lazy.

HEALTH PROBLEMS

Beagles may suffer from spinal problems, epilepsy, skin conditions and genetic eye diseases, such as glaucoma and cataracts. They also have a tendency to become obese.

Male: up to 16 in (41 cm)
22–25 lb (10–11 kg)
Female: up to 15 in (38 cm)
20–23 lb (9–10 kg)

Dachshund

These extraordinary "sausage" dogs come in a range of colors, sizes and coat types—it seems there's a sturdy little Dachshund for every taste, although most owners have decided preferences.

HISTORY

The Dachshund (pronounced dak sund) originated in Germany many hundreds of years ago—*Dachs* is the German word for badger. The Dachshund was bred to hunt and follow these animals to earth, gradually becoming highly evolved, with short-ened legs to dig the prey out and go down inside the burrows. Smaller Dachshunds were bred to hunt hare and stoat. Dachshunds have many "terrier" characteristics. They are versatile and courageous dogs and have been known to take on foxes and otters as well as badgers.

DESCRIPTION

Dachshunds come in two sizes—Standard and Miniature. All Dachshunds have a low-slung, muscular, elongated body with very short legs and strong forequarters developed for digging. The skin is loose and the coat comes in three distinct types: smooth, short and dense; longhaired, soft, flat and straight with feathering; and wirehaired with a short double coat, a beard and bushy eyebrows. The wirehaired is the least common and was developed to hunt in brushy thickets. The three coat types come in a range of solid colors, two-colored, brindled, tiger-marked or dappled. These dogs have a big bark for their size, which might be enough to intimidate intruders.

TEMPERAMENT

Alert, lively and affectionate, Dachshunds are great little characters, good company and reasonably obedient when carefully trained.

PET FACTS

 Brave, curious, lively

 Regular brushing

 Regular, moderate

 Ideal for apartment living

 Good watchdog

🐾 BE AWARE

• It is important to prevent these dogs from becoming obese as they are prone to spinal damage

• They are enthusiastic diggers and will wreak havoc in a garden

They can be slightly aggressive to strangers but make wonderful house pets. Miniatures are perhaps less suited to households with young children, as they are vulnerable to injury from rough handling.

Standard
Male: About 8 in (20 cm)
16–32 lb (7–15 kg)
Female: About 8 in (20 cm)
16–32 lb (7–15 kg)

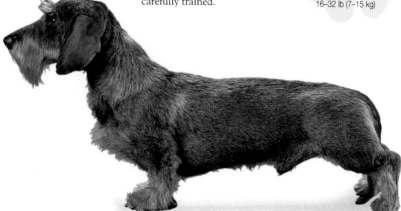

Miniature
Male: About 6 in (15 cm)
Up to 11 lb (5 kg)
Female: About 6 in (15 cm)
Up to 11 lb (5 kg)

GROOMING

Regular brushing with a bristle brush is appropriate for all coat types. Dry shampoo or bathe when necessary, but always make sure the dog is thoroughly dry and warm after a bath. The smooth variety will come up gleaming if you rub it with a piece of toweling or a chamois. Check the ears regularly.

EXERCISE & FEEDING

These are active dogs with surprising stamina and they love a regular walk or session of play in the park. They should be discouraged from jumping as they are prone to spinal damage. There are no special feeding requirements, but these dogs have a tendency to become overweight and lazy. This is a serious health risk, putting added strain on the back. Dachshunds seem prone to dental problems, so they should be given plenty of opportunities to chew.

HEALTH PROBLEMS

Herniated disks in the back can cause severe pain and paralysis of the hind legs. As they are a rather long-lived breed, Dachshunds also suffer problems common to aging dogs, such as obesity, diabetes and cardiac disease. They are also subject to genetic eye diseases and skin problems, including pattern baldness on the ears.

Basset Hound

The mournful face of this gentle, lovable hound belies its lively nature. When hunting, it is single-minded in following a scent, but it also makes a delightful pet in homes where there are young children.

HISTORY
While most Basset breeds originated in France (*bas* means "low" in French), the Basset Hound was developed in Britain only about 100 years ago. Its ability to concentrate on a particular scent quickly earned it respect as a hunting partner.

DESCRIPTION
This sturdy dog has short, stocky legs on which the skin is loose and folded. Much of the dog's weight is concentrated at the front of the long, barrel-shaped body. The shorthaired coat sheds only moderately and comes in combinations of white with tan, black and, occasionally, lemon. The ears are long and velvety.

TEMPERAMENT
Good-natured, sociable and gentle with children, Basset Hounds fit into family life well. With proper training, they are obedient, but when they pick up an interesting smell, it is sometimes hard to get their attention.

GROOMING
The smooth, shorthaired coat is easy to groom. Comb and brush with a firm bristle brush, and shampoo only when necessary. Wipe under the ears every week and trim toenails regularly.

EXERCISE & FEEDING
Plenty of moderate exercise will help to keep the Basset Hound healthy and happy but discourage it from jumping and stressing the front legs. Do not overfeed because extra weight places too great a load on the legs and spine. As they are prone to bloat, it is also wise to feed them two or three small meals a day instead of one large meal.

HEALTH PROBLEMS
Because the ears are long and heavy, they are susceptible to infection. These dogs also suffer from bloat and skin infections, such as seborrhea.

PET FACTS

 Gentle and loyal

 Weekly brushing, paying attention to ears and feet

 Regular, moderate

 Well suited to urban living

 Not a good watchdog

 BE AWARE

- These dogs may smell due to skin and ear infections

- Prone to overeating and becoming fat, if given the opportunity

Male: 12–15 in (30–38 cm)
50–65 lb (23–29 kg)
Female: 11–14 in (28–36 cm)
45–60 lb (20–27 kg)

Basenji

A handsome, muscular dog, the Basenji is as fastidious as a cat about its personal grooming, even washing itself with its paws. Although the breed is well known for being barkless, it is not silent, and "yodels" when happy.

HISTORY
These ancient dogs originated in Africa, where they were used for hunting and valued for their great stamina. They were introduced into Europe and then North America in the twentieth century.

DESCRIPTION
The Basenji is a compact, muscular, medium-sized dog, with a distinctive trotting gait. Their loose, silky, shorthaired coats come in combinations of white, tan, chestnut, brindle and black. When alert, the forehead is creased with wrinkles, giving the dog a worried look. The tail is tightly curled over the back. The breeding pattern is unusual, the bitch coming into season only once a year.

TEMPERAMENT
Alert, affectionate, energetic and curious, the Basenji loves to play and makes a good pet, as long as it is handled regularly from an early age. It is very intelligent and responds well to training.

GROOMING
The smooth, shorthaired, silky coat is easy to groom. Comb and brush with a firm bristle brush, and shampoo only when necessary.

EXERCISE & FEEDING
Vigorous daily exercise will keep the Basenji trim and fit—they have a tendency to become fat and lazy unless the owner is conscientious about their exercise regimen.

HEALTH PROBLEMS
This breed may suffer from kidney problems, which must be treated the moment any symptoms are noticed. They are also susceptible to progressive retinal atrophy and intestinal problems.

Male: 16–17 in (41–43 cm)
22–26 lb (10–12 kg)
Female: 15–16 in (38–41 cm)
20–25 lb (9–11 kg)

Whippet

Gentle, affectionate and adaptable, the Whippet makes a delightful companion and jogging partner. Clean and well behaved in the house, it settles happily into family routine.

History

This descendant of the Greyhound, perhaps with some terrier blood, was used for hunting rabbits in northern England. It was also pitted against its peers in a pastime known as rag racing, in which the dogs, when signaled with a handkerchief, streaked from a standing start towards their owners.

Description

The Whippet's lean, delicate appearance belies its strength and speed—it can accelerate rapidly to about 35 mph (55 km/h). The fine, dense coat comes in many colors or in mixes. The muzzle is long and slender and the overall impression is one of streamlined elegance.

Temperament

Gentle and sensitive, the Whippet makes a surprisingly docile and obedient pet, although it is inclined to be nervous when lively children are around. While it is easily trained, owners must take great care not to break its spirit by being harsh or overbearing.

Grooming

The smooth, fine, shorthaired coat is easy to groom. Brush with a firm bristle brush, and bathe only when necessary. A regular rub all over with a damp chamois will keep the coat gleaming. Keep the nails clipped.

Exercise & Feeding

Whippets kept as pets should have regular opportunities to run free on open ground as well as have long, brisk, daily walks on the leash. There are no special feeding requirements.

Health Problems

Because of their fine coats, Whippets are sensitive to cold and may get sunburned. Their bones are delicate and easily broken. They are also subject to genetic eye diseases such as cataracts and progressive retinal atrophy.

PET FACTS

- Sensitive, gentle, high strung
- Regular brushing
- Regular, moderate
- Adapts well to urban living, but needs plenty of space
- Not a good watchdog

BE AWARE

- These dogs will often hunt rather than obey, so may need to be leashed in public

Male: 19–22 in (48–56 cm)
20–22 lb (9–10 kg)
Female: 18–21 in (46–53 cm)
19–21 lb (9–10 kg)

Norwegian Elkhound

Surprisingly, the handsome Norwegian Elkhound can adapt to warmer climates than its homeland as the thick coat insulates it from both heat and cold. It makes a fine pet.

HISTORY
Dogs of this kind have been used to hunt bears, elk and moose since Viking times. They would chase and hold the prey until hunters arrived for the kill. They were also used to pull sleds.

DESCRIPTION
Although it is totally silent while tracking, the Elkhound is perhaps the most "talkative" dog of all. It has a whole vocabulary of sounds, each with a different meaning, and you will soon learn to recognize its way of telling you there are strangers about. A member of the Spitz family, the Elkhound has a shortish, thickset body with the tail tightly curled over the back. The coat comes in various shades of gray, with black tips on the outer coat, and lighter hair on the chest, underbody, legs and underside of the tail. There is a thick ruff around the neck.

TEMPERAMENT
While gentle and devoted to its owner, the Elkhound needs consistent training that is firm but never harsh. Although adaptable, it likes a set routine.

GROOMING
Regular brushing of the hard, coarse, weatherproof coat is important, with extra care when the dog is shedding its dense undercoat. At this time, the dead hair clings to the new hair and must be removed with a rubber brush designed for the task. Bathing is largely unnecessary.

EXERCISE & FEEDING
An agile, energetic dog, the Elkhound revels in strenuous activity. The more space it has to move around the better. There are no special feeding requirements.

HEALTH PROBLEMS
This hardy breed is used to a rugged life and suffers from few genetic diseases other than hip dysplasia and the common eye diseases.

Male: 19–21 in (48–53 cm)
50–60 lb (23–27 kg)
Female: 18–20 in (46–51 cm)
40–55 lb (18–25 kg)

Saluki

This ancient breed was used in Arabia, in association with falcons, for hunting gazelle and other game. While the falcons swooped over the quarry, the Salukis gave chase and held the prey for a mounted hunter to kill.

HISTORY

Related to the Greyhound, this fast and agile breed originated in Arabia—the name comes from the now-vanished city of Saluk. They are also known as Gazelle Hounds, although they hunted small animals other than gazelle. In Muslim society, they were thought of as "the sacred gift of Allah" and, traditionally, they were never sold, but could be presented as a gift to a friend or someone of importance.

DESCRIPTION

The athletic appearance is one of total grace and symmetry. Slim and fine-boned, Salukis are built for speed and capable of bursts of 40 mph (65 km/h) or more, but they also have exceptional endurance.

The galloping gait is unusual, and unique to sighthounds, with all four feet being off the ground at the same time when the animal is in full chase. This gives the impression that the dog is flying. There are two types of coat, smooth-haired and feathered. Both have feathering on the ears and on the long, curved tail, but the smooth variety has none on the legs. The soft, smooth, silky coat comes in black and tan, white, cream, fawn, gold and red, as well as various combinations of these. A dog with a small patch of white in the middle of its forehead is thought by Bedouin tribes to have "the kiss of Allah" and is regarded as special.

PET FACTS

Gentle, loyal and sensitive

Brush twice weekly

Regular, moderate

Adapts well to urban living if given adequate exercise

Not a good watchdog

BE AWARE

- These dogs are able to jump very high fences

- Cancer is a growing problem for this breed

The aristocratic head is narrow and well proportioned and the feathered ears are long and hanging.

TEMPERAMENT
Gentle, affectionate and intensely loyal, Salukis quickly become part of the family, although they may remain aloof with strangers. They are not at all aggressive but can be rather sensitive and, while easy to train, they become nervous and timid if the trainer's manner is overbearing or harsh.

GROOMING
The soft, smooth, silky coat is easy to groom and there is little shedding. Comb and brush with a firm bristle brush, and shampoo only when necessary. Be careful not to overbrush as this may break the coat. Trim the hair between the toes or it will matt and make the feet sore.

EXERCISE & FEEDING
Salukis should have regular opportunities to run free on open ground in addition to long daily walks—they make excellent jogging companions. There are no special feeding requirements, but they tend to be light eaters. They also drink less than other dogs, as you might expect, given their region of origin.

HEALTH PROBLEMS
These dogs are prone to cancer and genetic eye diseases, such as cataracts and PRA. Dogs with pale or mottled noses should have sunscreen applied regularly to such sensitive areas during the summer months.

Male: 23–28 in (58–71 cm)
50–60 lb (23–27 kg)
Female: 20–27 in (51–69 cm)
35–55 lb (16–25 kg)

Bloodhound

Brought to England by William the Conqueror, the solemn-looking Bloodhound has entered literature and legend as the archetypal sleuth dog, but it never kills its prey.

HISTORY

The Bloodhound's ancestry can be traced directly to eighth-century Belgium, and it is also known as the Flemish Hound. It is able to follow any scent, even a human's, a rare ability in a dog.

DESCRIPTION

Large and powerful, the Bloodhound looks tougher than it is. The skin is loose and seems several sizes too large for the body. The coat is short and dense, fine on the head and ears, and comes in tan with black or liver, tawny, or solid red. There is sometimes a little white on the chest, feet and the tip of the tail.

TEMPERAMENT

Sensitive, gentle and shy, a Bloodhound becomes devoted to its master, and gets along well with people and other dogs; it is rarely vicious.

GROOMING

The smooth, shorthaired coat is easy to groom. Brush with a firm bristle brush, and bathe only when necessary. A rub with a rough towel or chamois will leave the coat gleaming. Clean the long, floppy ears regularly.

EXERCISE & FEEDING

Bloodhounds love a good run and need a lot of exercise. However, if it picks up an interesting scent you may find it difficult to get its attention. As this breed is prone to bloat you should feed two or three small meals a day instead of one large one. Avoid exercise after meals.

HEALTH PROBLEMS

These dogs are susceptible to bloat and hip dysplasia. A well-padded bed is recommended to avoid calluses on the joints.

PET FACTS

  Gentle, sensitive affectionate

 Minimal

 Regular, vigorous

 Adapts to urban living, but needs plenty of space and exercise

 Too shy to be a very good watchdog

BE AWARE

- A bored Bloodhound's mournful howl may not be enjoyed by neighbors

- Prone to ear infections because of the long, heavy ears

Male: 25–27 in (63–69 cm)
90–110 lb (41–50 kg)
Female: 23–25 in (58–63 cm)
80–100 lb (36–45 kg)

Rhodesian Ridgeback

An all-weather, low-maintenance, dedicated watchdog, the Rhodesian Ridgeback bonds closely with its adoptive family in the early years of its life and makes a devoted, fun-loving pet.

HISTORY

The breed gets its name from a peculiarity of the coat—a well-defined dagger-shaped ridge of hair that lies along the spine in the opposite direction to the rest of the coat. Although they originated in South Africa, it was in what is now known as Zimbabwe that these dogs became prized for their ability to hunt lion and other large game.

DESCRIPTION

This is a strong, active dog with a dense, glossy coat that comes in solid shades of red to light wheaten with a dark muzzle and sometimes a little white on the chest. When alert, the brow is wrinkled.

TEMPERAMENT

Like many powerful dogs, the Rhodesian Ridgeback is a gentle, friendly animal, although it can be a tenacious fighter when aroused. It makes an outstanding watchdog and a devoted family pet. Intelligent and good natured, it is easy to train, but should be treated gently so as not to break its spirit or make it aggressive.

GROOMING

The smooth, shorthaired coat is easy to groom. Brush with a firm bristle brush, and shampoo only when necessary.

EXERCISE & FEEDING

These dogs have great stamina and you will tire long before they do, but they will adapt to your exercise regimen. They love to swim. There are no special feeding requirements, but beware of overfeeding.

HEALTH PROBLEMS

Rhodesian Ridgebacks are a hardy breed, able to withstand dramatic changes of temperature. They are, however, susceptible to hip dysplasia and occasional skin cysts related to their characteristic ridge of hair.

PET FACTS

- Brave, gentle, loyal
- Daily brushing
- Regular, moderate
- Adapts well to urban living, but needs plenty of space
- Outstanding watchdog

🐾 **BE AWARE**

- Training should be gentle and start young while the dog is still small enough to manage

Male: 25–27 in (63–69 cm)
80–90 lb (36–41 kg)
Female: 24–26 in (61–66 cm)
65–75 lb (29–34 kg)

Afghan Hound

While undeniably elegant and, when in peak condition, a thing of beauty, the Afghan Hound is not an easy-care pet. Choose one only if you are prepared to make a big commitment in time.

HISTORY
A hardy breed, agile and with great stamina, the Afghan Hound has been used for many centuries in its native land to hunt gazelle and other large prey, including snow leopards. It was especially favored by royalty.

DESCRIPTION
The coat is very long, straight and silky, except on the face and along the spine, and comes in all colors and some combinations. White markings are not liked by breed fanciers. Thick falls of hair on the legs protect the animal from cold.

The end of the tail should curl in a complete ring. The gait is free and springy.

TEMPERAMENT
The enormous popularity of these dogs during the seventies meant that many were acquired for the wrong reasons. Although they are intelligent, Afghan Hounds are not easy to train and, being quite large, they are not easy to handle either. They are definitely not a fashion accessory, and owners need to establish a genuine relationship with them. Too many of these dogs have been abandoned due to unrealistic expectations of owners.

GROOMING
The long, thick coat demands a great deal of attention and must be brushed every day. Dry shampoo when necessary and bathe once a month.

PET FACTS

Independent, lively, loving

Extensive

Regular, vigorous

Adapts well to urban living, but needs plenty of space

Not a good watchdog

BE AWARE
- These dogs are often very difficult to call back

EXERCISE & FEEDING
Afghan Hounds love open spaces and must be allowed to run free in a safe area as well as having long daily walks. There are no special feeding requirements.

HEALTH PROBLEMS
While the Afghan is generally a robust breed, some dogs may suffer from hip dysplasia and eye problems, such as cataracts.

Male: 26–29 in (66–74 cm)
55–65 lb (25–29 kg)
Female: 24–26 in (61–66 cm)
45–55 lb (20–25 kg)

Borzoi

The well-mannered Borzoi is a dog of grace and beauty, dignified and gentle. If you want a constant companion and can give it the exercise and love it craves, this may be the dog for you.

HISTORY

Also known as the Russian Wolfhound, Borzois were used in pairs by members of the Russian aristocracy to chase wolves. The prey was caught and held by the dogs until the mounted hunter arrived for the kill. They are probably descended from the "gaze hounds" of the Middle East, which they resemble.

DESCRIPTION

A tall, elegant dog, the Borzoi has a lean, muscular body designed for speed. The long, silky, often wavy coat is profusely feathered, and comes in all colors, usually white with colored markings. The small ears are pointed and well feathered.

TEMPERAMENT

Gentle, reserved and sometimes nervy around children, Borzois are affectionate with their owners and tolerant of other dogs, but they need plenty of attention.

GROOMING

The long, silky coat is easy to groom. Brush regularly with a firm bristle brush, and dry shampoo when necessary. Bathing presents problems with such a tall dog but shouldn't be required very often. Clip the hair between the toes to keep the feet comfortable and clean.

EXERCISE & FEEDING

To maintain their fitness these dogs need plenty of exercise, including regular opportunities to run off the leash. As they are susceptible to bloat it is a good idea to feed small meals two or three times a day and avoid exercise after meals.

HEALTH PROBLEMS

These large, deep-chested dogs are particularly prone to bloat. They occasionally suffer from thyroid and blood disorders.

PET FACTS

- Gentle, reserved, sensitive
- Regular brushing
- Regular, moderate
- Adapts well to urban living, but needs plenty of exercise
- Not a good watchdog

BE AWARE

- Borzois need a well-padded bed to prevent calluses and irritation to elbows

Male: At least 28 in (71 cm)
75–105 lb (34–48 kg)
Female: At least 26 in (66 cm)
60–90 lb (27–41 kg)

Greyhound

Agile and fleet of foot, this breed is one of the oldest known, long valued for its hunting prowess. The Greyhound's lean, elegant lines are often emblazoned on the coats of arms of royalty.

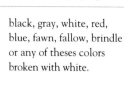

HISTORY
Greyhounds probably originated in the Middle East but also have a long history in Europe. They were much sought after as hunting dogs.

DESCRIPTION
Lean and powerful, these dogs are built for speed. Their long, muscular legs can propel them at up to 45 mph (70 km/h). At full stretch, their streamlined movement is a joy to watch. The close, short, fine coat comes in black, gray, white, red, blue, fawn, fallow, brindle or any of theses colors broken with white.

TEMPERAMENT
Gentle and sensitive, the Greyhound makes a surprisingly docile and obedient pet, given its hunting background. It does, however, retain a highly developed chase instinct and should always be kept on a leash in public. Greyhounds are good with children and settle happily into the family routine. While these dogs are easily trained, owners must be careful not to break their spirit by being harsh or overbearing.

GROOMING
The smooth, shorthaired coat is very easy to groom. Simply comb and brush with a firm bristle brush, and shampoo only when necessary.

PET FACTS	
🐕	Docile, loving and sensitive
〰	Occasional grooming
🐩	Regular, moderate
🏠	Adapts well to urban living if given plenty of exercise
🐾	Good watchdog

🐾 BE AWARE
- Should be leashed in public
- May be sensitive to some common anesthetics and flea-killing products

A rub with a chamois will ensure that the coat gleams.

EXERCISE & FEEDING
Greyhounds that are kept as pets should have regular opportunities to run free on open ground as well as have long, brisk walks, preferably at the same time every day. Greyhounds love a regular routine. There are no special feeding requirements, but it is better to give them two small meals a day rather than a single large one.

HEALTH PROBLEMS
Greyhounds are one of the only large breeds not to get hip dysplasia. They have very thin skin that tears easily and are unsuited to cold climates.

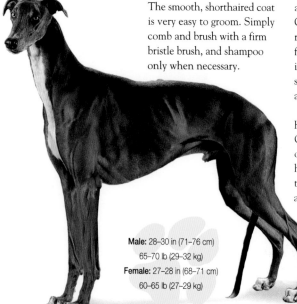

Male: 28–30 in (71–76 cm)
65–70 lb (29–32 kg)
Female: 27–28 in (68–71 cm)
60–65 lb (27–29 kg)

Irish Wolfhound

A true gentle giant, the Irish Wolfhound is affectionate and wonderful around children. It was once used to hunt wolves—so successfully that wolves have disappeared from the British Isles.

HISTORY
After working its way out of a job, the breed was brought back from the brink of extinction about 140 years ago by a British Army officer, Captain George Graham, who saw its potential for rescue work.

DESCRIPTION
A massive, muscular dog, the Irish Wolfhound is the tallest breed in the world. Its rough, wiry coat comes in gray, brindle, red, black, fawn and white. The paws are large and round, with markedly arched toes and strong, curved nails.

TEMPERAMENT
In spite of being a killer of wolves, this dog is gentle, loyal and very affectionate. It is trustworthy around children, although it might knock them over with its large tail. While disinclined to bark, its size alone should be daunting to intruders.

GROOMING
Unless the hard, wiry coat is combed often, it will become matted. Clip out any knots. Trim around the eyes and ears with blunt-nosed scissors.

EXERCISE & FEEDING
Irish Wolfhounds are inclined to be lazy and need a reasonable amount of exercise, but no more than smaller breeds. There are no special feeding requirements.

HEALTH PROBLEMS
Like many of the giant breeds, these dogs may suffer from heart disease. They are also subject to bloat, hip dysplasia and cataracts.

Male: 32–38 in (81–95 cm)
115–125 lb (52–57 kg)
Female: 28–32 in (71–81 cm)
100–110 lb (45–50 kg)

WORKING DOGS

Boxer

If your best friend is a Boxer, you can rely on it absolutely to take care of your property and to be waiting with the most enthusiastic welcome whenever you return home.

HISTORY
Developed in Germany from Mastiff-type dogs, the Boxer was originally used in bull-baiting and eventually crossed with the Bulldog to improve this ability. It was little known outside its country of origin until after World War II, when returning U.S. soldiers took some home.

DESCRIPTION
The body is compact and powerful and the shiny, close-fitting coat comes in fawn, brindle and various shades of red, with white markings. The tail is usually docked. In some countries, the ears are cropped.

GROOMING
The Boxer's smooth, shorthaired coat is easy to groom. Brush with a firm bristle brush, and bathe only when necessary.

EXERCISE & FEEDING
An active, athletic breed, Boxers need daily work or exercise. As well as a long, brisk, daily walk, they enjoy a session of play, fetching a ball. There are no special feeding requirements.

TEMPERAMENT
Intelligent and easily trained, Boxers have been widely used in military and police work. Training should start young and be firm and consistent—these exuberant animals need to be handled by a strong adult. They are reliable and protective with children and intensely loyal to their family. Excellent watchdogs, they will restrain an intruder in the same way a Bulldog does.

PET FACTS

- Lively, loving, loyal
- Occasional grooming
- Regular, vigorous
- Adapts well to urban living, but needs space
- Excellent watchdog

BE AWARE
- These dogs need a strong, energetic owner to play with
- May be aggressive with other dogs

HEALTH PROBLEMS
The shape of the nose can lead to sinus infections and breathing difficulties. They are prone to skin cancer; any skin lumps discovered during grooming should be investigated as they may be malignant tumors. Many boxers also have serious hereditary heart problems.

Male: 22–24 in (56–61 cm)
60–70 lb (27–32 kg)
Female: 21–23 in (53–58 cm)
55–65 lb (25–29 kg)

Schnauzer

Although known outside its native Germany for less than a century, the unusual-looking Schnauzer now has admirers worldwide, who are attracted by its high spirits, stamina and loyalty.

HISTORY

The Schnauzer is an ancient German breed, or more correctly, three breeds, since the three sizes, Giant, Standard and Miniature (see p. 384), are considered separate breeds. In the U.S., the Giant and Standard are classified as working dogs while the Miniature is considered to be a terrier. Many countries class all three together in a group known as utility dogs. The name comes from the German word for muzzle, Schnauze, a reference to the distinctive mustache of this breed, but these dogs were once also known as Wirehaired Pinschers. The Giant was originally used for herding cattle and as a guard dog. It was later harnessed to pull small traps. The Standard was prized as a ratter and often accompanied stage coaches and wagons.

DESCRIPTION

An angular, square-looking dog, strong and vigorous, the Schnauzer has a hard, wiry double coat that comes in pure black or salt and pepper colors, sometimes with white on the chest. The thick, prominent eyebrows and long mustache are often trimmed to accentuate the dog's overall square-cut shape. The feet are neat, round and compact, like a cat's paws, with well-arched toes and thick black pads. The tail is usually docked to be 1–2 inches (2.5–5 cm) at maturity.

TEMPERAMENT

These dogs are noted for their reliability and affectionate nature, and make excellent watchdogs. They are intelligent and independent but need firm, consistent training because they are inclined to be headstrong.

Standard
Male: 18–20 in (46–51 cm)
30–45 lb (14–20 kg)
Female: 17–19 in (43–48 cm)
30–40 lb (14–18 kg)

GROOMING

The wiry coat is reasonably easy to look after, but unless it is combed or brushed daily with a short wire brush, it will become matted. The undercoat is dense. Clip out knots and brush first with the grain, then against the grain to lift the coat. The animal should be clipped all over to an even length twice a year, in spring and fall, but this is a job best left to an expert. Trim around the eyes and ears with blunt-nosed scissors. Clean the whiskers after meals.

EXERCISE & FEEDING

These energetic dogs will take as much exercise as they can get, and relish play sessions during which they can run off the leash. At very least, they should be given a long, brisk daily walk. Don't overdo it with a very young pup, though, until the frame is strong and mature. There are no special feeding requirements.

HEALTH PROBLEMS

Schnauzers are fairly healthy dogs, although the Giant may suffer from hip dysplasia and orthopedic problems. Both the Giant and Standard are subject to epilepsy.

Giant
Male: 26–28 in (66–71 cm)
60–80 lb (27–36 kg)
Female: 23–26 in (58–66 cm)
55–75 lb (25–34 kg)

Note: Cropped ears are common in this breed. See p. 94 for more information

Samoyed

The Samoyed is almost always good-humored and ready for any challenge. With its pale, luxurious fur coat and thick, perky tail curled over the back to one side, it makes a spectacular pet.

HISTORY
Samoyeds are members of the Spitz family of dogs, which range throughout Arctic regions. They evolved as pack animals and sled dogs and were used by the nomadic Samoyed tribe of Siberia.

DESCRIPTION
The compact muscular body of this hard-working breed indicates its strength. The thick, silver-tipped coat comes in white, biscuit and cream.

TEMPERAMENT
The Samoyed is too friendly to be of much use as a watch-dog, although its bark will alert you to the presence of strangers. It willingly adapts to family life and gets on well with children. Start training at an early age.

GROOMING
Brushing two or three times a week is usually all that is needed, but extra care will be necessary when the dog is shedding. The long coat does not shed, but the woolly undercoat comes out in clumps twice a year. Bathing is difficult and mostly unnecessary, as the coat sheds dirt readily. Dry shampoo from time to time by brushing unscented talcum powder through the coat.

EXERCISE & FEEDING
Samoyeds need a reasonable amount of exercise, but take it easy during warm weather because the woolly undercoat inhibits loss of the heat built up during exercise. There are no special feeding requirements, but Samoyeds are particularly partial to fish.

HEALTH PROBLEMS
Samoyeds are prone to hip dysplasia, diabetes, glaucoma and cataracts. The heavy coat makes these dogs unsuited to life in very hot climates.

PET FACTS

- Gentle, friendly, good-natured
- Brush twice weekly; more when molting
- Regular, moderate
- Adapts well to urban living, but needs plenty of space
- Ineffective watchdog

🐾 BE AWARE
- It is difficult to find ticks in the dense, woolly undercoat
- Given to digging holes in which they lie to cool off

Male: 21–24 in (53–61 cm)
45–60 lb (20–27 kg)
Female: 19–21 in (48–53 cm)
45–60 lb (20–27 kg)

Siberian Husky

A member of the Spitz family, the Siberian Husky is able to haul heavy loads over vast distances in impossible terrain. Noted for its speed and stamina, it is often chosen for polar expeditions.

HISTORY
These dogs originated in Siberia and were developed to pull sleds and herd reindeer by the nomadic Chukchi people.

DESCRIPTION
Siberian Huskies are strong, compact working dogs. The face mask and underbody are usually white, and the remaining coat any color. Mismatched eyes are common. The large "snow-shoe" feet have hair between the toes for grip on ice.

TEMPERAMENT
Because they are friendly and bark little, Huskies make ineffective watchdogs. As puppies, they must be trained to come when called. Docile and affectionate, they enjoy family life and are depen-dable around children.

GROOMING
Brush the coarse, medium-length coat twice a week. The woolly undercoat comes out in clumps twice a year and requires extra care. Bathing is difficult and mostly unneces-sary, as the coat sheds dirt. An occasional dry shampoo should be enough to keep the coat looking clean. Clip the nails regularly.

EXERCISE & FEEDING
Siberian Huskies need a fair amount of exercise, but don't overdo it in warm weather. They need a large yard with a high fence, but bury the wire at the base of the fence because they are likely to dig their way out and go off hunting. Huskies are thrifty feeders and need less food than you might expect.

HEALTH PROBLEMS
The breed is comparatively free of breed-specific problems, apart from hip dysplasia and occasional eye problems, such as cataracts. Because of their heavy coats, these dogs are unsuited to life in hot climates and should not be excessively exercised in warm weather.

PET FACTS

- Playful, friendly, good-natured
- Brush twice weekly; more when molting
- Regular, vigorous
- Adapts well to urban living, but needs plenty of space
- Ineffective watchdog

BE AWARE
- Lack of exercise will make these dogs restless; if not securely enclosed, they will go off hunting by themselves

Male: 21–23 in (53–58 cm)
45–60 lb (20–27 kg)
Female: 20–22 in (51–56 cm)
35–50 lb (16–23 kg)

Alaskan Malamute

Despite its wolf-like appearance, this handsome and friendly breed makes a loyal and affectionate family pet. With its strong, powerful body and enormous stamina, it is ideal for work in the Arctic.

HISTORY

These sledding dogs of the Spitz family were named after a nomadic Inuit tribe from Alaska, the Malhemut.

DESCRIPTION

These are powerful, compact working dogs. Their under-body and face masking is always white, while the remaining coat may be light gray to black, gold to red and liver. The plumed tail is carried over the back.

TEMPERAMENT

Malamutes are very active and exceptionally friendly to people but not to other dogs. They look intimidating, but are not good watchdogs.

GROOMING

Brush the dense, coarse coat twice a week, with extra care during shedding—the under-coat comes out in clumps twice a year. Bathing is mostly unnecessary, as the coat sheds dirt readily. Dry shampoo occasionally.

EXERCISE & FEEDING

Malamutes need a reasonable amount of exercise, but don't overdo it in warm weather. They need a large yard with a high fence, but bury the base, because they are likely to dig their way out. They are thrifty feeders and need less food than you might expect. However, they tend to wolf down whatever is offered, which can lead to obesity and bloat.

PET FACTS

- Gentle, friendly, good-natured
- Brush twice weekly; more often when the undercoat is molting
- Regular, vigorous
- Adapts well to urban living, but needs plenty of space
- Ineffective watchdog

BE AWARE

- May be aggressive with other dogs

HEALTH PROBLEMS

The breed is subject to hip dysplasia, eye problems and blood clotting disorders. Malamutes are unsuited to life in hot climtes.

Male: 24–26 in (61–66 cm)
80–95 lb (36–43 kg)
Female: 22–24 in (56–61 cm)
70–85 lb (32–38 kg)

Rottweiler

Strong and substantial, the Rottweiler is not a dog for the average home nor for inexperienced owners. It makes an imposing and effective guard dog but needs firm handling and proper training.

HISTORY

The forebears of this breed were left behind throughout Europe many centuries ago by the withdrawing Roman army. In the area around Rottweil, southern Germany, these mastiff-type animals were crossed with sheepdogs to produce "butchers' dogs" capable of herding and guarding livestock.

DESCRIPTION

Compact, muscular dogs, Rottweilers have surprising speed and agility. The thick, medium-length coat conceals a fine undercoat and is always black with rich tan to mahogany markings. The tail is usually docked to leave one or two vertebrae.

TEMPERAMENT

Rottweilers are prized for their aggression and guarding abilities, yet they can, with proper handling, also be loyal, loving and very rewarding companions. They are highly intelligent and have proved their worth beyond question in police, military and customs work over many centuries. Training must begin young, while the dog is still small, and great care should be taken to ensure that the dog is not made vicious.

GROOMING

The smooth, glossy coat is easy to groom. Brush with a firm bristle brush, and bathe only when necessary.

EXERCISE & FEEDING

You can't give these robust dogs too much work or exercise—they thrive on it. There are no special feeding requirements, but avoid overfeeding.

HEALTH PROBLEMS

Rottweilers are fairly robust and adapt to any climate. However, they may suffer from elbow and hip dysplasia, and eye problems such as cataracts and progressive retinal atrophy.

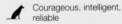

PET FACTS

 Courageous, intelligent, reliable

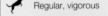 Occasional grooming

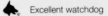 Regular, vigorous

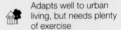 Adapts well to urban living, but needs plenty of exercise

Excellent watchdog

BE AWARE

- These formidable animals need kind and consistent training from a strong adult to be kept under control

- Rottweilers may be aggressive with other dogs and should be kept on leashes in public places.

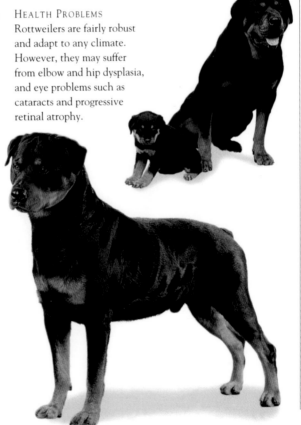

Male: 24–27 in (61–69 cm)
95–130 lb (43–59 kg)
Female: 22–25 in (56–63 cm)
85–115 lb (38–52 kg)

Akita

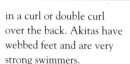

The national dog of Japan, many champions of this breed are considered national treasures. The handsome and much-loved Akita is renowned for its strength, courage and loyalty.

HISTORY
Displaying typical characteristics of the Spitz family, to which it belongs, the Akita has only recently become known outside of its native Japan, where it was used for hunting deer, wild boar and black bears. In feudal times, it was pitted in savage dog-fighting spectacles, but these are now outlawed and the dog has found work with the police and is a reliable guard dog.

DESCRIPTION
The largest of the Japanese Spitz-type breeds, the well-proportioned Akita has a muscular body and a waterproof double coat that comes in all colors with clear, dark markings. The tail is thick and carried in a curl or double curl over the back. Akitas have webbed feet and are very strong swimmers.

TEMPERAMENT
Despite the ferocity of many of its past activities, with diligent training the Akita can make an excellent pet. Care should always be taken, however, around other dogs. This dog likes to dominate and needs a strong, experienced adult to control it.

GROOMING
The coarse, stiff, shorthaired coat requires significant grooming and sheds twice a year. Brush with a firm bristle brush, and bathe only when absolutely necessary as bathing removes the natural waterproofing of the coat.

PET FACTS

- Brave, affectionate, loyal
- Regular brushing
- Regular, moderate
- Adapts well to urban living, but needs plenty of space and exercise
- Excellent watchdog

BE AWARE
- May be aggressive with other dogs

EXERCISE & FEEDING
The Akita needs moderate but regular exercise to stay in shape. There are no special feeding requirements.

HEALTH PROBLEMS
Illness is rare in this robust breed and Akitas don't need to be pampered. As with most large purebred dogs, there is some tendency to hip dysplasia and eye problems.

Male: 26–28 in (66–71 cm)
75–120 lb (34–54 kg)
Female: 24–26 in (61–66 cm)
75–110 lb (34–50 kg)

Bernese Mountain Dog

Once used as an all-around working dog in its native Switzerland, the Bernese Mountain Dog adapts easily to domestic life as long as it is given plenty of loving attention from the whole family.

HISTORY

The Bernese Mountain Dog, also known as the Bernese Sennenhund, made itself useful herding cattle, guarding farms and pulling carts in a specially made harness. It also shares the Saint Bernard's skill at finding people lost in snow. It is one of four Swiss breeds that are probably descended from Roman times.

DESCRIPTION

A large, powerful dog, the handsome Bernese is vigorous and agile. It has a gleaming, soft, wavy black coat with white and chestnut markings.

TEMPERAMENT

These gentle, cheerful dogs love children. They are very intelligent, easy to train and are natural watchdogs. They are very loyal and may have trouble adjusting to a new owner after they are 18 months old.

GROOMING

Daily brushing of the long, thick, silky coat is important, with extra care needed when the dog is shedding. Bathe or dry shampoo as necessary.

EXERCISE & FEEDING

Large, active dogs such as these need a regular exercise regimen. There are no special feeding requirements.

HEALTH PROBLEMS

Bernese Mountain Dogs are particularly prone to hip and elbow dysplasia. They also suffer from hereditary eye diseases and cancer.

PET FACTS

- Placid, cheerful, loving
- Daily brushing
- Regular, moderate
- Adapts well to urban living, but needs plenty of exercise
- Excellent w tchdog

BE AWARE

- These are one-owner dogs and may find it difficult to adjust to a new owner

Male: 24–28 in (61–71 cm)
85–110 lb (38–50 kg)
Female: 23–27 in (58–69 cm)
80–105 lb (36–48 kg)

Saint Bernard

Universally admired for its feats of rescue in the snows of the Swiss Alps, the Saint Bernard needs no introduction. For more than 200 years, its courage and skill have been the stuff of legends, and for some, the sight of this dog has signaled the end of an ordeal.

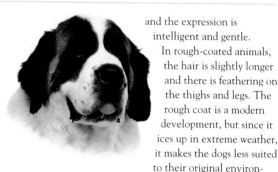

PET FACTS

Placid, affectionate, loyal

Daily brushing

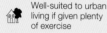
Regular, moderate

Well-suited to urban living if given plenty of exercise

Good watchdog

BE AWARE

• These dogs drool a lot and require regular exercise

• One of the most short-lived breeds; their life expectancy is about 11 years.

HISTORY

Saint Bernards are named after Bernard de Menthon, the founder of a famous hospice built in a remote alpine pass in Switzerland nearly 1,000 years ago to shelter mountain travelers. Exactly when the dogs started to be used at the hospice for rescue work is not known, however it is most likely to have been some time during the seventeenth century.

DESCRIPTION

These are very large, strong dogs. As long as the weight is in proportion to the height, the taller the dog is the better. There are two types of coat, rough and smooth, but both are very dense and come in white with markings in tan, mahogany, red, brindle and black in various combinations. The face and ears are usually shaded with black and the expression is intelligent and gentle.

In rough-coated animals, the hair is slightly longer and there is feathering on the thighs and legs. The rough coat is a modern development, but since it ices up in extreme weather, it makes the dogs less suited to their original environment. The feet are large, with strong, well-arched toes, making Saint Bernards surefooted in snow and on ice. They have a highly developed sense of smell and also seem to have a sixth sense about impending danger from storms and avalanches.

TEMPERAMENT

Dignified and reliable, the Saint Bernard is generally good with children, in spite of its size. It makes a good watchdog, its size alone an effective deterrent. It is highly intelligent and easy to train, however training should begin early, while the dog is still a manageable size. Bear in mind that an unruly dog of this size presents a problem for even a strong adult if it is to be exercised in public areas on a leash, so take control from the outset.

Male: 27 in (69 cm) or more
110–180 lb (50–81 kg)
Female: 25 in (63 cm) or more
110–180 lb (50–81 kg)

GROOMING
Both types of coat are easy to groom. Comb and brush with a firm bristle brush, and bathe only when necessary with mild soap—shampoo may strip the coat of its oily, water-resistant properties.

During spring and fall, there is considerable shedding. The eyes, which may be inclined to water, need special attention to keep them clean and free of irritants.

EXERCISE & FEEDING
A long walk each day will keep these dogs in good condition, although, of course, a great deal more was expected of them in the past. It is best not to allow puppies too much activity at one time until the bones are well-formed and strong. Short walks and brief play sessions are best until the dog is about two years old. As these dogs are prone to bloat, it is best to feed them two or three small meals a day instead of one large one.

HEALTH PROBLEMS
Like many of the giant breeds, Saint Bernards are particularly susceptible to hip dysplasia. They are also subject to epilepsy and bloat. They sometimes develop skin problems and the thick, warm coat makes them unsuited to life in very hot climates. There may be problems with out-turned eyelids, a condition called ectropion that causes irritation and weeping because the eyelids don't close completely.

Bullmastiff

Despite its size and aggressive looks, the Bullmastiff is a devoted family pet and a watchdog par excellence. The strong, silent type, it rarely barks, never loses its temper and is easy to train and control.

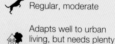
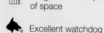
HISTORY

This powerful and intimidating dog was developed in Britain by crossing the fast and ferocious Bulldog with the Mastiff—an excellent tracker, large and very strong. The Bullmastiff was widely used by gamekeepers on large estates to deter poachers.

DESCRIPTION

Smaller and more compact than the Mastiff, the Bullmastiff is, nevertheless, a reliable and daunting watchdog. The dense, coarse coat is water-resistant and comes in dark brindle, fawn and red shades. The face and neck are darker and deeply folded. There are sometimes white marks on the chest.

TEMPERAMENT

Although the Bullmastiff is unlikely to attack, it will catch an intruder, knock him down and hold him. At the same time, it is tolerant of children, intelligent, even-tempered, calm and loyal.

GROOMING

The shorthaired, slightly rough coat is easy to groom. Comb and brush with a firm bristle brush, and shampoo only when necessary. There is little shedding with this breed. Check the feet regularly because they carry a lot of weight, and trim the nails.

EXERCISE & FEEDING

These dogs tend to be lazy so provide regular, moderate exercise. They are prone to bloat, so feed them two or three small meals a day instead of one large meal.

HEALTH PROBLEMS

While fairly robust, these dogs are susceptible to bloat, elbow and hip dysplasia and some eye problem . They do not tolerate extremes of temperature well.

Male: 25–27 in (63–69 cm)
110–133 lb (50–60 kg)
Female: 24–26 in (61–66 cm)
100–120 lb (45–54 kg)

Doberman Pinscher

Originally developed to deter thieves, the Doberman Pinscher is prized as an obedient and powerful watchdog, but with proper training from puppyhood, it can also become a devoted family pet.

HISTORY

These fearless and intimidating dogs were developed late in the nineteenth century by a German tax collector, Louis Dobermann. He drew on a number of breeds, including Rottweilers, German Pinschers, German Shepherd Dogs and Manchester Terriers to produce the ultimate guard dog—obedient and courageous.

DESCRIPTION

The Doberman Pinscher is an elegant, muscular and very powerful dog. It has a well-proportioned chest, a short back and a lean, muscular neck. Its hard, shorthaired, close-fitting coat generally comes in black, or black and tan, although blue-gray, red and fawn also occur. The tail is docked at the second joint.

TEMPERAMENT

This breed's reputation for aggression is generally undeserved, but firm training from puppyhood is essential. Fortunately, they are easy to school and make loyal and obedient watchdogs. They are fearless, alert, agile and energetic. However, being powerful animals, they should always be watched around young children.

GROOMING

The smooth, shorthaired coat is easy to groom. Comb and brush with a firm bristle brush, and shampoo only when necessary.

EXERCISE & FEEDING

These dogs are very active, requiring plenty of daily exercise. They are not suitable for apartments or houses with small yards. Feed these dogs two or three small meals a day.

HEALTH PROBLEMS

Unfortunately, this breed is subject to a number of health problems. In addition to such common diseases as bloat, hip dysplasia and eye problems, it is also prone to heart disease. Its short coat means that it should never be exposed to extreme cold.

PET FACTS

- Intelligent, loyal and fearless, but may be aggressive
- Occasional grooming
- Regular, vigorous
- Adapts to urban living if given enough exercise
- Superb watchdog

BE AWARE

- Can become aggressive if not trained from an early age
- Prone to heart problems

Male: 26–28 in (66–71 cm)
66–88 lb (30–40 kg)
Female: 24–26 in (61–66 cm)
66–88 lb (30–40 kg)

Note: Cropped ears are common in this breed. See p. 94 for more information

Great Pyrenees

The Great Pyrenees is a truly majestic animal that always impresses, but consider the commitment carefully—you must have the space, patience and, most important, time to meet all its needs.

HISTORY

Also known as the Pyrenean Mountain Dog, the Great Pyrenees has a long history in its native France as a guard dog of sheep and châteaux. It is also thought to have been used as a dog of war in ancient times when its temperament was less gentle than it is now.

DESCRIPTION

Fully grown, this is a very large animal with a solid, muscular body. The long, coarse outer coat is either straight or slightly wavy; the fine undercoat is soft and thick. The coat is waterproof and solid white or white with patches of tan, wolf-gray or pale yellow.

TEMPERAMENT

Although it is gentle and has a natural instinct for guarding, the Great Pyrenees must be well trained while young and small.

GROOMING

Regular brushing of the long double coat will keep it in good condition, but extra care is needed when the dog is shedding its dense under-coat. The outer coat doesn't mat, so care is relatively easy. Bathe or dry shampoo only when necessary.

EXERCISE & FEEDING

This dog needs plenty of exercise to stay in shape. It need not be vigorous, but it must be regular. There are no special feeding requirements.

HEALTH PROBLEMS

Like many large breeds, they may have problems with hip dysplasia and other orthopedic diseases. They are also prone to epilepsy, deafness and hereditary eye diseases.

PET FACTS

- Gentle, obedient, loyal
- Regular brushing
- Regular, extensive
- Adapts well to urban living, but needs plenty of space and exercise
- Very good watchdog

BE AWARE
- These dogs don't reach maturity until about two years of age

---

Male: 27–32 in (69–81 cm)
From 100 lb (45 kg)
Female: 25–29 in (63–74 cm)
From 85 lb (38 kg)

Mastiff

Few intruders would venture onto a property guarded by a Mastiff, but this magnificent animal also has a gentle side and, if properly handled, is utterly devoted to its own people.

PET FACTS

 Reliable, courageous, but can be aggressive

 Regular brushing

 Regular, moderate

Adapts well to urban living, but needs plenty of space

Outstanding watchdog

BE AWARE

• Firm but gentle training is essential to keep this dog under control

HISTORY

There are references to large Mastiff-type dogs going back to antiquity. They were ferocious and formidable fighters and were often used for military work as well as hunting. Today's animals are more correctly called Old English Mastiffs as they all trace their lineage to two surviving English strains.

DESCRIPTION

This large and powerful dog is an imposing sight. The shorthaired coat is dense, coarse and flat-lying and comes in shades of apricot, silver, fawn or darker fawn brindle. The muzzle, ears and nose are black and the wide-set eyes are hazel to brown.

TEMPERAMENT

An exceptional guard dog, the Mastiff must be handled firmly and trained with kindness if it is to be kept under control. Properly handled, it is docile, good natured and loyal, but it can become a big problem if it gets the upper hand.

GROOMING

The smooth, shorthaired coat is easy to groom. Brush with a firm bristle brush and wipe over with a piece of toweling or chamois for a gleaming finish. Bathe or dry shampoo when necessary.

EXERCISE & FEEDING

Mastiffs are inclined to be lazy but they will keep fitter and happier if given regular exercise. They should always be leashed in public. As these dogs are prone to bloat, feed two or three small meals a day, instead of one large one.

HEALTH PROBLEMS

Mastiffs may suffer from hip and elbow dysplasia, bloat and hereditary eye diseases.

Male: From 30 in (76 cm)
From about 160 lb (72 kg)
Female: From 27 in (69 cm)
From about 150 lb (68 kg)

Newfoundland

A naturally powerful swimmer, the Newfoundland has an outstanding record of sea rescues to its credit. It was prized by fishermen in its region of origin, along the east coast of Canada.

HISTORY

The Newfoundland is one of the few dogs native to North America and did invaluable work for early settlers pulling sleds, hunting and guarding.

DESCRIPTION

This massive dog comes in black, browns, or black with white markings—this variant being known as the Landseer after its depiction in a painting by Sir Edwin Landseer. Like some other water-loving breeds, it has webbing between the toes.

TEMPERAMENT

Famous as the "Nana" dog in *Peter Pan*, these dogs are renowned for being gentle with children. They are adaptable, loyal and courageous, with great strength and endurance.

GROOMING

Daily brushing of the thick, coarse, double coat with a hard brush is important. The undercoat is shed once or twice a year and extra care is required at these times. Avoid bathing unless absolutely necessary, as this strips away the coat's natural oils. Instead, dry shampoo from time to time.

EXERCISE & FEEDING

This gentle giant is quite content to laze around the house, but it will benefit from regular moderate exercise. It should have frequent opportunities to swim and frolic. There are no special feeding requirements, but don't overfeed.

HEALTH PROBLEMS

In these large, heavy dogs, hip dysplasia and other orthopedic problems are common, as are genetic heart conditions. The thick black coat makes these dogs unsuited to hot climates.

PET FACTS

- Intelligent, gentle, loyal
- Daily brushing
- Regular, moderate
- Adapts well to urban living, but needs plenty of space
- Good watchdog

BE AWARE

- Teach pups to be gentle before they grow large

Male: 27–29 in (69–74 cm)
130–150 lb (59–68 kg)
Female: 25–27 in (63–69 cm)
100–120 lb (45–54 kg)

Great Dane

Ancestors of this aristocratic breed have been known in Germany, where they probably originated, for more than 2,000 years. They are surprisingly gentle for their size.

DESCRIPTION
Large, tall, muscular dogs, Great Danes come in fawn, striped brindle, black, blue and harlequin.

TEMPERAMENT
Gentle, loyal, affectionate, playful and patient with children, the Great Dane is well behaved and makes a good watchdog. Start training before it gets too large and socialize to avoid shyness.

HISTORY
Among the tallest of dog breeds, the powerful, fast and agile Great Dane was originally favored by the German aristocracy for hunting boar and stags.

GROOMING
The smooth, shorthaired coat is easy to groom. Comb and brush with a firm bristle brush, and dry shampoo when necessary. Bathing this giant is a major chore, so it pays to avoid the need by daily grooming. The nails must be kept trimmed.

PET FACTS

- Gentle, loyal, affectionate
- Daily brushing
- Regular, moderate
- Adapts well to urban living, but needs plenty of space
- Very good watchdog

☙ BE AWARE
- Prone to bloat, so avoid exercise after meals

EXERCISE & FEEDING
Great Danes need plenty of exercise, at the very least a long daily walk. They are prone to bloat so feed small helpings and avoid exercise after meals. Ideally, the food dish should be raised so that the dog can eat without splaying its legs.

HEALTH PROBLEMS
Being very large and heavy, Great Danes are prone to hip dysplasia and some genetic heart problems.

Male: 30–34 in (76–86 cm)
120–160 lb (54–72 kg)
Female: 28–32 in (71–81 cm)
100–130 lb (45–59 kg)

TERRIERS

Cairn Terrier

The vivacious little Cairn Terrier will delight you with its antics and steal your heart with its courage and fun-loving ways. It makes an ideal pet, adaptable, friendly and alert.

PET FACTS

Alert, frisky, friendly

Regular brushing

Regular, moderate

Ideal for apartment living

Good watchdog

BE AWARE

• Prone to skin allergies

HISTORY

All terriers have much in common, being natural hunters bred to dig their prey out of burrows. They have powerful jaws with large teeth to hold the prey once caught. The Cairn Terrier is one of the oldest of the terriers and has contributed attributes to many varieties through cross-breeding. It originated in the Scottish Highlands, where it hunted among the many cairns that dot the landscape there.

DESCRIPTION

This compact little animal has a hard, shaggy, weather-resistant outer coat that comes in cream, wheaten, red, sandy, gray, brindle, black, solid white or black and tan, with ears and mask often darker. The thick undercoat is soft and furry.

TEMPERAMENT

A strong, fearless and companionable dog, the Cairn Terrier is always ready to play or be petted. Energetic and always on watch, it will alert you to the presence of strangers by its growling and on-guard stance. Cairn Terriers are intelligent and easily trained.

GROOMING

That shaggy "natural" look actually takes quite a bit of maintenance and a neglected coat soon becomes a sorry, matted mess. Brush several times a week, being gentle with the soft undercoat. Once a month, bathe the dog and brush the coat while it dries. Trim around the eyes and ears with blunt-nosed scissors and clip the nails regularly.

EXERCISE & FEEDING

This dog will get enough exercise running around a small garden, but if you live in an apartment, it will need a daily walk or a romp in the park. There are no special feeding requirements.

HEALTH PROBLEMS

Generally healthy, but prone to allergic skin problems, blood clotting disorders, dislocating kneecaps and hereditary eye diseases.

Male: 10–13 in (25–33 cm)
14–18 lb (6–8 kg)
Female: 9–12 in (23–30 cm)
13–17 lb (6–8 kg)

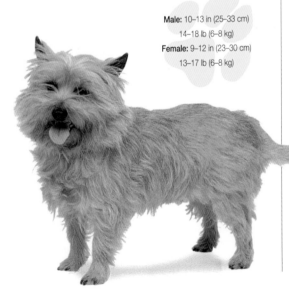

Norwich Terrier

A feisty, short-legged little dog, the Norwich Terrier has a big heart and is happiest when looking after its human family. It makes a very good watchdog and devoted companion.

HISTORY

Until 1964, this breed comprised what later became two groups, those with prick ears and those with ears that fell forward. After that date, drop-eared Norwich Terriers became known as Norfolk Terriers in Britain, and, despite being virtually identical, they are now officially recognized as different breeds. US recognition followed in 1979. The original Norwich Terriers came from East Anglia in Britain.

DESCRIPTION

These lovable dogs are among the smallest of the working terriers. Both breeds have short, sturdy bodies and short legs. Their coats are wiry and straight and come in red, tan, wheaten, black and tan, and grizzle, occasionally with white marks. The faces sport jaunty whiskers and eyebrows. The tails are usually docked.

Male: About 10 in (25 cm)
10–13 lb (5–6 kg)
Female: About 10 in (25 cm)
10–13 lb (5–6 kg)

TEMPERAMENT

Although good natured and friendly with people, including children, the Norwich Terrier can be scrappy with other dogs and often bears the scars of brief encounters. It is alert, smart and easy to train.

GROOMING

Care of the shaggy, medium-length, waterproof coat is relatively easy, but daily combing and brushing is important. Take extra care when the dog is molting. Little clipping is required and bathe or dry shampoo only when necessary.

EXERCISE & FEEDING

These energetic little dogs were bred to work and they thrive on an active life, but they won't sulk if you miss a day now and then. There are no special feeding requirements.

PET FACTS

🐾	Fearless, lively, loyal
🪮	Daily combing and brushing
🦴	Regular, moderate
🏠	Ideal for apartment living, but needs plenty of exercise
🐕	Very good watchdog

🐾 **BE AWARE**

• To avoid fights, always keep on the leash when other dogs are around

HEALTH PROBLEMS

The breed is hardy and long-lived, although some dogs may suffer from genetic eye diseases, such as cataracts.

Jack Russell Terrier

Admired for its courage and tenacity, the Jack Russell Terrier will take on all challengers. An excellent watchdog, this little dog will also keep your property free of small interlopers, such as snakes.

HISTORY

Although still not universally recognized as an official breed, the Jack Russell Terrier has been around for about 100 years. It takes its name from the English "hunting parson" who developed the dog. It was specially bred with the speed, stamina and agility to hunt foxes. There is a longer-legged type, known as the Parson Russell Terrier, that is regarded as a separate breed.

DESCRIPTION

This tough little dog is clean and a convenient size for a house companion. The coat may be either smooth and short or rough and a little longer and comes in white, or white with black, tan or lemon markings.

TEMPERAMENT

Jack Russell Terriers are happy, excitable dogs that love to hunt. In fact, they'll chase just about anything

that moves. They make vigilant watchdogs, but are sometimes scrappy with other dogs. Smart and quick witted, they must be firmly trained from an early age, but settle well into family life and make devoted pets.

GROOMING

Both smooth and rough coats are easy to groom. Comb and brush regularly with a firm bristle brush, and bathe only when necessary.

EXERCISE & FEEDING

The Jack Russell Terrier is very adaptable and will exercise itself in a small garden, but it is in its element with space to run, hunt and play. There are no special feeding requirements.

HEALTH PROBLEMS

This robust breed has few genetic problems, but may suffer from dislocating kneecaps and some hereditary eye diseases.

Male: 10–15 in (25–38 cm)
15–18 lb (7–8 kg)
Female: 9–14 in (23–36 cm)
14–17 lb (6–8 kg)

Australian Terrier

Although its talents as a rat and snake killer are called on less frequently now, the playful little Australian Terrier, nevertheless, retains the best characteristics of a working dog.

The topknot is lighter and there is a thick ruff. The tail is generally docked to less than half its length.

TEMPERAMENT
Keen and smart, the Australian Terrier responds well to training and makes a delightful pet. It is always eager to please and loves being around children.

HISTORY
Developed over the past 150 years in Australia as a working terrier, the lively little Australian Terrier combines the attributes of the several British terrier breeds that contributed to its makeup, mainly Cairn, Yorkshire and Norwich Terriers. Its current role is mainly as a pet.

DESCRIPTION
A sturdy, low-set dog with a straight, weather-resistant, double coat in blue and rich tan, clear reds or sand shades.

GROOMING
The long, stiff, shaggy coat is easy to care for and doesn't need clipping. Simply brush several times a week, being gentle with the soft under-coat. Brushing stimulates the natural oils and will soon bring the coat to a high gloss. Once a month, bathe the dog and brush the coat while it dries. Trim around the eyes and ears, if necessary, with blunt-nosed scissors. Be sure to clip the nails regularly.

PET FACTS	
🐕	Bold, good-natured, friendly
🪮	Regular brushing
🐕	Regular, gentle
🏠	Ideal for apartment living
🐕	Too friendly to strangers to be a good watchdog

🐾 BE AWARE

- These dogs are avid hunters

- Quiet and affectionate, great with children, elderly or handicapped.

EXERCISE & FEEDING
The Australian Terrier is an adaptable little dog and will happily adjust to as much or as little exercise as you are able to provide—it is quite content in a garden of reasonable size. There are no special feeding requirements.

HEALTH PROBLEMS
While Australian Terriers are generally tough and hardy dogs, they may suffer from dislocating kneecaps, deterioration of the hip joint and skin problems.

Male: 9–11 in (23–28 cm)
9–14 lb (4–6 kg)
Female: 9–11 in (23–28 cm)
9–14 lb (4–6 kg)

West Highland White Terrier

A perfect mascot or companion, the West Highland White Terrier has all the terrier charm and vitality, plus brains and beauty in one neat package. It makes a bright and entertaining pet.

HISTORY

With similar ancestry to the other Highland working terriers, especially the Cairn Terrier, the "Westie" was selectively bred for its white coat so as to be highly visible in the field. It was formerly known as both the Poltalloch and Roseneath Terrier.

DESCRIPTION

This is a sturdy little terrier with an all-white coat and bright, dark eyes. The ears are small, pointed and erect, giving the animal an alert, ready-for-anything look. The tail is carried jauntily and should not be docked.

TEMPERAMENT

Friendly, playful, alert and self-confident, this dog just loves companionship. It is bold, strong and brave, and makes a very good watchdog, despite its size.

GROOMING

The harsh, straight, short-haired double coat is fairly easy to groom and sheds very little. Simply brush regularly with a stiff bristle brush. Brushing should keep the coat clean, so bathe only when necessary. Trim around the eyes and ears with blunt-nosed scissors. The whole coat should be trimmed about every four months and stripped twice a year.

EXERCISE & FEEDING

These dogs enjoy a regular walk or sessions of play in the park but won't be too upset if they miss a day. There are no special feeding requirements.

HEALTH PROBLEMS

Westies are a generally hardy breed, although they may be subject to bad allergic skin problems. They are also prone to hereditary jaw problems and deterioration of the hip joint.

Male: 10–12 in (25–30 cm)
15–18 lb (7–8 kg)
Female: 9–11 in (23–28 cm)
13–16 lb (6–7 kg)

Scottish Terrier

The sturdy, active little Scottish Terrier is so distinctive that it has become something of an unofficial emblem of its native Scotland. While a little stubborn, it nevertheless makes a wonderful pet.

HISTORY

Perhaps the best known, if not the oldest, of the Highland terriers, the modern Scottish Terrier hails from Aberdeen and was developed at least 150 years ago. The correct standard for the breed was hotly debated in Britain until it was formalized in 1880.

DESCRIPTION

This sturdy little dog has very short legs and the way it is groomed makes them look even shorter. Even so, it is a strong, active animal and surprisingly agile. The rough-textured, weather-resistant, broken coat comes in black, wheaten, or brindle of any color. The undercoat is short, dense and soft. Sharply pricked ears give the Scottish Terrier a thoughtful look.

TEMPERAMENT

Although somewhat dignified in its behavior, the Scottish Terrier makes a very good watchdog. It is inclined to be stubborn, however, and needs firm handling from an early age or it will dominate the household.

GROOMING

Regular brushing of the harsh wiry coat is important and extra care should be taken when the dog is molting. Bathe or dry shampoo as necessary. The dog should be professionally trimmed twice a year. The hair on the body is left long, like a skirt, while the hair on the face is lightly trimmed and brushed forward.

EXERCISE & FEEDING

Given a yard of reasonable size, the sporty Scottish Terrier will exercise itself, but it will happily accompany you for a walk or play session in the park and delights in fetching sticks and balls.

PET FACTS	
🐕	Happy, brave, loyal
〰	Regular brushing
🐕	Regular, moderate
🏠	Ideal for apartment living
🐕	Very good watchdog

🐾 BE AWARE

- Likes to go wandering
- Prone to skin ailments, including flea allergies

There are no special feeding requirements, but overfeeding will cause obesity and laziness.

HEALTH PROBLEMS

A generally robust breed, but sensitivity to fleas may cause skin problems. Cramp may also be a recurrent problem.

Male: 10–11 in (25–28 cm)
19–23 lb (9–10 kg)
Female: 9–10 in (23–25 cm)
18–22 lb (8–10 kg)

Border Terrier

A plain, no-nonsense little working dog, the Border Terrier is game for anything. It loves being part of a family and is unrestrained in its displays of affection, especially in greeting.

HISTORY

Once known as the Reedwater Terrier, the brave little Border Terrier evolved in the rugged border country between England and Scotland, sharing a common ancestry with other terriers. It was used to hunt foxes, otters and vermin and is perhaps the toughest of the terrier breeds.

DESCRIPTION

One of the smallest of the working terriers, the Border Terrier has a wiry little body to go with its wiry double coat. It comes in reds, blue and tan, grizzle and tan, or wheaten. The muzzle and ears are usually dark and the undercoat very short and dense. The loose skin, which feels thick, enables the dog to wriggle into tight burrows. The head is somewhat different from other terriers and is often described as being otter-like.

TEMPERAMENT

Reliable and intelligent, Border Terriers are easily trained, obedient, sensible and bright. They are generally not aggressive with other dogs but may hunt your cat and drive it crazy.

GROOMING

The durable, wiry coat needs little grooming. Clip out any knots and brush occasionally with a bristle brush. The object is a completely natural look with no artifice. Bathe only when necessary.

PET FACTS

🐕 Energetic, affectionate, loyal

〰 Minimal

🐕 Regular, moderate

🏠 Ideal for urban and apartment living, but needs plenty of exercise

🐾 Good watchdog

🐾 BE AWARE

- A bored Border Terrier can become destructive and chew things

- Start gentle training from a very early age

EXERCISE & FEEDING

These dogs have great vitality and stamina, and need plenty of exercise. There are no special feeding requirements.

HEALTH PROBLEMS

These hardy dogs have few genetic problems, but do suffer from dislocating kneecaps and occasional kidney problems.

Male: 13–16 in (33–41 cm)
13–16 lb (6–7 kg)
Female: 11–14 in (28–36 cm)
11–14 lb (5–6 kg)

Fox Terrier

The look and stance of super-alertness and expectation is the hallmark of the Fox Terrier. Wire and Smooth Fox Terriers are remarkably similar in nearly every way, except in their coats.

PET FACTS

Keen, alert, independent

Regular brushing; Wire more than Smooth

Regular, moderate

Ideal for urban or apartment living, but needs plenty of exercise

Good watchdog

BE AWARE

- Fox Terriers are enthusiastic diggers

- Prone to allergic skin conditions

HISTORY

Fox Terriers are among the oldest of the terrier breeds and were bred to dig down into burrows to flush out foxes or to catch small animals in their powerful jaws. They were also highly prized as ratters, more than earning their keep around the stables. The Wire was bred for use in rough country, its skin being less vulnerable to damage than that of the Smooth. While the two types are sometimes regarded as a single breed, since 1984 they have been classed as separate breeds in the U.S.

DESCRIPTION

These popular, firm-bodied dogs are familiar to most people. The flat coat of the Smooth is mainly white, with tan, or black and tan markings. The coarse, broken coat of the Wire is dense and wiry, with a soft, short under-coat, and comes in the same colors. The feet of both varieties are small and neat and the V-shaped ears fold and fall forward. The tail is usually docked to three-quarters of its length.

TEMPERAMENT

Keen, alert and independent, the Fox Terrier needs to be firmly trained from an early age. It is generally an easy dog to live with, and enjoys being part of the family. Amazing stories are told of the animal's loyalty and devotion. It is quite reliable with children, although it can be argumentative and feisty with other dogs, even large ones. Fox Terriers make good watchdogs, although the

Male: 14–16 in (36–41 cm)
15–20 lb (7–9 kg)
Female: 13–15 in (33–38 cm)
13–18 lb (6–8 kg)

ring. However, if the dog is simply a family pet, the same straightforward care as for the Smooth will suffice to keep the dog clean and comfortable and looking neat and smart.

high-pitched barking can be annoying and may cause problems with neighbors. They may be too boisterous for elderly owners.

GROOMING

The shorthaired coat of the Smooth is easy to groom. Brush with a firm bristle brush, and bathe or dry shampoo when necessary. The coat of the more common Wire presents a few more problems if the dog is to look smart and shapely, since the coat must be kept well trimmed. Professional groomers have quite a bag of tricks to keep the Wire looking its best for the show

EXERCISE & FEEDING

Given a small garden, these irrepressible and athletic dogs will get enough exercise running around by themselves, but if you live in an apartment, you will need to take them for regular long walks or romps in the park, off the leash if possible. Keep on the leash, however, if there are small animals about, as the urge to hunt is strong and they are likely to take off after cats or rabbits. There are no special feeding requirements, but measure the amount of food against the level of activity.

HEALTH PROBLEMS

A hardy breed, these dogs are subject to few genetic weaknesses, although they do have trouble with skin allergies. They are also susceptible to genetic eye diseases, such as dislocatiing lenses and cataracts.

Miniature Schnauzer

*A dog of clean habits and neat size, the perky Miniature
Schnauzer makes a delightful little companion for an apartment
dweller or someone with a small house and yard.*

HISTORY

The Miniature Schnauzer
is the smallest of the
three Schnauzer breeds
(see pp. 358–9), all of which
originated in Germany. They
are only classified as terriers
in the U.S.; most countries
classify all Schnauzers as
utility or working dogs.

DESCRIPTION

A strong, angular, square-
looking dog, the Miniature
Schnauzer has a harsh, wiry
double coat that comes in
salt and pepper or any solid
color, sometimes with white
on the chest. The thick,
prominent eyebrows and
long mustache are often
trimmed to accentuate the
dog's square-cut shape and
the tail is usually docked.

TEMPERAMENT

These dogs are noted for their
reliability and affectionate
nature and make excellent
watchdogs. They are spirited
and brave, and while not
aggressive they will take on
much larger dogs should they
feel the need.

GROOMING

The wiry coat is reasonably
easy to look after, but unless
it is combed or brushed daily
with a short wire brush, it
will become matted. Clip
out any knots. The animal
should be clipped all over to
an even length twice a year,
in spring and fall, but this is a
job best left to an expert. Trim
around the eyes and ears with
blunt-nosed scissors and clean
the whiskers after meals.

EXERCISE & FEEDING

These energetic little dogs
enjoy long, brisk, daily walks,
and relish play sessions off
the leash. There are no
special feeding requirements.

HEALTH PROBLEMS

Schnauzers are reasonably
healthy dogs, although they
may suffer from bladder
stones, liver disease, diabetes
and epilepsy.

PET FACTS

- Spirited, lively, affectionate
- Daily brushing
- Regular, moderate
- Ideal for apartment living, but needs plenty of exercise
- Excellent watchdog

✱ BE AWARE

- The ears are sometimes cropped, but this practice is illegal in Britain. In many countries, breeders are now leaving the tails of Schnauzers undocked

Male: 12–14 in (30–36 cm)
11–18 lb (5–8 kg)
Female: 11–13 in (28–33 cm)
10–15 lb (5–7 kg)

Bull Terrier

Although surprisingly gentle, the Bull Terrier is a powerful and determined animal and needs firm handling. Even the much smaller Miniature is not a dog for timid or inexperienced owners.

Miniature
Male: Up to 14 in (36 cm)
Up to 20 lb (9 kg)
Female: Up to 14 in (36 cm)
Up to 20 lb (9 kg)

PET FACTS

 Determined, fearless, playful

 Regular brushing

 Regular, moderate

 Adapts well to urban living, but needs space to exercise

 Excellent watchdog

BE AWARE

• May be aggressive with other dogs

HISTORY

Bull Terriers were developed in Britain by crossing Bulldogs with Whippets and a variety of terriers. They were once used to bait bulls and for dog fighting, and were prized for their courage, tenacity, agility and speed. The Miniature was developed to have the same qualities in a dog of more manageable size.

DESCRIPTION

A thick-set, muscular, well-proportioned animal, the Bull Terrier has a short, dense coat that comes in pure white, black, brindle, red, fawn and tricolor. Its most distinctive feature is its head, which is almost flat at the top, sloping evenly down to the end of the nose. The eyes are small, dark and closely set.

TEMPERAMENT

A tenacious fighter, the Bull Terrier is more of a danger to other dogs than to people. When properly trained it is usually sweet natured, gentle and playful. Some dogs, however, suffer from obsessive compulsive behaviors, such as tail chasing.

GROOMING

The smooth, shorthaired coat is easy to groom. Brush with a firm bristle brush, and bathe or dry shampoo as necessary. The coat will benefit from a rub with a piece of toweling or chamois.

EXERCISE & FEEDING

Bull Terriers need plenty of exercise, but keep them leashed at all times in public. There are no special feeding requirements, but don't over-feed as they are inclined to become overweight and lazy.

HEALTH PROBLEMS

While generally hardy dogs, Bull Terriers may suffer from blood clotting disorders and dislocating lenses. Some pups are born deaf.

Standard
Male: 21–22 in (53–56 cm)
52–56 lb (23–25 kg)
Female: 21–22 in (53–56 cm)
45–60 lb (20–27 kg)

Staffordshire Bull Terrier

A trustworthy, all-purpose dog, the Staffordshire Bull Terrier is intelligent and affectionate, very good with children and an excellent watchdog that will intimidate any intruder.

PET FACTS

Tough, brave, reliable

Daily brushing

Regular, moderate

Adapts well to urban living, but needs plenty of exercise

Excellent watchdog

BE AWARE

- Can be aggressive to other dogs. Must be leashed in public

HISTORY

A ferocious fighter, the medium-sized Staffordshire Bull Terrier was used in England for bull baiting and dog fighting until both of these pastimes were outlawed. It was also used to hunt badgers. Like the Bull Terrier, it has Bulldog blood in its makeup, giving it that broad-chested look of immovability.

DESCRIPTION

A substantial, muscular, well-proportioned animal, the Staffordshire has a short, dense coat that comes in white or solid reds, fawn, brindle, black or blue, or any of these colors with white.

TEMPERAMENT

Usually adored and adoring within its own family circle, the Staffordshire needs firm and consistent training to curb its instinct to fight with other dogs. As pups, they tend to chew a great deal so make sure you provide them with plenty of chew toys.

GROOMING

The smooth, shorthaired coat is easy to groom. Brush every day with a firm bristle brush, and bathe or dry shampoo as necessary. The coat will gleam if rubbed with a piece of toweling or chamois.

EXERCISE & FEEDING

Staffordshire Bull Terriers must have plenty of regular exercise, but keep them on the leash in public places at all times. There are no special feeding requirements, but don't overfeed.

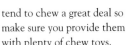

HEALTH PROBLEMS

Staffordshire Bull Terriers are relatively free of genetic problems, although some dogs may suffer from cataracts. They may also be subject to breathing problems and can become overheated in very hot weather.

Male: 14–16 in (36–41 cm)
25–38 lb (11–17 kg)
Female: 13–15 in (33–38 cm)
23–35 lb (10–16 kg)

American Staffordshire Terrier

Stoic and reliable, the American Staffordshire Terrier is a dog few strangers would mess with, yet with its own family, this powerful, fine-looking animal is devoted, gentle and loving.

PET FACTS

 Tough, reliable, courageous

 Daily brushing

 Regular, moderate

 Adapts well to urban living, but needs plenty of exercise

 Excellent watchdog

BE AWARE

• To avoid dog fights, keep leashed in public

HISTORY

Developed independently after early Staffordshires were taken to the U.S. during the nineteenth century, the American Staffordshire Terrier is now larger and bigger-boned than its British cousin. It has been recognized as a separate breed since 1936, the qualification "American" being added in 1972.

DESCRIPTION

The American Staffordshire looks much like the British, although it is a larger dog overall. It probably bears an even closer resemblance to Bulldogs of about a century ago, from which it is directly descended. The coat comes in all colors.

TEMPERAMENT

The American Staffordshire should never be confused with the notorious Pit Bull Terrier. Although it is a courageous and tenacious fighter if provoked, and needs firm, kind training to control this instinct, its basic temperament toward people is gentle and loving.

GROOMING

The smooth, shorthaired coat is easy to groom. Brush every day with a firm bristle brush, and bathe or dry shampoo as necessary. A rub with a piece of toweling or chamois will make the coat gleam.

EXERCISE & FEEDING

American Staffordshire Terriers must have plenty of regular exercise, but keep them leashed in public to avoid fights with other dogs. There are no special feeding requirements, but don't overfeed these dogs as they are inclined to put on weight and become lazy.

HEALTH PROBLEMS

Although not particularly long-lived, this breed is reasonably free of genetic weaknesses. Some dogs, however, develop hip dysplasia or cataracts.

Male: 17–19 in (43–48 cm)
40–50 lb (18–23 kg)
Female: 16–18 in (41–46 cm)
35–45 lb (16–20 kg)

Bedlington Terrier

In full show trim, the Bedlington Terrier looks more like a lamb than a dog, but it has retained its terrier qualities and is a surprisingly fast runner. It makes a devoted companion.

HISTORY
Once known as the Rothbury Terrier, the Bedlington Terrier gets its speed, agility and grace of movement from its Whippet blood. These attributes once made it popular with poachers, and it earned the nickname of Gypsy Dog. Its work also included ratting in the Northumberland mines.

DESCRIPTION
The body is flexible and muscular, covered in a thick and slightly curly coat with a woolly undercoat. It comes in solid blue, liver and sandy beige, or particolored tan with any of these colors. The eyes are dark to light hazel, depending on the coat color.

TEMPERAMENT
Although they can be stubborn, Bedlington Terriers are relatively easy to train and very affectionate. They love to be the center of attention and make very good watchdogs.

GROOMING
The coat does not shed and requires specialized clipping every six weeks, so it is probably best if you learn to do this yourself. The coat is thinned and clipped close to the head and body to accentuate the shape. Shave the ears closely, leaving a tassel on the tips. On the legs, the hair is left slightly longer. Have a professional groomer show you how to do it. Brush the dog regularly and clean and pluck inside the ears.

PET FACTS

 Alert, intelligent, curious

 Specialized

 Regular, moderate

 Adapts well to urban and apartment living, but needs plenty of exercise

Very good watchdog

BE AWARE
- It is an enthusiastic digger
- Can be scrappy with other dogs and is a formidable fighter when provoked

EXERCISE & FEEDING
These active dogs need plenty of exercise and, like other terriers, will be bored and mischievous without it. There are no special feeding requirements.

HEALTH PROBLEMS
Bedlington Terriers may have a serious inherited liver problem known as Copper Storage Disease. They are also prone to hereditary kidney disease and eye problems, such as cataracts and retinal disease.

Male: 16–17 in (41–43 cm)
18–23 lb (8–10 kg)
Female: 15–16 in (38–41 cm)
18–23 lb (8–10 kg)

Irish Terrier

Known for its fighting spirit, the game little Irish Terrier is not for everyone, but it is very adaptable and its courage and loyalty are unquestioned. The breed has a growing band of admirers.

HISTORY
Among the oldest of the terriers, the Irish Terrier is only now regaining some of the immense popularity it once enjoyed. Admired for its pluck and unconquerable spirit, it was widely used as a guard dog and for hunting foxes, badgers and otters. Later, it excelled in the dog-fighting ring. It is closely related to the Wire Fox Terrier (see p. 385) but is slightly longer and larger.

DESCRIPTION
The Irish Terrier looks a little like a small version of the Airedale Terrier (see p. 391). Its hard, short, wiry coat may be solid red, red-wheaten or yellow-red. The tail is docked to three-fourths of its length.

TEMPERAMENT
While sociable with people and devoted to its owner, this dog has an often uncontrollable urge to fight with other dogs, which makes it unsuitable for inexperienced owners.

GROOMING
The hard double coat is easy to groom and rarely sheds. Brush regularly with a stiff bristle brush and remove the dead hair with a fine-toothed comb. Bathe only when necessary.

PET FACTS

- Intelligent, loyal, brave
- Regular brushing
- Regular, vigorous
- Adapts well to urban living, but needs plenty of exercise
- Excellent watchdog

BE AWARE
- Very argumentative with other dogs

EXERCISE & FEEDING
Being bred for active work, these dogs need plenty of regular exercise. When walking in public, always keep the dog firmly under control on a leash so that it doesn't fight with other dogs. There are no special feeding requirements.

HEALTH PROBLEMS
Irish Terriers are a robust breed but may suffer from a hereditary urinary problem as well as foot and eye diseases.

Male: 16–19 in (41–48 cm)
25–30 lb (11–14 kg)
Female: 15–18 in (38–46 cm)
23–28 lb (10–13 kg)

Soft-coated Wheaten Terrier

A jolly creature, the Soft-coated Wheaten Terrier seems to retain its carefree puppy ways into adulthood. Its enthusiasm and zest for life make it a delightful companion and pet.

HISTORY

The Soft-coated Wheaten Terrier is now rare in Ireland, where it is thought to have originated, as well as most other parts of the world. An exception is the U.S., where it currently enjoys wide popularity. Like the Irish Terrier, it once earned its keep by performing guard duties, herding sheep and hunting badgers, otters, rats and rabbits.

DESCRIPTION

This is a strong, medium-sized dog with good proportions and great stamina. The soft single coat is long and wavy and doesn't shed. It comes in wheaten shades (pale yellow to fawn).

The face is adorned with a beard and mustache, with lots of hair falling over the eyes. The tail is usually docked.

TEMPERAMENT

Friendly and appealing, the Wheaten is intelligent and easy to train. It makes an excellent watchdog.

GROOMING

Frequent, even daily, combing of the long, profuse coat with a medium-toothed comb is recommended to keep it free of tangles, beginning when the dog is a puppy. The object is to achieve a natural look and brushing can make the soft coat fuzzy.

Clean the eyes and check the ears carefully. Bathe or dry shampoo when necessary.

EXERCISE & FEEDING

These dogs can get by with moderate exercise as long as it is regular. There are no special feeding requirements.

HEALTH PROBLEMS

Wheatens are hardy dogs, but may suffer from hip dysplasia, skin allergies and eye problems, such as PRA. They are also subject to hereditary kidney disease.

Male: 18–20 in (46–51 cm)
35–45 lb (16–20 kg)
Female: 17–19 in (43–48 cm)
30–40 lb (14–18 kg)

Airedale Terrier

A lively, water-loving dog, the Airedale Terrier is very adaptable and fits in well with family life as long as it has plenty of exercise and is not allowed to rule the roost.

HISTORY
Largest of the terriers, the Airedale was developed in Yorkshire to hunt otters, badgers and wolves, becoming particularly popular in the Aire Valley. It has since been used extensively in police and military work.

DESCRIPTION
A medium-sized dog with a strong, straight back, the Airedale has a jaunty, alert stance. The stiff, wiry, waterproof coat comes in a combination of dark grizzle or black with red and tan markings, and the face is adorned with beard, mustache and bushy eyebrows. The straight tail, usually docked to the same height as the head, is carried erect. The small, V-shaped ears fold forward to the sides.

TEMPERAMENT
Airedales are intelligent, reliable and loyal. They are not difficult to train, but they don't respond to harsh or overbearing training methods. They are naturally lively and love children.

GROOMING
The Airedale's hard, short-haired, double coat is easy to groom and sheds very little.

Brush regularly with a stiff bristle brush to remove the dead hair and bathe only when necessary.

EXERCISE & FEEDING
Being bred for active work, these dogs need plenty of exercise. An adjusted omega-6:omega-3 fatty acid ratio in the diet is recommended if the dog suffers from dry, itchy skin.

HEALTH PROBLEMS
While a generally robust breed, the Airedale may suffer from eye problems, hip dysplasia and skin infections.

PET FACTS

- Reliable, loyal, lively
- Regular brushing
- Regular, moderate
- Adapts well to urban living, but needs plenty of exercise
- Good watchdog

BE AWARE
- These dogs are incorrigible diggers and are easily bored, so keep them occupied

Male: 23–24 in (58–61 cm)
40–50 lb (18–23 kg)
Female: 22–23 in (56–58 cm)
40–45 lb (18–20 kg)

TOY DOGS

Chihuahua

Adored by its owners, the intriguing Chihuahua is prized for its tiny size. Although not the best dog for young children, this bright-eyed, dainty creature is perfect for apartment dwellers.

PET FACTS

Affectionate, alert, playful

Regular brushing

Regular, gentle

Ideal for apartment living

Poor watchdog

BE AWARE

• These dogs tend to snap out of fear, so be especially careful when handling

HISTORY
Little is known about the Chihuahua (pronounced chu-wah-wah) before its discovery in Mexico about 100 years ago, although the breed is believed to date back to at least the ninth century.

DESCRIPTION
This is the smallest breed of dog in the world and there are two distinct coat types: smooth and short, or long. The dogs are otherwise identical and can occur in the same litter, although, in Britain, the two are considered separate and never interbred. Every coat color and color combination occurs.

TEMPERAMENT
The Chihuahua is intensely loyal and becomes very attached to its owner, even to the point of jealousy. When strangers are present, it follows its owner's every move, keeping as close as possible. It learns quickly and responds well to training.

GROOMING
The smooth, shorthaired coat should be gently brushed occasionally or simply wiped over with a damp cloth. The long coat should be brushed daily with a soft bristle brush. Bathe both types about once a month, taking care not to get water in the ears. Check the ears regularly and keep the nails trimmed.

EXERCISE & FEEDING
Although it is tempting to carry these dainty creatures about, they will keep fitter if taken for walks. A body harness is safer than a collar. There are no special feeding requirements, but feed small amounts twice a day.

HEALTH PROBLEMS
Although reasonably healthy, Chihuahuas do suffer from eye problems, collapsing trachea, dislocating kneecaps and heart disease.

Male: 6–9 in (15–23 cm)
2–6 lb (1–3 kg)
Female: 6–8 in (15–20 cm)
2–6 lb (1–3 kg)

Pekingese

Venerated since ancient times by the Chinese, the tiny Pekingese is, perhaps, the ultimate lapdog, a devoted companion quite content to loll on a cushion or a lap for as long as one is available.

HISTORY

These fabled dogs once led a pampered life in the Imperial Court of Peking, where the smallest specimens were sometimes carried around in the sleeves of royalty.

DESCRIPTION

This is one of the few breeds in which the female is heavier than the male. The extravagant, long, straight, flowing coat has profuse feathering and comes in all colors, except albino and liver. The face is flat with a dark, wrinkled muzzle and drooping heart-shaped ears. These tiny, heavy-boned dogs have a characteristic rolling gait.

TEMPERAMENT

Although small, Pekingese are excellent watchdogs. They are loyal, alert, courageous and good tempered, and fit in well with the family routine.

GROOMING

Daily combing and brushing of the very long, double coat is essential. Take extra care around the hindquarters, which can become soiled and matted. Females shed the undercoat when in season. Dry shampoo regularly. Clean face and eyes daily and check the hairy feet for burrs and objects that stick there.

EXERCISE & FEEDING

Pekingese are disinclined to take walks and, although they don't need much exercise, they will stay in better health if given regular sessions of play activity. There are no special feeding requirements, but Pekingese will quickly become obese if overfed.

HEALTH PROBLEMS

Pekingese often encounter difficulty when giving birth

PET FACTS	
🐕	Intelligent, devoted, determined
	Special care is needed
	Regular, gentle
	Ideal for apartment living
	Excellent watchdog for its size

🐾 BE AWARE

- Eyes are vulnerable to injury and to corneal ulcers
- Breathing problems may require surgery to correct

and should be under the care of a veterinarian at this time. Like other short-nosed breeds, they are subject to breathing problems. The prominent eyes are very sensitive, and prone to corneal ulcers and injury.

Male: 6–9 in (15–23 cm)
10–14 lb (5–6 kg)
Female: 6–9 in (15–23 cm)
10–14 lb (5–6 kg)

Papillon

A real charmer, the Papillon steals hearts with its dainty elegance and amusing antics. It loves to be the center of attention and enjoys being fussed over, so it makes a delightful companion or family pet.

HISTORY
The origin of the Papillon (French for "butterfly" and pronounced pah-pee-yon) is uncertain, but by the sixteenth century it had become a breed cherished among the European nobility.

DESCRIPTION
Because of the tail, which is long and plumed and carried curled over the back, the Papillon was once called a Squirrel Spaniel. Its long, lustrous coat is white with patches of any color, except liver. The "butterfly" ears are heavily fringed and there is a well-defined white noseband.

TEMPERAMENT
Intelligent and adaptable, these animated little dogs have perky, friendly natures, but tend to become quite possessive of their owners. As watchdogs, their usefulness is limited by their tiny size, but at least they will alert you to unusual noises or the arrival of strangers.

GROOMING
Daily combing and brushing of the long, silky, single coat is important and fairly straightforward. These dogs are usually clean and odorless. Bathe or dry shampoo when necessary. Keep the nails clipped and have the teeth cleaned regularly because they tend to accumulate tartar.

EXERCISE & FEEDING
These playful little dogs love to go for a run but won't fret too much if confined to the house for days at a time. Like any dog, they benefit from a regular exercise regimen. There are no special feeding requirements for this breed.

PET FACTS

- Animated, friendly, alert
- Daily brushing
- Regular, gentle
- Ideal for apartment living
- Not a good watchdog

BE AWARE

- Sensitive to some commonly used anesthetics
- Papillons are small enough to wriggle through fences that might appear to be secure

HEALTH PROBLEMS
In general, Papillons are a fairly robust breed although they do suffer from some eye and knee problems.

Male: 8–11 in (20–28 cm)
8–10 lb (4–5 kg)
Female: 8–11 in (20–28 cm)
7–9 lb (3–4 kg)

Pomeranian

While the Pomeranian adores pampering and petting, it also loves to play and be active. In other words, it is a most accommodating creature, ready to fit in with the needs of any type of owner.

anything unusual by setting up a commotion of barking. Although excitable, it is obedient and easily calmed.

HISTORY
The Pomeranian resembles the much larger sled-pulling Spitz-type dogs from which it is descended. It was deliberately bred down in size during the nineteenth century, when toys and miniatures were very popular.

DESCRIPTION
This little dog looks like a walking powderpuff of black, gray, blue, orange, cream, shaded sable or particolored hair. Its small, cheeky, fox-like face peers out from an outsize ruff. The spectacular tail is carried over the back.

TEMPERAMENT
Easy to train, the happy little Pomeranian makes a good watchdog, despite its tiny size. It will alert you to

GROOMING
Frequent brushing of the very long, double coat is recommended. If you work from the head, parting the coat and brushing it forward, it will fall neatly back in place, so the task, although time-consuming, is relatively easy. The cottony undercoat is shed once or twice a year. Dry shampoo when necessary. Clean the eyes and ears daily and take the dog for regular dental checkups.

EXERCISE & FEEDING
There is no need to make special provision for exercise if there is a small area for the dog to play in. Otherwise, a session of play in the park from time to time will suffice.

PET FACTS

	Lively, loyal, friendly
	Frequent brushing
	Regular, gentle
	Ideal for apartment living
	Good watchdog despite its size

BE AWARE
- Barking can become a problem if not curbed from an early age
- Will lose teeth early if not well cared for

There are no special feeding requirements for this breed.

HEALTH PROBLEMS
The breed is subject to eye problems and the knees are susceptible to dislocation. Many animals lose their teeth as they get older.

Male: 7–12 in (18–30 cm)
3–7 lb (1–3 kg)
Female: 7–12 in (18–30 cm)
3–7 lb (1–3 kg)

Yorkshire Terrier

Originally, Yorkshire Terriers were pressed into service as ratters, a job they did very well. Later, they claimed the spotlight with their unusual appearance and quickly became a favored breed as pets.

HISTORY

Developed only a little more than a century ago, the Yorkshire Terrier is a mysterious blend of various terriers, English, Scottish and Maltese. The toys we see today are much smaller than their forebears and the breed enjoys great popularity.

DESCRIPTION

The ultra-long, fine, silky coat parts along the spine and falls straight down on either side. It is steel-blue on the body and tail, and tan elsewhere. Puppies are usually black and tan. The tail is usually docked to half its length. If the dogs are not for showing, many owners opt for a natural shaggy look.

TEMPERAMENT

Alert, indomitable and spirited, the Yorkshire Terrier is also admired for its loyalty. Despite its diminutive size, it makes an excellent watchdog, defending its territory in no uncertain manner.

GROOMING

For show purposes, there are many tricks to caring for the Yorkshire Terrier's long, single coat, and strict guidelines must be adhered to. For the ordinary pet owner, daily combing and brushing and regular shampooing are necessary to keep the lustrous hair in top condition. This involves quite a commitment in time and effort.

EXERCISE & FEEDING

Although it doesn't need a lot of exercise, this lively little warrior will benefit from regular opportunities to run and play. There are no special feeding requirements.

HEALTH PROBLEMS

Yorkshire Terriers are subject to eye problems, including cataracts, progressive retinal atrophy and dry eye. They also suffer from deterioration of the hip joint, dislocation of the knee and collapsing trachea. If they cannot be encouraged to chew hard foods, their teeth will need to be scaled regularly.

PET FACTS

 Brave, feisty

 Daily, extensive

 Regular, gentle

 Ideal for apartment living

Good watchdog despite its size

BE AWARE

- Barking can cause problems with neighbors

- These dogs are not good with children

Male: 7–9 in (18–23 cm)
4–7 lb (2–3 kg)
Female: 7–9 in (18–23 cm)
3–7 lb (1–3 kg)

Japanese Chin

The lovely little Japanese Chin is truly a dog to dote on and will gladly return the love that is unfailingly lavished upon it. It is a superlative lapdog with few, if any, flaws or vices.

HISTORY
These gorgeous little dogs have been known in Western countries for only about 150 years. However, they were the pampered pooches of wealthy Japanese, including royalty, for many centuries, having been introduced to Japan from China in ancient times. They are probably distantly related to the Pekingese.

DESCRIPTION
The Japanese Chin looks like a tiny toy. The profuse, straight, longhaired coat comes in white with markings either of black or shades of red. The gait is graceful with the feet lifted high off the ground.

TEMPERAMENT
The engaging little Chin is a lively, happy, sweet-tempered animal, the perfect size for small living spaces. With its gentle ways and charming manners, it is perhaps best suited to homes in which there are no small children.

GROOMING
Although the coat looks as though it might be difficult, a few minutes each day will keep it looking beautiful. Comb out tangles and brush lightly, lifting the hair to leave it standing out a little. A professional dog groomer can show you the correct technique. Dry shampoo occasionally and bathe only when necessary. Clean the eyes every day and check the ears regularly for any signs of infection.

EXERCISE & FEEDING
While they don't require a great deal of exercise, Chins love a daily walk and an opportunity to play in the open. There are no special feeding requirements, but they prefer to "graze" on small meals and tidbits.

HEALTH PROBLEMS
The large and prominent eyes are vulnerable to damage and subject to cataracts and progressive retinal atrophy.

PET FACTS

- Intelligent, lively, gentle
- Daily brushing
- Regular, gentle
- Ideal for apartment living
- Poor watchdog

BE AWARE
- Matted hair must be clipped off the feet

Male: 7–11 in (18–28 cm)
Up to 9 lb (4 kg)
Female: 7–11 in (18–28 cm)
Up to 9 lb (4 kg)

Silky Terrier

Bred purely as a lively companion, the dainty Silky Terrier exhibits the best traits of its several forebears. It is a confident, entertaining little dog with a charm all its own.

HISTORY

Derived from several toy and terrier varieties, including the Yorkshire Terrier, which it resembles, the Silky Terrier was developed in New South Wales, Australia in very recent times. It is also known as the Sydney Silky. It was never intended to work, but in spite of its tiny size, it is an excellent watchdog.

DESCRIPTION

The body is small and strong with a silky coat that falls straight down on either side of a spinal parting. The coat is long except on the face and ears, and comes in either blue or gray-blue with tan. The tail is usually docked.

TEMPERAMENT

Alert and intelligent, the Silky Terrier is easy to train.

GROOMING

Daily combing and brushing and a regular shampoo are necessary to keep the lustrous hair in top condition. This involves quite a commitment from its owners. After bathing, make sure the dog is thoroughly dry and warm. The coat must be trimmed occasionally, and the hair on the legs from the knees down is often trimmed short. If the hair that falls over the eyes is tied up in a topknot, the dog will find it easier to see.

EXERCISE & FEEDING

This energetic little dog delights in extended play sessions and has surprising stamina. It needs regular exercise and activity to stay fit and happy. There are no special feeding requirements for this breed.

PET FACTS

Courageous, alert, affectionate

Daily, extensive

Regular, moderate

Ideal for apartment living, but needs plenty of exercise

Excellent watchdog for its size

BE AWARE

- It is an enthusiastic digger

- Can be jealous and may pick fights with other dogs

HEALTH PROBLEMS

These hardy dogs generally enjoy good health, although they may suffer from genetic eye diseases and, like many of the toy breeds, they are subject to collapsing trachea.

Male: 9–10 in (23–25 cm)
8–11 lb (4–5 kg)
Female: 9–10 in (23–25 cm)
8–11 lb (4–5 kg)

Maltese

Celebrated since Roman times and perhaps even earlier, the main purpose in life of the glamorous little Maltese has always been to lift the spirits of its countless doting owners.

HISTORY

Especially favored by women through the ages, the gentle Maltese is featured in many famous paintings.

DESCRIPTION

With its compact little body, short legs and silky, dazzlingly white coat, this dog is sure to be the center of attention. The oval eyes are large and dark, with black rims. The profuse single coat falls long and straight, parting along the spine and eventually reaching the ground, concealing the legs and feet completely. It is always white, sometimes with lemony or beige markings. The tail arches gracefully over the back.

TEMPERAMENT

Intelligent and easy to train, the Maltese enjoys being groomed, petted and fondled. Lively and alert, it will let you know by barking if strangers are about.

GROOMING

Daily combing and brushing of the long coat is important, but be gentle as the coat is very soft. Clean the eyes daily to prevent staining, and clean the beard after meals for the same reason. Bathe or dry shampoo regularly, making sure the animal is thoroughly dry and warm afterward. Clean the ears and pull out hairs growing inside the ear canal. The eyes should be checked regularly and cleaned if necessary. The hair on the top of the head is often tied up in a topknot to keep it away from the eyes.

EXERCISE & FEEDING

Maltese enjoy a regular walk or play session and remain playful well into old age. Do not overfeed. To avoid dental problems, encourage these dogs to chew on hard, crunchy foods.

PET FACTS

- Even-tempered, affectionate
- Regular, extensive. Be gentle with soft coat
- Regular, gentle
- Ideal for apartment living
- Adequate watchdog

BE AWARE

- The eyes are inclined to weep from time to time, staining the face
- These dogs can be difficult to house-train

HEALTH PROBLEMS

This breed is generally long-lived, hardy and healthy. Like most purebred dogs, however, they are subject to genetic eye diseases.

Male: 8–10 in (20–25 cm)
4–6 lb (1.5–3 kg)
Female: 8–10 in (20–25 cm)
4–6 lb (1.5–3 kg)

Shih Tzu

Entertaining little dogs that love company, Shih Tzus like nothing better than to sit on your lap and be groomed—which is just as well, because the magnificent coat demands extensive care.

HISTORY

A number of similarities suggest that the Shih Tzu (pronounced shidzoo) is descended from Tibet's Lhasa Apso, possibly as a result of being crossed with the Pekingese after it was introduced into China. The Shih Tzu is also known as the Chinese Lion Dog or the Chrysanthemum Dog.

DESCRIPTION

This is a proud-looking little dog with a long body and short legs. The thick, long, luxuriant coat can be any color, but a white blaze on the forehead and a white tip on the tail are very desirable.

TEMPERAMENT

Endowed with loads of character, the gentle, loyal Shih Tzu makes friends easily and responds well to training.

Male: Up to 11 in (28 cm)
9–16 lb (4–7 kg)
Female: Up to 11 in (28 cm)
9–16 lb (4–7 kg)

GROOMING

Daily combing and brushing of the long, soft, double coat with a steel comb and a bristle brush is essential, with extra care during shedding. The long hair on the top of the head is usually tied in a topknot to keep it out of the dog's eyes. Dry shampoo as necessary and bathe once a month. Check the ears regularly for infection and remove food scraps from the beard after meals. Clip out any matting on the feet.

EXERCISE & FEEDING

These are naturally active little dogs but, if allowed, like to lounge about in their own particular spot. They should be encouraged to get out and about and will keep fitter with a daily walk. There are no special feeding requirements, but don't overfeed or they will quickly become fat.

HEALTH PROBLEMS

The prominent eyes are prone to injury and tend to get dry from exposure, causing them to ulcerate. Shih Tzus are also subject to ear infections and inherited kidney problems, and they may suffer breathing difficulties in hot weather.

PET FACTS

 Friendly, playful, independent

 Extensive

 Regular, gentle

 Ideal for apartment living

 Adequate watchdog

 BE AWARE

- Ear infections are common due to the abundance of hair around the ears

- Prone to heatstroke

Toy Poodle

The dainty Toy Poodle loves company and is the perfect pet for an older or less active person with time to pamper this diminutive natural clown and be amused by its antics.

HISTORY

The Toy Poodle is the smallest version of the Poodle (see pp. 414–5), originally used in Germany and France as a retriever of waterfowl. Later, it was favored by circus performers for its comic appearance and because it was easy to train.

DESCRIPTION

This active little dog has a dense, woolly coat of springy curls. The hair keeps growing and is not shed and, for this reason, the Toy Poodle is often recommended as a pet for people with allergies. The coat comes in solid red, white, cream, brown, apricot, black, silver and blue.

TEMPERAMENT

Sensitive and remarkably intelligent, the Toy Poodle is highly responsive and very easy to train. It makes a very good watchdog for its size.

GROOMING

Poodles must be bathed regularly and clipped every six to eight weeks. Clean and check the ears frequently for wax or infection and pull out hairs growing inside the ear canal. The traditional clips were developed to lighten the weight of the coat for swimming and to protect the joints and chest from cold and thorns, but many pet owners opt for a plain lamb clip, the same length all over. The teeth need regular scaling.

EXERCISE & FEEDING

Although they love to go for a walk, and will keep in better humor and be fitter if given regular opportunities to run free and play, Toy Poodles are not demanding as far as exercise goes. There are no special feeding requirements.

PET FACTS

Very intelligent, loyal

Comb and brush daily

Regular, gentle

Ideal for apartment living

Very good watchdog for its size

BE AWARE

- When purchasing a puppy, check carefully for genetic disorders

- These dogs prefer to live indoors

HEALTH PROBLEMS

Toy Poodles are subject to dislocated knees, epilepsy, diabetes and genetic eye diseases, such as progressive retinal atrophy and cataracts.

Male: Up to 11 in (28 cm)
6–9 lb (3–4 kg)
Female: Up to 11 in (28 cm)
6–9 lb (3–4 kg)

Pug

Not at all pugnacious, this lovable softie is even-tempered and good with children. Pugs love company and only want to be your best friend, but they will sulk if left out of family activities.

PET FACTS

 Smart, sociable, mischievous

 Daily brushing

 Regular, moderate

Ideal for apartment living if given enough exercise

Good watchdog

🐾 **BE AWARE**

• A Pug's prominent eyes are prone to injury

• Prone to sinus and breathing problems

HISTORY

Although dogs very similar to Pugs appear on ancient Chinese porcelain and paintings, the origin of the breed is shrouded in mystery. They seem always to have been house dogs or pets rather than dogs bred for any particular task.

DESCRIPTION

While not exactly handsome, the Pug, nevertheless, has a certain appeal. It has a square, thickset, stocky body with a sleek, soft coat that comes in fawn, apricot, silver and black, all with black muzzle and velvety ears. Moles on the cheeks are considered beauty spots. The tail lies in a tight curl, or even, in the best specimens, a double curl on the back. The jaunty, rolling gait is quite distinctive.

TEMPERAMENT

Intelligent, easily trained, and with a big bark for its size, the Pug makes a good watchdog. It is playful, loyal and affectionate and makes a captivating companion that will shadow your every move or curl up on your lap.

GROOMING

The smooth, shorthaired coat is easy to groom. Brush and comb with a firm bristle brush, and shampoo only when necessary. Clean the creases on the face regularly.

EXERCISE & FEEDING

Strong dogs with short straight legs, Pugs enjoy energetic games and will keep in better health if given regular exercise. Don't overfeed, as Pugs will eat more than is good for them, quickly becoming obese and living much shorter lives.

HEALTH PROBLEMS

Pugs are stressed by both hot and cold weather and are accustomed to living indoors. They are prone to allergies and the short muzzle contributes to chronic breathing problems.

Male: 12–14 in (30–36 cm)
13–20 lb (6–9 kg)
Female: 10–12 in (25–30 cm)
13–18 lb (6–8 kg)

Miniature Pinscher

The Min-Pin, as it is often called, is a very active terrier-type of dog. Its courage is undoubted, and it was valued in Germany, where it originated, as a ratting dog of outstanding vigilance and tenacity.

PET FACTS

🐕 Brave, lively, playful

🪮 Daily brushing

🦴 Regular, gentle

🏠 Ideal for apartments, but barking can be a problem

🐾 Excellent watchdog for its size

🐾 **BE AWARE**

- These inquisitive dogs will take off at any opportunity

- Prone to chew small objects that may choke them

HISTORY

Known only in Germany until about 100 years ago, these dogs are now popular throughout the world.

DESCRIPTION

A small, neat dog with a characteristic high-stepping, "hackney" gait, this breed makes a lively and delightful pet. The coat comes in black, blue and chocolate, all with sharply defined tan markings on the face and matching patches on the chest and above the eyes. Solid reds are also seen. The tail is usually docked short.

TEMPERAMENT

This brave, playful little dog will bark and nip at intruders and, for its size, makes an excellent watchdog. It is not suited to families with small children because, if handled roughly, it is likely to be injured and react aggressively.

GROOMING

The smooth, shorthaired, hard coat is easy to groom. Comb and brush with a firm bristle brush, and shampoo only when necessary. Loose hair can be removed by wiping over with a warm, damp washcloth.

EXERCISE & FEEDING

These dogs don't require a lot of exercise but should be given regular opportunities to run and play. Any yard in which they run loose needs to have a fence high enough to prevent their determined efforts to escape and explore. There are no special feeding requirements.

HEALTH PROBLEMS

Miniature Pinschers are robust animals on the whole, but are subject to eye and joint problems. Bitches often have difficulty giving birth and should be under the care of a veterinarian at this time.

Male: 10–12 in (25–30 cm)
8–10 lb (4–5 kg)
Female: 10–11 in (25–28 cm)
8–9 lb (about 4 kg)

Chinese Crested

If you are looking for a novelty, this may be just the pet for you, but choose a Chinese Crested only if you are ready to return the affection this dainty little creature is so eager to give.

HISTORY

It is not known how or even where this breed originated, although it seems to have existed in ancient China. There are many similarities to the Mexican Hairless.

DESCRIPTION

There are two distinct varieties of this unusual dog: one is hairless, except for its head, feet and tail, and called, not surprisingly, the Hairless; the other, the Powderpuff, has a coat of long, soft hair. Both come in numerous colors, either solid or mixed, or all-over spotted. Strangely, the two types often occur in the same litter.

TEMPERAMENT

Chinese Cresteds tend to become very attached to their owners and have difficulty adjusting to new ones. They crave constant companionship.

GROOMING

Daily combing and brushing of the long, fine, double coat of the Powderpuff is important, with extra care required when the dog is shedding. The woolly under-coat becomes matted if neglected. Bathe the Hairless frequently and massage a little oil or cream into the skin to keep it supple.

EXERCISE & FEEDING

Although these dogs enjoy brisk walks, they do just as well with regular sessions of play. There are no special feeding requirements, but do not overfeed these dogs, as they will become obese if given the chance. They may be reluctant to chew hard foods as they often have an incomplete set of teeth.

HEALTH PROBLEMS

The skin of the Hairless reacts to contact with wool and must be protected from sunburn. This variety is also unsuited to cold climates.

PET FACTS

Lively, gentle, devoted

Powderpuff needs daily brushing. Hairless needs little attention

Regular, gentle

Ideal for apartment living

Not a good watchdog

BE AWARE

- The Hairless is allergic to wool and vulnerable to sunburn

Male: 9–13 in (23–33 cm)
Up to 12 lb (5 kg)
Female: 9–13 in (23–33 cm)
Up to 12 lb (5 kg)

Cavalier King Charles Spaniel

A fearless, lively little dog with a cheerful disposition, the Cavalier King Charles Spaniel is friendly and sociable with both people and other dogs, and is far more hardy than the average toy breed.

PET FACTS

 Lively, friendly, playful

 Regular brushing

Regular, gentle

Ideal for apartment living

Adequate watchdog

BE AWARE

- These dogs are highly prone to heart disease

tricolored black, tan and white. The coat is long and silky and free of curls, although it is sometimes wavy. The ears are long, silky and well feathered, as are the legs and feet.

HISTORY

Developed from a cross between a King Charles and a Cocker Spaniel (see p. 326), the Cavalier differs greatly from its forebears. Its breeders were trying to reproduce a toy dog similar to those seen in portraits from the time of England's Charles II—he was said to dote on these animals.

DESCRIPTION

Compact and handsome, the Cavalier is slightly larger than the King Charles and has a longer muzzle, but comes in the same colors: solid reds, chestnut and white, black and tan, and

TEMPERAMENT

The Cavalier is easily trained, clean and sensible, and makes a delightful and diverting companion.

GROOMING

The smooth, longhaired coat is easy to groom. Comb or brush with a firm bristle brush, and bathe or dry shampoo as necessary. Always make sure the dog is thoroughly dry and warm after a bath. Check the eyes and ears carefully for any signs of infection.

EXERCISE & FEEDING

Whatever exercise you can provide will be just fine with this adaptable dog, although it does enjoy a good romp in the park. There are no special feeding requirements.

HEALTH PROBLEMS

Although it is classed as a toy, the Cavalier has little of the fragility usually associated with these breeds. However, heart disease is very common. They are also subject to hereditary eye diseases and dislocating kneecaps, and the long, well-feathered ears are prone to infection.

Male: 12–13 in (30–33 cm)
10–18 lb (5–8 kg)
Female: 12–13 in (30–33 cm)
10–18 lb (5–8 kg)

Italian Greyhound

A graceful and delicate-looking dog, the Italian Greyhound is a perfect miniature of its larger forebear. A clean, odorless animal, it will adapt happily to any reasonably quiet, loving home.

PET FACTS

- Obedient, loving, sensitive
- Minimal
- Regular, moderate
- Adapts well to urban living if kept in a quiet household
- Not a good watchdog

BE AWARE
- Prone to broken legs and slipped kneecaps

HISTORY
The Italian Greyhound has been around since ancient Egyptian times. Whatever its original purpose, perhaps flushing birds, chasing small game or killing rats, it has been bred for the past few centuries purely as a pet. In most countries it is classified as a toy breed.

DESCRIPTION
Lithe and streamlined, these dogs are capable of short bursts of speed. The glossy, satiny coat comes in various shades of fawn, cream, white, red, blue, black and fawn, and white splashed with any of these colors.

TEMPERAMENT
As it tends to be timid and must be handled very gently, this is a pet for a quiet household where there are no lively children. In stressful situations it needs constant reassurance by stroking.

GROOMING
This dog is one of the very easiest to groom. All that is needed to keep the fine, silky coat gleaming is a rubdown with a piece of rough toweling or chamois. If absolutely necessary, the animal can be bathed, but make sure it is thoroughly dry and warm afterward.

EXERCISE & FEEDING
Italian Greyhounds are active little dogs and love to run free and play as well as have regular walks. There are no special feeding requirements.

HEALTH PROBLEMS
Italian Greyhounds are prone to broken legs and slipped kneecaps, especially when they are young. They are also susceptible to hereditary eye problems and seizures, and because of their fine coats they should not be exposed to extreme weather conditions.

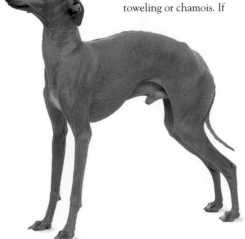

Male: 12–15 in (30–38 cm)
6–10 lb (3–5 kg)
Female: 12–15 in (30–38 cm)
6–10 lb (3–5 kg)

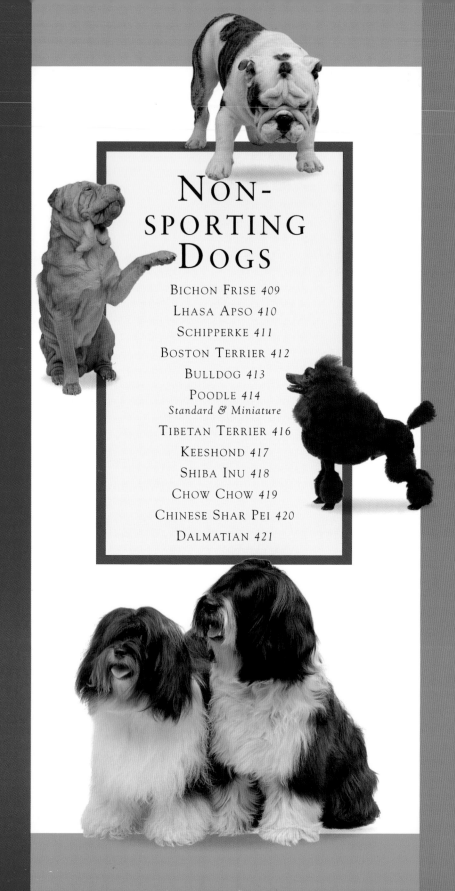

NON-SPORTING DOGS

Bichon Frise

It's easy to see why people are enchanted by the fluffy Bichon Frise. It loves to be the center of attention and is always eager to please—altogether a delightful and amusing companion.

HISTORY

Although it first came to notice as the darling of French royalty during the sixteenth century (*bichon* is French for lapdog; *frisé* means curly), the Bichon Frise is thought to have originated in the Canary Islands and was once called the Teneriffe. Its French or Belgian forebears may have been taken there by sailors.

DESCRIPTION

This sturdy, confident little dog has a lively, prancing gait and a puffy white coat, sometimes with cream or apricot markings. The eyes are round and dark and the large, round nose is black.

TEMPERAMENT

A gregarious individual, the Bichon Frise is playful and merry and not aggressive to people or other dogs. It is intelligent and easy to train.

GROOMING

Daily brushing of the long, soft coat with a stiff bristle brush is essential. The fine, silky hair falls naturally in curls and is usually cut with scissors to follow the contours of the body and brushed out to a soft cloud. Dry shampoo as necessary and bathe once a month. Trim around the eyes and ears with blunt-nosed scissors and clean the eyes meticulously to prevent staining.

EXERCISE & FEEDING

These are active little dogs and play will take care of most of their exercise needs, but they do love a walk and especially a romp in the open. There are no special feeding requirements.

HEALTH PROBLEMS

Bichon Frises are a fairly sturdy breed, although some of them may suffer from epilepsy and dislocating kneecaps. They are also subject to eye problems, such as cataracts and blocked tear ducts, the last of which can cause the eyes to run, staining the white coat.

PET FACTS

- 🐕 Charming, friendly, alert
- 〰 Extensive
- 🐕 Regular, gentle
- 🏠 Ideal for apartment living
- 🐕 Good watchdog

🐾 **BE AWARE**
- If neglected, the coat quickly becomes a sorry, matted mess

Male: 9–12 in (23–30 cm)
7–12 lb (3–5 kg)
Female: 9–11 in (23–28 cm)
7–12 lb (3–5 kg)

Lhasa Apso

This bewitching creature seems to be composed entirely of hair, but the Lhasa Apso is neither a toy nor a lapdog. It is a rugged little animal that earns its keep as a companion and watchdog.

HISTORY
Rarely seen outside Tibet until fairly recently, the Lhasa Apso was bred in monasteries as a temple and palace sentinel. It takes part of its name from the Tibetan capital, Lhasa.

DESCRIPTION
This shaggy little dog looks like a small version of the Old English Sheepdog. Gold, creams and honey are the most popular colors, but the coat also comes in dark grizzle, smoke, slate and particolors of black, white or brown.

TEMPERAMENT
Adaptable, affectionate and loyal, these hardy little dogs thrive on human companionship and don't like to be left alone. Their hearing is acute and they will alert you to any unusual sounds and to the approach of strangers. They are playful, intelligent, easily trained dogs and make delightful companions.

GROOMING
The long topcoat parts along the spine and falls straight on either side. Daily combing and brushing is important. The thick undercoat will become matted if neglected. Dry shampoo as necessary. Some owners opt for easier care with a short all-over clip. Check the feet for matting and for foreign matter stuck there. Clean eyes and ears meticulously.

EXERCISE & FEEDING
Although they love to walk and scramble about and will be fitter and happier if given regular opportunities to run free and play, Lhasa Apsos don't demand exercise. There are no special feeding requirements, but clean any dribbles of food off the beard after each meal to avoid staining and matting.

HEALTH PROBLEMS
Lhasa Apsos are relatively free of health problems, although they may suffer from genetic kidney problems. Poor ventilation of the ears may cause ear infection.

PET FACTS

- Playful, devoted, alert
- Daily, extensive
- Regular, gentle to moderate
- Ideally suited to apartment living
- Very good watchdog

BE AWARE
- They need a lot of grooming
- Nervous around strangers

Male: 10–11 in (25–28 cm)
14–18 lb (6–8 kg)
Female: 9–10 in (23–25 cm)
12–16 lb (5–7 kg)

Schipperke

While the agile, hardy and independent little Schipperke is remarkably self-sufficient, it is sociable, adapts well to family life and makes a well-behaved, loyal and affectionate pet.

HISTORY
The name possibly derives from the Flemish for "little boatman," because Schipperkes (pronounced skipper-keys) were popular watchdogs on Belgian barges, keeping rats and mice in check. They are probably related to the Groenendael, a Belgian Shepherd Dog.

DESCRIPTION
These small dogs have a harsh double coat, usually black, but gold and some other solid colors do occur. The hair is smooth on the fox-like head, elsewhere more erect, and the male has a standing ruff around the neck. Schipperkes are often born without a tail. If a tail is present, it is closely docked within a few days of birth.

Male: 10–13 in (25–33 cm)
12–16 lb (5–7 kg)
Female: 9–12 in (23–30 cm)
10–14 lb (5–6 kg)

TEMPERAMENT
This plucky little dog backs down for nobody and makes an excellent watchdog. It is alert and very curious, and nothing escapes its attention. Undemanding and devoted to its owner, it looks on itself as part of the family.

GROOMING
The Schipperke is very clean and pretty much takes care of its own grooming, but to keep the medium-length double coat in top condition, comb and brush regularly with a firm bristle brush. Dry shampoo when necessary.

EXERCISE & FEEDING
In general, Schipperkes are an active breed. While some will be content with sessions of free play in a yard or park, others will want at least a long daily walk. There are no special feeding requirements.

PET FACTS

- Curious, brave, loyal
- Minimal
- Regular, moderate
- Adapts well to urban living and is ideal for an apartment if given plenty of exercise
- Excellent watchdog

BE AWARE
- This dog tends to be very suspicious of strangers

HEALTH PROBLEMS
This breed is remarkably free of genetic problems, apart from the common eye diseases and occasional hip problems. Some dogs get mild skin infections, but these are easily treated.

Boston Terrier

Besides being an excellent watchdog, the Boston Terrier has much to recommend it—easy-care, handy size and a delightful disposition. No wonder it is one of the most popular breeds in the US.

HISTORY
The Boston Terrier's direct forebears are English and French Bulldogs and the White English Terrier. It was developed in the US only about 150 years ago as a fighting dog, a pastime that has since been outlawed. Although it is still always ready to scrap with other dogs, its behavior toward people is not aggressive.

DESCRIPTION
Boston Terriers are compact and well-muscled dogs. Their faces are unmistakeable, with short, wide muzzles, prominent eyes set far apart and short, erect ears. These dogs come in brindle or black, both with white markings.

TEMPERAMENT
Playful and very affectionate, they like to be part of the family. They are reliable with children, intelligent, easy to train and, despite being relatively small, make excellent watchdogs.

GROOMING
The smooth, shorthaired, fine, glossy coat is easy to groom. Comb and brush with a firm bristle brush, and bathe only when necessary. Wipe the face with a damp cloth every day and clean the prominent eyes carefully. Check both the ears and eyes for grass seeds. The nails should be clipped from time to time.

EXERCISE & FEEDING
Regular walks or sessions of free play in a fenced yard are all Boston Terriers need to stay in shape. In summer, they should be exercised only in the cooler parts of the day. There are no special feeding requirements.

PET FACTS

	Playful, devoted, fearless
	Daily brushing
	Regular, moderate
	Ideal for apartment living
	Excellent watchdog

BE AWARE

- Bitches often experience difficulties giving birth to their large-headed pups

HEALTH PROBLEMS
These short-faced dogs may have breathing difficulties when stressed by exertion. Whelping is often difficult as the pelvis is narrow, and the large-headed pups are often delivered by Cesarean section. Heart and skin tumors are common problems in this breed. The prominent eyes are prone to injury.

Male: 11–15 in (28–38 cm)
15–25 lb (7–11 kg)
Female: 11–15 in (28–38 cm)
15–25 lb (7–11 kg)

Bulldog

These stalwarts have come to epitomize determination and the broad-chested stance certainly suggests immovability, if not downright stubbornness. Yet Bulldogs make loving and lovable pets.

HISTORY

In earlier times, Bulldogs were fighting dogs that would take on opponents such as bulls, bears, badgers, or even other dogs in the ring. When such bloodsports became unpopular, breeders concentrated on developing the breed's non-ferocious traits.

DESCRIPTION

The coat comes in reds, fawn, brindle or fallow, or white pied with any of these colors. The muzzle is sometimes dark. With its stocky legs set squarely at each corner of its compact, muscular body, the Bulldog's deliberate gait has become a waddle.

TEMPERAMENT

Absolutely reliable, and although its appearance can be somewhat intimidating, it is among the gentlest of dogs. Just the same, it will see off any intruder, and few would risk a close encounter with a dog brave enough to bait a bull.

GROOMING

The smooth, fine, shorthaired coat is easy to groom. Comb and brush with a firm bristle brush, and bathe only when necessary. Wipe the face with a damp cloth every day to clean inside the wrinkles and prevent them from becoming smelly.

EXERCISE & FEEDING

Bulldogs would just as soon not take any exercise, but they will stay fitter if given

some regular, not overly strenuous activity such as walking. Be careful not to overfeed them as they easily become obese. They can also be somewhat possessive of their food.

HEALTH PROBLEMS

Whelping is difficult and the large-headed pups are usually delivered by Cesarean section. Bulldogs are prone to breathing difficulties because of their short muzzles. Some have small windpipes as well. They are also stressed by exertion and hot or cold weather.

PET FACTS

 Reliable, gentle, kind

Daily brushing

Regular, moderate

Adapts well to urban living

Very good watchdog

BE AWARE

- Bulldogs tend to drool and snore

- Prone to chronic respiratory problems

Male: 14–16 in (36–41 cm)
45–55 lb (20–25 kg)
Female: 12–14 in (30–36 cm)
35–45 lb (16–20 kg)

Poodle

Once a Poodle owner, always a Poodle owner—fanciers of this breed seldom become attached to another. The winning ways of these clever animals captivate almost everyone.

HISTORY

Known since the thirteenth century, the Poodle is a gundog originally used in Germany and France as a retriever of waterfowl. Later, it was favored by circus performers for its comic appearance and because it was very easy to train. Despite the claims of several other countries, France has now been officially recognized as its country of origin, and the breed occupies a special place in the affections of the French. Its ancestors probably include the French Barlut and the Hungarian Water Hound.

DESCRIPTION

Poodles come in three officially recognized sizes, Standard (the largest), Miniature and Toy (the smallest, see p. 404). They are active, sure-footed dogs with excellent balance, moving lightly and easily with a springy, trotting gait. Their dense, woolly coats of springy curls are either brushed out to a soft cloud and clipped in one of several standard styles, or simply combed for a more natural look. The fine, harsh-textured hair keeps growing and is not shed, and for this reason the Poodle is often recommended as a pet for people with allergies. The coat comes in solid white, cream, brown, apricot, black, silver and blue. Puppies' tails are usually docked at birth to half their length in Standard dogs and two-thirds of their length in Miniatures and Toys.

PET FACTS

Very intelligent, loyal

Comb and brush daily

Regular, moderate

Ideal for apartment living, but needs plenty of exercise

Very good watchdog, particularly the Standard

BE AWARE

• When purchasing a puppy, check carefully for genetic disorders

• These dogs fret if not given enough human company

TEMPERAMENT

Considered by many the most intelligent of all breeds, the Poodle makes a very good watchdog for its size, seldom becoming aggressive. It has a great sense of fun, loves to play and will feel slighted if left out of family activities. Somewhat sensitive, it may become jealous of children.

Miniature
Male: 11–15 in (28–38 cm)
15–17 lb (7–8 kg)
Female: 11–15 in (28–38 cm)
15–17 lb (7–8 kg)

GROOMING

Poodles must be bathed regularly and clipped every six to eight weeks. Check the ears frequently for mites and pull out hairs if necessary. The traditional clips were developed to reduce the weight of the coat for swimming and to protect the joints and chest from cold and thorns, but many pet owners opt for a plain lamb clip, the same length all over, because it is easier and more economical to maintain. The teeth, especially of Miniatures, need regular scaling.

EXERCISE & FEEDING

Poodles adore water and love to go for walks, but are not demanding as far as exercise goes. They will, however, keep happier and fitter if given regular opportunities to run and play off the leash. The Standard retains its sporting instincts, has great stamina and needs more activity than the smaller varieties. To prevent bloat, feed two or three small meals a day instead of one large one, and avoid exercise after meals.

HEALTH PROBLEMS

A long-lived breed, Poodles are, nevertheless, subject to many genetic diseases. Cataracts and progressive retinal atrophy may cause blindness, and allergies and skin conditions are common. Miniatures are subject to diabetes, epilepsy and heart disease, and Standards to hip dysplasia, cancer and bloat.

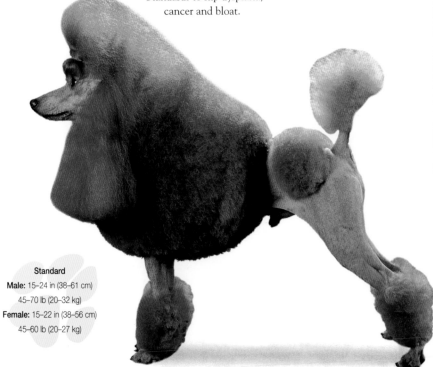

Standard
Male: 15–24 in (38–61 cm)
45–70 lb (20–32 kg)
Female: 15–22 in (38–56 cm)
45–60 lb (20–27 kg)

Tibetan Terrier

While it is treasured in its native Tibet as a symbol of good luck, you will probably cherish your appealing little Tibetan Terrier more for its delightful ways and joyous zest for life.

HISTORY

Still something of a rarity in Western countries, the Tibetan Terrier was little known outside Tibet until about 70 years ago. It is not a true terrier as it does not dig prey out of burrows. In its homeland it is something of an all-purpose farm dog.

PET FACTS

Loving, alert, playful

Regular combing

Regular, gentle

Ideal for apartment living

Good watchdog

BE AWARE

- They are very energetic dogs, requiring regular play

- They are good jumpers, so escape-proof your yard

DESCRIPTION

This compact little animal is nimble and sure-footed—it will stand on its hind legs and jump quite high to see what is on a table, especially if senses food. The shaggy coat is fine and long, falling over the face. It comes in white, golden, cream, gray shades, silver, black, particolor and tricolor. The tail is well feathered and carried proudly curled over the back.

TEMPERAMENT

These gentle, engaging animals are easy to train, alert and full of bravado. They will certainly let you know if strangers are around.

GROOMING

Comb the long, double coat every second day with a metal comb to keep it free of tangles. The dense, fine, woolly undercoat is shed twice a year and extra care is needed during shedding. Bathe or dry shampoo as necessary.

Trim around the eyes with blunt-nosed scissors and check the ears regularly.

EXERCISE & FEEDING

Sessions of play and regular walks will keep this lively dog fit and happy. There are no special feeding requirements, but if allowed they can become finicky about their food.

HEALTH PROBLEMS

Tibetan Terriers are generally fairly robust, although they do suffer from some genetic eye diseases and occasional thyroid problems.

Male: 14–16 in (36–41 cm)
18–30 lb (8–14 kg)
Female: 13–15 in (33–38 cm)
16–25 lb (7–11 kg)

Keeshond

A natural watchdog, the Keeshond is a great favorite in its native Holland, in spite of not being considered a pure-bred. It is a long-lived dog and becomes deeply attached to its owners.

HISTORY

Originally used as watchdogs on barges in Holland, the Keeshond (pronounced kays-hond) was sometimes called the "smiling Dutchman" for its perpetual good-natured grin. It is a member of the Spitz group of dogs and has the typical tightly curled tail.

DESCRIPTION

Keeshonden are compact, muscular animals with a cream or pale gray undercoat and a luxurious outer coat that comes in shades of gray with black tips and stands away from the body. The markings are quite definite and there are distinctive pale "spectacles" around the eyes.

TEMPERAMENT

Reliable, adaptable, easy to care for and loyal to its family, the Keeshond is a natural watchdog and easy to train for other tasks.

GROOMING

Grooming is not as onerous as you might expect, but daily brushing of the long coat with a stiff bristle brush is important. Brush with the grain first, then lift the hair with a comb, against the grain, and lay it back in place. Bathe or dry shampoo only when necessary. The dense undercoat is shed twice a year, in spring and fall.

EXERCISE & FEEDING

These dogs will readily adapt to an exercise regimen, whether it be demanding or easy, but they will keep fitter with regular activity. Don't use a choke chain as it will spoil the spectacular ruff. There are no special feeding requirements, but beware of overfeeding as they put on weight quickly.

HEALTH PROBLEMS

While generally robust, some Keeshonden are subject to diabetes, heart defects and genetic eye diseases.

PET FACTS

- Gentle, intelligent, devoted
- Daily brushing
- Regular, moderate
- Ideal for apartment living, but needs plenty of exercise
- A natural watchdog

BE AWARE
- Ticks are hard to locate in the dense undercoat

Male: 17–19 in (43–48 cm)
55–65 lb (25–29 kg)
Female: 16–18 in (41–46 cm)
50–60 lb (23–27 kg)

Shiba Inu

Because of its convenient size and vivacious, outgoing personality, the Shiba Inu is now the most commonly owned pet dog in its native Japan, and is gaining in popularity worldwide.

HISTORY

The Shiba Inu is the smallest of the Japanese Spitz-type dogs and was originally bred to flush birds and small game from brushwood areas. The name Shiba possibly comes from a Japanese word for brushwood, or it may derive from an old word meaning small (*inu* means dog).

DESCRIPTION

The Shiba looks like a much smaller version of the Akita (see p. 364). Agile and well proportioned, it has a strong body and alert bearing. The double coat usually comes in red tones, sable or black and tan, with pale shadings on the legs, belly, chest, face and tail.

TEMPERAMENT

Lively and good natured, Shibas are smart but some-what difficult to train. They are very independent and choose which commands to obey. Although extremely sociable, they can be aggressive to unfamiliar dogs.

GROOMING

The coarse, stiff, shorthaired coat is easy to groom. Brush with a firm bristle brush, and bathe only when absolutely necessary as this removes the natural waterproofing of the coat.

EXERCISE & FEEDING

This is an active dog needing lots of exercise. There are no special feeding requirements.

HEALTH PROBLEMS

The breed is generally hardy and healthy with few genetic weaknesses. Its waterproof, all-weather coat protects it in both cold and hot conditions, so it can live outdoors if you have a secure yard of reasonable size. However, it does regard itself as part of the family and doesn't like to be left alone outside.

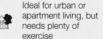

Male: 14–16 in (36–41 cm)
20–30 lb (9–14 kg)
Female: 13–15 in (33–38 cm)
18–28 lb (8–13 kg)

Chow Chow

An appealing, unusual-looking dog, the Chow Chow is less exuberant than many of its fellows, but nevertheless affectionate and loyal. It has a growing band of devotees around the world.

HISTORY
Physically very similar to fossilized remains of ancient dogs, the Spitz-type Chow Chow probably originated in Siberia or Mongolia. Used as a temple guard, it later became the favored hunting dog of Chinese emperors. It was almost unknown in the West until about 120 years ago.

DESCRIPTION
The two most distinctive features of the Chow Chow are its blue-black tongue and its almost straight hind legs, which make its walk rather stilted. Its dense, furry, double coat is profuse and comes in solid black, red, fawn, cream, blue or white, sometimes with lighter or darker shades, but never particolored. The ears are small and rounded and there is a huge ruff behind the head, which gives it a lion-like appearance.

TEMPERAMENT
Although something of a challenge to train, the strong-willed Chow Chow makes a very good watchdog. It has a reputation for ferocity, probably undeserved, but is a tenacious fighter if provoked.

GROOMING
Regular brushing of the long outer coat is important to maintain the lifted, standing-out look. Extra care is needed when the dog is shedding its dense undercoat. Dry shampoo when necessary.

EXERCISE & FEEDING
Chow Chows can be lazy, but they will keep fitter with regular exercise. There are no special feeding requirements, but don't overfeed.

HEALTH PROBLEMS
These dogs have problems with hip and elbow dysplasia and are prone to genetic eye diseases.

Male: 18–23 in (46–56 cm)
50–65 lb (23–29 kg)
Female: 18–22 in (46–53 cm)
45–60 lb (20–27 kg)

Chinese Shar Pei

The Chinese Shar Pei is thought to be about 2,000 years old. The loose, wrinkled skin gives these animals an appealingly worried, forlorn look.

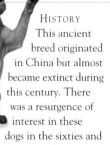

HISTORY

This ancient breed originated in China but almost became extinct during this century. There was a resurgence of interest in these dogs in the sixties and they are now popular pets.

DESCRIPTION

Both heavily wrinkled dogs with large heads and smaller-headed dogs with tighter-looking skins occur in this breed. The stiff, short, bristly coat feels rough to the touch and comes in black, red, fawn, apricot and cream, often with lighter tones on the backs of the hindquarters and tail. The small ears fall forward and the tail is carried in a curl. Like the Chow Chow, these dogs have a blue-black tongue.

TEMPERAMENT

Once used as fighting dogs, the well-mannered Chinese Shar Pei has a surprisingly friendly, easy-going nature and makes a delightful companion, although it may be aggressive toward other dogs. It needs firm but gentle training and is a good watchdog.

GROOMING

Regular brushing with a bristle brush is enough to keep the unusual coat in good condition. Dry shampoo or bathe when necessary and keep an eye out for mites.

EXERCISE & FEEDING

Chinese Shar Peis need regular exercise, but keep them on a leash in public. There are no special feeding requirements.

PET FACTS

Amiable, intelligent, independent

Regular brushing

Regular, moderate

Adapts well to urban living, but needs plenty of space

Good watchdog

🐾 BE AWARE

- These are high-maintenance dogs as they require a great deal of medical attention. Many have chronic skin problems and require corrective eye surgery

HEALTH PROBLEMS

There may be problems with in-turned eyelids, a condition known as entropion that can result in blindness and usually requires corrective surgery. Chinese Shar Peis are also prone to chronic skin problems, including allergies, infections and mites.

Male: 18–20 in (46–51 cm)
40–55 lb (18–25 kg)
Female: 18–20 in (46–51 cm)
40–55 lb (18–25 kg)

Dalmatian

Exuberant and fun-loving, the Dalmatian is an excellent choice for anyone with the time to exercise and train it. Although it always turns heads, it is much more than a mere fashion accessory.

HISTORY
The handsome Dalmatian's origins are obscure, but in nineteenth-century Europe, and particularly Britain, its main work was to run beside horse-drawn carriages. This may have been to protect the travelers inside or perhaps merely for appearance. It also kept the stables clear of rats.

DESCRIPTION
A picture of elegance, the Dalmatian is of medium size with the lean, clean lines of the Pointer, to which it may be related. It is well muscled and has a short, hard, dense coat of pure white with well-defined, black or liver-colored spots randomly splashed over it. The feet are round with well-arched toes and the nails are either white or the same color as the spots.

TEMPERAMENT
Spirited and playful, these dogs adore children and can be trusted with them. They are rather sensitive, so training takes patience and gentle but firm handling. They like to spend time with their owners.

GROOMING
The smooth, lustrous, short-haired coat is easy to groom. Comb and brush with a firm bristle brush, and bathe only when necessary.

EXERCISE & FEEDING
A Dalmatian is not an ideal dog for apartment dwellers unless it can be taken out for a brisk walk or run several times a day. It needs plenty of vigorous exercise. There are no special feeding requirements.

HEALTH PROBLEMS
Dalmatians have problems with skin allergies and urinary bladder stones. They are also prone to deafness.

PET FACTS

- Gentle, sensitive, energetic
- Daily brushing
- Regular, vigorous
- Adapts well to urban living, but needs plenty of space
- Good watchdog

🐾 BE AWARE

- Newborn pups are spotless; markings develop during the first year
- Make sure a puppy's hearing has been checked before purchasing

Male: 19–23 in (48–58 cm)
50–65 lb (23–29 kg)
Female: 19–23 in (48–58 cm)
45–60 lb (20–27 kg)

HERDING DOGS

Shetland Sheepdog

The Sheltie, as it is affectionately known, is well endowed with both beauty and brains. Intuitive and responsive to its owner's wishes, it makes a charming family pet, becoming deeply attached.

History

This beautiful dog looks like a small version of the Collie (see p. 431), but it has developed over centuries on the Shetland Islands where it was used for herding sheep. Other Shetland animals, notably ponies and sheep, are also miniaturized.

Description

Strong, nimble and lightly built, the Sheltie is a fast runner and can jump well. The most common colors for the long, shaggy coat are sable, blue merle and tricolor, but it also comes in black with white or tan.

Temperament

Alert and remarkably intelligent, the sensitive Sheltie likes to feel like part of the family. It is easy to train, but may be shy with strangers.

Grooming

The coat is easier to care for than you might expect, but regular brushing is important. Mist the coat lightly with water before you begin and tease out mats before they get bad, but use the comb sparingly. The dense undercoat is shed twice a year, in spring and fall. The coat readily sheds dirt and mud and Shelties are quite fastidious about their cleanliness. Bathe or dry shampoo only when absolutely necessary.

Exercise & Feeding

This active, graceful dog needs lots of exercise, preferably running free. There are no special feeding requirements.

Health Problems

While Shelties are generally healthy, some dogs may suffer from cataracts and progressive retinal atrophy, as well as liver and skin disease. Blue merles should be checked for any signs of deafness.

PET FACTS

- Obedient, loyal, intelligent
- Regular brushing
- Regular, moderate
- Ideal for apartment living, but needs plenty of exercise
- Good watchdog

BE AWARE

- Excessive barking can be a problem with this breed
- Sensitive to some heartworm preventatives

Male: 13–15 in (33–38 cm)
14–18 lb (6–8 kg)
Female: 12–14 in (30–36 cm)
12–16 lb (5–7 kg)

Pembroke Welsh Corgi

Long associated with royalty, especially the British monarchy, the Pembroke Welsh Corgi is a widely recognized and popular pet. Its neat size and affectionate nature alone recommend it.

HISTORY
The Pembroke and Cardigan Welsh Corgis have been considered separate breeds for only about 70 years. The origins of both are open to conjecture, but the Pembroke is thought to have been taken to Wales from Belgium by weavers about 1,000 years ago. It was greatly valued for herding sheep and cattle in the steep hills.

DESCRIPTION
The long, powerful little body is set on short, well-boned legs. The coat comes in red, sable, fawn, tan and black, all with or without white. The most noticeable difference from the Cardigan is in the tail. The Pembroke's is quite short or docked very close to the body.

TEMPERAMENT
Pembrokes adore children, but because their way of getting sheep or cattle to move is to nip at their heels, they have a tendency to also nip people. This trait should be firmly discouraged from an early age. They are wary of strangers and make very good watchdogs.

GROOMING
The soft, medium-length, water-resistant coat is easy to groom. Comb and brush with a firm bristle brush, and bathe only when necessary. The coat is shed freely twice a year.

EXERCISE & FEEDING
Naturally active little dogs, they should always be encouraged to remain so. There are no special feeding requirements, but don't overfeed or they will become obese and lazy.

PET FACTS

- Affectionate, loyal, independent
- Regular brushing
- Regular, gentle
- Ideal for apartment living, but needs plenty of exercise
- Very good watchdog

BE AWARE
- Heavy shedding twice a year and some year-round dropping of hair

HEALTH PROBLEMS
This breed is reasonably healthy. However, the short legs and long back make it prone to slipped disks in the spine. There may also be problems with epilepsy and hereditary eye diseases, such as cataracts and progressive retinal atrophy.

Male: 10–12 in (25–30 cm)
25–30 lb (11–14 kg)
Female: 10–12 in (25–30 cm)
24–28 lb (11–13 kg)

Cardigan Welsh Corgi

Although it has not attained the widespread popularity of the Pembroke, the Cardigan Welsh Corgi is a great favorite in Wales, and in fact predominates in many rural communities.

the coat comes in any color, except pure white. Slightly longer in the body than the Pembroke, the Cardigan also differs by having a long, thick tail and larger, more widely spaced ears.

PET FACTS

 Obedient, alert, intelligent

 Regular brushing

 Regular, gentle

 Ideal for apartment living, but needs plenty of exercise

 Very good watchdog

BE AWARE
- These dogs may suffer from spinal problems

HISTORY

The Cardigan Welsh Corgi may have arrived in Wales from Scandinavia, but whatever its origins, it has become indispensable for the herding of cattle in parts of that country's rugged terrain. The dogs nip at the heels of the large beasts, then duck out of the way of vengeful kicks.

DESCRIPTION

A tough, fearless little animal, it can move very fast on its short, well-boned legs. The face is quite fox-like and

TEMPERAMENT

Intelligent and easy to train, Cardigans make obedient little workers. Like Pembrokes, they should be firmly discouraged from nipping. Because of their tendency to nip, they are not well suited to households with children. Wary of strangers, they make very good watchdogs.

GROOMING

The wiry, medium-length, water-resistant coat is easy to groom. Comb and brush with a firm bristle brush, and bathe only when necessary. The coat is shed twice a year.

EXERCISE & FEEDING

Even more active than the Pembroke, Cardigans must

have regular exercise. There are no special feeding requirements, but don't overfeed or they will become obese and lazy.

HEALTH PROBLEMS

While generally hardy, they share with the Pembroke a susceptiblity to spinal problems and some inherited eye disorders.

Male: 10–13 in (25–33 cm)
25–30 lb (11–14 kg)
Female: 10–13 in (25–33 cm)
25–30 lb (11–14 kg)

Puli

*The "dreadlocks" worn in such a carefree way by the Puli are
a special adaptation to protect the animal from extremes of
weather. In mature coat, these dogs are an amazing sight.*

HISTORY

This fabulous dog is currently enjoying unprecedented popularity in its native Hungary, where it was originally prized as an excellent sheepdog and guard. Before this, it may have lived in Central Asia. Like a few other herding breeds, it jumps on or over the backs of the sheep while moving them along.

DESCRIPTION

The wiry, medium-sized Puli is among the most unusual-looking dogs in the world. Its long, dense, water-resistant double coat falls in naturally matted cords, eventually reaching the ground and hiding its legs completely. The hair is usually black, often reddish or tinged with gray, but it also occurs in white, gray, or apricot. The gait is quick and skipping. The tail is of medium length and curled over the back.

TEMPERAMENT

Pulis, or more correctly Pulik, are agile, intelligent creatures that respond well to training—they are used successfully as police dogs in Hungary and make great companions.

GROOMING

This coat does not shed and is often left in its natural state—simply separate the strands with your fingers from time to time. The dog can be bathed when necessary, but disturb the cords as little as possible. Clean around the ears and eyes regularly. Some owners prefer to clip their dog and not allow the coat to cord.

EXERCISE & FEEDING

Pulik are energetic and lively and enjoy plenty of regular activity, but take it easy on hot days. There are no special feeding requirements.

HEALTH PROBLEMS

These dogs are fairly hardy, although they may suffer from hip dysplasia and eye problems. They are not suited to hot climates.

Male: 16–18 in (41–46 cm)
25–35 lb (11–16 kg)
Female: 14–16 in (36–41cm)
20–30 lb (9–14 kg)

Australian Cattle Dog

The Australian Cattle Dog, also known as a Heeler, has in its make-up the best characteristics of its several antecedents. If you need a working dog, this is as good as they get.

PET FACTS

 Diligent, courageous, loyal

 Minimal

 Regular, vigorous

 Adapts well to urban living, but needs plenty of exercise

 Excellent watchdog

BE AWARE
- Check puppies for any signs of deafness before purchasing

DESCRIPTION

Not your average pampered pooch, this tough, medium-sized dog was bred for hard work. There are two coat colors: speckled blue, with tan or black markings, or speckled red, with dark red markings.

HISTORY

A potent cocktail of blood runs in the veins of the Australian Cattle Dog: blue merle Collie, Dalmatian, Old English Sheepdog, Australian Kelpie, the little-known Smithfield and the native Dingo. The result is a working dog with few equals, ready, willing and able to drive cattle across vast distances under harsh, hot, dusty conditions. Both its guarding and herding instincts are very strong and may extend to people and other pets.

TEMPERAMENT

The Australian Cattle Dog is absolutely loyal and obedient to its master, but it is something of a one-person dog. It may also feel compelled to establish dominance over other dogs.

GROOMING

The coarse, shorthaired, weather-resistant coat needs little care and is very easy to groom. Just comb and brush with a firm bristle brush, and bathe only when necessary.

EXERCISE & FEEDING

These animals have incredible stamina and will enjoy all the activity you can give them. Exercise is of paramount importance—without enough they can be bored and destructive. There are no special feeding requirements.

HEALTH PROBLEMS

While Australian Cattle Dogs are extremely hardy, they may suffer from hereditary deafness and occasional eye problems, such as progressive retinal atrophy.

Male: 17–20 in (43–51 cm)
32–35 lb (15–16 kg)
Female: 17–19 in (43–48 cm)
30–35 lb (14–16 kg)

Border Collie

Ready, willing and able sums up the Border Collie asleep at your feet. You might think you've succeeded in tiring him out, but move a muscle and he'll be instantly alert, ready to learn a new trick.

HISTORY
Developed for herding sheep in the rugged Scottish border country, the Border Collie's speed and stamina made it an outstanding worker and now a favorite worldwide.

DESCRIPTION
These athletic little dogs have well-proportioned bodies, lean and well muscled. The medium-length, double coat comes mainly in black with white, sometimes tricolored with tan, and also blue merle with white markings. There is often lavish feathering on the legs, underbody and tail, and a ruff behind the head. It is noted for the way it mesmerizes sheep with its eyes.

TEMPERAMENT
Highly intelligent and eager to please, Border Collies are easily obedience trained, but harsh training can make them submissive. They are wonderful pets, especially in homes with energetic children, but can be scrappy and jealous with other dogs.

GROOMING
Regular combing and brushing will keep the coat gleaming, with extra care needed when the soft, dense undercoat is shedding. Bathe or dry shampoo only when necessary. Check the ears and coat regularly for ticks.

EXERCISE & FEEDING
Fast and agile, these lively little dogs have boundless energy and thrive on hard work and play. They are a delight to see streaking after a ball, or bringing straying sheep back to the fold. They also love to swim. There are no special feeding requirements, but don't allow them to become overweight and lazy.

HEALTH PROBLEMS
Although generally hardy, the breed is subject to some joint problems and genetic eye diseases, such as progressive retinal atrophy.

PET FACTS

- Intelligent, cooperative, joyful
- Regular brushing
- Regular, vigorous
- Adapts well to urban living, but needs plenty of space
- Good watchdog

BE AWARE

- These dogs must have enough exercise—boredom leads to bad habits
- They are sensitive to some heartworm preventatives

Male: 19–22 in (48–56 cm)
30–45 lb (14–20 kg)
Female: 18–21 in (46–53 cm)
27–42 lb (12–19 kg)

Australian Shepherd

Highly regarded in farming circles as an outstanding working dog long before its official recognition as a breed, the Australian Shepherd is not yet widely appreciated beyond this sphere.

HISTORY

Despite the misleading name, the Australian Shepherd is not Australian at all but was developed entirely in the U.S. to work as a herding dog on ranches. It is possible that the name was derived from one of the dog's ancestors. The breed's principal forebears were most likely Spanish dogs that accompanied the Basque shepherds and herds of fine Merino sheep exported to both America and Australia in the early days of the colonies. At some point, it was probably crossed with Collie stock. It has only quite recently gained recognition as a distinct breed.

DESCRIPTION

A medium-sized dog, the Aussie, as it is known, has a lean, muscular body and coarse, medium-to-long coat, which is well feathered on the ears, chest and underbody and the tops of the legs. There is a thick ruff on the chest and neck. The coat color and pattern are remarkably varied. The tail is very short or missing. If present, it is usually docked.

TEMPERAMENT

Extremely intelligent, easily trained, obedient and very responsive, these dogs seem to know exactly what is required of them.

GROOMING

The coat is easy to groom and needs very little attention.

Brush occasionally with a firm bristle brush, and bathe only when necessary.

EXERCISE & FEEDING

This energetic working dog needs plenty of vigorous exercise to stay in shape, or better yet some real work to do. There are no special feeding requirements.

HEALTH PROBLEMS

Australian Shepherds are healthy and hardy, although they can suffer from hip dysplasia and eye problems.

Male: 19–23 in (48–58 cm)
40–70 lb (18–32 kg)
Female: 18–22 in (46–56 cm)
35–65 lb (16–29 kg)

Bearded Collie

The friendly, even-tempered Bearded Collie is an attractive family pet, but as it needs lots of exercise and care and is fairly long-lived, potential owners should consider their commitment carefully.

HISTORY

A working sheepdog for most of its known history, especially in Scotland, these dogs were formerly called Highland Collies. They are thought to have developed from Polish Lowland Sheepdogs taken to Scotland about 500 years ago.

DESCRIPTION

Well proportioned and compact, the Bearded Collie looks a bit like a small Old English Sheepdog with an undocked tail. It has a shorter muzzle than other collies. The harsh, long double coat comes in all shades of gray, slate, black, red, brown and fawn, with or without white markings. There is a long, silky beard and abundant feathering.

TEMPERAMENT

Intelligent, responsive and fearless, Bearded Collies are willing workers with great stamina and endurance. They love children, but due to their size and herding instinct they may frighten a small child.

GROOMING

Daily brushing of the long, shaggy coat is important—mist the coat lightly with water before you begin. Tease out mats before they get bad and give extra attention when the dog is molting. Use the comb sparingly. If you prefer, the coat can be professionally machine clipped every two months or so. Bathe or dry shampoo when necessary. It is difficult to locate ticks in the thick undercoat, so check regularly.

EXERCISE & FEEDING

This is an active dog that needs lots of exercise, preferably running free. There are no special feeding requirements.

HEALTH PROBLEMS

Bearded Collies are a hardy breed with few genetic weaknesses, although hip dysplasia and eye defects do occasionally occur. Some dogs may react badly to certain heartworm preventatives, so consult your vet before administering medication.

PET FACTS

Energetic, alert, playful

Daily brushing

Regular, vigorous

Adapts well to urban living, but needs plenty of exercise

Good watchdog

BE AWARE

• If not discouraged from an early age, Bearded Collies tend to bark a lot

Male: 21–22 in (53–56 cm)
45–55 lb (20–25 kg)
Female: 20–21 in (51–53 cm)
40–50 lb (18–23 kg)

Collie

Instantly recognizable to generations of children who were brought up watching the television series "Lassie," the Collie is now one of the most popular dogs in the world.

HISTORY

The Collie was used in the Scottish Lowlands as a hard-working sheepdog. Its name derives from the term used for the local black sheep, colleys. There are two types, identical except for the length of their coats: the Rough Collie and the less common Smooth Collie. The Rough Collie is by far the most popular variety and is generally referred to simply as the Collie. Its magnificent coat provides protection from the cold.

DESCRIPTION

A large, strong dog, the Collie often has the typical markings of white collar, chest, feet and tail tip. The main colors of the long, thick double coat are sable, tricolor and blue merle. The head is long and tapered, and the facial expression is gentle and knowing.

TEMPERAMENT

Very sociable and dependent on human company, Collies can be aloof with strangers. They are family oriented and good with children. Intelligent and easy to train, they make good watchdogs but can be terrible barkers.

GROOMING

The spectacular stiff coat sheds dirt readily; a thorough weekly brushing will keep it in good condition. Clip out any mats and bathe or dry shampoo as necessary.

EXERCISE & FEEDING

Collies need plenty of exercise, preferably some of it off the leash. There are no special feeding requirements, but these dogs should be encouraged to chew hard foods to keep their teeth clean.

HEALTH PROBLEMS

Collies are subject to epilepsy, hip dysplasia, skin infections and eye problems, such as progressive retinal atrophy and a condition known as collie eye anomaly (CEA). They are sensitive to some heartworm preventatives.

Male: 24–26 in (61–66 cm)
60–75 lb (27–34 kg)
Female: 22–24 in (56–61 cm)
50–65 lb (23–29 kg)

PET FACTS

 Independent, good natured, energetic

 Regular brushing

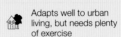 Regular, moderate

 Adapts well to urban living, but needs plenty of exercise

Good watchdog

BE AWARE

• May be sensitive to some heartworm preventatives. Check with your vet

Belgian Shepherd Dog

The picture of power and grace, the Belgian Shepherd makes its appearance in several guises, but beneath its skin-deep beauty is a reliable, hard-working and very adaptable animal.

HISTORY

The dogs used in Belgium to guard and herd sheep are all closely related but in recent times have evolved into one basic type with four distinct varieties differentiated by appearance. They are the Groenendael, Laekenois, Malinois and Tervuren (or Tervueren). In the U.S., the rare Laekenois has not yet been officially recognized and the other three are classified as separate breeds. The popular Groenendael is known simply as the Belgian Sheepdog.

DESCRIPTION

Similar to German Shepherd Dogs, with well-shaped heads and long muzzles, each variety is distinguished by its coat. The Belgian Sheepdog has an abundant, glossy, longhaired, black coat, sometimes with small white markings. The Tervuren is also longhaired, but comes in fawn, gray and mahogany and any shade in between. The hair is tipped with black and the mask and the tips of the ears are also black. Both of these dogs have a generous ruff around the neck, larger in the male. The Malinois is fawn to mahogany with the same black tips and shaded areas as the Tervuren, but the hair is shorter. Around the neck, the hair thickens to a deep collar. The Laekenois has similar coloring to the Malinois, but the short hair is harsh and wiry.

PET FACTS

- Obedient, willing, intelligent
- Regular brushing for shorthaired coats, more extensive for longhaired coats
- Regular, vigorous
- Adapts well to urban living, but needs plenty of exercise
- Very good watchdog

BE AWARE

- Thorough training is essential

Male: 24–26 in (61–66 cm)
65–75 lb (29–34 kg)
Female: 22–24 in (56–61 cm)
60–70 lb (27–32 kg)

TEMPERAMENT

Essentially working dogs, Belgian Shepherds are easily trained, reliable and obedient. Their training should always be patient, firm and consistent—if you are harsh or overbearing they will become uncooperative. They make excellent police and guard dogs, and this type of work is currently their main occupation. They do, however, make excellent pets, ever-watchful, alert and loyal, and they thrive on loving companionship.

GROOMING

The smooth, shorthaired coat of the Malinois is easy to maintain. Brush regularly with a firm bristle brush, and bathe only if absolutely necessary as bathing removes the waterproofing of the coat. Care of the longer-coated Belgian Sheepdog and Tervuren is more demanding. Their coarse, straight outer coats are heavy and of medium length; the undercoats are very dense.

Daily combing and brushing is important, with extra care when the animals are shedding. Clip out mats that form, particularly in the ruff and on the legs, and clip hair from between the toes and on the outer ears. The rough, wiry coat of the Laekenois needs only an occasional brushing with a firm bristle brush. It should be rough-looking but never curled. Again, bathing is not recommended.

EXERCISE & FEEDING

Remember that these are working dogs, used to an active outdoor life. As such, they need a lot of exercise, preferably off the leash as much as possible. There are no special feeding requirements, but do not overfeed as all varieties tend to become obese and lazy.

HEALTH PROBLEMS

These are hardy, healthy animals with few genetic diseases, although some get hip dysplasia and eye problems.

Old English Sheepdog

If you have endless patience and lots of time to spend exercising and grooming the Old English Sheepdog, your reward will be the love of a faithful and supremely glamorous companion.

HISTORY
Commonly called Bobtails, Old English Sheepdogs were developed for herding livestock, both sheep and cattle, in England's West Country.

DESCRIPTION
This large, hardy, thickset, muscular dog has a distinctive low-pitched, loud, ringing bark. The shaggy coat, which is free of curls, may be gray, grizzle, blue or blue merle, with or without white markings. When the dog is not naturally bobtailed, its tail is docked close to the body.

TEMPERAMENT
These playful, intelligent dogs learn quickly, but training should be started while the animal is still of a manageable size.

GROOMING
The coarse, longhaired coat needs constant care to keep it in top condition. Unless it is combed and brushed right through to the dense, waterproof undercoat at least three times a week, it will become matted and the dog may develop skin problems or be plagued by parasites. Clip out any tangles carefully so as not to nick the skin. A grooming table will make the whole job easier. If you prefer, the coat can be professionally machine-clipped every two months or so. In former times, these dogs were shorn along with the sheep. Trim around the eyes and rear end with blunt-nosed scissors.

PET FACTS

🐕 Intelligent, playful, loyal

🪮 Daily, extensive

🐾 Regular, vigorous

🌳 Adapts well to urban living, but needs plenty of space

🐕‍🦺 Good watchdog

🐾 **BE AWARE**

- If bored and lonely, these dogs can be mischievous
- It doesn't take long for the coat to get out of control

EXERCISE & FEEDING
These dogs were developed for hard work and love a good run. There are no special feeding requirements.

HEALTH PROBLEMS
Being thick coated, this breed is not suited to hot climates. Like many heavy dogs, they are subject to hip dysplasia. They are also susceptible to genetic eye diseases.

Male: 22–24 in (56–61 cm)
From 65 lb (29 kg)
Female: 20–22 in (51 cm)
From 60 lb (27 kg)

German Shepherd Dog

It seems as if the incredibly versatile German Shepherd Dog can be trained to do any job. Admired the world over for its intelligence and excellence as a guard dog, it seems to thrive on a life of service.

HISTORY

Known also as Alsatians, German Shepherd Dogs were originally bred as herding dogs. Nowadays, their tasks include police, rescue, tracking and military work. They also make devoted companions and watchdogs.

DESCRIPTION

Handsome, well proportioned and very strong, they must be firmly trained to obedience from an early age. The coat most often comes in black with tan, sable or all black, but other colors do occur. The nose is always black.

TEMPERAMENT

These dogs seem ever-vigilant and constantly on duty. They are both loved and feared, with good reason. They are inclined to be reserved and you must win their friendship, but from then on their loyalty is unquestioned.

GROOMING

Daily combing and brushing of the thick, coarse coat is important, and take extra care when the dog is shedding its dense undercoat. At this time, the dead woolly hair clings to the new hair and must be removed with a slicker brush designed for the task. Bathe or dry shampoo only when necessary.

PET FACTS

Fearless, loyal, intelligent

Daily brushing

Regular, vigorous

Adapts well to urban living, but needs plenty of space

Outstanding watchdog

BE AWARE

- These dogs require firm, consistent handling by a strong adult
- This breed suffers from many genetic diseases

EXERCISE & FEEDING

German Shepherd Dogs revel in strenuous activity, preferably combined with training of some kind. Feed them two or three small meals a day instead of one large meal.

HEALTH PROBLEMS

This breed suffers from many health problems, including skin ailments, hip and elbow dysplasia, bloat, genetic eye diseases, epilepsy and heart defects.

Male: 24–26 in (61–66 cm)
75–95 lb (34–43 kg)
Female: 22–24 in (56–61 cm)
70–90 lb (32–41 kg)

Briard

A gentle giant, the Briard is now becoming better known and appreciated outside its native France, where it is highly regarded as an excellent working dog and devoted pet.

TEMPERAMENT

A long history of working with humans has made Briards sweet natured and gentle. They are intelligent and easy to train, making wonderful family pets and very good watchdogs.

HISTORY

The Briard's lineage goes back more than 1,000 years, although today's dog is more elegant than those of earlier times. In its native France it has long been regarded as a shepherd dog, and during World War I soldiers were impressed by its abilities as a messenger and by the way it pulled supply wagons. It first appeared in the U.S. in the late eighteenth century.

DESCRIPTION

A large, muscular animal, the Briard has a smooth gait that appears almost effortless. The long, shaggy coat comes in solid colors, especially black and fawns, the darker the better. The hind legs have double dewclaws.

GROOMING

If the dog is kept outdoors, the coat (which doesn't shed) seems largely to take care of itself. If the dog spends a lot of time indoors, you may wish to brush the long coat regularly and bathe or dry shampoo as necessary.

EXERCISE & FEEDING

These working dogs require plenty of vigorous exercise. There are no special feeding requirements.

HEALTH PROBLEMS

This breed is generally healthy, although hip dysplasia, cataracts and PRA do occur.

Male: 23–27 in (58–69 cm)
70–80 lb (32–36 kg)
Female: 21–25 in (53–63 cm)
65–75 lb (29–34 kg)

Bouvier des Flandres

Everything about the Bouvier des Flandres says dependability—
from its workmanlike body to its calm, steady manner. Today,
its work includes police duties and guiding services for the blind.

TEMPERAMENT

Adaptable and even tempered, the Bouvier goes about its business quietly and calmly. It is easy to train and is an excellent watchdog.

GROOMING

If the dog is kept outdoors, the harsh, dry coat seems to look after itself, shedding dirt and water easily. If the animal lives in the house, you may wish to brush the long coat regularly and bathe or dry shampoo when necessary. This will certainly enhance the appearance and both dog and owner will enjoy the contact. Trim the coat occasionally, if necessary.

HISTORY

The Bouvier des Flandres, or Ox-Drover of Flanders, originated in pastoral regions around the Franco-Belgian border, where it was used for herding and guarding. During World War I, it was used as a messenger and an ambulance dog.

DESCRIPTION

First and foremost a working dog, the Bouvier is powerful and short in the body. The rough, long, shaggy double coat comes in black, gray, brindle, salt and pepper, and fawn, sometimes with a white mark on the chest. A thick beard and mustache adorn the face. The tail is usually docked.

EXERCISE & FEEDING

Energetic and active, the Bouvier needs plenty of exercise. There are no special feeding requirements.

HEALTH PROBLEMS

These hardy dogs are used to harsh conditions and are rarely ill. However, some dogs may suffer from hip dysplasia and eye problems, such as cataracts.

Male: 23–28 in (58–71 cm)
75–90 lb (34–41 kg)
Female: 22–27 in (56–69 cm)
60–80 lb (27–36 kg)

Every dog must have his day.

JONATHAN SWIFT (1667–1745),
English writer and satirist

INDEX *and* GLOSSARY

INDEX *and* GLOSSARY

In this combined index and glossary, bold page numbers indicate the main reference, and italics indicate illustrations and photographs.